DRIVEN TO SURVIVE

DRIVEN TO SURVIVE

Selected Papers by
Cordelia Schmidt-Hellerau

IPBOOKS.net
International Psychoanalytic Books

International Psychoanalytic Books (IPBooks)
New York • http://www.IPBooks.net

International Psychoanalytic Books (IPBooks),

Queens, NY 11102

Online at: www.IPBooks.net

Cover graphic by Karola Schmidt-Hellerau

Interior book design by Maureen Cutajar, gopublished.com

ISBN: 978-1-7320533-4-2

For Fred Busch
My companion in life and psychoanalysis

TABLE OF CONTENTS

FOREWORD

When I was seventeen, a good friend gave me Freud's "Outline of Psychoanalysis," suggesting it might interest me. And it did! Despite the challenge it poses as an introduction to Freud's work, I was fascinated by its bold expedition into the universe of the human mind. Freud's take on healthy and neurotic experiences and how to understand psychic processes altogether became the center of what I wanted to learn about when I embarked on my studies of literature, philosophy, and psychology in Heidelberg and Zürich. Today, fifty years and a whole professional career later, I still feel inspired by the writings of Freud and by what psychoanalysts in the various branches of our field have been developing since these early years.

As much as I still enjoy reading Freud's work and thinking about it, I never felt I had to worship him or shy away from scrutinizing his ideas. The first puzzle I involved myself in was his second drive theory of 1920. Together with introducing a life and a death drive, Freud had reshuffled a number of his other concepts that didn't seem to fall well into place thereafter. In the wake of my studies to sort this out, resulting in my monograph on his whole metapsychology*, I resurrected Freud's

---

* *Life Drive and Death Drive, Libido and Lethe: A Formalized Consistent Model of Psychoanalytic Drive and Structure Theory* (1995 in German; 2000 in French; 2001 in English; 2002 in Russian).

1

self-preservative drive, elaborating and integrating it into our contemporary theory of the mind. To me, this opened a door to a new, still–unexplored, and mostly unconscious part of the mind.

In fact, it is curious that despite the richness of our psychoanalytic ideas, we have neglected self- and object preservation, an urge so powerful and primal in human nature that it should be a staple of all clinical considerations. *We are driven to survive*—not only in the rare event of a life-threatening catastrophe, but in every move that steers us—subtly or not so subtly—through all the days of our life. How could we not have noticed? The answer is: we didn't really have a concept of it; we lacked the notion, the language with which to think and talk about it. Hence, strangely, *survival* stayed beyond our framework—as Wittgenstein would have it: "The limits of my language mean the limits of my world" (Tractatus logico-philosophicus, 5.6).

This blind spot is also curious because Freud initially did conceptualize self-preservation as a primal drive activity and even gave it an axiomatic place in his theory of the mind. But he didn't have much to say about it. Self-preservation received some early recognition as the force that represses unacceptable sexual wishes, but never reached the center of Freud's inquiries as an independent drive. Over the years, the self-preservative drives merely coasted alongside their more exciting antagonists, the sexual drives. Thus, being simultaneously there and not there, neither taken into account nor ever discarded, the self-preservative drives were relegated to a shadowy existence in our psycho-analytic understanding of the human mind.

With the papers in this volume, I want to turn a spotlight onto this forgotten dimension of our mental life. I have selected essays that expand and develop the trunk of Freud's original notion into a differentiated concept that now can be used as an integral part of our theoretical and clinical thinking. My hope is that the reader will gain a new sense of self- and object-preservative needs and anxieties, which are pervasive but often almost unnoticeable as they pave the ground in the depths of an unconscious territory that waits to be revealed and analyzed.

This book is organized into four sections preceded by an *introduction* in which I present a brief and easily accessible summary of the main ideas pertinent to the understanding of the chapters to come. Readers who prefer not to linger on theoretical considerations (such as those discussed in chapters 1 – 6) can then immediately proceed to the second section, while others may find the introduction helpful as a rough outline before entering the first section with its more detailed theoretical reflections.

Metapsychology and Drive Theory. This first section presents in a certain way the evolution of my ideas as I tried to clarify the major conceptual breaks and contradictions in Freud's theory of the mind. I begin with Freud's "Project for a Scientific Psychology" (1895), focusing on its historico-scientific context and structural congruence with all later metapsychological developments, and I then proceed to develop a formalized framework for the reexamination of the logical consistency of Freud's theory of the mind. These reflections have led me to develop new conceptions for aggression and the preservative and death drives. The last paper in this section, "Surviving in Absence," is the one within which I place the final piece of the puzzle in my revised view of drive theory; it had taken me ten years after having finished my monograph on Freud's metapsychology to understand how it makes sense to think of the preservative drives as part of the death drives. To capture this connection theoretically and clinically seems to me to yield invaluable benefits for our work with our patients.

The Oedipus Complex. We are used to thinking of the Oedipus complex as a group of conflicts between sexuality and aggression, love and hate, in a triangular relation with the parental objects. In this section, I explore the hidden yet essential function of the preservative drives in this classical concept, drawing on myth, literature, and clinical examples. The results have surprised even me. I do not question what we have previously learned, but my examination considerably widens and adds to our understanding of the many challenges around this core conflict of neuroses.

Clinical Applications. This section is devoted to various clinical observations of the workings of the preservative drives. Drawing on a number of examples, I explore difficulties we frequently face with our patients and new ways of understanding them, e.g., caregiving issues between mothers and daughters, the negative therapeutic reaction, and moral masochism and the root of its insistent blaming. I also present detailed reflections on the choices we face when addressing and interpreting our patients' material.

Musings. In this last section, I include papers that linger more broadly on cultural questions. An early article, previously published in German, addresses personal and professional integrity, which I reflect on with regard to the behavior of German psychoanalysts during the Third Reich. In more recent, previously unpublished short essays, I muse on the intricate relationships between reality, fantasy, and fiction. And finally, I relate some of the ways in which we age and die to the needs of the preservative drives and the final upsurge of the death drive.

When Arnold Richards invited me to publish a selection of my papers in his series of International Psychoanalytic Books (IPBooks), I was delighted to accept. I am grateful for his interest in and support of this project, and I also wish to thank Tamar Schwartz and Lawrence L. Schwartz for their assistance in realizing this book. Many papers in it were originally published in *The Psychoanalytic Quarterly;* I am very appreciative of the excellent editorial advice and support I received from its then-Editor, Henry F. Smith, whose careful reviews contributed a great deal to making my papers more accessible to readers. Over the years, Gina Atkinson has done a wonderful job in editing my papers for *The Psychoanalytic Quarterly,* which, given that English is not my first language, was at least in the beginning no small task; to collaborate with her and discuss particular phrasings has always been interesting and enjoyable. I am thankful that she agreed to edit all the new papers included in this book, which she did with her usual care and sensitivity. I am particularly indebted to my sister, Karola Schmidt-Hellerau, who, over the years, has produced countless diagrams for my various presentations and publications; her creativity generated many easily interpretable graphic images, which were a decisive help in making my abstract thoughts about theory more accessible. All the graphics in this book, as well as the graphic on its cover, are designed by her, for which I am deeply grateful. With the exception of three earlier publications, the papers in this book have all been written since I moved from Zürich to Boston in 2000, and I am deeply grateful to my husband, Fred Busch, for helping me in the beginning to sharpen my English-language skills, and for his interest and engagement in the development of my thinking. In the chain of our countless intriguing discussions, he helped me clarify and articulate my thoughts, which makes him an invaluable partner on my analytic journey. Finally, I am much obliged to my patients on both sides of the Atlantic, who shared with me their fears, hopes, and dreams, allowing me to sense, think, and muse alongside them on these amazing analytic journeys through their unique psychic lives; they are the latent coauthors of the papers in this book.

Cordelia Schmidt-Hellerau
Chestnut Hill, MA
March 2018

Why drives—and which ones?

How does the mind work? Given its complexity, will we ever be able to grasp at least some of it? And why did Freud devote so much time to it, or why would we nowadays care about it? As psychoanalysts, we treat patients who suffer. So isn't it enough to help our analysands resolve their problems? But how can we do this? Do we simply need to be empathic, gifted, and eventually experienced in what we are doing? Clearly, those qualities, while desirable, wouldn't distinguish us from a well-meaning friend or from anyone practicing any form of psychotherapy.

In order to *analyze* specific mental disturbances, we need a general theory of how the mind *normally* works, because this allows us to see more clearly how exactly particular problems occur.

Psychoanalysis assumes—as all other sciences about humans do—that there are certain *general laws,* in this case laws that determine the functioning of the mind. These laws or principles of mental functioning, partly derived from clinical work and partly inferred from other forms of thinking, are organized in Freud's *metapsychological model of the mind* (his "psychic apparatus"). Metapsychology evolved over the course of more than four decades in sometimes complicated or roundabout ways, which makes it difficult to comprehend its main threads. Here I will present in straight, simple terms some general guidelines of a psychoanalytic theory of the mind with special emphasis on the concept of *drives*.

The basic model of the mind rests on only two notions, *drive*[1] and *structure*.[2] The drives provide the mind with energy; the structures organize and balance these energies (homeostasis). The drives link the physiological with the psychological needs and desires (body-mind connection); the structures represent, based on experiences (memory traces), what these needs and desires are. To put it differently: without drives we wouldn't want anything; and without structures we wouldn't know what we want. The drives move us toward the object; the structures guide these moves and represent the object. Thus we can say: the drives link the body with the mind and the subject with the object.

Drive theory is essentially an object-relations theory. All elements of our experience are associated and represented in the form of structures. It's the investment of these structures with drive energies that activates them and gives us the ideas we pursue. We could say: structures are like light bulbs—they only shine when they receive electric (drive) energy. So it's quite puzzling to me when psychoanalysts claim that we can do without the drives. I'd say: without drives we'd be stuck in the dark.

Freud, informed by Darwin's insight that self-preservation and pro-creation are the driving forces in the evolution of all species, started out postulating two primal or basic drives: a self-preservative and a sexual drive (hunger and love). Whether on purpose or merely by intuition, he arranged them as antagonists in his theory—an essential step, because the interaction between two antagonists can keep a system (like the mind) in a dynamically stable position. Freud refers to this tendency toward stability as the *pleasure principle*, stipulating that an increase of energetic excitation is registered as a threat to the system, felt as dis-pleasure, thus activating mechanisms to get it back to a more stable position, felt as pleasure. Hence the antagonism of the two primal drives

---

[1] As a general rule, I have used the notion *drive* for Freud's word *Trieb*, instead of Strachey's misleading translation of *Trieb* into *instinct*.

[2] Freud initially organized his theory around the more common (at the time) notions of *system*, *agency*, or *representative*—which all fall into the category of (macro- or micro-) structures. Only around 1923 did he start to think about the mind as structured. But in contemporary language, we can use the unifying term *structure* for all these entities, including *representations*.

accounts for these homeostatic regulations: an energetic increase in one direction needs to be countervailed by an energetic increase in the other direction. We find this principle represented in pairs such as drive (pressure) and repression, wish and defense—even conscious and unconscious; it manifests in conflicts, compromise formations, symptoms, dreams, ambivalence, and in fact in all mental operations; all are generated, energized, and held by the two antagonistic drives.

From 1895 until 1920, Freud defined the drives as *the body's demand on the mind* and distinguished between the needs of self-preservation and the desires of sexuality as primal motivating forces. His main interest centered around the exploration of the sexual drives with their libidinal energies (he didn't succeed in finding an equivalent energy term for the self-preservative drives). During these years, the place of aggression in his theory shifted somewhat; in 1905, Freud understood aggression as a capacity of the sexual drives, necessary to overcome any resistance of the sexual object. In 1909, he saw it as a potential of both primal drives, since both needed to be able to override obstacles on their way to satisfaction. Finally, in 1915, Freud thought that aggression initially arose in the service of self-preservation since the infant's delicate organism needed a way to fight off life-threatening stimuli. In all three versions of Freud's conception, aggression was seen as merely a means to an end, an energetic enhancement in the service of the successful assertion of one or both drives—in other words, satisfaction.

It was only in 1920, in his famous essay *Beyond the Pleasure Principle*, that Freud fundamentally changed this conception. He now defined the drive as *an urge to return to an earlier state of being* and named the two primal drives *life drive (Eros)* and *death drive*. However, he struggled with the transition from his first to his second drive theory. While the sexual drives easily fit under the umbrella of a life drive or Eros, their previous antagonist, the self-preservative drives, seemed to contradict the notion of a death drive. Not without seesawing, Freud eventually tried to resolve this problem by uniting the self-preservative and sexual drives under the broader concept of a life drive, now appointing libido as the energy of both—while aggression and destruction were seen to represent the death drive. In consequence of this shift, aggression was

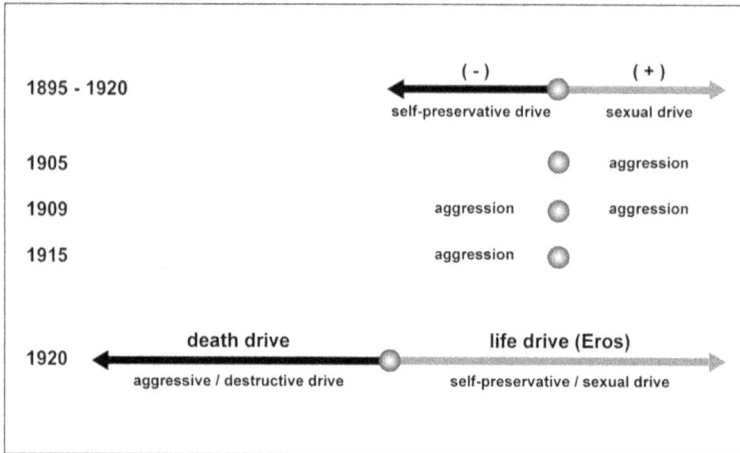

Diagram 1: Here the antagonism of the two drives is indicated by the algebraic signs (-) and (+).

no longer understood as a means to an end but as an end in itself; it was elevated to the position of a primal drive (still without a fitting energy term other than the provisional notion of *aggressive energy*). And the self-preservative drives, always at the margins of Freud's research and now submerged as *libidinal* under the notion of Eros, almost completely faded from his further clinical and theoretical consideration. Ever since 1920, then, psychoanalysis has operated with *sexuality and aggression as the two primal drives* and motivating factors in mental life.

I think this last move was a mistake, a misconception that lies at the root of psychoanalytic disenchantment with the drives. Bowlby was among the first to declare that it doesn't seem right to reduce all the infant's strivings to sexuality and aggression; what he noticed instead was the infant's *need for attachment* to the caregiver, which he didn't consider to be erotic but rather all about survival. So it's easy to see that his attachment theory falls squarely into the task area of what Freud's forgotten self-preservative drives could have conceptualized.

Also, it simply made no sense—as implied by the idea of aggression as a primal drive—that we would attack or destroy anything solely to satisfy our aggressive or destructive drives. Instead, it does make sense to say that we become assertive and ultimately aggressive or even destructive when we feel threatened in our survival or in the pursuit of our sexual interests. Thus, Freud got it right in his postulation that both the sexual and the self-preservative drives need the capacity to become aggressive. Hence we should understand (and analyze) *aggression as an intensified expression of either a preservative need or a sexual desire* (or both at the same time), arising whenever the goals of this need or desire are or appear to be thwarted.

Most stunning, however, seems the fact that, since 1920, psychoanalysis has turned a blind eye toward the urge to *preserve* oneself and one's objects. This urge is immediate, spontaneous, irrepressible, and powerful: *we are driven to survive!* When our health, safety, or well-being—in short, our survival—is at risk, all we think and care about, all we do, is aimed at preserving and protecting ourselves. And the same is true for our objects. If they are endangered, we rush to protect them from harm. Whether by flight or fight, whether anxiously or furiously—and notably, whether the danger is real or the perceived threats are the fruit of infantile or neurotic imagination, *we are driven to preserve ourselves and our objects.* The need for self- and object preservation may turn aggressive and destructive, depending on the level of the experienced threat. And while we fight for safety and survival, our sexual strivings are put on hold. Clearly, the preservative drives have to be called primal and essential, requiring a place right next to the sexual drives.

Why did this basic fact of human mental life lie dormant for one hundred years, a sort of Sleeping Beauty? Freud's preoccupation with the culture of sexual repression in turn-of-the-century Vienna comes to mind as a relevant factor. Then both World Wars pushed the matter of aggression and destruction to the fore. Thereafter, narcissism and borderline personality disorders seemed to best capture the demands of a widening scope of analytic patients. Has the time finally come to focus on how we do or don't preserve ourselves, our objects, and our environment? Has psychoanalysis anything important to say about that?

I think that there are a number of reasons why psychoanalysis has not yet paid attention to self- and object preservation as drive activities. A few decades ago, the concept of drives itself was marginalized, if not obliterated. It was suggested that it is clinically more useful, more humane—maybe more benign?—to speak about wishes or motivations, to focus on affects (rather than fantasies), and to talk about the body instead of the drives. This turn eliminated or smoothed the uncanny, wild, and scary element of human irrationality that Freud pointed out—namely, that we are powerfully driven by unconscious forces, and that our ego, this relatively weak rider on the horse of nature, must struggle to even begin to control and steer these urges. Was this an exaggeration? Shouldn't we think of ourselves as *homo sapiens*—hence, knowing what we are doing?

Yes, but remember: we humans share 98.4% of our genome with the chimpanzee! So we'd better not delude ourselves about our superior capacity to tame the primitive urges of our animalistic nature. Under the surface of even our patients' most articulate communications, the force of drives is continuously at work. Psychoanalysts need to know that.

But if psychoanalysts decide to reintegrate this basic idea that *we are driven*, the question of how to understand and position a preservative drive as well as Freud's *death drive* (for most analysts, quite an uncomfortable and unlikely notion), and how this whole drive theory should actually *work*, theoretically and practically, has to be answered. For without an idea of the usefulness of drive theory on both accounts, psychoanalysts won't engage in studying it seriously. Here in a nutshell is my solution for these problems with drive theory (see Diagram p. 13):

We begin with and maintain Freud's assumption of a life drive and a death drive, both striving virtually endlessly, each in its own direction, one toward eternal life and the other toward final death. We conceive of the infant's hunger as a sense of *starvation* eliciting the fear of death (a drive toward death / a *death drive*). It is then the *interference* of the nursing object that stops this rush toward death and *introduces* for the first time what self-preservation is at this point—namely, being fed, held, kept clean and safe, etc. *Thus, it is the object that introduces self-preservation by structuring and limiting the death drive and building protective screens against the surge toward death, screens that define the specific ranges and functions of the various partial preservative drives.*

If these (energy-absorbing, containing, and guiding) structures aren't solidly enough established, a "draft toward death" will remain over time, posing a risk to the survival of self and/or object. And the same process can be stipulated on the side of the life drives: it's the structuring inter-vention of the loving object that introduces the erotic pleasures of sexuality.

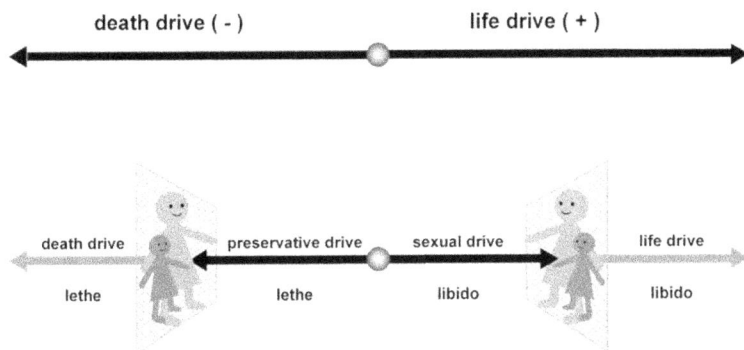

Finally, there is another subtle but important reason for the lack of traction of Freud's self-preservative drives—better to call them simply *preservative* drives, since they aim at preserving not only the self but also the object—namely, the missing energy term, which made it difficult to talk about their activities, appearances, investments, and functions. When we speak about a patient's libidinal (rather than concretely sexual) strivings, investments, or objects, we immediately understand that we mean sexuality in the widest sense, including all the sublimated and derivative forms of its expressions. In that very sense, we should think of self- and object preservation not only regarding the physical survival of ourselves and our objects, but also in terms of all derivative and subli-mated forms of care and attentiveness. To better address this wide-range perspective, as well as for practical reasons, we need a *theoretical* energy term for the preservative (and death) drives, one that is as removed from everyday language as *libido*. That's why I've suggested calling the energy of the preservative drives *lethe* (in Greek mythology, *lethe* is the name of a river that flows from the world of the living to the underworld of the dead). The term *lethe* allows us to think and talk about lethic feelings, lethic fantasies, lethic tendencies, lethic objects, and the like.

But how exactly does psychoanalytic drive theory—which is first and foremost part of metapsychology—translate into clinical work? The answer is easy in principle and not so easy in practice. The easy part refers to Freud's insight that every drive elicits ideas that are in keeping with its aims. Basically: if we are hungry, a sandwich may come to mind; if we are sexually excited, we think of our lover. *Our ideas always speak the language of our drives.* We can distinguish between two major categories: *lethic ideas* are concerned with caretaking, protection, health and disease, hygiene, fatigue, envy, greed, danger, misery, feelings of sadness, comfort, sorrow, guilt, mourning, etc. *Libidinal ideas* revolve around love, curiosity, enjoyment, jealousy, rivalry, exploration, excitement, competition, invention, art, beauty, fun, happiness, etc.

The not-so-easy part relates to the conception of drive "mixtures"; that is, our ideas always integrate both libidinal and lethic elements. I have argued that from the beginning, structures come about by combining the energies and ideas of both primal drives with regard to self and object in a dynamically stable unit (they are compromises of wish and defense that relate self to object and hence are *drive-repression* units). Still, despite the complicating factor of these "mixtures," through their combinations, we can recognize particular leanings. For instance, if we speak of cooking or dining out, we may tend toward a preoccupation with either the health value of the meal (lethic interest) or with the deliciousness and beauty of its arrangement (libidinal interest); or we might buy a pair of shoes following ergonomic and practical considerations (lethic) or with an eye for their elegance and beauty (libidinal)—or, ultimately, we may chose the middle ground, coming up with a compromise (elegant enough shoes that are still comfortable and practical). With the concept of preservative and sexual drives, psychoanalysts may notice these leanings, may more clearly see conflicts about the one or the other side, and may also learn how patients tend to resolve these conflicts or prioritize various factors.

Moreover, listening to a patient's continuous stream of thoughts, memories, deliberations, and associations will eventually reveal what we are used to calling a *pattern* (a structural term) but what is actually the *trajectory* of his or her general tendencies—namely, a predominance of one drive's or the other's activities that underlies and/or undermines the patient's efforts, an imbalance that creates the specificity of the presenting problems. For instance, is there a preoccupation with lethic concerns about the self (e.g., hypochondria) or about the other (e.g., the helicopter parent, the "helper syndrome") or a flagrant lack thereof (e.g., risk-taking behavior, neglect, carelessness)? Or are there abundant fantasies about libidinal pleasures regarding the self (e.g., narcissistic or romantic daydreams) or the other (idealization of objects), or are these totally missing (lack of love for and interest in self or other)? And if so, the question is *why*? *What are the unconscious lethic or libidinal fantasies that lie at the bottom of these problems?*

It is this *general trajectory* of the clinical material in a particular phase or in the analysis overall that may expose the organization of significant unconscious drive activities that would otherwise remain obscured under the multifaceted surface of the patient's daily reports, stories, memories, and musings. The theory of the two primal drives enables us to realize these different tendencies and analyze their particular functions (including defensive ones) at any point in the analysis.

For the reasons outlined above, I advocate the reintroduction of drive theory into our clinical and theoretical thinking, and particularly the elaboration and exploration of the preservative drives. The development, workings, challenges, and deviations of self- and object preservation have not yet been sufficiently focused on and are far from being fully understood in psychoanalysis. There remains much to explore, to learn, to reconsider—or shall I say to care about? The papers in this volume begin to do just that.

Metapsychology and Drive Theory

CHAPTER 1

The Birth of Metapsychology

On the currency of Freud's Project for a Scientific Psychology (1895)*

Freud's Project for a Scientific Psychology of 1895 is generally assigned to his pre-analytical writings, that is, the pre-analytical part of his oeuvre, from which in later years the author would distance himself. Contrary to Freud's appraisal, and that of many of his disciples, the Project can, however, be read as a metatheory that resolves the problem associated with the timeworn issue of whether psychoanalysis is a natural science or belongs to the humanities: the interaction of the disciplines of soma and psyche, otherwise invariably separated, can be understood as conceptualized in the Project on a meta-level, beyond how they are generally accounted for as physiological and psychological processes by the natural sciences and the humanities. From this viewpoint, the Project emerges as a theoretical document of astonishing modernity with contemporary relevance, because Freud attempts in it to conceptualize the interaction of neurophysiology and psychology by transcending the body-soul schism. Freud's metapsychology, still contentious today, elaborates this in detail.

It worth drawing attention to an unacknowledged anniversary: salvaged from the furthest recesses of a fractured friendship and all too swiftly

* Die Geburt der Metapsychologie. Zur Aktualität des "Entwurfs einer Psychologie" (1895). (1995). Psyche 49:1156-1195. Translated from German into English by Helen Shiner.

banished again to the historical cabinet of scientific curiosities, the hundredth anniversary of metapsychology could be celebrated this year (1995) with *A Project for a Scientific Psychology*. After Freud had ventured to propose some theoretical hypotheses on psychological processess in previous works, he formulated for the first time in a neuropsychological study written in September/October 1895 the essential outlines of his *comprehensive approach* to a "psychic apparatus", that he would further develop and extend over the following forty years. In the same year as the *Studies on Hysteria* (Freud, 1895), he conceived the fundamental theoretical model of psycholoanalysis, a scientific undertaking that on February 13, 1896, Freud would name, "*meta*psychology" (Freud, 1985, p. 172). It was, however, more than half a century later before the *Project* (in an abridged version) was made available to the public; and, thus, a whole generation of founding fathers of psycholoanalysis represented Chapter VII of *The Interpretation of Dreams* (1900) as the foundation of psychoanalytical theory without knowing that this foundation had, in fact, been taken from the overarching structure of the *Project*.

Anatomy of a Paradigm Shift

Only one month after finishing the final chapter of his *Studies on Hysteria*, Freud got to work on what was probably the most ambitious project of his research career: he wanted to develop a "Psychology for Neurologists" (1985, p. 127), in which the functional theory of a normal psyche would be presented from a purely quantitative viewpoint. "I have never before experienced such a high degree of preoccupation," he confessed to Fließ on April 27, 1895 (*ibid.*); he was "overflowing with new ideas" (*ibid.*, p 131), wrestling intently with his "psychological construction" (*ibid.*), particularly in attempting to outline his "theories on defense" (*ibid.*), and also seemed very happy with the high demands put upon him by his project,

"I feel so well that there need be no question of hurry. My heart is wholly with the psychology. If I succeed in this, I will be satisfied with everything else. It will be hard on me that in the meantime I have to keep it to myself." (Letter of June 17, 1895, *ibid.*, p. 132).

In a state of mind bordering on impatience, therefore, Freud looked forward to September 4, which he had cleared for his "private congress" with Fließ (*ibid.*, p. 135). The meeting must have clarified and confirmed things so well for him that even on his journey home, he began "writing, as well as possible, a first draft of the psychology" (*ibid.*, p. 138). As early as October 8, he sent two full notebooks to his friend in Berlin together with an accompanying letter, which conveyed the powerfully emotional state in which he had found himself during this time.

"Now, the two notebooks. I scribbled them full at one stretch since my return, and they will bring little that is new to you. I am retaining a third notebook that deals with the psychopathology of repression, because it pursues its topic only to a certain point. From there on I had to work once again with new drafts and in the process became alternately proud and overjoyed and ashamed and miserable—until now, after an excess of mental torment, I apathetically tell myself: it does not yet, perhaps never will, hang together. What does not yet hang together is not the mechanism—I can be patient about that—but the elucidation of repression, the clinical knowledge of which has in other respects greatly progressed.

But I am not succeeding with the mechanical elucidation; rather, I am inclined to listen to a quiet voice, which tells me that my explanations are not adequate.

My yearning for you and your company this time came somewhat later, but was very great. I am alone with a head in which so much is germinating and, for the time being, thrashing around. I am experiencing the most interesting things, which I cannot talk about and which for lack of leisure I cannot commit to paper. (I am enclosing a fragment for you.) I do not want to read anything, because it plunges me into too many thoughts and stunts my gratification in discovery. In short, I am a wretched hermit. Now, moreover, I am so exhausted that I shall just throw the rubbish aside for a while." (*ibid.*, p. 141).

Despite recurrent moments of despondence, Freud was filled with a fascination and 'the pleasure of discovery' during these weeks of autumn and winter, as he would never be again in any of his later work. "I was in the throes of writing fever, believed that I had found the secret," (*ibid.*, p. 144) he wrote to his friend. His "feverish work" alternated between "enticing hopes and disappointments"; he made "a few genuine findings" and all of that "gives me a kind of faint joy—for having lived some forty years not quite in vain—and yet no genuine satisfaction because the psychological gap in the new knowledge claims my entire interest." (*ibid.*, p. 145) What was the *discovery* that forced itself upon him? In order to be able to assess this, we must bring to mind the scientific consensus of the period on which Freud's thought built.

In the 1860s, physiology at the Helmholtz School[1] in Vienna, represented by *Ernst von Brücke* (1819-1892), had developed to become the most interesting and most modern branch of science. Its credo was "to assert the truth that *no other forces are operative within the organism than the common physico-chemical ones*," and to employ no other method in its research than the "physico-mathematical" (Bernfeld, 1944, p. 62f., emphasis of the author). It would prove exceptionally inspirational for a whole generation of researchers, including Freud in his early years. In substantial accordance with this fundamental position, a positivist, strictly science-oriented tendency in psychiatry had simultaneously asserted itself, its chief exponent being *Wilhelm Griesinger* (1817-1869), who, as the leading proponent of an organic-oriented line of research, supported the hypothesis that "mental illnesses are illnesses of the brain" (Ellenberger, 1970, p. 342).[2] *Theodor Meynert* (1833-1892), who was a

---

[1] The Helmholtz School was founded by Bernfeld (1944) and financed by Emil Du Bois-Reymond (1818-1896), Ernst von Brücke (1819-1892), Hermann von Helmholtz (1821-1894), and Carl Ludwig (1816-1895). From 1876 until 1882, Freud worked in the laboratory of Ernst von Brücke, the Viennese representative of this group, under whose guidance he carried out a series of histological tests on nerve cells, also making the acquaintance there of Brücke's successor, Sigmund Exner (1846-1891), and of Josef Breuer (1842-1925), his co-author on *Studies on Hysteria*. The far-reaching significance of the physicalistic physiology of the Helmholtz School for Freud has been examined notably by Bernfeld (1944, 1949) and Amacher (1965); Pribram & Gill (1976) saw the opportunity to further develop psychoanalysis on the basis of this by combining it with modern neurophysiology, Holt (1965) recognised its limits, at least in respect of the utility of metapsychology.

[2] Although Griesinger evidently considered himself to be somatician at one with this fundamental position, his teachings also incorporated a dynamic psychological element, which, by applying the associational psychology of Johann Friedrich Herbart (1776-1841), took into consideration the role played by unconscious psychical processes. This psychological element would then be disregarded again by Theodor Meynert.

disciple of Griesinger, and recognized as a European authority on brain anatomy alongside Flechsig, expanded this approach to a theory of functional specialization, in which psychic disturbances were explained as impairments of, or damage to, the structures, above all, of the forebrain or any one of the vascular centers in the brain (Meynert, 1878).[3] In his eagerness to classify all mental and psychopathological phenomena as specific neuronal structures, over time, however, he began to pass off known regions of the brain as new discoveries, thus increasingly losing himself in the field of what was known as "brain mythology", for which the positivist neuroscientists especially at that time displayed a particular weakness (Ellenberger, 1970, pp. 591, 656).

The scientific paradigm current in the late 19th century defined mental disturbances as neurological or neurophysiological disorders, and, as a consequence, employing scientific methods, the role of research was to prove the somatic basis of the various psychopathological or neurotic phenomena (for instance, the presence of an organic lesion in the case of hysteria). This objective was also mandatory for Freud, when he went to the Salpêtrière in Paris, "the Mecca for neurologists" (Jones, 1953, p. 248), in 1885 to work with *Jean-Martin Charcot* (1825-1893), after his years of apprenticeship under Brücke and Meynert. It can perhaps be seen as a stroke of luck that Freud was intensively engaged again here in research on brain anatomy – such as a case of infantile cerebral hemiplegia entrusted to him by Charcot, which, in his autopsy findings, Freud attributed to an embolism with a sclerotic lesion in the temporal lobe (Jones, 1953, p. 251f.). *At the same time,* he attended Charcot's famous staged, extraordinarily impressive presentations of

---

[3] Between 1883 and 1885, Freud worked under Meynert both on the psychiatric ward and in his laboratory, where he continued to be involved with the production and examination of preserved anatomical specimens. He proved to be so skilful and innovative in doing so, that the elderly Meynert wanted to transfer the anatomical element of his teaching duties to him, in order to devote more time to psychiatry – an offer that Freud "declined, in alarm at the magnitude of the task; it is possible, too, that I had guessed already that this great man was by no means kindly disposed towards me." (Freud, 1925, p. 11).

patients with hysterical paralysis.[4] Now it was obvious that he would undertake a scientific comparison between cerebral and hysterical paralysis, an interesting, fruitful idea, that he addressed as early as 1887 in a lecture and the following year in an essay that, nonetheless, would only be published five years later in *Archives de Neurologie* (Jones, 1953, p. 277).

This article entitled, "Some Points for a Comparative Study of Organic and Hysterical Motor Paralyses" (1893) seems to me to have played a very important role in the development of Freud's theoretical thought.[5] Its argumentation is impressively simple and clear and aimed at "indicating a line of thought that might lead to a conception which does not contradict the properties of hysterical paralysis in so far as it differs from organic cerebral paralysis." (1893, p. 169) After briefly differentiating in symptomatological terms between *periphero-spinal or projection paralysis* and *cerebral paralysis*—Freud proposed the use of the terms, *"projection paralysis"* and *"representation paralysis"* (*ibid.*, p. 161) – Freud demonstrated that hysterical paralysis never simulated the peripheral form, but instead always resembled cerebral, especially cortical paralysis (monoplegia), nonetheless failing to exhibit their clinically typical characteristics (for instance, the peripheral element, say, the hand, would always be worse affected by paralysis than the central one, say, the shoulder). Thus, one could equally term hysterical paralysis *"representation paralysis"*, although it was a specific kind of representation. Hysterical paralysis, in fact, proceeded from *another representation or conception of the body*, whereby the organs corresponded to a simple perception or conception, being grouped anatomically in a layman's sense: "the leg is the leg as far up as its insertion into the hip, the arm is the upper limb as it is visible under the clothing" (ibid., p. 169) – and corresponding to the sleeve. Charcot characterized hysterical paralysis as "purely dynamic or functional" (*ibid.*, p. 168), since it was

---

[4] Charcot's clinical demonstrations of *"grande hystérie"* were memorably captured in the painting by A. Brouillet.

[5] For a detailed discussion of this paper, see *Where Models Intersect: A Metapsychological Approach* in this volume.

not possible to prove any kind of organic lesion behind it. Freud, however, opposed even this less strident view:

> "I, on the contrary, assert that the lesion in hysterical paralysis must be completely independent of the anatomy of the nervous system, since in its paralyses and other manifestations hysteria behaves as though anatomy did not exist or as though it had no knowledge of it." (*ibid.*, p. 169)

At this point, Freud recommended that researchers transfer their work onto the *psychological level*. Hysterical paralysis comes about, he wrote, because "the paralysed organ or the lost function is involved in a subconscious association, which is provided with a large quota of affect, and it can be shown that the arm is liberated as soon as this quota is wiped out" (*ibid.*, p. 171). Thus, Freud had hit upon a clear *differentiation* between the *neurological* and the *psychological conception* – and *representation* – of the organism, and its ability to be influenced.

What is significant about this small study is that, at a stroke, Freud was calling into question the dominant paradigm under which all brain anatomists and physiologists were working at the time. Kuhn (1962) precisely describes this situation, which instigated the overthrowal of a prevailing theory: the change began with the realization that there was an anomaly, that is, that a natural phenomenon could not be explained by means of scientific expectations based on a paradigm. Anomalies of this kind exposed the failure of scientific rules that had held sway thus far, triggering the search for new theories, which then only went on to be acknowledged by the history of science as the basis for further research work (even in the face of minor resistance), if they were *sufficiently innovative* and *open-ended* to attract a stable group of researchers to investigate them, and to employ them in order to confront a series of potential, as yet unresolved, problems.

Today, a hundred years later, we know that Freudian psychoanalysis precisely fulfilled both of these criteria, which is why it became the leading paradigm internationally for a large group of scientists involved in psychoanalytical work, who, since then, have produced innumerable valuable research findings. It is, therefore, worth investigating this moment of paradigm shift in greater detail.

It is possible to say that Freud's thorough grounding in neuroanatomy under Meynert, followed by his work under Charcot, were the precise preconditions needed for his *discovery*[6] of the decisive difference between *organic* and *mental paralysis* – and thus for his rejection of any kind of functional specialization, as advocated in particular by Meynert. Freud developed this position further in his monograph, *Zur Auffassung der Aphasien* (1891).[7] In it, following Hughlings Jackson's theory, he criticized any attempt to propose a neuro-anatomical functional specialization of mental elements or processes by referring to the *fact* that physiological and psychological processes operate on *two levels of variant complexity and organization*, and direct parallels between them cannot be found[8] (on this matter, see also Rubinstein, 1965). It was a very crucial step – but with it came a very serious problem for the moment, the issue of how these two

---

[6] Kuhn distinguishes between *discoveries* that relate to a *fact*, a *new kind of truth* and *inventions* or *new theories* that provide an answer to previous paradigmatic crises. In this sense, one can say that in the case of Freud's *discovery* that hysteria (neurosis) takes no account of anatomy, is concerned with the working out of a *fact, a new kind of truth*, and that the notion of the *mental representation* of the body (body image), which is subject to mental associations and unconscious suppression, gave birth to a new theory. – While it is true that Charcot did not accept this differential criterion, today generally established in neurological science, he did not want to contradict Freud's findings, and he supported him in the publication of his "Comparative Study" in the *Archives de Neurologie* (Jones, 1953, p. 212f.). Thus, Freud's *Project* presented in this study his *invention* of a new *theory*, following on from his above-mentioned *discovery* (referred to in his writings as a "pleasure of discovery").

[7] Freud considered this study on aphasia to be the "the most valuable of his neurological works" (Jones, 1953, p. 213). Solms and Saling (1986) saw it as offering the most important connection between neuroscience and psychoanalysis, and Leuschner even deemed it to be "a very specifically targeted operation to provide a scientific foundation and secure footing for psychoanalysis" (Leuschner, 1989, p. 539).

[8] The decisive, oft-cited passage is as follows: "The relationship between the chain of physiological events in the nervous system and the mental processes is probably not one of cause and effect. The former do not cease when the latter set in; they tend to continue, but, from a certain moment, a mental phenomenon corresponds to each part of the chain, or to several parts. The psychic is, therefore, a process parallel to the physiological, 'a dependent concomitant'." (Freud, 1953, p. 55). According to Leuschner, this *psychophysical parallelism* of Freud's marks the "fundamental position in respect of psychology/biology that he maintained throughout his life" (1989, p. 543).

fields, conceived as separate, were to cooperate after this baffling "leap from a mental process to a somatic innervation" (Freud, 1909, p. 157) – and vice versa; because Freud was,

> "not at all inclined to leave the psychology hanging in the air without an organic basis. But apart from this conviction I do not know how to go on, neither theoretically nor therapeutically, and therefore must behave as if only the psychological were under consideration. Why I cannot fit it together [the organic and the psychological] I have not even begun to fathom." (Freud, 1985, p. 326).

This assertion, "...I have not even begun to fathom", seems to me to be a downright *negation* and, thus, a disclosure by Freud of something theoretically preconscious – but let us see what followed:

Three years after Freud's study on aphasia, and a year following the publication of his "Comparative Study", *Sigmund Exner* (1846-1891) presented his *Entwurf zu einer physiologischen Erklärung der psychischen Erscheinungen* (1894) – a synthesis, so to speak, of the teachings of Brücke and Meynert (Ellenberger, 1970, p. 658). In it, he pursued the intention of "ascribing the most important mental phenomena to the nuances of the states of arousal of the nerves and nerve centers [and] thus to everything that appears to our consciousness as multiplicity, to quantitative relationships, and to the diversity of the central connections of the otherwise essentially similar nerves and centers" (1894, p. 3). Reading this book against the backdrop of knowledge about Freud's *Project* is really exciting, since Exner anticipates a great deal, in terms of thematic content, of what Freud would introduce only a year later in the two notebooks that he sent to Fließ.[9] However, it is unmistakable that

---

[9] Exner (1894) was extensively preoccupied with the formation, conduct and processing of the *intracerebral arousal*, the *summation* of stimuli and the *threshold* for arousal, (unlike Brücke and Meynert) distinguishing between a *reflex movement* and an *instinctive* one, introducing the new concepts of central *restraint* and *facilitation*, and presenting comprehensive reflections on attention (attentional facilitation), the difference between (sensory) *perceptions* and *feelings* (generated by the arousal of inner organs, such as the brain) (Freud's *endogenous stimuli*), on *feelings of pleasure and displeasure, perceptions* and *imaginings* and on *consciousness*.

Exner's argument still takes the old reductive position of the paradigm that had held sway until then as its starting point, since his deliberations are not yet informed by knowledge of this *scientific conundrum*; of how to *conceive* this mysterious leap from the mental organizational level to the somatic one – this being the *specific difference* in the thought of both researchers. This is precisely the reason that Exner's ideas are today considered to be obsolete, whereas Freud's theory heralded a new era of understanding of mental and psychophysical processes.

Thus, we come to Breuer and his chapter entitled "Theoretical" in *Studies on Hysteria*, which was published only a year after Exner's *Entwurf*. Breuer, who exchanged ideas constantly with Freud, now attempted to strictly separate the physiological level from that of psychological observations:

> "In what follows little mention will be made of the brain and none whatever of molecules. Psychical processes will be dealt with in the language of psychology; and, indeed, it cannot possibly be otherwise. If instead of 'idea' we chose to speak of 'excitation of the cortex', the latter term would only have any meaning for us in so far as we recognized an old friend under that cloak and tacitly reinstated the 'idea'. For while ideas are constant objects of our experience and are familiar to us in all their shades of meaning, 'cortical excitations' are on the contrary rather in the nature of a postulate, objects which we hope to be able to identify in the future. The substitution of one term for another would seem to be no more than a pointless disguise. Accordingly, I may perhaps be forgiven if I make almost exclusive use of psychological terms." (Breuer in Freud, 1895, p. 185).

The defensive attitude evident in the last sentence was directed at exponents of the reductionist paradigm, by means of which it was held that anything mental should ultimately be explained using neuronal – and not psychological terminology. Against this backdrop, Breuer's theoretical chapter was already a notable attempt to create *independent* space for the psychological alongside the physiological, when, after making reference to the useful example of the erection, he continued: "In conformity with our experience of a large number of physiological processes, such as the secretion of salvia or tears, changes in the action of the heart, etc., it is possible and plausible to assume that one and the same process may be set in motion equally by ideas and by peripheral and other non-psychical stimuli." (Breuer in Freud, 1895, p. 187). He then added almost defiantly: "The contrary would need to be proved and we are very far short of that" (*ibid*.). His new argument might be summed up as "both x and y" – a position that Breuer was, nonetheless, able to sustain in a precarious balancing act:

> "But the fundamental pathological change which is present in every case and enables ideas as well as non-psychological stimuli to produce pathological effects lies in an abnormal excitability of the nervous system. How far this excitability is itself of psychical origin is another question." (Breuer in Freud, *ibid*., p. 191).

Without this last sentence, everything would again have been attributed to "an abnormal excitability of the nervous system"; but here Breuer raised the question of a psychical origin for this neuronal excitation – thus standing the current doctrine on its head. This is what is truly revolutionary in this otherwise rather modest theoretical section of *Studies on Hysteria* when seen from the viewpoint of today's understanding of metapsychology. Breuer could not answer his own question, and he stuck far too closely to specific physiological and mental facts. He was presumably still too bound to the current scientific criteria of his time.

However, then it was Freud's turn! Four weeks only after finishing his concluding chapter for *Studies on Hysteria*, he threw himself with great enthusiasm into a daring scientific enterprise, which would entirely absorb him: *A Project for a Scientific Psychology*. Analysts tend to ask, *why then particularly*? Why was it that Freud started on this project so shortly after completing his most comprehensive publication to date, an impressive book after all (even if co-authored with Breuer) – at a time when he could have at least stopped to enjoy for a moment what he had achieved, when he could have been satisfied with this first successful stage of his career – and why did he commence what was probably the most complex and difficult work he would ever write? Why this impatience? I believe that it demonstrates his dissatisfaction with Breuer's chapter, "Theoretical", in *Studies on Hysteria*.[10] Or conversely: had the hypothesis outlined there satisfied him for the time being, had it contained everything that he was capable of thinking in theoretical terms at this moment, then Freud certainly would not have started to develop a "Psychology for Neurologists", which would outclass Breuer's chapter decisively, even before the study on hysteria had been published. There is no doubt that Breuer noticed this; on July 5, 1895, he wrote to Fließ, "Freud's intellect is soaring at its highest. I gaze after him as a hen at a hawk." (Jones, 1953, p. 242).

One is used to discerning the discord between Freud and Breuer from their disagreements about the etiological role of sexuality in the causation of neuroses, and Breuer's dismissive stance in this respect is, indeed, documented. Perhaps, however, there is another, silent reason that can be found in the differing attitudes of both men to their theoretical positions. The image of a hen and a hawk exemplifies this difference: Breuer bravely accompanied Freud one step over the boundary of the old paradigm (although his submissive plea for forgiveness for employing "psychological terms" might be read as an indication that he was already in two minds about this); but that was it. What Freud developed over the following months appears not to be something that Breuer was prepared to support. And so, Freud rose like a hawk, looking down sharp-sightedly from a bird's-eye view, to apprehend the two

---

[10] It is for this reason that Sulloway (1979), referencing Stewart (1967), considered that Freud's *Project* can be read as the scientist's own version of Breuer's chapter, "Theoretical". Kris noted the differing mind-set of the two researchers, which would ultimately lead to their mutual estrangement: "Freud's ideas were conceived and developed in an erratic manner, whereas the older, more cautious Breuer was unable to give him his allegiance. Even as early as their first joint publication, Freud reported to Fließ that there were conflicts with Breuer ... Breuer had been willing to follow Freud with his first fundamental assumptions ... At the time *Studien* was published, they still found it possible to bridge over their differences of opinion for the outside world" (Kris, 1950, in Freud, 1985, p. 527f.).

levels of the mental and somatic, conceived thus far as separate – and it was from this *meta*-position, I would argue, that he was able to conceive the theory outlined in his *Entwurf,* the fundamental concept of *metapsychology.* What then was this theory?

At first glance, the *Project* appears to be a "neurone theory" (1950c/1950, p. 297). In it Freud speaks very specifically about neurons and saltatory conduction, sensory stimuli and certain structures in the brain; he dedicates a chapter to the "Biological Standpoint" (*ibid.,* p. 302ff.), another to "Consciousness" (*ibid.,* p. 311ff.), and debates "The Problem of Quantity" (*ibid.,* p. 305f.) and "The Problem of Quality" (*ibid.,* p. 307ff.). He feels his way forward on the somatic terrain, and then on the psychological one – and it is repeatedly reminiscent of the corresponding sections in Exner's *Entwurf.* However, there is something that distinguishes Freud's *Entwurf* from all other contemporary attempts to relate the psychological with the physiological.

The interesting thing about this text is that Freud establishes a new overriding level of argumentation by introducing three *constructs,* the φ (phi), ψ (psi) and ω (omega) systems, that constitute the foundation for the meta-status of his hypothesis. These systems, φ, ψ and ω do not correspond to anything concrete or real, they denote neither neuroanatomical structures in the brain nor any kind of mental experiential entity; instead they are abstract concepts that permit him to *think* about the constitutional ordering of complex (mental) processes within the framework of a *model.* By employing them, Freud succeeds in sketching the basic outlines of a theory that delineated the *organizational principles* of the living organism on a *superordinate level,* as a dynamic, stable and modulated system. It was precisely these assumptions about the measures taken by the system to maintain its inner balance that could refer both to the mental as well as the somatic levels – and it is for this reason that Freud's theory can absolutely be understood as *meta-psycho-physiology* (Schmidt-Hellerau, 1993).

Freud *invented* this meta-theory in 1895. Nonetheless, he wrote to Fließ in 1898: "Why I cannot fit it together [the organic and the psychological] I have not even begun to fathom" (Freud, 1985, p. 326). Or did he foresee that "the organic and the psychological" could combine *in theory* on this meta-level? We know from letters to Fließ that Freud was really flying high with his theory during his *Entwurf* period, but that his mood was repeatedly interrupted by sudden descents into despondency – perhaps, after all, he did sense that he was on the track of something completely new, a theoretical meta-level, for which there were yet no concepts, no terminology, and that, for this reason, he could not yet grasp it? Because it would not be for another good half-century before Norbert Wiener would develop *cybernetics*, a method that would, for the first time, enable scientists to describe, and thus think about, specific, empirically researchable processes (with a number of unknowns) in the form of abstract models (so-called regulatory circuits) – that is, divorced from their material substrate (Wiener, 1948). Aside from Jones (1953), Strachey was one of the first to link this "resemblance to certain modern approaches" in Freud's work (Strachey in Freud 1950c/1950a, p. 292), that is, that there was "more than a hint or two at the hypotheses of information theory and cybernetics in their application to the nervous system" (*ibid.*); but he also found fault with the "uncomfortable divorce between the clinical and theoretical" (*ibid.*) and criticized the fact that the *Project* was "in the main built up on theoretical and a priori foundations." (*ibid.*, p. 291). That, however, is precisely its forte; it is in this separation of the clinical and theoretical observation (Schmidt-Hellerau, 1993), or, in other words, in this development of a new superordinate level that the innovative potential of the *Project* – and that of metapsychology – as yet not fully tapped, lies. It is the *construction of an abstract model of thought* that ensures that Freud's *Project* is *not* simply a "late offshoot" from the main stem of an outdated "dynamic, speculative philosophy" of a Herbartian kind (Ellenberger, 1970, p. 656), or the last legacy of a century of "brain mythology" (*ibid.*, p. 658) – but is instead the breakthrough to an entirely new dimension in theoretical thought.

Strachey's ambivalent assessment of the *Project* throws light on the issue, still unresolved today, of whether metapsychology has a consistently tenable position: what status should one accord to this theory? Does the *Project* contain – as many, who attribute it to Freud's pre-analytical period, consider to be the case – only some of the obsolete neuron theory from the start of the last century, or do the terms and concepts belonging to his later metapsychology[11] already hint at Freud's transition towards a "pure" psychological theory? It is possible to state that the entire controversy around metapsychology in the sixties and seventies (on this, see Mertens, 1981, Schmidt-Hellerau, 1993) was precisely to do with the problem of positioning: centred on *natural science versus the humanities*, resulting finally in the rather disappointed-sounding title of an essay by Gill: *Metapsychology is not Psychology* (1976). Thus, for a large group of psychoanalysts, it seemed to have become unusable in part, even "completely unacceptable" (Peterfreund, 1971, 1975).

It is, however, possible to answer the question about the scientific status of metapsychology in another way: not with an *either-or* or a *both-x-and-y*, but instead with *neither-nor*. It is possible to state that this theory, its main features formulated in their entirety for the first time in the *Project*, can be read – regardless of how Freud categorized it himself – as a metatheory standing above and beyond the descriptions of physiological and psychological processes as found in the natural sciences and the humanities. By introducing the three constructs, the φ, ψ and ω systems, Freud makes a first attempt to separate his thought from the constraints of one after another discipline, and, in this manner, he succeeds in taking a step forwards in the pursuit of getting a grip *conceptually* on the problem of the interaction of the two domains of soma and psyche, divided thus far.[12] One could also align oneself with Strachey's

---

[11] In fact, the *Entwurf* already contained detailed statements about the principles of *inertia, constancy, pleasure* and *unpleasure, primary* and *secondary processes,* the distinction between the *unconscious,* the *preconscious* and the *conscious,* the *ego* as a separate entity, *cathexis, discharge, inhibition, defence* and *repression, hallucination* and *reality testing,* the *wish-fulfilling tendency of dreams* and its similarity to neurotic symptoms, the meaning of language and approaches to a theory of cognition – and, clearly outlined, the fundamentals of the psychoanalytic *drive and structural theories.*

[12] Grubrich-Simitis (1987, p. 1021) considers it probable that this contribution to the overcoming of the body-mind schism will one day rank alongside the discovery of unconscious and infantile sexuality, and the invention of the psychoanalytical method, as one of Freud's lasting achievements, and "that precisely on this 'intermediate terrain' the modernity and capacity for development of his thought will be able prove itself again." See also Kernberg (1993, p. 47).

view that the *Project* is only ostensibly a neurological document, and that, rather, it "contains within itself the nucleus of a great part of Freud's later psychological theories... it actually threw light for the first time on some of the more obscure of Freud's fundamental hypotheses" (Strachey in Freud, 1950c/1950, p. 290).

Were one to choose not to cling to the neuronal detail in his description, then it becomes evident that Freud's primary interest, and the most interesting and productive sections for metapsychology, are devoted to the functioning of the psychic apparatus with its three systems, φ, ψ and ω, as well as everything that may be developed from this construct – and then a theory would be generated before our eyes, ingeniously simple in its basic assumptions and complex in its opportunities for development. Since, however, this theory is embedded in a thicket of complicated, interwoven threads of argument, reading the *Project* becomes a conceptually extraordinarily demanding project of disinterment, in which it is repeatedly a matter of finding the continuance of the guiding principles of Freud's fundamental concept. In the following summary of some of the key positions of the *Project*, this preliminary work has been undertaken; the findings of this analysis, ordering and, in part, new interpretation thus trace the trajectory of a highly specific epistemological interest, solely oriented towards the structures of Freud's theoretical concept. They do not take into account the full variety of the themes addressed in the *Project*, nor does this account seek to exclude any other readings of this complex text.[13]

---

[13] I present a detailed working out of the theory outlined in the *Project* in my book on metapsychology (Schmidt-Hellerau, 2001). In it, I also demonstrate how the later development of metapsychology repeatedly makes reference to the fundamental assumptions of the *Project*. – There are accounts and discussions of the *Project* from various perspectives, among others, in Jones (1953), Pribram (1962), Wollheim (1972), Sulloway (1979), and Drews and Brecht (1982); Peters (1960), Pribram (1969) and Basch (1975) detail the extraordinary importance of the *Project* for the foundation of psychoanalytical theory. Pribram & Gill (1976) examine Freud's "Psychology for Neurologists" in particularly great detail, and demonstrate, using a number of examples, that Freud's *Project* anticipated, in many respects, later neurophysiological research findings, especially in relation to the electrical concomitant phenomena of neuronal activities (Gill (1976), p. 66ff.). They conclude that the *concept* of neurons presented by

The Theory behind the Project[14]

(a) Initial Position

Freud opens the "Project" by declaring his "intention . . . to furnish a psychology that shall be a natural science: that is, to represent psychical processes as quantitatively determinate states of specifiable material particles, thus making those processes perspicuous and free from contradiction" (1950, p. 295). He thereby shows that he is concerned in this work not with the *experiential dimension* of the psychic—its contents, the "what" of psychic life; not, that is, with a *theory directed toward understanding-but* with the "quantification" of psychic processes at least to the extent that they can be assigned a *plus* or *minus* sign, or, as the case may be, a *zero* symbol, and arranged within a model in quantitative terms (i.e., as *more* or *less);* and the constituents of this model are Freud's quasi-"material particles." The initial hypothesis underlying his "general scheme" (ibid.) is thus that psychic processes conform to specific (logical and mathematical) laws and that they can be represented on a formalized level within a model (the psychical apparatus).

(b) First Principal Theorem: The "Principle of Inertia"

Freud immediately states that the system to be constructed (the psychical apparatus) is to have the tendency to remain in a permanent (stable) state; if it is driven out of this state by the action of forces of some kind, every form of activity is to have the aim of returning it to the original state. In other words, if the psychical apparatus, starting from its initial position, is exposed to the "supply" of a certain quantity of excitation, it will immediately attempt to get rid of it by "discharge": the supply of excitation (plus) and its discharge (minus) together satisfy what we may call the zero principle: $(+e) + (-e) = 0$. Since zero (i.e., any value arbitrarily taken as

---

Freud, and his outlining of nerve functions remain barely flawed even today (Gill, 1976, pp. 34, 61).

[14] The text of the following chapter was translated into English by Philip Slotkin; it was first published in (2001) Life Drive & Death Drive, Libido & Lethe, A Formalized Consistent Model of Psychoanalytic Drive and Structure Theory. New York: Other Press, pp. 49-69.

zero) is to be the *stable* initial position of the system, the *zero principle* (Freud's *principle of inertia*) is, in purely formal terms, simply a principle of regulation in the service of *homeostasis* (or, if you will, of the system's *dynamic stability*). This is the proposition of the first principal theorem and the fundamental principle of the model: *any departure (in this case, a supply of incoming excitation) from the reference value (in this case, zero) leads to measures on the part of the system (in this case, discharge) that restore the system's state to its reference value—that is, equilibrium—through homeostatic regulation (in this case, the principle of inertia).* The simplest way of representing this is as follows:

input variable (+e) → law: zero principle → output variable (−e)

(c) The φ System

The activator of the psychical apparatus is in each case a quantitative stimulus. Freud distinguishes between exogenous and endogenous stimuli. The quantities of the *exogenous* or *environmental stimuli* (e.g., a ray of light falling on the eye, or a blow on the hand) are broken down by the "nerve-ending apparatuses" of the sense organs into quotients of their physical magnitude, and then pass via afferent pathways to a group of neurones, which Freud calls φ (i.e., peripheral) neurones, that together form the φ *system* (p. 302), whence they are "discharged" again via the motor neurones of the efferent pathways. The principle of inertia is thus satisfied in the φ system by way of a *reflex movement,* in which the discharge ("flight from the stimulus") is proportional to the supply (magnitude of the stimulus)—thus restoring the initial position of the system (homeostasis):

exogenous / sensory supply of stimulus → φ system → motor discharge

(d) The ψ System

The situation is more complicated in the case of the *endogenous* stimuli, such as "the major needs: hunger, respiration, sexuality" (p. 297); here, simple motor discharge would not eliminate the cause of the stimulus, because new quantities of excitation are constantly being produced inside the organism. These arise continuously, but it is only periodically, by "summation," that they attain a given minimum necessary stimulatory value, which then passes directly to the nucleus of the "ψ group of neurones" (ψ meaning psychic), the ψ *system*. The ψ system is "exposed" to this quantity of "Qs … without protection and in this fact lies the *mainspring* of the psychical mechanism" (p. 315f.): the result is an urgency for discharge of the stimulus, which in this case means an urgency for satisfaction of the need; this, however, is possible only "subject to particular conditions, which must be realized in the external world" (p. 297), so that what Freud calls a "specific action" is now necessary. The paradigm of such a process is the following series: hunger—screaming/search behavior—appearance of the nourishing object/nourishment—supply of nourishment—termination of the hunger stimulus. The sequence is now:

Endogenous stimulus → ψ system → specific action → termination of stimulus

(e) *Principle of Constancy*

As Freud acknowledges, this sequence extends beyond the model of a simple reflex movement: the specific action constitutes a much more complex process than simple discharge; it is an accomplishment that consumes more energy than is supplied by the cause of the stimulus alone.

In consequence, the nervous system is obliged to abandon its original trend to inertia (that is, to bringing the level [of Qή][15] to zero). It must put up with [maintaining] a store of Qή sufficient to meet the demand for a specific action. Nevertheless, the manner in which it does this shows that the same trend persists, modified into an endeavor at least to keep the Qή as low as possible and to guard against any increase of it–that is, to keep it constant. All the functions of the nervous system can be comprised either under the aspect of the primary function or of the secondary one imposed by the exigencies of life. [p. 297][16]

---

[15] Qή stands for endogenous quantities.

[16] Freud distinguishes between Q (quantity in general, of the order of magnitude in the external world) and Qή (quantity of the intercellular order of magnitude).

Hence "the exigencies of life" develop the *principle of constancy* out of the "trend to inertia": the ψ group of neurones must equip itself with (i.e., must store) a minimum of quantities of excitation in order to be capable at all times of effectively countering an increase in quantities of endogenous excitation within the organism by the performance of the specific action. However, even if the system deviates from its "zero level," the new term *principle of constancy* already indicates the persistence of the "principle of inertia": a new homeostatic ("zero") value is established, which must now be kept constant and restored whenever it is departed from.

(f) Second Principal Theorem: The "Neurone Theory"

To facilitate understanding of this process of storage—of both the quantity of excitation and the specificity of the action—Freud formulates what he calls his *neurone theory,* which is interesting in that it already contains essential propositions of his subsequent structure theory and theory of structural development. He writes:

> The main substance of these new discoveries is that the nervous system consists of distinct and similarly constructed neurones, which have contact with one another through the medium of a foreign substance, which terminate upon one another as they do upon portions of foreign tissue, [and] in which certain lines[17] of conduction are laid down in so far as they [the neurons] receive [excitations] through cell-processes [dendrites] and [give them off] through an axis-cylinder [axon]. They have in addition numerous ramifications of varying calibre.
>
> If we combine this account of the neurones with the conception of the Qή theory, we arrive at the idea of a *cathected* neurone filled with a certain Qή while at other times it may be empty. The principle of inertia finds its expression in the hypothesis of a *current* passing from the cell's paths of conduction[18] or processes [dendrites] to the axis-cylinder. A single neurone is thus a model of the whole nervous system with its

---

[17] [Translator's note: Freud's word *Richtungen* should actually be translated as "directions."]
[18] [Translator's note: This is a translation of the German word *Zelleitungen.* The complete German edition (1950c [1895]), however, has *Zelleib,* which means "cell's body."]

dichotomy of structure, the axis-cylinder being the organ of discharge. The secondary function [of the nervous system], however, which calls for the accumulation of Qή, is made possible by the assumption of resistances which oppose discharge; and the structure of neurones makes it probable that the resistances are all to be located in the contacts [between one neurone and another], which in this way assume the value of *barriers.* [p. 297f.]

Freud is here focusing on the nerve cell as a "model of the whole nervous system"—in other words, he is concerned not so much with the process within a concrete nerve cell as with a principle possessing general validity within the system as a whole. The most important point here is that there is a "certain *Richtung* [direction] of conduction," in which the "current" flows; moreover, it flows from the "cell-processes" (dendrites) in the afferent direction via the *"Zelleib"* ["cell body"] (nerve cell) to the "axis-cylinder" (axon) in the efferent direction. In the language of the model, this may be expressed as follows. The process is *directional:* the input variable (supply of a quantity of excitation [plus]) and the output variable (discharge of a quantity of excitation [minus]) are vectorial magnitudes (that is, they are determined by value and direction). The principle of inertia is the homeostatic regulation that proceeds from the nerve cell in the direction of the axon; hence the nerve cell operates as a switch, as a control center, or, if you will, as a controller that contains the homeostatic law. This is illustrated by Figure I–1.

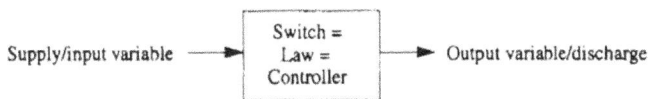

Supply/input variable ⟶ | Switch = Law = Controller | ⟶ Output variable/discharge

Figure I–I

This basic principle also applies within the afferent and efferent pathways: in order to reach a "central" switch or controller, the stimulus must cross a number of thresholds in the contact barriers; its discharge is likewise controlled by such thresholds. The above configuration can therefore be subdivided again—in principle, any number of times—the contact barriers also being assigned the function of switches, or, so to speak, of subcontrollers or microcontrollers (subordinate levels) in relation to a central main controller or macrocontroller (supraordinate level), as shown in Figure I-2.

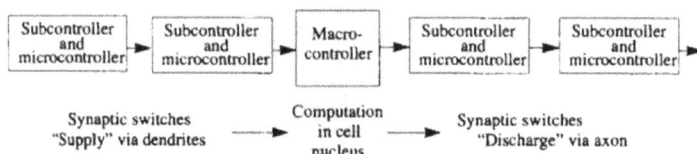

Figure I–2

(g) Facilitation

Since the paths of conduction (of the nervous system) have multiple segments, the endogenous stimuli must overcome various resistances or thresholds before they reach the neurones of the ψ system. At each barrier in the path of conduction, therefore, a summation of the quantities of excitation is initially necessary; the barriers controlling conduction to the ψ system become permeable only when a given quantity is reached. At this point a *facilitation* arises and *partially persists* after the passage of the excitation-and, moreover, "the facilitation which remains after the passage of Q consists, not in the lifting of every single resistance but in its reduction to a necessary remaining minimum" (p. 317). This is now significant for the direction of future passages, as the next passage of endogenous excitation preferentially involves pathways (neurones) whose contact resistances already have a lower threshold value—that is, pathways that are *facilitated* and thus allow faster discharge. Freud thus assumes that "the process of conduction itself will create a differentiation in the protoplasm and consequently an improved conductive capacity for subsequent conduction" (p. 298f.). This interesting point in his theory must not be underestimated, because it states that the (repeated) passage of certain quantities of excitation through the "neuronal" pathways influences the controller value or switching principle (the synapse): in other words, the *process of conduction itself is structure-forming: the energetic activity of the system leads to the formation of structure!*[19]

(h) "Information Processing" by the System ("Complication")
With the introduction of facilitation through the partial lowering of resistances, Freud finds an initial answer to the question of how the system he has constructed can *learn.* However, a second question then immediately arises: Does a quantitatively greater stimulus in this case always produce a stronger psychic effect in ψ? Freud makes a distinction:

Here a special contrivance seems to be present, which once again keeps off Q from ψ. For the sensory path of conduction in ψ[20] is constructed in a peculiar fashion. It ramifies continually and exhibits thicker and thinner paths, which end in numerous terminal points-probably with the following significance: a stronger stimulus follows different pathways from a weaker one. For instance, [I] Qή will pass only along pathway I and will transfer a quotient to ψ at terminal α. [2] (Qή) will not transfer a double quotient at α, but will be able to pass also along pathway II, which is narrower, and to open up another terminal point to ψ (at β). [3] (Qή) will open up the narrowest path [III] and will transfer through γ as well. This is how the single φ path is relieved of its burden; the larger quantity in φ will be expressed by the fact that it cathects several neurones in ψ instead of a single one. The different cathexes of the ψ neurones may in this case be approximately equal. If Qή in φ gives rise to a cathexis in ψ, then [3] (Qή) is expressed by a cathexis in ψ1+ ψ2+ ψ3. Thus quantity in φ is expressed by *complication* in ψ. By this means the Q is held back from ψ, within certain limits at least [p. 314f.].

---

[19] Already in 1960, Rapaport had declared structure formation to be one of the central issues of psychoanalytic theory. Applegarth (1971), who also believes that the central question of psychoanalysis, as a general psychology, has to do with the nature of psychic structure and the mechanisms of structure formation sees the "Project" as an ambitious attempt by Freud to develop a structural theory of this kind (ibid., p. 397) and, moreover, as an attempt to do so in such a way that *a connection between psychology and neurophysiology becomes unavoidable* (ibid., p. 386).

[20] [Translator's note: The *Standard Edition* here has the Greek letter misprinted as φ.]

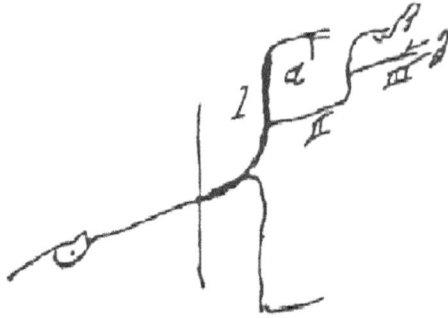

Figure I–3

This can be imagined in simplified form as follows: a quantum of excitation exceeds the threshold of pathway I; pathway I passes only a certain quantity; there remains a residual quantity that is sufficient to pass through the "thinner" pathway II, and so on. Hence a larger quantum will give rise not to a greater threshold reduction in pathway I, and a consequent stronger stimulus in ψ, but to the distribution of the excitation over a number of pathways, and will thereby—and this is the crucial point in Freud's assumption of "complication" (divergence*)—generate a specific pattern of excitation,* which will be different in each case. In other words, the *information* corresponding to a given quantum of excitation is in effect converted, transformed, or "reformatted," so that information is preserved while the transfer of excitation, or consumption of energy, decreases.[21] In this way the "Project" not only reflects the

---

[21] Pribram and Gill (1976) emphasize the importance of the distinction between energy and information, which originates in thermodynamics, whose first law concerns the *conservation* of energy and whose second law relates to its *organization*. The first states that an interaction between systems is limited by the fact that each action gives rise to an equal and opposite reaction. The principle of inertia enunciated in the "Project" corresponds to this. The second law deals with the quantitative change in the organization of energy systems involved in these interactions (conversion of energy). A similar distinction proved relevant in communications engineering: the quantity of energy required to maintain a system (radio, for example) does not bear any direct relation to the information processing carried out (e.g., a news bulletin, a symphony, a sports commentary, or merely the station's call sign). The amount of *organization* that charac-

hierarchical "construction of the nervous system out of several systems" (p. 306), but is, from its very design, already a surprisingly modern information processing model.

(i) The System's Memory

Freud's purpose in introducing the concept of contact barriers is wholly concrete. It is clear to him that a "psychological theory deserving any consideration must furnish an explanation of 'memory'" (p. 299). The problem of such an explanation lies in the fact that "it must assume on the one hand that neurones are permanently different after an excitation from what they were before, while nevertheless it cannot be disputed that, in general, fresh excitations meet with the same conditions of reception as did the earlier ones" (ibid.). The problem is solved by his assumption that the thresholds of the contact barriers in the neuronal pathways are permanently changed, whereas the (input) receptors of the neurones remain unaltered. The learning process of the ψ *neurones* (i.e., the memory of the ψ system) then consists firstly in the reduction of the resistance of the contact barriers, a reduction that differs in each case by virtue of the magnitude (quantity) and frequency (also a quantity) of a stimulus—that is, in the *facilitation* of the pathways—and secondly in the *distribution* ("complication") of the passages of excitation, that is, the different paths—associations (patterns)—that are thereby established. Now associations consist of nothing other than connections, or switches, that link different "neurones" together. Freud thus comes to the following general conclusion: "*Memory is represented by the facilitations existing between the ψ neurones*" (p. 300). Again, since memory after all has to do with the *particular* "preferred pathways" taken by the passage of an excitation, Freud immediately adds that "*memory is represented by the differences in the facilitations between the ψ neurones*" (ibid.).

(j) Building Blocks of a Hierarchical Organization

It is impossible to overlook the paramount importance of the contact-

---

terizes a communication was given the name *information* by Claude Shannon and Warren Weaver in 1949, a good half-century after Freud's "Project."

barrier theory of the "Project" for metapsychology's subsequent theory of structural development. However, we shall now specifically show once again that it also demonstrates the great parsimony of the basic theoretical assumptions and the *stringency* of the entire model design. As we have seen, the principle of inertia set forth in the first principal theorem can be reduced to the formula in Figure I–4.

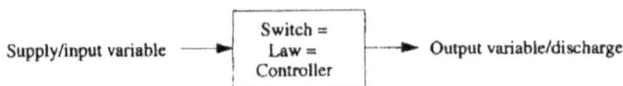

Figure I–4

We have recognized that the working of the contact barriers in Freud's "neurone theory" is based on the application of this principle of inertia: the contact barriers in the pathways also function as controllers of this kind, classifiable according to their position as microcontrollers, subcontrollers, or macrocontrollers. The various controllers (barriers in the pathways) incorporate modifiable laws (threshold values), differing according to the degree of their facilitation and their position, which they apply in order to restore the initial state of *homeostasis*. Any measure (switching operation) that brings the system, at whatever stage of its organization, into a *dynamically stable equilibrium* (the principle of inertia or of constancy) can be understood as a form of homeostatic control. These few assumptions already contain the foundations of the "psychical apparatus" model, as described not only in the "Project" but also in the later versions of Freud's metapsychology: *the entire system is hierarchically structured, regulated specifically according to hierarchical level, and made up simply of (input and output) variables (the subsequent drives) and controllers or switches (the subsequent structures).*

(k) Cathexis

Freud's reflections on the contact-barrier theory had started from the assumption that the psychical apparatus (and, within it, the ψ system in particular) had to lay up a certain store of quantity in order to perform the specific action. This process of "storing" quantities of excitation can now be imagined roughly as follows: if the passage of an excitation proceeds from its source via the φ and/or ψ neurones to some kind of "discharge," climbing through the various interposed contact barriers as if up a staircase—that is, if the thresholds become higher" (the pathways "narrower") step by step (relative to the magnitudes transported)—then a certain store of quantities of excitation can as it were "get stuck" on each step; this will be precisely the store of excitation that is no longer strong enough to cross the next threshold in the sequence. Freud calls this storage of quantities of excitation at each level of the hierarchy a "cathexis." *The facilitation of the contact barriers and the cathexis of the ψ nuclear neurones[22] are therefore the result of one and the same quantitative passage.*

(l) Inhibition

On the basis of this assumption of a cathexis of the ψ group of neurones, Freud now develops a "third powerful factor," *inhibition.* He writes:

> If an adjoining neurone is simultaneously cathected, this acts like a temporary facilitation of the contact-barrier lying between the two, and modifies the course [of the current], which would otherwise have been directed towards the one facilitated contact-barrier. A *side-cathexis* thus acts as *an inhibition of the course of Qἠ. . . .* If we suppose that a Qἠ enters a neurone *a* from outside (φ), then, if it were uninfluenced, it would pass to neurone *b*; but it is so much influenced by the side-cathexis *a—α* that it gives off only a quotient to *b* and may even perhaps not reach *b* at all. [p. 323f.)

---

[22] Within the ψ system, Freud distinguishes between the ψ *nuclear neurones* and the ψ *neurones of the pallium:* since the excitation of the φ system (which receives the exogenous stimuli) itself gives rise to an endogenous stimulus within the psychical apparatus, and the latter after all is supposed to be capable of distinguishing precisely between exogenous and endogenous stimuli—i.e., between *outside* and *inside*—he introduces a *topography of representation* by suggesting that "the ψ neurones should be divided into two groups: the neurones of the *pallium* which are cathected from φ and the *nuclear* neurones which are cathected from the endogenous paths of conduction" (p. 315).

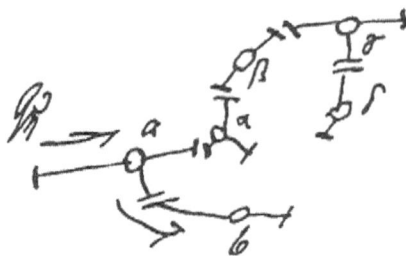

Figure 1–5 Ibid., p. 324.

This completes the development of the deciding factors that both control and (quantitatively) modify the passage of excitations within the psychical apparatus. To recapitulate, the passage of excitation leads to *facilitation* of the contact barriers—to a change in the controllers' resistance (that is, in their switching laws)—so that the excitation is routed in specific divergent directions (those of least resistance); the neurones' *divergence* and *cathexis* reduce (modify) the quantities of excitation and contribute to a further control of their passage, because each cathexis, in the form of a *"side-cathexis,"* can effect a further facilitation; this kind of control constitutes an additional *inhibition* for the course of the excitation. Here, then, Freud is already introducing his theory of the *primary* and *secondary processes* (for the secondary process is substantially characterized by the inhibition of discharge). All these considerations show him at work on a theory of the *control of passages of excitation within his model;* in other words, he is attempting to establish on a general level why a given stimulus follows an absolutely specific path, and which path it follows.

(m) Introduction of the "Ego"

These theses now prove important for the introduction of the ego. The ego is conceived as a *hierarchically supraordinate (macro) structure*—namely, as an *organization* in ψ that influences the passages of excitation in a particular way. Freud imagines its genesis as follows:

> [T]he regularly repeated reception of endogenous Q$\acute{\eta}$ in certain neu-
> rones (of the nucleus) and the facilitating effect proceeding thence will

produce a group of neurones which is constantly cathected and thus corresponds to the *vehicle of the store* required by the secondary function. Thus the ego is to be defined as the totality of the ψ cathexes, at the given time, in which a permanent component is distinguished from a changing one. [p. 323]

This is a *formal* definition of the ego. It states that the ego is composed, or consists, of a group, or network, of cathected neurones; in other words, it is the totality of "a complex of neurones which hold fast to their cathexis, a complex, therefore, which is for short periods at a constant level" (p. 369)—that is, a series of controllers whose operation is integrated (i.e., associated controllers), which, at least "for short periods," operate together by switching principles on approximately the same level—and in the process it so happens that "a permanent component is distinguished from a changing one." This means that the ego has at its disposal, firstly, a *permanent* part made up of cathected ψ neurones with a relatively higher level of organization—corresponding to constant homeostatic regulation at ego or secondary-process level-and, secondly, an additional *changing* part consisting of neurones that are manifestly only temporarily cathected (to a higher degree) and therefore do not belong to the ego's primary stock of neurones. This *interaction* of the ego's permanent nuclear stock, which is no doubt greater, with the fluctuating proportions of elements (neurones) that operate only temporarily at ego level, already constitutes the rudiments of the *dynamic organization of the ego*.

(n) Satisfaction of Needs: Origins of on Object-Relations Theory
Having sketched out this formal ("neurophysiological") model of the ego, Freud develops its *psychological* counterpart, by demonstrating the consequences of *interaction with an object* for the formation of the ego's structure: if, for example, "hunger"—that is, the endogenous stimuli corresponding to hunger—has overcome the various contact barriers and reached the ψ nuclear neurones, then, according to Freud, "ψ is at the mercy of Q, and it is thus that in the interior of the system there arises the impulse which sustains all psychical activity. We know this

power as the *will*—the derivative of the *drives*" (p. 317).[23] What now occurs is as follows.

The filling of the nuclear neurones in ψ will have as its result an effort to discharge, an *urgency* which is released along the motor pathway. Experience shows that here the first path to be taken is that leading to *internal change* (expression of the emotions, screaming, vascular innervation). But . . . no such discharge can produce an unburdening result, since the endogenous stimulus continues to be received and the ψ tension is restored.[24] The removal of the stimulus is only made possible here by an intervention which for the time being gets rid of the release of Qή in the interior of the body; and this intervention calls for an alteration in the external world (supply of nourishment, proximity of the sexual object) which, as a *specific action,* can only be brought about in definite ways. At first, the human organism is incapable of bringing about the specific action. It takes place by *extraneous help,* when the attention of an experienced person is drawn to the child's state by discharge

---

[23] Here as nearly everywhere else in the *Standard Edition,* Strachey translates Freud's term *Trieb* as *instinct;* sometimes, however, it is rendered as "motive" (e.g., *Triebkraft* as *motive force*). Freud in fact distinguished very precisely between *Trieb* and *Instinkt.* In my theoretical reformulation of his drive theory, *Trieb* is understood in a very specific formalized sense (to denote a vector, or unidirectional force), which differs fundamentally not only from the ethological notion of instinct (as a complex structured action or fixed pattern of action) but also from the more complex psychological concept of "motive." For this reason *instinct* and *instinctual* have here been replaced by *drive* in all quotations from the *Standard Edition.* This has occasionally necessitated minor stylistic amendments. *Instinct* is retained only where Freud himself uses the word *Instinkt .* Holt, who advocates the abolition of the concept of *Trieb* and its replacement by "wish," points out "that Freud worked productively for his first 15 years as a psychoanalyst without the concept of *Trieb,* relying primarily on wish as his motivational term" (Holt 1976, quoted in Pribram and Gill1976, p. 57). The passage quoted above, however, proves that Freud worked from the beginning with the idea of the *drive,* even if it only appears explicitly for the first time in his published oeuvre in an insertion, dating from 1915, in the *Three Essays on the Theory of Sexuality ,* in a form analogous in every respect to his 1895 conception: "The source of a drive is a process of excitation occurring in an organ and the immediate aim of the drive lies in the removal of this organic stimulus" (Freud 1905, p. 168).

[24] [Translator's note: "and restores the ψ tension" would be a more accurate translation.]

along the path of internal change. In this way this path of discharge acquires a secondary function of the highest importance, that of *communication,* and the initial helplessness of human beings is the primal source of all *moral motives.* [p. 317f.]

It is thus clear that Freud incorporates the "external object" into his theory of the psychical apparatus from the beginning. The description of the first decisive interactions between mother and child thus contains the *basic schema* of every relationship between *inside and outside*—and hence the origin and nucleus of a *psychoanalytic theory of object relations*—*while* at the same time furnishing a pattern for the structuring processes, or processes of adaptation and learning, within the psychical apparatus: a "helpful object" for the first time makes possible the "specific action" that eliminates the urgency and, at the same time, the cause of the endogenous excitation, namely hunger. The result is an experience of satisfaction "which has the most radical results on the development of the individual's functions" (p. 318). What happens is that links are forged between (1) the specific neurones of the ψ nucleus that are affected by this urgency, (2) a cathexis of specific neurones of the ψ pallium that are excited by the (visual, olfactory, gustatory, tactile, auditory, etc.) perception of the helpful object, and (3) the "information of the reflex discharge" (which also takes the form of sensory excitations) that leads to a cathexis elsewhere in the ψ pallium, where it so to speak produces a "motor image" of the specific action. "A facilitation is then formed between these cathexes and the nuclear neurones" (ibid.). By virtue of this facilitation, every new endogenous excitation of the same kind—that is, every urgency generated by a *need stimulus* from the same source—will lead, in accordance with the "basic law of *association by simultaneity*", to a series of sensory excitations (equivalent to an *"object image"*) and "sensory excitations (from the skin and muscles)" (ibid.)—that is to say, a *"motor image."* Hence an *endo-senso-motor association* between *need, object, and action* is facilitated—and this association forms the basis of *hallucination.*

(o) The ω System

A fresh difficulty now arises. If the object images and motor images once associated are recathected—that is, "remembered" (hallucinated)—

upon each drive stimulus from the same source, how is the psychical apparatus then to tell whether the image of the object summoned up by an endogenous stimulus is a hallucination (reproduction) or a perception of reality (reception), and, consequently, to decide when it is appropriate to perform a motor action?

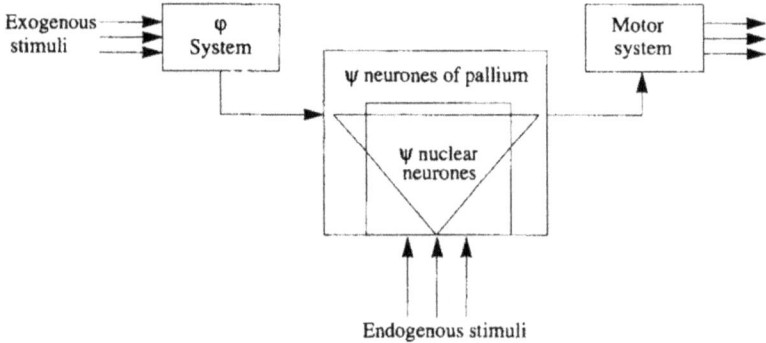

Figure I–6 Diagrammatic representation of the φ-ψ system. The three vertices of the triangle stand for the need *(drive stimulus)* (bottom),the *object image* (left). and the *motor image* (right), which are all excited together in hallucination, combined into a pattern of association (that is, a wish).

Freud links the answer to this question, at least in part, to the conception of *consciousness*—and the phenomenon of consciousness, which every psychology both finds interesting and needs to explain, has, after all, not yet been elucidated within his model. He reflects as follows.

> During perception the φ and the ψ systems are in operation together; but there is one psychical process which is no doubt performed exclusively in ψ—reproducing or remembering—and this, speaking generally, is *without quality*. Remembering brings about *de norma* [normally] nothing that has the peculiar character of perceptual quality. Thus we summon up courage to assume that there is a third system of neurones—ω perhaps [we might call it]—which is excited along with perception, but not along with reproduction, and whose states of excitation give rise to the various qualities—are, that is to say, *conscious sensations.* [p. 308f.]

> Here consciousness is the subjective side of one part of the physical processes in the nervous system, namely of the *m* processes; and the omission of consciousness does not leave psychical events unaltered but involves the omission of the contribution from *ω*. [p. 311]

At first sight, Freud seems to be trying to resolve the issue of perception and consciousness tautologically by the introduction of neurones of perception or consciousness (ω for its resemblance to the "*W*" of *Wahrnehmung,* the German word for perception)—that is, with the aid of an ω *system:* consciousness is equated with the activity of neurones of consciousness, and omission of consciousness with the inactivity of these neurones. However, with the complex of the ω neurones, Freud is introducing a *third* system; this fact alone should preserve us from the temptation to dismiss the ω neurones overhastily as a tautological pseudo-explanation for consciousness. For all the variant forms of Freud's models are characterized by a *duality of variables* and a *triad of controllers* —*for* example, the systems φ, ψ, and ω, the *Ucs., Pcs.,* and *Cs.;* or the structures id, superego, and ego. Does this ω system, then, have some special aspect that could not be conceptualized by the two systems introduced previously?

Let us now follow Freud as he sets about incorporating the ω neurones into his system. The idea is that the ω system is excited *upon every external perception* from φ via ψ, or direct from φ; the ω excitation will then result in an ω discharge, information of which will in turn pass to ψ because ψ registers all *changes* (whether increases or decreases) in endogenous excitations, and hence also those in φ and ω. "*The information of the discharge from ω is thus the indication of quality or of reality for ψ*" (p. 325). This applies in the first place to all simple perceptual processes.

However, an intense endogenous excitation in ψ alone—that is, if "the wished-for object is abundantly cathected" (ibid.) or sought—could give rise to an indication of quality of this kind in ω. The initial question as to the distinction between a mnemic image (hallucination or wish) and a perception of reality, which is so important for the organism's self-preservation, can therefore be answered *quantitatively* only by saying that the processes in ψ must be subject to a (quantitative) inhibition in order for them not to trigger an indication of *reality* in ω. This inhibition is now made possible by the ego, that "network of cathected neurones well facilitated in relation to one another" (p. 323), which, precisely, distributes a part of the quantities of excitation in the direction of the facilitated contact barriers among the cathected neurones (including "side-cathexes"), binding the quantity of excitation present and thus reducing the level of excitation. By the "hypothesis of what is, as it were, a *bound state*" in the neurones, Freud reconciles two opposing requirements, "strong cathexis and weak displacement" of quantities; and this is the very state that makes the process of thought, or intense attention, possible (p. 368f.)—characterizing the *secondary process* as opposed to the *primary process.* The residual "unbound" ("freely mobile") quantities in ψ then no longer suffice to produce in ω the indication of quality for the perception of reality. This allows Freud to add the following explanation: "It is accordingly *inhibition by the ego which makes possible a criterion for distinguishing between perception and memory*" (p. 326).

(p) The Function of Speech

However, the process of remembering is also able, and intended, to reach consciousness, and what is conscious is, after all, supposed to be connected with discharge, however minimal, in ω. The problem is as follows:

> Indications of quality come about normally only from perceptions; it is thus a question of obtaining a perception from the passage of Qή. If a discharge were linked to the passage of Qή (in addition to the [mere] circulation), then, like every movement, it [the discharge] would furnish information of the movement. After all, indications of quality themselves are only information of discharge. . . . It is a question, however, of receiving discharges of this kind from all cathexes. They are not all motor, and for this purpose, therefore, they must be brought into a secure facilitation with motor neurones.
>
> This purpose is fulfilled by *speech association.* This consists in the linking of ψ neurones with neurones which serve sound-presentations

and themselves have the closest association with motor speech-images.
.. In any case, from the sound-image the excitation reaches the word-image and from it reaches discharge. Thus, if the mnemic images are of such a kind that a part-current can go from them to the sound-images and motor word-images, then the cathexis of the mnemic images is accompanied by information of discharge, which is an indication of quality and also accordingly an indication of the consciousness of the memory. [p. 364f.]

Remembering or thinking can thus become conscious only subject to the use of "motor word-images," or "*indications of speech-discharge*": "they put thought-processes on a level with perceptual processes, lend them reality and *make memory of them possible*" (p. 366). The slight innervation of the motor apparatus of speech, triggered by an activated associative network, produces the indications of discharge (i.e., the quantitative amount) necessary for satisfying the criteria of consciousness within the model. That is to say, *conscious thinking is always coded in the form of speech.* We now have a firm criterion for a quantitative distinction between perception and ideation (conscious or unconscious reproductive thinking, or memory), and all that remains to be shown is how the two can be made to coincide, for example for the purpose of need satisfaction.

(q) The "Reality Principle"

If it is borne in mind "that perceptual cathexes are never cathexes of single neurones but always of complexes" of neurones (p. 327), and, in addition, that the need likewise excites an entire associative chain of neurones belonging to the ψ nucleus and the ψ pallium—that is, also a *specific complex* of neurones—it will readily be conceived that "[b]iological experience" (the requirement of the principle of constancy—in this case, the persistence of states of disequilibrium) will teach "that it is unsafe to initiate discharge if the indications of reality do not confirm the whole complex but only a part of it" (p. 328). This is an interesting point, because we are now dealing with the excitation of two neuronal complexes connected in parallel, one of which (the perceptual complex) is required to confirm the other (the need complex, or wish). The "activation of the wish" will therefore trigger, or "cathect," a specific pattern, a specific associative series, in ψ, and lay it down as a reference for the overall perception in the searching movement (selective perception); it is only upon the appearance of a perception in the outside world, which activates a corresponding matching pattern in ω via the φ and ψ neurones of the pallium, that the specific quantitative amplification (a kind of "doubling") that initiates final "discharge" will occur via the feedback to ψ. This could also be put as follows. The associative pattern of the memory trace in ψ contains the neuronal excitations of the need stimulus, the satisfying object, and the satisfying action; the associative pattern of the (external) perception in ω contains (in favorable cases) only the excitation values of the (matching) satisfying object; hence the performance of the satisfying action completes the pattern in combination with the need stimulus and thereby makes it a better match overall. From this point of view, matching, too, would in formal terms be simply a kind of "equilibrium state" of two patterns of excitation (on a higher hierarchical level).

The postulate of the ω system thus introduces a *reference value* that manifestly performs the function of an *integration* or, if you will, comparison of pattern formations of neuronal (or psychic) excitation complexes. This can be pictured as follows. In the simple process of "disinterested contentment"—that is, what might be described as a need-free perception (as, for example, in the situation of "evenly suspended attention")—the ψ neurones of the pallium and the ω neurones are excited from φ, and their discharge, as an indication of quality or reality, gives rise to the amplification of excitation in the ψ neurones of the pallium that results in the phenomenon of conscious perception. Conversely, in a state of need-induced tension, a specific pattern of associated neurones is excited in the ψ nucleus and the ψ pallium; the pattern of excitation of any merely random perception will not match this pattern (it will seem "insignificant"), and will therefore remain quantitatively subliminal overall, because a comparison of patterns between the excitation complexes in ψ and ω, which are superimposed like two filters, now occurs —and it is only in the event of an optimum match between the patterns that the necessary quantitative amplification takes place for triggering in ω the indication of reality for conscious perception of the object "that promises satisfaction." In other words, then, ω is the system crucial both to consciousness and to distinguishing between internal and external perceptions—mainly by comparing and, where appropriate, integrating and processing the patterns of different excitation complexes on two levels; the ω system thus operates on a more complex level than the ψ system, so that it belongs on a higher hierarchical plane. Moreover, since Freud links consciousness to ω, the ω system by definition corresponds to the later *system Cs.,* while the ψ processes of the 1895 ego may be said to correspond to the system *Pcs.;* similarly, in the eventual structure theory of 1923, the ego would have its roots in ψ and include ω.

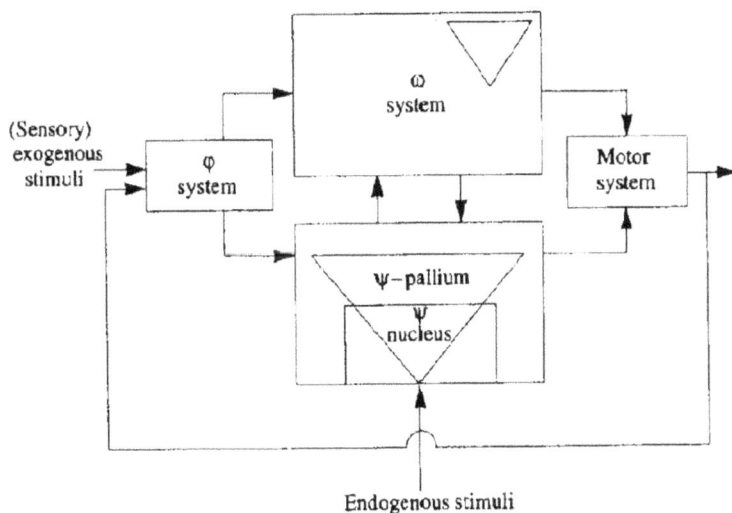

Figure 1-7. This diagram is merely a simplified representation of the systems construct-ed by Freud in the "Project" and the referencing processes that take place within them. In the process of need satisfaction in reality, the smaller triangle in the ω system (the perceptual pattern) is required to be brought into coincidence with the larger triangle in the ψ system (the need pattern—i.e., the wish); the need pattern is the reference for orientation and coordination with the perceptual pattern: the latter makes the organism better able, on each succeeding occasion, deliberately to bring about an experience of satisfaction, and/or to perform a "specific action."

That completes my presentation of several key assumptions of the *Project*. Up until this point, Freud's theoretical deliberations proved to be successful. They conformed without problem with an interesting, viable model, that would later become the basis of what he termed his "psychic apparatus". I do not wish to discuss here his failed attempts to introduce the repression of a "mechanistic resolution" to psychopathology, and thus to incorporate it into his system (on this subject, see Schmidt-Hellerau, 2001); although the concept had already been applied to his hypothesis, Freud became bogged down in ever more complicated additional assumptions, that fundamentally contradicted "that simplification ... for which we strive in scientific work" (Freud 1930, p. 119). Despite this, he continued to work intensively on this demanding project:

> "I keep returning to psychology; I cannot escape its compelling call. What I have is probably neither a million, nor yet a kreuzer—but a lump of ore containing unknown quantities of precious metal. On the whole, I am satisfied with my progress, but am contending with hostility and live in such isolation that one might imagine I had discovered the greatest truths." (Letter to Fließ, dated 16 March 1896; Freud, 1985, p. 178f.).

A third notebook, dedicated to the problem of repression, that he kept back when sending his missive to Fließ, was never completed, and until today no trace of it has been found.[25] In his correspondence with Fließ, Freud turned increasingly, from spring 1896, to other subjects – it is

---

[25] Jones (1953, p. 287ff.) related the story of what happened to the *Project*: Freud left both notebooks with Fließ; after Fließ died (in 1928), his widow sold Freud's letters and scientific notes, including the *Project*, to the Berlin-based book dealer, Reinhold Stahl, who fled France to escape the National Socialists, selling the entire package to Marie Bonaparte for 100 pounds; she took the documents to Vienna, and spoke to her analyst, Freud, about them, who showed himself to be very annoyed about it, and seemingly wished for the papers to be destroyed; Marie Bonaparte defied him; after the invasion of the National Socialists, she took the texts back to Paris, from where they were taken to London at the end of the war. In 1950, an abbreviated version of the *Project* was published by Marie Bonaparte, Anna Freud and Ernst Kris alongside a selection of Freud's letters to Fließ; the full version of the *Project* with comprehensive commentaries was published in 1966 in volume 1 of Freud's *Standard Edition*.

doubtful whether he had finished his reflections on the remaining open questions of his *Entwurf*, since in December 1896, he suddenly and abruptly confessed within an entirely different context (a commentary on Fließ's theory of periodicity and pheromones): "Hidden deep within this is my ideal and woebegone child—metapsychology" (Letter to Fließ dated December 17, 1896; Freud, 1985, p. 216).

Ambivalence towards a difficult inheritance

"No other document in the history of psychoanalysis has brought about such a tangled mass of conflict with so little agreement as has Freud's *Project*" (Sulloway, 1979, p. 176; consult this for an extended description of the disputes, p. 177ff.). Sulloway attributed the controversies around the discovery of the *Project*, above all, to the fact that, at this point, the already well-established history of Freud's intellectual development was suddenly apparently inflected by an unwelcome prehistory to metapsychology (unwelcome because it concerned neurology). From the start, reactions were divided: there was idealized admiration and recognition of the enormous significance of the *Project*, on the one hand, and denigration and an attempt to immediately assign this early outline to Freud's "preanalytical" period, on the other, thus to exclude it again from the accepted body of psychoanalytical writings. So, for instance, Kris (1950, p. 541f.) stressed the bravery and consistency with which Freud had attempted in the *Project* to comprehend brain physiology and psychology as a whole, but he also called his study a *tyrant* that Freud had supposedly *banished* due to lack of ongoing interest. Jones termed the *Project* a "magnificent *tour de force*...of great value to the student of Freud's psychology because it throws light on many of his later conceptions" (Jones 1953, p. 383), but simultaneously criticized the "richness of the ideas contained in the Project, and the extraordinarily close relationship subsisting among them" (*ibid.*), and accusing it of "relative sterility" (*ibid.*, p. 384). Strachey, it is true, admitted that the "Project, in spite of being ostensibly a neurological document, contains within itself the nucleus of a great part of Freud's later psychological theories" (Strachey in Freud 1950, p. 290), but insisted that "The *Project* must remain a torso, disavowed by its creator" (1950, p. 293). While, with reference to these first commentaries, above all to the authoritative judgment of Strachey, some perceived a radical break between the "neurological" *Project* and the "psychological" *Interpretation of Dreams*,[26] others (Holt, 1965, Klein, 1973, 1976, Schafer, 1976, Stolorow, 1978) emphasized the continuity in Freud's thought, and extrapolated from it from then onwards, using it as the foundation for their own various efforts at revision. It is evident that of all of Freud's works the *Project* seemed to possess the greatest potential for irritation. Herein lies the germ cell for innumerable debates about the position of metapsychology between the natural sciences and the humanities – the outcome of these debates, it was feared, would be altogether decisive for the value and future of psychoanalysis.

Since I have dealt with the arguments featured in these debates elsewhere (1993, 1995, 2001), finally, I would like here to briefly discuss the actual *subjective* – rather than the assumed *objective* – reasons that played a perhaps too rarely considered role in the debates around the value or lack of value of the *Project* – and of metapsychology.

One would be glad to be rid of something that caused one such difficulties. It is for this reason that the entire "for" and "against" argumentation in respect of the *Project* also *has* a markedly emotional aspect, which, nonetheless, largely remained hidden behind well-schooled rationalisations. Freud repeatedly brought our attention to the limitations of the formation of our opinions,[27] and these naturally apply equally to analysts. Even in his case – as with all other researchers –

---

[26] The idea of a radical break between a *neurological* and a "purely" *psychological* theory overlooks that the model of the "psychic apparatus", developed in chapter VII of the *Interpretation of Dreams*, recoups almost all the assumptions of the *Entwurf* – for which reason, Freud was able to declare: "*The Interpretation of Dreams* ... was finished in all essentials at the beginning of 1896 but was not written out until the summer of 1899." (Freud, 1914, p. 22).

[27] It was in this manner, for instance, that Freud spoke about *unconscious motives*: "it is an event of daily occurrence for a person—even a healthy person—to deceive himself over the motives for an action and to become conscious of them only after the event, provided only that a conflict between several currents of feeling furnishes the necessary condition for such a confusion." (Freud, 1907, p. 66)

personal motives occasionally had a determining influence on his declared scientific opinions. In the case of the *Project:* perhaps one would rather not be numbered among those within the scientific community who are still concerned with the ideas about neurology from the late 19th century? Would it not be better to affiliate oneself with current thought, which considers these early theoretical efforts by Freud – as well as his drive and energy concepts, by the way, and even to some degree the whole of metapsychology – to be obsolete? The discrediting of psycholoanalysis *ex cathedra*, well covered in the media (Grawe et. al., 1994), exerts a considerable, often underestimated pressure on individuals, and exacerbates a tendency towards opportunism, which is the enemy of any kind of scientific progress (because it undermines interest in a subject, spoils any pleasure taken in researching it, and directs the gaze away from the object of knowledge towards personal prejudice). Many researchers are almost ashamed today to still be arguing in psychoanalytical terms, employing a theory that is now over a hundred years old.

In such a case of rejection, motivated in this way, of the original ideas of the old master – at least in respect of one or another of his concepts – the other side comes into play, which may be deemed something specific to psychoanalysis. No other science has such a markedly personal relationship with its founder as this one does. This goes beyond any acknowledgment of Freud's great achievements, and does not just concern him as a historically important figure. People seem to feel almost personally indebted to him. However, there is a negative side to such proximity,[28] whereby the conflict between being *true to the father of psychoanalysis* and the *urge to disempower the dominant father figure* is pre-programmed. The *Project* appears to offer an outlet of a kind: since Freud himself spoke out against the publication of papers from the Fließ estate, one can finally for once let go of the reins with one's criticism. Nonetheless, sensitized by their

---

[28] The willingly undertaken attempts by investigative journalism, to knock Freud down from his pedestal (for instance, Masson, 1984), have regularly pervaded the history of psychoanalysis until the present day.

métier, analysts do not misjudge the castrating dimension of their insurrection against the founding father, and thus attempt, employing sophisticated rhetorical strategies, to salve their consciences. An interesting (and amusing) example of denial of such castrating desires (marked with a [c] in the following quotation) and their projection (marked with a [p] in the following quotation) onto the reader, is offered by Laplanche, for instance: first of all, Laplanche refers to the *Entwurf* as " the most important [text] for Freud's metapsychology, if one acknowledges that the attempt then to combine sexuality and repression organically from the inside to form a single theory was most developed in it" (1988, p. 48). Then he continues:

"It is surely not easy, to remove concepts belonging to a terminological context from their conceptual apparatus, which is in part obsolete, making any approach to the *Project for a Scientific Psychology* difficult. This will certainly make readers of today [p] uncomfortable as they read this text. Either they will enter into the form of representation employed by Freud, until they come back to their senses and have to ask themselves, whether they have not just stumbled into a monstrous pseudo-scientific machinery [c], that has little [to do] with psychological realities", or they try again from the start to distinguish what within it is a vehicle for early psychoanalytical experience, from the remnants of a banal scientistic pattern of thought [c]. And yet if one adopts this second attitude, then one must admit, that the greater part of the *Project* must be repudiated [c]. Nonetheless, we have not, despite the opinion of many historians of Freud's teaching [p] and despite Freud's own judgment [p], surrendered to systematically responding, for the time being, to the complex labyrinth of this text and to subjecting ourselves to such a forbidding "technicity" [c]; we will allow ourselves to be guided by the certainty that a great work – one fed by rich experience – would not [denial] easily allow itself to be cut up into good and bad parts [c]" (1988, p. 48f.).

Should all criticism be vilified as a "triumph over the old gentleman"? Certainly not. However, the contradiction in Laplanche's statements draws our attention to the fact that we – in positive and negative cases – will not get anywhere with ad personam argumentation.[29]

When Strachey acknowledges the similarities of the deliberations in the *Project* with the "hypotheses of information theory and cybernetics in their application to the nervous system" (Strachey in Freud 1950, p. 292) and admits that: "Such resemblances, and others, if they were confirmed, would no doubt be fresh evidence of the originality and fertility of Freud's ideas" (*ibid.*, p. 293), and yet simultaneously closes the door to this new dimension with the justification that because "there is a risk that enthusiasm may lead to a distortion of Freud's use of terms and may read into his obscure remarks modern interpretations that they will not bear" (Strachey in Freud, 1950, p. 293), then he is arguing *ad personam*, suggesting that we should understand and interpret Freud's writing only in so far as he himself understood them – or at least wanted them to be understood. This claim is entirely unanalytical. It sounds like the defense of an analysand who objects to an interpretation by pleading that he meant what he said in a different way, and that is how he wants it to be understood. Should we only understand in Freud's writings what he himself understood? Or should we also attempt to understand what manifests, develops and is expressed in these texts? What *Freud personally* meant and wanted, when he understood and employed a concept (for instance, a neurological one), is primarily of biographical interest.

---

[29] Even Anzieu argues in *absentia* by analyizing Freud: "One comprehends that Freud did not intend to publish the *Project*. It was, for him, an underdeveloped text, with which he declared himself very swiftly to be unsatisfied. Certainly, some intuitions are inherent within it, and several concepts, which would later become some of the permanent achievements of psychoanalysis, are formulated here for the first time. In this sense, this text forms a compromise. To be precise: due to his scientific mind-set, and, as we will see, *owing to his personal hysterophobic psychopathological organisation, Freud required a conceptual framework, which kept the phenomena to be investigated at a distance*, without obscuring them; in this way *he could risk seeing them* as they were, with acuity and foresight – *and inspect them* … Today, as in 1895, the epistemological situation is the same: one can only observe the wish, the fantasy, the repression, the representability and the derivatives of the unconscious, when one departs from any schema that uses systems created by humans as a model" (1988, p. 62f., emphasis of the author).

Of scientific interest, on the contrary, is what kind of *theory* is contained in his metapsychological works – and here in the *Project*. And if we are to be fair to him: Freud himself did not intend it any other way, when he appraised his "Psychology for Neurologists" – despite the high demands it placed on him – soberly, clearly and far from any kind of idealization or invalidation, saying, "What I have is probably neither a million, nor yet a kreuzer—but a lump of ore containing unknown quantities of precious metal." (Freud, 1985, p. 179). He gave us a lump of unworked ore as a legacy, from which who knows how much precious metal can be won – what an exciting task he has handed to us!

References

Amacher, P. (1965): Freud's Neurological Education and Its Influence on Psychoanalytic Theory. *Psychol. Issues*, 4, Monographie 16.

Anzieu, D. (1988): *Freuds Selbstanalyse*. vol. 1, 1895-1898. Munich/Vienna (Verlag Internationale Psychoanalyse) 1990.

Applegarth, A. (1971): Comments on Aspects of the Theory of Psychic Energy. *J. Amer. Psychanal. Assn.*, 19, 379-416.

Basch, M. F. (1975): Perception, Consciousness, and Freud's "Project". *Annual of Psychoanal.*, 3, 3-19.

Bernfeld, S. (1944): Freuds früheste Theorien und die Helmholtz-Schule, in: S. Bernfeld and S. Cassirer Bernfeld *(1988): Bausteine der Freud-Biographik*. Frankfurt (Suhrkamp), 54-77.

Bernfeld, S. (1949): Freuds wissenschaftliche Anfänge, in: S. Bernfeld and S. Cassirer Bernfeld *(1988): Bausteine der Freud-Biographik*. Frankfurt (Suhrkamp), 112-147.

Braitenberg, V., and A. Schütz (1989): Cortex: hohe Ordnung oder größtmögliches Durcheinander? in: *Chaos und Fraktale, Spektrum der Wissenschaft*, 164-176.

Drews, S., and K. Brecht (1982): Psychoanalytische Ich-Psychologie. *Grundlagen und Entwicklung*. Frankfurt (Suhrkamp).

Ellenberger, H.F. (1970): Die Entdeckung des Unbewußten. *Geschichte und Entwicklung der dynamischen Psychiatrie von den Anfängen bis zu Janet, Freud, Adler und Jung*. Zürich (Diogenes) 1985.

Exner, S. (1894): *Entwurf zu einer Physiologischen Erklärung der Psychischen Erscheinungen.* Leipzig (Franz Deuticke).

Freud, S. (1891): On Aphasia: A Critical Study, ed. and trans. E. Stengel. London: Imago, 1953.

Freud, S. (1893): Some Points for a Comparative Study of Organic and Hysterical Motor Paralyses. *SE* 1.

Freud, S. (1895): Studies on Hysteria. *SE* 2.

Freud, S. (1900): The Interpretation of Dreams. *SE* 4-5.

Freud, S. (1905): Three Essays on the theory of sexuality. *SE*, 7.

Freud, S. (1907): Delusions and Dreams in Jensen's "Gradiva". *SE* V9.

Freud, S. (1909): Notes upon a case of obsessional neurosis. *SE* 10.

Freud, S. (1914d): On the History of the Psycho-Analytic Movement. *SE* 14.

Freud, S. (1925): "An Autobiographical Study". *SE* 20.

Freud, S. (1930a): Civilization and its discontents. *GW* 21.

Freud, S. (1950): Project for a Scientific Psychology. *SE 1.*

Freud, S. (1953): On Aphasia. A Critical Study. New York, International Universities Press INC.

Freud, S. (1985): The Complete Letters of Sigmund Freud to Wilhelm Fließ, 1887-1904. *Translated and Edited by* J.M. Masson, The Belknap Press of Harvard University Press, Cambridge, Massachusetts and London 1985.

Gill, M. (1976): Die Metapsychologie ist keine Psychologie. *Psyche*, 38 (1984), 961-992.

Grawe, K., R. Donati and F. Bernauer (1994): Psychotherapie im Wandel. *Von der Konfession zur Profession.* Göttingen/Bern (Hogrefe).

Grubrich-Simitis, I. (1987): Trauma oder Trieb – Trieb und Trauma. Lektionen aus Sigmund Freuds phylogenetischer Phantasie von 1915. *Psyche*, 41, 992-1023.

Hebb, D.O. (1955): Drives and the C.N.S. (conceptual nervous system). *Psychol. Rev.*, 62, 243-254.

Holt, R. (1965): A Review of Some of Freud's Biological Assumptions and Their Influence on His Theories, in: N.S. Greenfield and W.C. Lewis (eds.): *Psychoanalysis and Current Biological Thought.* Madison/Milwaukee (University of Wisconsin Press), 93-124.

Holt, R. (1976): Drive or Wish? A Reconsideration of the Psychoanalytic Theory of Motivation, in: M. Gill and P.S. Holzman (eds.): *Psychology versus Metapsychology. Psychoanalytic Essays in Memory of George S. Klein. Psychol. Issues, 9, Monograph 36*. New York (International Universities Press), 158-197.

Jones, E. (1953): The Life and Work of Sigmund Freud, vol. 1, New York: Basic Books, Inc.

Kernberg, O.F. (1993): The Current Status of Psychoanalysis. *J. Amer. Psychanal. Assn.*, 41, 45-62.

Klein, G.S. (1973): Two Theories or One? *Bull. Menn. Cl.*, 37, 102-132.

Klein, G.S. (1976): Psychoanalytic Theory. *An Exploration of Essentials*. New York (International Universities Press).

Kris, E. (1950) Einleitung für den Auswahlband der Briefe an Fließ sowie der Erstpublikation des Entwurfs unter dem Titel: Aus den Anfängen der Psychoanalyse. *Citations here from the reprint in Freud, 1985c*, 519-561.

Kuhn, T.S. (1962): *Die Struktur wissenschaftlicher Revolutionen*. Frankfurt (Suhrkamp) 1978.

Laplanche, J. (1988): Leben und Tod in der Psychoanalyse. Translation from French to German by Peter Stehlin. Frankfurt: Nexus Verlag.

Leuschner, W. (1989): Zur Entstehungsgeschichte psychoanalytischer Begriffe. Freuds Auseinandersetzung mit der Aphasielehre, in: H. Bareuther, H.-J. Busch, D. Ohlmeier and T. Plänkers (eds.): *Forschen und Heilen. Auf dem Weg zu einer psychoanalytischen Hochschule. Beiträge aus Anlaß des 25 jährigen Bestehens des Sigmund-Freud-Instituts*. Frankfurt (Suhrkamp), 536-552.

Masson, J. (1984): *The Assault on Truth: Freud's Suppression of the Seduction Theory*. London (Faber & Faber).

Mertens, W. (ed.) (1981): *Neue Perspektiven der Psychoanalyse*. Stuttgart (Kohlhammer).

Meynert, T. (1878): *Über Fortschritte im Verständnis der krankhaften psychische Gehirnzustände*. Vienna (Wilhelm Braumüller K. K. Hof- und Universitätsbuchhändler).

Peterfreund, E. (1971): Information, Systems, and Psychoanalysis. *An Evolutionary Biological Approach to Psychoanalytic Theory. Psychol. Issues, 7, Monograph 25/26*. New York (International Universities Press).

Peterfreund, E. (1975): The Need for a New General Theoretical Frame of Reference for Psychoanalysis. *Symposium on The Ego and the Id After Fifty Years. Psychoanal. Quarterly*, 44, 534-534.

Peters, R. (1960): *The Concept of Motivation*. 2nd edition. London New York (Humanities Press).

Pribram, K.H. (1962): The Neuropsychology of Sigmund Freud., in: A.J. Bachrach (Ed.) (1962): *Experimental Foundations of Clinical Psychology*. New York (Basic Books).

Pribram, K.H. (1969): The Foundation of Psychoanalytic Theory: Freud's Neuropsychological Model. *Brain and Behaviour*, 4, 395-432.

Pribram, K.H. and M.M. Gill (1976): Freud's "Project" Re-assessed. *Preface to Contemporary Cognitive Theory and Neurology*. New York (Basic Books).

Rapaport, D. (1960): Die Struktur der psychoanalytischen Theorie. *Versuch einer Systematik*. Stuttgart (Klett) 1973.

Rubinstein, B. (1965): Psychoanalytic Theory and the Mind-Body-Problem, in: N.S. Greenfield und W.C. Lewis (ed.): *Psychoanalysis and Current Biological Thought*. Madison/Milwaukee (University of Wisconsin Press), 35-56.

Schafer, R. (1976): *Eine neue Sprache für die Psychoanalyse*. Stuttgart (Klett-Cotta) 1982.

Schmidt-Hellerau, C. (1993): Überbau oder Fundament? Zur Metapsychologie und Me-tapsychologiedebatte. *Psyche*, 47, 1-30.

Schmidt-Hellerau, C. (1995): Lebenstrieb & Todestrieb, Libido & Lethe. *Ein formalisiertes konsistentes Modell der psychoanalytischen Trieb- und Strukturtheorie*. Stuttgart (Verlag Internationale Psychoanalyse).

Solms, M., and M. Saling (1986): On Psychoanalysis and Neuroscience: Freud's Attitude to the Localizationist Tradition. *Int. J. Psychoanal.*, 67, 397-416.

Stewart, L. (1967): Freud before Oedipus: Race and Heredity in the Origins of Psychoanalysis. *Journal of the History of Biology*, 9, 215-228.

Stolorow, R.D. (1978): The Concept of Psychic Structure: Its Meta-Psychological and Clinical Psychoanalytic Meanings. *Int. J. Psychoanal.*, 5, 313-320.

Sulloway, F.J. (1979): Freud, Biologe der Seele. *Jenseits der psychoanalytischen Legende*. Cologne (Hohenheim) 1982.

Wiener, N. (1948): Kybernetik. *Regelung und Nachrichtenübertragung im Lebewesen und in der Maschine.* Düsseldorf (Econ) 1963.

Wollheim, R. (1972): *Sigmund Freud.* Munich (Deutscher Taschenbuch Verlag).

CHAPTER 2

Libido and Lethe

Fundamentals of a Formalized Conception of Metapsycholgy[*]

On the basis of a chronological review of some of Freud's principal metapsychological writings, I inquire into the logical consistency of the theoretical foundations of psychoanalysis. Particular attention is devoted to the functions ascribed by Freud to the two basic axioms of his model of the psyche, namely the two antagonistic drives (originally called the sexual and self-preservative drives and ultimately the life and death drives) on the one hand, and a balancing principle (inertia, constancy, pleasure or Nirvana) on the other. I adopt a formalized view of these concepts, considering the drives as vectors and concentrating on their directionality. The psychical apparatus as modelled by Freud is then seen to be constructed along homoeostatic lines, the dynamic stability of the psyche as a system being assured by the combination of, firstly, a (+)drive and a (-)drive as variables and, secondly, a structure, in accordance with the relevant regulating principle. I show that Freud remained faithful to this basic idea throughout his career notwithstanding all the changes in his theory. Preserving this consistency and with a view to the exploration of a fresh dimension of the mind, I suggests the introduction of a new concept, lethe, for the energy of the death drive.

---

[*] (1997) International Journal of Psycho-Analysis, 78:683-697. Translated from German into English by Philip Slotkin, MA (Cantab.), MITI.

Metapsychology has in the last few decades been subjected to detailed, fundamental criticism from many points of view, highlighting the weaknesses of its concepts and their definitions and drawing attention to its lack of systematization. Serious doubts have in consequence been cast on its utility, especially as regards the further development of clinical work and theory. However, one question has remained open, an answer to which could in my view place the function of metapsychology in a new perspective and offer a boost to clinical and interdisciplinary research. That question is as follows: *is the basic theoretical model of psychoanalysis, which we call metapsychology, logically consistent?* Rapaport did not doubt that it is:

> The theory of psychoanalysis grew by successive spurts in the fifty years of Freud's work. Additions and revisions make it appear more like a patchwork than an architectonic design … Yet psychoanalytic theory does have an impressive structured unity, though it is hidden under the layers of progressive additions and modifications, and has not been disentangled and independently stated (1960p. 101, my italics).

What Rapaport is here suggesting is tantamount to an *archaeology of the argument structure* that underlies the metapsychological papers. If we are interested in the argument *structure* of the theoretical foundations of psychoanalysis, we focus not on the *contents* or *propositions* of the arguments *as such* but on the *links* between them. In so doing, we treat the metapsychological concepts developed and modified over a period of some three decades as integral parts of a theoretical corpus that presents a model in the sense of an '*imaginary entity*, an *experiment in thinking* that will bring some measure of order to the raw data of psychoanalysis derived from the psychoanalytic situation itself' (Modell, 1981 p. 393, my italics). The following is true of this model: 'models are not things, are not concretizations, but are only efforts to *describe relationships*: they are not explanations of relationships, but … they can set up questions in ways that can lead to fruitful answers or explanations' (Wallerstein, 1977p. 532, my italics). To obtain as clear as possible a view of these relationships, which Freud describes within his model of the 'psychical apparatus', it is a good plan to consider his metapsychological notions and concepts from the purely formal point of view. The implications of this approach are described below.

A central question that runs consistently through Freud's metapsychological papers is how the equilibrium of the psychical apparatus is maintained. A more modern formulation would be: what conditions are necessary for the psyche as a system to be capable of maintaining a state of homoeostasis or dynamic stability? Freud answers this question by postulating *two antagonistic drives* (originally called the sexual drive and the self-preservative drive, and finally the life drive and the death drive) as well as a *principle of regulation* (the zero principle, the principle of constancy, the pleasure-unpleasure principle, the reality principle and ultimately the Nirvana principle), which is responsible for maintaining or restoring psychical equilibrium. The sexual drive may thus be said to be directed *outwards*, towards the external love object, while the self-preservative drive is focused *inwards* on the preservation of the subject's own person. *Outwards* and *inwards* are opposites like *life* and *death, waking* and *sleeping, drive* and *repression, yes* and *no*, or, more generally, *plus* and *minus*. Consideration of the situation in these terms—that is, disregarding the *experienceable meanings* of, for example, sexuality and self-preservation and envisaging the drives in the sense of vectors, solely from the point of view of their opposing (+/-)-directionality—is what I understand by a *'formalized'* view of these concepts. According to this approach, the notions and concepts of psychoanalytic theory interest us only as 'auxiliary constructions' —i.e. as *constructs* or *a priori propositions* —that allow us to conceive in *thought* of certain connections and sequences, and also to arrive at a clear idea of the *manner* in which we conceive them in thought. Hence the question is not 'What did Freud think (or intend)?' but '*How* did he think?' What are the basic assumptions and movements of his theorizing, which remained *constant* through all the revisions of his metapsychology?

Even if, from this point of view, we dissect out of the metapsychological papers the aspect of an abstract *high-level* theory (Rubinstein, 1965), which, in the sense of a *'boundary theory'* between psyche and physis, can be contemplated in strict separation from its clinical-empirical connotations (Schmidt-Hellerau, 1993), the metapsychological considerations that follow from it are by no means irrelevant to the practice of psychoanalysis. They are instead the necessary first step towards insight, clarification and orientation when it comes to the question of *how* we as psychoanalysts perceive, think and arrive at our conclusions, whether practical or theoretical. After all, even if one has long adopted a critical distance from them, the metapsychological assumptions remain, as in the past, 'also contained in the less inferential clinical theory, and influence the analyst even when he believes that he is listening without a trace of prejudice' (Thomä & Kächele, 1987p. 14). The clinical facts we establish and their formulation are thus never entirely independent of theory (Cooper, 1996); and that is already reason enough to continue to grapple with the theoretical foundations of psychoanalysis, namely metapsychology—which in the present context means the question of the latter's logical structure and consistency.

1895: The basic model

Let us begin with the 'Project for a scientific psychology' (Freud, 1950), the initial version of the metapsychology that already contains the most important positions of the later elaboration of the 'psychical apparatus' (for a more detailed analysis of the 'Project', see Schmidt-Hellerau, 1995a, b).

The 'Project's' 'First Principal Theorem' formulates the so-called 'principle of inertia': Freud declares that the system to be constructed (the psychical apparatus) is to tend to remain in a lasting (stable) state; if it is displaced from this state by the action of some force or other, the aim of any kind of activity will be to return it to the original state. In other words, if the psychical apparatus is subjected, from its initial situation, to the 'charge' of a certain quantity of excitation, it will immediately endeavour to get rid of it by 'discharge': the charge of excitation (plus) and the discharge of excitation (minus) together satisfy the 'zero principle'. Since zero (i.e. any value conventionally deemed to be *zero*) is taken to be the *stable* initial position of the system, what Freud calls the *zero principle* or *principle of inertia* is, in purely formal terms, nothing other than a principle of regulation in the service of *homoeostasis* (or of the system's *dynamic stability*). That is the proposition presented in the

First Principal Theorem and the basic principle of the model: *any depar-ture (in this case, a charge) from the reference value (in this case, zero) leads to measures on the part of the system (in this case, discharge) which restore the reference value—i.e. the equilibrium of the system—and this is a homoeostatic regulation, here called the principle of inertia.*

According to this principle, exogenous excitations (e.g. a blow on the hand) are conducted afferently to the so-called φ-system (φ stands for peripheral) and thence discharged again efferently via the motor neu-rones. That is to say, the principle of inertia operates on the φ-system by triggering a reflex movement in which the *discharge* is proportional to the *charge*—thus restoring the initial situation of the system, homoeo-stasis. The simplest notation for this is as follows:

(+e) Input Variable → Zero-Principle → (-e) Output Variable

The situation with the endogenous stimuli (Freud mentions the exam-ples of hunger and sexuality) is more complicated. Simple motor discharge is of no avail for these excitations, because the cause of the stimulus in the interior of the organism constantly produces new quan-tities of excitation. These endogenous stimuli excite the so-called ψ-system (ψ stands for psychical), and here, according to Freud, is the *mainspring* of the psychical mechanism: the onset of a pressure towards satisfaction of need. However, the need can be satisfied only by way of a 'specific action', which, being more complicated than a reflex discharge, is a task which, as Freud says, consumes more energy than is supplied by the current stimulus.

> In consequence, the nervous system is obliged to abandon its original trend to inertia (that is, to bringing the level [of Qη] to zero). It must put up with [maintaining] a store of Qη sufficient to meet the demand for a specific action. Nevertheless, the manner in which it does this shows that the same trend persists, modified into an endeavour at least to keep the Qη as low as possible and to guard against any increase of it—that is, to keep it constant (1950 p. 297, my italics)

The new term *principle of constancy* that arises out of these considerations thus takes over the basic idea of the original *principle of inertia*. The only change is that a new homoeostatic 'zero' value has been established, which is now to be kept constant and restored after every deviation. Thus, the change from the zero principle to the principle of constancy involves not a new *principle* but a new *level* with a more complex structure —because the *principle* of organization of all processes within the psychical apparatus remains directed, as before, towards maintaining the equilibrium of the system: towards homoeostasis.

This also applies to the 'Project's' 'Second Principal Theorem', what Freud calls 'The Neurone Theory', in which he focuses on the neurone as 'a *model* of the whole nervous system' (p. 298, my italics)—and hence as a prototype for description on the micro-level of the processes within the psychical apparatus. The most important point here is that there is said to be a specific *direction* of conduction of the excitation, namely an afferent flow from the dendrites to the neurone and an efferent flow from the neurone to the axon. It follows in turn, as expressed in the language of the model, that the processes are directional: the charge of a quantity of excitation (*plus*) is followed by the discharge of a quantity of excitation (*minus*), and the principle of inertia is the homoeostatic regulation performed by the neurone. The neurone thus functions as a switch or regulator containing the homoeostatic law:

Charge / Input Variable → Switch / Law /Regulator → Discharge / Output Variable

This simple basic principle can now be expanded to any scale: since the nervous system has a multiple structure, the stimulus must cross a number of thresholds or contact barriers—thus undergoing *multiple* switching —and since a homoeostatic law modified specifically in accordance with the degree of facilitation and cathexis is activated at each individual switch, the stability of the system as a whole is multiply safeguarded. These few assumptions thus already contain the fundamental construction elements of the model of the psychical apparatus; the entire system is organized hierarchically, regulated specifically according to the hierarchical level and operates with nothing other than the incoming and outgoing quantities of excitation, i.e. the input and output variables (the later *drives*) and the zero principle or principle of constancy, implemented by the system's regulators or switches (the later *structures*).

This basic conception now affords us a better appreciation of the significance of the need-satisfaction paradigm. What happens when an endogenous stimulus—e.g. hunger —reaches the ψ-system? The baby screams and kicks, but this does not get rid of the hunger; however, the mother—the breast —appears, the baby's motor action changes from aimless kicking to aim-directed sucking, and in this way the cause of the endogenous excitation is eliminated. This gives rise to an experience of satisfaction, 'which has the most radical results on the development of the individual's functions' (p. 318): an association (stored as a neuronal pattern of excitation) arises between the *drive*, the *object* and the *specific action*. In other words, there arises in the system ψ a facilitation that will henceforth have the consequence that every new endogenous excitation of the same kind—i.e. every drive-related stimulus from the same source (hunger)—will, according to the 'basic law of *association by simultaneity*' (p. 319), cathect the image of the object (mother/breast) and activate the motor image (the specific action). An *endo-sensori-motor association* has arisen between the *drive*, the *object* and the *action*. Moreover, this association (as a whole) is now—in relation to the hypothetical first regulator of the system —already a *modified regulator*, whose switching law implements the principle of constancy and no longer the zero principle. Even on such a primitive level, this is a highly complex structure that henceforth allows regulation of the charge and discharge of excitation according to the nature of the specific action.

1900: The wish, a DPM association

Freud returns to these assumptions from the 'Project' in Chapter VII of *The Interpretation of Dreams* (1900). The psychical apparatus introduced by him in 1900 is made up of a number of systems: at one end is the perceptual (*Pcpt.* or P) system and at the other the motor or M system, with the so-called mnemic systems in between. Freud states that psychi-cal processes have 'a sense or *direction* [...]. Psychical processes advance in general from the perceptual end to the motor end' (1900 p. 537, my italics).

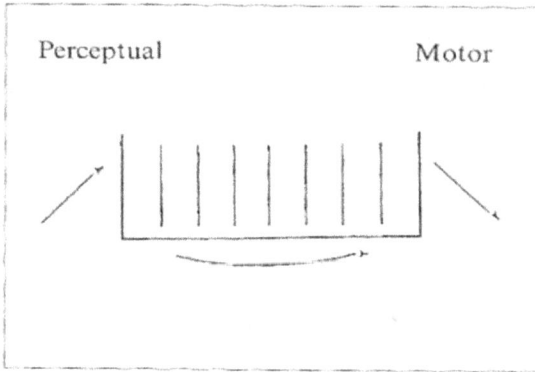

The function to be performed by this apparatus is again 'to avoid an accumulation of excitation', because that 'is felt as unpleasure and ... it sets the apparatus in action with a view to repeating the experience of satisfac-tion, which involved a diminution of excitation and was felt as pleasure' (p. 598). The same *simple basic configuration* is thus observed again here: a charge of excitation (+ e) causes the principle of regulation established in the structures of the psychical apparatus to adopt a measure that consists in the reduction of excitation (- e), thereby restoring the equilibrium of the system. Freud then returns to the need-satisfaction paradigm of the 'Project'. After describing the ineffectiveness of aimless motor discharge in the case of the hunger stimulus, he continues:

> A change can only come about if in some way or other (in the case of the baby, through outside help), an 'experience of satisfaction' can be achieved which puts an end to the internal stimulus. An essential com-ponent of this experience of satisfaction is a particular perception (that of nourishment, in our example) the mnemic image of which remains associated thenceforward with the memory trace of the excitation pro-duced by the need. *As a result of the link that has thus been established,*

next time this need arises a psychical impulse will at once emerge which will seek to recathect the mnemic image of the perception and to re-evoke the perception itself, that is to say, to reestablish the situation of the original satisfaction. An impulse of this kind is what we call a wish (pp. 565-6, my italics).

This enables us to distinguish precisely between the *drive* and the *wish*. The drive is an excitation process in the organism—in formal terms, an input variable that triggers homoeostatic regulation measures in the switch or in a structure of the psychical apparatus —namely 'A current … starting from unpleasure and aiming at pleasure' (p. 604). The *path* of this current, registered in the mnemic systems, has an origin (the excitation due to the need, i.e. the drive), a direction (towards the satisfying object) and an end (the successfully accomplished action of satisfaction). The combination of these three fixed points in the sequence constitutes the wish. *The wish is thus an association between the drive, the image of the object and the motor image—i.e. a sequence that involves the drive system, the perceptual system and the motor system—*or, in brief, extending Freud's sketch downwards to include the dimension of the drive and inserting an initial for the drive system in the same way as for the other systems, a DPM association.

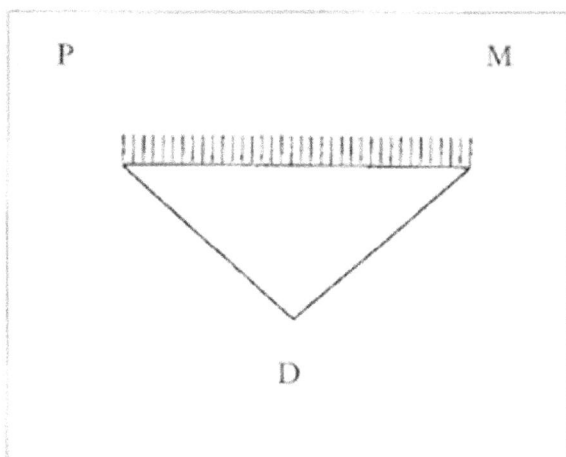

The wish is thus a more complex concept than the drive, because it includes not only the drive but also the associated object and motor images. However, if the wish is seen as a *unity*, the directional force resulting from it can also—on a more complex plane—be conceived *formally* in the sense of a drive, which causes the psychical apparatus to undertake the relevant homoeostatic regulation measures.[1]

1910: Repression as a drive

Let us now leap forward in time to a short contribution dating from 1910, 'The psychoanalytic view of psychogenic disturbance of vision', in which precisely this concept is taken up again, i.e. the notion 'that every instinct [drive] tries to make itself effective by activating ideas that are in keeping with its aims' (191) p. 213). That is *the concept of the wish*. An important addition now follows. Freud explains:

> These drives are not always compatible with one another; their interests often come into conflict. *Opposition between ideas is only an expression of struggles between the various drives.* From the point of view of our attempted explanation, a quite specially important part is played by the undeniable opposition between *the drives which subserve sexuality*, the attainment of sexual pleasure, and those other *drives which have as their aim the self-preservation of the individual—the ego-drives*. As the poet has said, all the organic drives that operate in our mind may be classified as 'hunger' or 'love' (1910 pp. 213-5, my italics).

The postulate of the antagonism between the sexual drives on the one hand and the self-preservative or ego drives on the other is thereby

---

[1] This clearly brings out the difference between drive and instinct. The ethological concept of instinct concerns a complex pattern that includes a triggering stimulus, a defined object and a specific action, i.e. for our purposes, a DPM association. The term drive, on the other hand, is more consistent with the formal conception proposed here, in the sense of a unidirectional (vectorial) magnitude constituting only one component of a DPM association. To preserve this perspective, in the Freud quotations that follow I have replaced the word instinct in Strachey's translation of Trieb by drive.

formulated. This antagonism is the basis for Freud's identification of the conflict resulting from the irreconcilability of different ideas activated simultaneously, to which the following statement applies: '*Opposition between ideas is only an expression of struggles between the various drives*'. The result of the struggle is that one group of ideas gives rise to 'the unconsciousness' of the other; Freud goes on to define this process:

> [There is] an interplay between forces that favor or inhibit one another. If in any instance one group of ideas remains in the unconscious, psycho-analysis … maintains that the isolation and state of unconsciousness of this group of ideas have been caused by an active opposition on the part of other groups. The process owing to which it has met with this fate is known as repression (p. 213).

In the process of repression, therefore, one of the two drives—and the ideational patterns associated with it—conquers the other, together with its associated ideational patterns. In *formal* terms, this means that *repression is nothing other than the activity of whichever drive is in the antagonistic position in any particular instance.*

The question of the nature of repression —a constant subject of debate in the psychoanalytic community, said by Sulloway (1979) to be one of the main unsolved problems of psychoanalytic theory—is here given a clear and simple answer by Freud within the logic of his model, as follows. If there are to be only two basic drives, either of which has the power to repress the other, then *repression must be conceived as a process in the nature of a drive*. Hence the activation of the sexual drive has the effect, in the structure it excites, of activating the self-preservative drive in a repressing function; while, conversely, the excitation of the self-preservative drive on the switch of a structure gives rise to the excitation of the sexual drive. In other words, the self-preservative drive represses the sexual drive and the sexual drive represses the self-preservative drive. This means that, considered in *formal* metapsychological terms, the drive-repression theory appears in the simple guise of an antagonistic drive theory; hence, within the model of the psychical apparatus, there now effectively remain only, on the one hand, *plus* and *minus drives* as variables and, on the other, *structures* as switches for the implementation of whichever homoeostatic principle of regulation applies in the particular case.

1911: Hallucination, a double DPM association

As we have seen, Freud regards the learning process within the psychical apparatus as the linking of a specific drive to the image of an object and to a motor image; a link of this kind to a DPM association he calls a wish. Hence, if each drive manifests itself by the ideas that correspond to it, this basic assumption must apply to *both* antagonistic drives—that is, not only to the drive but also to the repression; and if we formally distinguish the two antagonistic drives—or drive and repression—by giving them opposite signs, we then have a (+)-wish and a (-)-wish.

Precisely this is relevant to the *metapsychological conception of hallucination* put forward by Freud in his 'Formulations on the two principles of mental functioning' (1911). The paradigm is once again that of need-satisfaction: after a number of identical positive experiences, the hungry baby will produce a hallucination of the earlier experience of satisfaction. He cannot of course stop at the hallucination, because this is ultimately not satisfying, but must take a further developmental step, namely that of acceding to the level of the 'reality principle'. But let us take a closer look at how Freud *conceives* hallucination.

Hallucination is the presentation of a situation of satisfaction, i.e. the cathexis of a memory trace that contains and brings about a reduction in tension, even if only temporary; to that extent the hallucination, even if inadequate, serves for homoeostatic regulation. The situation can be formalized as follows: the baby is hungry (i.e. an impulse from the self-preservative drive makes itself felt); by his screaming he induces the mother to give him the breast (i.e. to satisfy his need); however, satisfaction as such does not exist in the psychical apparatus, so that on the *formal* level the statement 'nourishment *satisfies* the drive' is equivalent to the statement 'nourishment *represses* the drive'—because, from the metapsychological point of view, satisfaction means return to homoeostasis, or *zero* tension. So, if we give a drive a *plus* sign and its repression a *minus* sign—or, conversely, as presented by Freud in his example, if we give hunger (as a deficiency) a *minus* sign and then nourishment a *plus* sign—the two combine in the desired result of the initial or equilibrium state of *zero*. It follows that the hallucination of *need-satisfaction* invoked in the service of the pleasure principle is composed, *in terms of its conception*, of *both* a *drive* presentation *and* a *repression* presentation, a (-)'hunger' presentation *directed inwards* or *towards the 'self'* and a (+)'breast' presentation *directed outwards* or *towards the 'object'*—that is, of a (-)*self-preservative drive* presentation and a (+)*sexual drive* presentation. In other words, on closer inspection, it is seen to be made up of *two* wishes, a (-)wish and a (+)wish (whose 'superimposition' gives rise to the 'fit' that is a prerequisite for its perceptibility —whereas the edges are as it were 'lost'); the hallucination is thus a (±)wish—or a *double* DPM association.

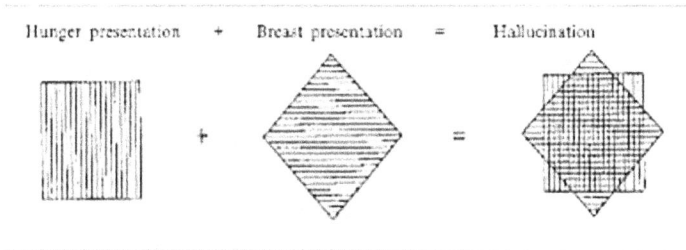

Hunger presentation + Breast presentation = Hallucination

The extent to which the level of tension increases in consequence of a drive-related excitation is determined firstly by the zero principle *set* as the initial state of the model; secondly by the real situation of satisfaction *introduced* by an external object; and lastly by the principle of constancy *acquired* in this interaction. The hallucination is the first manifestation of such an externally set intrapsychic boundary for the self-preservative drive; it becomes possible only when the psychical apparatus is able to retain this experience of a self-object-related drive limitation structurally—i.e. in the form of a *modification* of its switching laws—and, in the case of a fresh drive-related excitation of the same kind, automatically initiates the process of repression at this boundary, and hence a reduction in the system's overall excitation. It can be said that *the hallucination arises at this boundary, is located precisely at the changeover point between drive and repression, and contains and connects the self- and object-presentations of both drives (the self-preservative drive and the sexual drive).* The following general proposition could now be derived from this: *psychical structure arises at the precise time and place at which a drive tendency changes over into a repression tendency, so that it always represents a specific (homoeostatic) relationship of the two drives to each other.*

1920: Lethe, a concept for the energy of the (-)death drive

Finally, let us turn to *Beyond the Pleasure Principle,* the last version of Freud's drive theory. He begins with the 'new and remarkable' observation that, besides the striving for pleasure in psychic life, there is also an *unconscious tendency* to reproduce unpleasant experiences *repeatedly.* The regularity and inexorability of this painful process are indicative of a 'compulsion to repeat'. Since, according to Freud, the aspirations of the unconscious always exert pressure towards discharge but this discharge must give rise to unpleasure in the case of the painful, the analysand maintains a certain resistance to the analyst's efforts to make the unconscious conscious. Freud concludes that 'the patient's resistance arises from his ego, and we then at once perceive that the compulsion to repeat must be ascribed to the unconscious repressed' (1920 p. 20).

However, why should the compulsion to repeat be ascribable only to the unconscious repressed? Does the ego, with the same constant arsenal of repression responses to the recurring pressure of the unconscious, not also manifestly obey a compulsion to repeat? *Is this entire sequence of pressure and repression not therefore also subject to a compulsion to repeat?* As Freud had shown paradigmatically by the example of the need-satisfaction experience, psychical processes repeatedly follow whichever pathways are best 'facilitated'. This assumption allows us to conceptualize also the *repetition* of infantile or traumatic scenes as a drive-related activation of such well-facilitated, associatively linked *structures*, which summon up specific 'cathected' object, affect and motor images. From this point of view the compulsion to repeat would not be confined to the repressed, the unconscious, but should be seen as a property inherent in all systems of the psychical apparatus, falling within the functional sphere of structure. In other words, *the compulsion to repeat is a structural phenomenon.*

The clarification of this theorem has far reaching consequences: Freud derives both his new general definition of the drive and his introduction of the death drive from his 'at once' characterization of the compulsion to repeat as a 'manifestation of the power of the repressed', which appears to him 'more primitive, more elementary, *more driven* than the pleasure principle which it over-rides' (p. 23, my italics). From this he concludes: '*It seems, then, that a drive is an urge inherent in organic life to restore an earlier state of things*' (p. 36).

This new conception of the drives appears to Freud himself as 'strange', because the drives, seen in this way, are no longer 'a factor impelling towards change and development' but 'the precise contrary— an expression of the *conservative* nature of living substance' (p. 36). That is precisely the point: this new definition of the drive is formulated in *finalistic* terms and for that reason alone is irreconcilable with the exiguous basic conditions of our formalized model. If drives are assigned an 'intention' '*to restore an earlier state*' (p. 36), the drive necessarily becomes an *intelligent* magnitude that *knows* what it wants and *remembers* what has been. However, this means that the definition of the drive is being mixed with that of structure; in other words, the differing functions we have attributed within the model to the drive (variable) on the one hand and the structure (switch) on the other are here being combined. For 'an expression of the *conservative* nature of living substance'—and hence also of the '*compulsion to repeat*'—as well as 'the expression of the inertia' have their basis in the *structural* situation of the system and not in the drive element in itself. In the formalized conception, the drive is merely a directional magnitude (vector), which with a virtual lack of limitation takes one direction only. Hence it is the law of the structure (the principle of inertia, the principle of constancy, the pleasure principle or the reality principle) that determines *when* the earlier or sought-after 'zero' state has been reached, *what* this state consists of, i.e. when the drive should cease to exert its pressure—and *not* the drive. In other words, *a system's memory consists in its structures* and not in its variables, the drives.

It is a logical consequence of this sequence of ideas that Freud calls the drive that seeks to return to an earlier state—ultimately a cosmological primal state—a *death drive*. The death drive is therefore the first of all the drives and strictly speaking—because the lifeless existed before the living—the only drive directed towards repetition. For Freud, a drive always needs an antagonist, and the antagonist of a death drive can be nothing other than a *life drive*—and in this way the two new drives are now put to work.

This extension of the notion of the drive need by no means appear alien to a formal conception of metapsychology. Freud may be said here to be merely drawing out the line of the *directionality* of the two drives and prolonging it from the *individual* (sexuality and self-preservation) to the *general* (life and death). The idea of a (+)life drive and a (-)death drive is entirely consistent with the arbitrary assignment of a *plus* sign to the sexual drive and of a *minus* sign to the self-preservative drive. However, Freud allows himself to be confused by the *meaning level* of his concepts: it bothers him that the self-preservative drives should be mere satellites of the death drive, and for this reason he abolishes this classification and now includes *both* the self-preservative drives *and* the sexual drives among the life drives.

But this gives rise to a new problem: Freud must now find at least one representative for the death drive just created. He arrives, via sadism-masochism, at aggression and destruction. From this derives the opposition, which is still accepted today, of the *sexual drive and the aggressive drive*—which is additionally related by a minority of analysts to the opposition of the *life and death drives*. This connection or identification (already suggested by Freud) of the death drive with the aggressive or destructive drive is in my view metapsychologically (and indeed also clinically) problematical. Let us consider Freud's argument in greater detail:

> We started out from the great opposition between the life and death drives. Now object love itself presents us with a second example of a

similar polarity—that between love (or affection) and hate (or aggressiveness) ... From the very first we recognized the presence of a sadistic component in the sexual drive ... *But how can the sadistic drive, whose aim it is to injure the object, be derived from Eros, the preserver of life?* Is it not plausible to suppose that *this sadism is in fact a death drive* which, under the influence of the narcissistic libido, has been forced away from the ego and has consequently only emerged in relation to the object? (pp. 53-4, my italics).

This passage raises two problems for the logic of our model conception of the notions of *drive* and *structure*: (1) the representative of the *death drive* is here derived from the *sexual drive*—namely, from *object love* with its two manifestations of love and hate (aggression) —so that the representative of the death drive is defined not as an independent variable but as *dependent* on the sexual or life drive. (2) Freud defines death as damage to or destruction of life, but this definition has consequences for his conception of the death drive. For the sake of clarity, let us formulate this in everyday language. We now no longer have a simple *vectorial* definition of the drive, for which an antagonism would be roughly as follows: *the death drive wants to die* and *the life drive wants to live*. Freud's suggestion, by contrast, is that *the death drive wants the life drive not to live*; as he puts it, the death drive wants 'to lead what is living into an inorganic state' (1940 p. 148). That is to say, the death drive is here defined as a 'negation' of the life drive; strictly speaking, this means that it is defined not as a drive but as a *vicissitude of a drive*—or, in formalized metapsychological terms, a drive-repression connection involving a structure.

To explain sadism, Freud again invokes 'the oral stage of organization of the libido', in which 'the act of obtaining erotic mastery over an object coincides with that object's destruction' (1920 p. 54), and for him the *intention to harm* follows from this *destruction*. However, Freud could instead have used the formulation that erotic mastery at the oral stage still coincides with the *incorporation* of the object—in which case he would have merely described a *process directed entirely inwards*, whereas the destruction and intention to harm are deliberately directed *outwards*. Here a further conceptual problem arises with this new view of the drives: we now have *two outward-directed drives*: the sexual drive (as the representative of the life drive) aims at the 'external' object, while sadism (as the representative of the death drive), with its intention to harm, also aims at the 'external' object. Freud did of course notice that his system, with its two *unidirectional* drives, could no longer be regulated homoeostatically, and so he hastens to make a correction: the antagonist to the *outward-*directed life drive is now to be an originally *inward-*directed death drive, for which a *primary masochism* can be taken as the representative. However, in spite of this important correction, Freud retains the death drive's *intention to harm*—thus raising the question whether this *fits* theoretically.

If the antagonism of the drives is expressed by use of the opposite signs (+) and (-), the characterization of love and hate (or aggression) at first seems to fit in very well with a (+)life drive and a (-)death drive: love is so to speak a positive, 'good' drive activity and hate (or aggression) a negative, 'bad' one. But a *formalized* conception of the psychical apparatus excludes such *properties* or *qualities*; it can operate only with (+) or (-)*quantities*. Ought the original (-)activity of the aggressive drive therefore to balance out the (+)activity of Eros, for example in such a way that the primary masochistic aggressive drive, directed inwards, ensures that the Eros directed towards the external object does not go too far outwards? However, this is quite irreconcilable with Freud's insight that a 'surplus of sexual aggressiveness will turn a lover into a sex-murderer, while a sharp diminution in the aggressive factor will make him bashful or impotent' (1940 p. 149). The aggression here is applied not in a (-) but in a (+)function: (+)Eros and (+)aggression turn the lover into a sex murderer, while insufficient (+)aggression makes him bashful or impotent. In this way, aggression is inadvertently being used again in an outward-directed function, so that the vectorial sum again fails to add up to a balance of the two (+/-)drives.

Freud was not unaware of this logical error in the construction of his model; as late as 1932 he remarked: 'Why have we ourselves needed such a long time before we decided to recognize an aggressive instinct [drive]?' (1933 p. 103). He presumes that his hesitation, as well as the rejection met with by his final drive theory, is attributable to wishful thinking about the moral nature of man. I do not believe that this explanation is correct, but rather that his question touches upon a sore point in his last theory of the drives, and that his misgivings have to do with his abandonment of a conceptually necessary (-)activity of the death drive.

In *Beyond the Pleasure Principle* Freud had conceded the existence of such (-)trends of the death drive as well, for example, in acknowledging that 'the death drives seem to do their work *unobtrusively*' (1920 p. 63, my italics); later he notes that these drives 'are by their nature *mute*' (1923 p. 46, my italics), 'desire to be at *peace* and … *to put … to rest*' (p. 59, my italics), in accordance with 'the *Nirvana principle, belonging as it does to the death drives*' (1924 p. 160, my italics; Rechardt & Ikonen (1993) have emphasized these non-destructive peace-striving functions of the death drive). It is *these* passages in *Beyond* and later works that express a tendency of the death drive that operates positively in the *opposite direction* to the idea of aggression and destruction. Conceived as it were in the shadow—*as a negative*—of a phenomenally active, extroversive defensive measure, namely aggression, the death drive with its silent, passive, introversive traits here shows itself as a quietistic agent: silently, inconspicuously and with the function of repressing the noisy pressure of the life drive, it makes its contribution to the internal equilibrium of the organization.

This reversal again reveals the *constants of Freud's model conception*: a (+)life drive and a (-)death drive and their connection to a structure by a defined principle of regulation together guarantee the dynamic stability of the entire system.

We can now see why Freud was never able to find a suitable name for the *energy* of the death drive. In 1938 he admits: 'We are without a term analogous to libido for describing the energy of the destructive drive' (1940 p. 150). The lack of a term for the energy of the death drive is a serious problem, because without a conception of this energy it is not easy to think about the effects the cathectic processes emanating from the death drive are in fact supposed to have. For this reason, in view of the quietistic tendencies of the death drive established above, I suggest that the energy attributable to it be given the name of *lethe*, borrowed from Greek mythology; the word means *forgetting*: a river in Hades or at the boundary of the realm of the dead bears the name of *Lethe*. Greek mythology, to which Freud so often had recourse for the naming of his theoretical concepts, can thus once again be pressed into service, because the word *lethe* seems to me to correspond in every respect to the requirements postulated by Freud for a *term to denote the energy* of the death drive:

    i.   The concept of *lethe* is both analogous and equivalent to that of *libido*.

    ii.   The meaning of the term *lethe* (i.e. forgetting) emphasizes the outside-to-inside directionality of a (-)drive and hence also its orientation towards the *unconscious*.

    iii.   *Lethe* is a term used in everyday language in precisely the sense considered here: we describe a person's behavior as *lethargic*, and speak of a *deleterious* condition, a *lethal* dose, etc. (even if the etymological relationship of the last two words is questionable). This at the same time indicates a change in the affective points of reference: whereas Freud took as his basis the opposites of love and hate, the pair of terms *libido* and *lethe* are associated more with opposites such as lively/apathetic, cheerful/ gloomy or happy/sad.

    iv.   Last but not least, the term *lethe* is consistent with the language of metapsychology: we can speak just as legitimately of a *lethic cathexis* as we customarily do of a *libidinal* cathexis.

Because precisely the psychoanalytic concept of energy has been subjected to almost unanimous destructive criticism, the introduction of an additional, second energy related concept, *lethe*, calls for a brief commentary. In accordance with our formalized conception of metapsychology, we must here be conceiving energy in 'dematerialized' terms (Pribram, 1989). Hence the concept of *drive energy* is an *ideational construct*, a pure *proposition*, which enables us to conceive *in thought* of Freud's postulate of the antagonism of the drives and to formulate this postulate. As before, the notion of the *drive* should be understood in the sense of a directional (vectorial) magnitude, whereas that of drive *energy* should be regarded as the amount (of the cathexis)—a scalar—whose direction is determined by the drive. In order to satisfy strictly this distinction between vector and scalar, we ought really to speak always of life-drive cathexis, death-drive cathexis, sexual-drive cathexis, self-preservative drive cathexis, etc. However, considerations of intellectual economy must militate in favor of the pragmatically shorter (albeit inexact) expression *libidinal cathexis or lethic cathexis*.

Concluding remarks

The introduction of the new energy concept *lethe* as an antagonist to *libido* allows us in formal terms to retain the metapsychological proposition of the (+/-)directionality of the two antagonistic drives. Moreover, this does not invalidate the previous conception of the principles of regulation (the principle of constancy and the pleasure principle) in their function as guarantors of a dynamic stability (homoeostasis) of the system constituted by the psychical apparatus. This means that Freud's basic assumptions about the functioning of the psychical apparatus are preserved through all stages in the evolution of his metapsychology. *That is the consistent basis of his model of psychoanalytic theory*. His late postulate of the opposition of the life and death drives constitutes the most general version of an antagonism of drives and, within the model, represents fundamental psychophysiological functions, for which we could invoke examples such as *waking* and *sleeping* or, more generally, differing degrees of instantaneous psychical *extroversion* or *introversion*. Freud's original opposition of the sexual and the self-preservative drives is therefore not abolished; on the contrary, it seems appropriate to retain these two more specific drives as issuing from the next hierarchical level of the model—after all, they are clinically by far the most relevant drives —and then to derive from them the entire gamut of component drives with which we are familiar from Freud's genetic reflections on the sexual drive; there is no problem in extrapolating these to the self-preservative drive (see Schmidt-Hellerau, 1995a). We should then have conceived a system of drives expandable to successive levels and backed up by a structural system also amenable to successive stages of differentiation.

The obvious question now arises as to the place of aggression/destruction in this conception. Is it appropriate, within the approach here developed, to accept Freud's equation of an 'drive of death, or destruction' (1924 p. 163) and hence to postulate an original, primary aggressive *drive*? It would in my view be more accurate to speak not of an aggressive *drive* but of *aggression* in the sense of an *affect* or *affective action*, which happens to serve the purpose of self-preservation or to be in the service of sexuality—because we are not of course concerned with the abolition or with a lethic reinterpretation of the *phenomenon* of aggression. At any rate, it makes a significant difference not only metapsychologically but also clinically whether we conceive of aggression as a primary drive that seeks satisfaction or instead take as our starting point a self-preservative drive and a sexual drive whose striving for satisfaction may in certain circumstances also assume destructive features. After all, it should not be forgotten that the metapsychological postulate of a (-)drive—whether it be the death drive or the self-preservative drive—focuses our attention on the *lethic dimension* of psychic processes, for which we could account only indirectly by taking aggression as our measure of the energy of the death drive.

References

Cooper, S. (1996). Facts all come with a point of view: some reflections on fact and formulation from the 75th Anniversary Edition of the Int. J. Psycho-Anal. *Int. J. Psycho-Anal.*, 77:255-273.

Freud, S. (1900). *The Interpretation of Dreams. S.E.* 4-5.

Freud, S. (1910). The psycho-analytic view of psychogenic disturbance of vision. *S.E.* 11.

Freud, S. (1911). Formulations on the two principles of mental functioning. *S.E.* 12.

Freud, S. (1920). *Beyond the Pleasure Principle. S.E.* 18.

Freud, S. (1923). *The Ego and the Id. S.E.* 19.

Freud, S. (1924). The economic problem of masochism. *S.E.* 19.

Freud, S. (1933). *New Introductory Lectures on Psycho-Analysis. S.E.* 22.

Freud, S. (1940). *An Outline of Psycho-Analysis. S.E.* 23.

Freud, S. (1950). Project for a scientific psychology. *S.E.* 1.

Modell, A. (1981). Does metapsychology still exist? *Int. J. Psycho-Anal.*, 62:391-402.

Pribram, K. H. (1989). Psychoanalysis and the natural sciences: the brain-behavior connection from Freud to present. In *Dimensions of Psychoanalysis*, ed. J. Sandler. London: Karnac Books, pp. 139-163.

Rapaport, D. (1960). *The Structure of Psychoanalytical Theory: A Systematizing Attempt.* New York: Int. Univ. Press.

Rechardt, E. & Ikonen, P. (1933). How to interpret the death drive? *Scand. Psychoanal. Rev.*, 16:84-99.

Rubinstein, B. (1965). Psychoanalytic theory and the mind-body problem. In *Psychoanalysis and Current Biological Thought*, ed. N. S. Greenfield & W. C. Lewis. Madison, Milwaukee: Univ. of Wisconsin Press, pp. 35-56.

Schmidt-Hellerau, C. (1993). Überbau oder Fundament? Zur Metapsychologie und Metapsychologiedebatte. *Psyche*, 47: 1-30.

Schmidt-Hellerau, C. (1995a). *Lebenstrieb & Todestrieb, Libido & Lethe. Ein formalisiertes konsistentes Modell der psychoanalytischen Trieb- und Strukturtheorie.* Stuttgart: Verlag Internationale Psychoanalyse.

Schmidt-Hellerau, C. (1995b). Die Geburt der Metapsychologie. Zur Aktualität des Entwurfs einer Psychologie (1895). *Psyche*, 49: 1156-1195.

Sulloway, F. J. (1979). *Freud, Biologist of the Mind. Beyond the Psychoanalytic Legend.* New York: Basic Books.

Thomä, H. & Kächele, H. (1987). *Psychoanalytic Practice. Vol. 1: Principles.* Trans. M. Wilson and D. Roseveare. Berlin/Heidelberg/New York: Springer-Verlag.

Wallerstein, R. S. (1977). Psychic energy reconsidered. Introduction. *J. Am. Psychoanal. Assoc.*, 25: 529-535.

CHAPTER 3

Why Aggression?

*Metapsychological, Clinical and Technical Considerations**

On the basis of a formalized view of metapsychology, I briefly consider the problems inherent in the Freudian notion of a death drive or aggressive drive and then go on to develop a new theoretical conception of aggression. Aggression is understood as an affect, action or affective action and, in relation to these, as an expression of the intensity with which a drive— whether it be the sexual drive with its libidinal cathexes or the self-preservative drive with its lethic cathexes—seeks to attain its object. In this

---

* In his exchange of letters with Albert Einstein published under the title 'Why war?', Freud confirms Einstein's supposition that there is a 'drive for hatred and destruction' and summarizes his drive theory as follows: 'According to our hypothesis human drives are of only two kinds: those which seek to preserve and unite—which we call "erotic", exactly in the sense in which Plato uses the word "Eros" in his Symposium, or "sexual", with a deliberate extension of the popular conception of "sexuality"—and those which seek to destroy and kill and which we group together as the aggressive or destructive drive' (19333b, p. 209). This paper develops a different conception of aggression. It is a continuation of my elaboration and reformulation of metapsychology (Schmidt-Hellerau, 1995, 2000, 2001), in which I presented a formalized view of metapsychological concepts and also introduced the term 'lethe' to denote the energy of both the self-preservative drive and the death drive. For a discussion of the death drive, see also Schmidt-Hellerau (1997). [Translator's note: Throughout this text the word Trieb is translated as 'drive' so as to distinguish it from the ethological notion of instinct. Where it was originally rendered as 'instinct' in quotations from the Standard Edition, 'drive' has been tacitly substituted.]

2002 International Journal of Psycho-Analysis 83(6):1269-1289. Translated from German into English by Philip Slotkin, MA (Cantab.), MITI.

context I regard the regulation of closeness and distance with respect to the 'psycho-geometric locus' of the relevant drive object as being of central importance. I contend that neurotic personalities suffer from specific distortions in the perception of the psycho-geometric locus of their drive objects, which may give rise to an intensification of the drive tendencies prevailing in these individuals at any given time so that these tendencies take on an aggressive character. Based on these considerations I present two clinical vignettes to emphasize the resulting technical consequences for interpretation.

Introduction

Aggression is one of the most complex and important phenomena of human behavior, and understanding it is crucial to the development and course of our patients' analyses. Whereas analysts of all schools agree that this is so, appreciable differences, as well as a far-reaching lack of clarity concerning certain aspects, exist with regard to the psychoanalytic conception of aggression. We may on occasion fail to realize how far our explicit theories, or even our perhaps only vaguely formulated theoretical assumptions, influence our clinical work. However, for the sake of example, let us briefly consider the implications of just three different possibilities. First, in the view of Freud (post-1920), Melanie Klein and the majority of analysts, aggression is a primary drive that seeks satisfaction and must be 'tamed'; second, aggression may be seen as a secondary reaction to frustrations of all kinds (cf. Dollard et al., 1939; Stern, 1974; Rizzuto et al., 1993) or to a danger confronting the self (Ornstein & Ornstein, 1990; Fonagy et al., 1993; Mitchell, 1993; Kohut, 1977); and third, aggression may be regarded, at least in part, as an energy that promotes psychic development or the 'motoric element' of that energy, used for the purpose of self-assertion, self-delimitation, adaptation and exploration of the world (Spitz, 1953, 1969; Parens, 1979; Winnicott, 1984; Stechler & Halton, 1987). Consideration of these different perspectives will give us an impression of the diversity (in accordance with our theoretical assumptions) of our understanding of the aggressive expressions of our analysands, and hence of the extent to which our theoretical conception tacitly determines the focus of our attention and interpretation.

As Mitchell not unjustly notes, "It would be hard to find an issue that has generated more controversy during the history of psychoanalytic ideas than aggression" (1993, p. 351). The reasons for these disagreements are of many different kinds. They lie partly in the general psychoanalytic orientation (e.g. classical, Kleinian or French drive theory, self-psychology, or the relational school) into which the concept of aggression is to be fitted, or is supposed to fit; they are also connected with the degree to which the relevant authors' interests center on the *cause, function* or *purpose* of aggression; and, finally, they are partly based on the different weightings accorded, in the argument over the conceptualization of aggression, to theoretical considerations, clinical material or experimental observational data. The result is a situation that allows something relevant to be found in all theoretical positions: hardly anyone would dispute that aggression is something 'driven', inherent in human nature (that is, biogenetically based); it is equally correct to say that it arises in response to frustration and danger and within object relationships; and it is virtually self-evident that, besides hostile (malignant) aggression, there is also useful (benign) aggression. Rather than casting doubt on the differing results of this research extending over many years, we should be asking whether it is possible to develop a psychoanalytic conception of aggression within which these varying explanatory models can be integrated.

The Metapsychological Presuppositions as a Starting Point

As I have shown in detail elsewhere (Schmidt-Hellerau, 1995, 1997, 2000, 2001), interesting vistas present themselves if we consider the concepts of metapsychology in a less concrete, less phenomenally oriented way, and instead allow them to remain on a purely theoretical level—that is, within an overall model of mental functioning—on which they serve as tools that enable us to reconstruct and think about certain psychic processes. In accordance with this approach, I drew attention to two basic assumptions upon which Freud constructs his model of the 'psychical apparatus': first, he assumes the existence of two antagonistic drives (the sexual versus the self-preservative drive, or the life drive versus the death drive) which 'drive' virtually without limitation in opposite directions as, for example, a (+)life drive and a (−)death drive, with the (+)sexual drive tending, as it were, 'outwards' towards the external object and the (−)self-preservative drive tending 'inwards' towards the preservation of the subject; and second, he postulates a regulating principle (e.g. the principle of inertia or the pleasure principle) that guarantees the homoeostasis or dynamical stability of the psyche as a system. According to Freud, the pleasure principle is part of the basic equipment of the psychical apparatus. More differentiated principles of regulation—such as the 'principle of constancy' (1895) or the 'reality principle' (1911)—are acquired during the course of an individual's developmental history by way of a series of successful and unsuccessful interactions with the outside world, and are stored in the structures of the system. Hence, what are stored in the form of micro-structures are self and object representations, identifications and object relationships, fantasies, memories and the affects associated with each of these (Kernberg, 1976)—together these regulate the psychic equilibrium of the entire system.

Until 1920, Freud had taken the opposition of the sexual drive and the self-preservative drive as the foundation of his model of the psychical apparatus. In so doing, he concentrated mainly on the sexual drive, with the result that the self-preservative drive tends by comparison to lead no more than a shadowy existence in both his clinical and his meta-psychological writings. During these years, different approaches to the explanation of aggression may be found within his meta-psychology, as follows.[1]

From the early writings on 'hysteria' to the *Three Essays on the Theory of Sexuality* of 1905, Freud sees the aggressive impulses not as constituting an independent drive but as sadistic components of the sexual drive which pursue the necessary aim of overcoming the possible resistance of the sexual object (1905, p. 158).

---

[1] See also Diagram 1 in the Introduction.

In 1909, too, he categorically rejects the assumption of "the existence of a special aggressive drive alongside of the familiar drives of self-preservation and of sex", but takes a view "which leaves each drive its own power of becoming aggressive" (p. 140f.).

In 1915, he changes his mind again and assigns aggression to the "drives of self-preservation", pointing out that hate, "as a relation to objects, is older than love" and is connected with the rejection of stimuli from the outside world that give rise to unpleasure (1915a, pp. 137, 139).

In 1920, Freud reorganizes his entire drive theory by postulating a life drive and a death drive as primary. The sexual drive fits in easily with his concept of the life drive; however, the self-preservative drive seemed to contradict the notion of a death drive, and so Freud includes it too within the life drive. In seeking a representative for his death drive, Freud eventually arrives, by way of sadism (see Schmidt-Hellerau, 1995, 1997, 2000, 2001), at aggression, which is now, after all, declared to be a drive in its own right. In this way the life drive and the death drive—or the "sexual drive" and the "aggressive drive", which are closer to the practical experience of the majority of analysts—are identified as the two new drive antagonists, and have been accepted as such ever since.

The vital role of the obstacle on the path to satisfaction of the drive is clearly evident in the first three versions of his conception of aggression. It is only in *Beyond the Pleasure Principle* (1920) that aggression comes to be defined no longer as *a means to an end* but as *an end in itself*. It is, in my view, important to be fully aware of this turning point: whereas for Freud before 1920 there was only the satisfaction of the tendencies of the self-preservative and sexual drives—which was in certain circumstances to be attained by means of aggression—aggression/destruction was elevated, with the introduction of the "drive of death, or destruction" (1924b, p. 163), to the status of a basic drive that imperiously demanded satisfaction for reasons inherent in itself.

For the sexual and life drive, Freud had introduced the term *libido* to denote the drive energy assigned to it; this proved to be practical in so far as we can then simply speak of *libidinal tendencies or cathexes* whenever we are referring to a sexual impulse regardless of the particular component-drive that might thereby be meant. Freud temporarily called the energy of the self-preservative drive *interest* or *ego interest*; this was a comparatively impractical term, with which neither he nor his colleagues liked to work and which completely disappeared after Freud had placed the self-preservative drives under the heading of the life drives and emphasized that they were "of an erotic kind" (1933b, p. 209)—the self-preservative drives had thus become libidinal. For the newly introduced death drive, Freud, after some vacillation, identified aggression as the energy equivalent. However, he was not convinced of the validity of this solution (1938, p. 150), which also led to a number of both conceptual and logical problems (see Schmidt-Hellerau, 1995, 1997, 2000, 2001). As it happens, Freud's 1920 approach proved to have enormously far-reaching implications: the self-preservative drive, which (as he had certainly acknowledged in his earlier writings) corresponds to one of the most fundamental human tendencies, namely "the drive of nutrition, that is of hunger" (1905, p. 135)—and could as such also include other *self-preservative needs* such as digestion, hygiene, warmth, physical well-being and sleep (or growth and immunological defense) in their psychological dimensions—came to be totally lost from view for the psychoanalysts. Laplanche, who interprets the death drive as the uncivilized aspect, or, if you will, the free energy, of the sexual drive and thereby deprives it of its status as a drive in its own right, includes the self-preservative drive, too, as a "biological instinct" within the antithesis to the psychoanalytic notion of the drive, and excludes it from metapsychology:

> I have insisted… on the fact that self-preservation is expelled from this theory… I shall say that self-preservation (instinct) in the life of every one of us is 'put out of play', disqualified, just as self-preservation is set aside in the movement of Freud's thought after 1915 (1979, p. 153).

However, just as Laplanche sees self-preservation as a biological instinct, so too could sexuality be deemed a biological instinct. That is to say, the biological in itself does not disqualify self-preservation in its psychological dimension from being conceptualized metapsychologically as a drive. In other words, what distinguishes the psychoanalytic notion of the drive from the biological or ethological concept of instinct is the psychic dimension of bodily processes and human behavior, and this applies equally to sexuality and to self-preservation.

For these and other reasons (see Schmidt-Hellerau, 1995, 1997, 2000, 2001), I have deviated in part from Freud in adopting the following classification or assignment: the 'outward'-aiming drive is (as before) the *sexual drive* which is directed towards the object, and is called, in its extension, the 'life drive', whereas, conversely, the primarily 'inward'-aiming drive is (as in the first classification of drive theory) to be, and also to remain, the *self-preservative drive* directed towards the subject; and in the line of prolongation of the self-preservative drive, I have reinserted the *death drive*, as Freud also attempted to do for a moment when he formulated the "opposition between the ego or death drives and the sexual or life drives" (1920, p. 44), only to shortly after reject it again. In this connection between the self-preservative drive and the death drive, however, the death drive is *not* to be linked to aggression and thereby characterized as a primarily destructive drive. If this view is accepted, the opposition between the sexual and self-preservative drives (prolonged into the dualism of life and death drives) remains as the basic drive antagonism.

I have, then: first, separated aggression from the death drive; second, placed the self-preservative drive back on the vectorially inward-directed line which, with effect from a certain extreme extension, is to continue to be known by Freud's appellation *death drive*; and third, proposed the term *lethe* to denote the energy of this overall, primarily inward-directed drive tendency of the self-preservative and death drive. The term *lethe* ('oblivion' in Greek), borrowed from Greek mythology, incorporates the death drive's 'quiet' forms of expression, recognized by Freud (the forms directed towards the idea of a Nirvana), while at the same time corresponding to the equally quiet sides of a self-preservative drive (for example, the need to sleep for the purposes of digestion and recreation). Also, this drive should be called simply the *preservative drive* because, just as the sexual drive can cathect the object as well as the subject's own self thereby expressing *object-love* or *self-love* (narcissism), so too the so-called self-preservative drive can cathect not only the self but also the object—for example, a child or partner—and consequently functions in the service of either *self-preservation* or *object-preservation*. The introduction of the energy term *lethe* is intended to facilitate the clinical perception of this drive with its many predominantly silent tendencies—an *essential quietive of the psyche*, which seeks satisfaction. I contend that, just as we perceive libidinal tendencies and cathexes in the multiplicity of diverse psychic manifestations and forms of expression, we shall be in a better position to recognize—either in alternation with or in the shadow of these tendencies—*lethic* tendencies and cathexes (and their excesses and pathologies) and to distinguish them from their libidinal counterparts if we possess an appropriate concept for them in our overall model of psychic functioning.

Aggression as Action, Affect or Affective Action

However, we should then have to rethink the metapsychological conception of aggression. If we decide to regard it no longer as a primary drive and antagonist of the sexual drive, it is an obvious course to see aggression as *action* or *affective action* (e.g. destruction) or as *affect* (e.g. hate). Kernberg reversed the relationship between drive and affect. For him, affects are primary and the drives are derived from them: "In my view, affects are instinctive structures—that is, biologically given, developmentally activated psychophysiological patterns. It is the psychic aspect of the patterns that becomes organized to constitute the aggressive and libidinal drives Freud described" (1992, p. 5). Kernberg thereby confirms Freud's final drive theory, which postulates an opposition between the sexual drive and the aggressive drive, but *not* Freud's concept (1915b, p. 152f.) of affect as the quantitative expression of the drive. While accepting Kernberg's distinction between primitive affects and derived affects that have a more complex structure, I would apply the characterization of primitive affects, which include "a subjective experience of a pleasurable and rewarding or painful and aversive nature" (ibid.) equally to the sexual drive and the preservative drive—the experience of pleasure to the satisfaction, and the experience of pain to the non-satisfaction or disturbance. In other words, pleasure and pain, 'good' and 'bad', are, according to my conception, not the organizers of libido and aggression (or, if you will, of the two drive antagonists), but the indicators of satisfaction and non-satisfaction of libidinal and lethic tendencies—that is, of both the sexual drive and the preservative drive. If, therefore, we accept Freud's view of action, in the sense of the *specific action*, as the 'motoric element of the drive' leading to satisfaction, and if we understand affect as the quantitative (and phenomenologically qualitative) "subjectively experienced expression of the drive" (1915b, p. 152f.), the view of aggression as an affect or affective action not only retains the connection with drive activity but at the same time proves applicable to *both* drives. However, since the sexual and preservative drives can find expression in a wide variety of actions, affects and fantasies—most of which are surely regarded as non-aggressive—it remains an open question how it might be possible to understand and conceive aggression in these terms. Let us begin on the phenomenological level.

Affect: We may find a person quite nice, like him/her, be very fond of him/her, love him/her or be madly in love with him/her; or we may be slightly sad, quite distressed, very miserable or desperately unhappy. These distinctions each correspond to quantitative increments within a feeling dimension, increasing, as it were, from small to large "quotas" or "quanta of affect".

Action: We may look at another person, point to him/her, touch him/her, push him him/her, punch him him/her, knock him him/her down or kill him/her. The dominant term in this series has to do with *motoricity*, and thus with the *strength*, and also the *speed* (i.e. time), for example, with which my arm moves through the particular distance to the object, as well as with the aim with which the movement comes to its intended end or to a standstill (that is to say, for instance, whether the object is held in my hand or squashed).

Let us now turn to aggression. The definition of aggression given by Laplanche & Pontalis is: the "tendency or cluster of tendencies finding expression in real or phantasy behavior *intended to harm other people, or to destroy, humiliate or constrain them etc."* (1973, p. 17, my italics). This definition, according to which aggression primarily constitutes an action within an object relationship, conforms to ordinary linguistic usage, in which aggression is something bad, malicious and negative. However, it is tendentious and limiting.

After all, an aggressive act may also be controlled and then in every way be constructive, useful, and good. Or else an aggressive reaction may arise spontaneously, in the form of a reflex—for example, in the situation of danger, which calls for a defense—and, in this case, we may see it not only as appropriate but also, according to the circumstances, as necessary for survival. However, whereas these examples are based on an ideally mature personality structure capable of appropriate actions directed towards a specific end, in psychoanalysis we are predominantly concerned with neurotic aggression.

To avoid biasing our reflections on the conceptualization of aggression, I should like to adopt a value-neutral approach to the question of aggression, based on the meaning of the Latin *aggredi*, which signifies *going towards, approaching* or *seizing* in the descriptive sense of these notions. Understood in this way, aggression *per se* is neither something bad nor something good, but instead an indication of the degree of firmness or vigor—or, if you will, *intensity*—with which a drive tendency, of whatever kind, is pursued, or aggresses its goal. (This idea is to some extent included in Freud's notion of the *drive for mastery*, although the idea of mastery relates to a much more specific intention than what I mean here by firmness, vigor or intensity.) *Any* drive tendency may be pursued or implemented with *more intensity* or *less intensity*; this applies equally to the libidinal tendency (which corresponds to the sexual or life drive) and to the lethic tendency (corresponding to the preservative or death drive). The term *intensity* here has two connotations. First, it relates to the *quantitative* element, as expressed, for example, in Freud's fine idea that a "surplus of sexual aggressiveness will turn a lover into a sex-murderer, while a sharp diminution in the aggressive factor will make him bashful or impotent" (1938, p. 149). Second, *intensity* implies the element of *speed*—that is, the path-time dimension of a psychic process. I shall elaborate on these notions below with the aid of our metapsychological concepts.

What is the Meaning of Intensity?

We generally assume that actions and affects are more intense and more primitive the deeper the regression. The underlying concept here is the distinction between primary and secondary process. Freud developed the idea that primary processes (being the province of the *Ucs.*) aim for immediate discharge and are more violent and less differentiated, whereas secondary processes (being ascribed to the *Pcs.* and the *Cs.*) take place in a structured manner—that is to say, they are differentiated and at the same time inhibited, so that their expression is more measured. Containment, inhibition and differentiation of drive processes are a function of structures; they increase with the number of structures involved in a process, because each structure, like a switch, contributes to the regulation of drive excitation.

The intensity of a drive's expression thus depends on two factors: the quantity of drive energy mobilised and the number of regulating structures involved in a psychic process. I have attempted elsewhere (Schmidt-Hellerau, 2001, p. 163f.) to illustrate this by a hypothetical calculation.

Let us stipulate that in a drive excitation a given *quantum* (+/−) of energy is released for the cathected process within one or all of the system's subsystems—for example, (+/−) 10 [Q]. Let us further specify that the passage of excitation, from its presumed commencement to its end point, takes one *unit time* [*t*]; in a given unit time, the same quantum of energy then passes through, say, ten *switches* or *structures* [S] in the less structured primary process and, for example, 100 [S] in the highly structured secondary process (the number of switches stands for path length). On this presupposition, *speed* in secondary-process cycles is much higher (100/1) than in their primary-process counterparts (10/1). Now let the *intensity factor* [*I*] of a psychic process cycle correspond to the quotient obtained by dividing the quantity of drive energy released [Q] by the speed of the process cycle (the path-time dimension, or *S/t*), i.e.

$$I = Q \div (St)$$

This yields the following intensity quotients:

for the *Ucs.*: $I = 10[Q] \div (10[S]/I[t]) = 1$
for the *Cs.*: $I = 10[Q] \div (100[S]/I[t]) = 0.1$

Hence, although the processes of the *Ucs.* are slower, their lower structural density (number of switching points) means that they have a higher intensity quotient than the secondary processes of the *Cs.*, which take place at much higher speed although the intensity of the process cycles is less, and which, accordingly, also exhibit an inhibition ition of drive discharge (output).

This description is also consistent with the psychoanalytic idea of the greater intensity of affective experiencing, actions and reactions in children (in whom, by virtue of their stage of development, a deficiency of psychic structures relative to the level of excitation of the two drives may be assumed), as well as in adults in regressive states (during which entire structural areas are temporarily deactivated). However, an increase in the intensity of excitation processes presents a potential threat to the functioning of the psychical apparatus—at least at times when the system as a whole moves out of balance, that is, when the excitation values permissible for homoeostasis, or dynamical stability, are substantially exceeded. This kind of overloading of the processing capacities of the structures, constituting a threat to the system as a whole, by the overwhelming intensity of the processes of psychic excitation, might correspond to the painful intensification described by Freud (1896, p. 214)—that is, a pain of tension (experienced as an 'attack') and anxiety (concerning a disintegration of the system); that is why the emergency measure adopted by the psychical apparatus, aggression, is qualitatively associated with something negative, bad or undesirable. This has the paradoxical consequence that the intense excitation of, for example, a self-preservative need aims for the necessary satisfaction, namely the elimination of a threatening state of tension, while at the same time the very intensity of the excitation threatens the psychical apparatus (with disintegration). The intense excitation of the drive itself may, therefore, be experienced as a threat and, hence, qualitatively as something bad, dangerous and traumatizing.

This connection was thoroughly explored by Melanie Klein. In her description of weaning as the phase involving 'the fullest activation and development of sadistic tendencies flowing from every source', with oral-sadistic fantasies of gaining 'possession of the contents of [the] mother's breast' (1932, p. 128), she is portraying a situation of drive tension of the utmost intensity working within the ego in two directions:

> In the first place it [anxiety] implies the *annihilation* of [the child's] *own body* by his destructive impulses, which is a *fear* of an *internal drive² danger;* but in the second place it focuses his fears on his *external object*, against whom his sadistic feelings are directed, as a *source of danger* (p. 127, my italics, except for the word 'external').

Klein's description of the 'good breast' as the feeding breast that is present and of the 'bad breast' as the absent, non-satisfying breast indicates that it is the drive need in relation to the psycho-geometric locus of the satisfying object (see following section) that determines the intensity of a drive excitation and, hence, also whether a drive, its subject or its object is experienced as 'good' or 'bad'. Klein espoused Freud's notion of the death drive as a destructive drive primarily directed against the subject's own organism; this inward-directed destruction is 'regarded by the ego as a danger' (p. 126), which triggers annihilation anxiety. She concludes, 'Therefore anxiety would originate from aggression' (p. 126). If we regard aggression and destruction in general terms as the intensification of a drive impulse, and see the preservative or death drive as a basic drive directed inwards, on to the subject him/herself and his/her organism, it becomes clear how our conception can be linked to Klein's, even if it is formulated in different language. What is feared as potentially destructive seems to be the *intensity* of the tendencies directed towards both the self and the object.

---

² Translator's note: 'instinctual' in the original.

Subject and Object in Psycho-Geometric Space

The path-time dimension considered so far was related wholly to the 'spatiality' of the psychical apparatus—that is, to internal structures and the number of switching points involved in a drive process. However, psychic behavior takes place in concrete geometric space in relation to both animate and inanimate objects and, here too, distance plays a decisive part. Of course, everything we perceive 'outside' must be represented 'inside' in order to be perceived, so that these 'external perceptions'—or the corresponding data supplied by the sense organs—must in turn be processed as 'internal perceptions'. Within an object relationship, the question of closeness/distance regulation is important from the outset and at all times thereafter. Closeness needs vary during the course of development and in terms of the relevant drive excitation, just as the form in which they manifest themselves differs according to the circumstances. We want our love object to be close and the object that arouses anxiety to be distant, far away. 'Close' and 'distant' here are relative terms, which are determined not only by the measuring tape but also by whatever psychic need is predominant at any given time. For a child who has eaten his/her fill and feels safe, the mother is close enough if she is somewhere in the house, but for a child who is hungry or anxious, the mother is much too far away if she is only in the room next door. In other words, every drive tendency, whether it be endogenous or reactive in relation to a perception, raises the question of *where* the object of satisfaction is and whether the distance from this object is correct in relation to the need situation prevailing at that time, or is experienced as insufficient or excessive.

In formal terms we can say that the psychical apparatus is constantly 'computing'—computing both the distance from the object and the speed or intensity necessary to reach it, to drive it away, to escape from it or to destroy it. During the course of psychic development, these computations are learned as a complex process, just like the grasping movement of a child who, in his/her first attempts, misses the aimed-for and desired object or overturns it, and learns only gradually how far to extend his/her arm in order to catch hold of the object, how fast he/she must do so if he/she is to be able to grasp the object if it is moving, and how firmly to hold it in order not to lose it but also not to crush it. Computations of this kind are computations of the necessary quantities within the path-time to the object. They are learned, stored in the memory systems (i.e. the structures of the psychical apparatus) and anticipated accordingly. In other words, however undeveloped or mature these structures of the psychical apparatus are at any given time, these computations and the resulting *anticipations* become the basis for assessing the drive energy to be mobilized within an object relationship.

Learning in the field of motoricity and adaptations in geometric space is a relatively basic process which, given healthy brain function, every individual succeeds in mastering more or less well, but certainly to the point of normal functionality. By contrast, however, our perception and regulation of distance in the relevant psycho-geometric space are much more difficult and fragile. Two different and partially overlapping configurations are contained in the notion of psycho-geometric space.

This notion relates first to *the geometric locus of the object in relation to the psychic locus of the subject*. The psychic locus of the subject here is substantially determined by its drives' needs and desires, while the geometric locus of the object indicates how far the subject must reach out and how long it must endure the drive tension before the satisfying action can take place.

Second, the term encompasses *the psychic locus of the object in relation to the psychic locus of the subject*. The psychic locus of the object means the psychic presence or absence of the object, whether it is turned towards or away from the subject, or, in general, also the object's psychic availability, empathy or, as the case may be, aversion, in relation to the subject's psychic situation.

The relevance of the psycho-geometric space thus always results from the subject's needs or desires at any given time. The psychical apparatus must constantly *measure out* this space so that the specific actions intended to lead to satisfaction can be performed successfully. The result of this measurement determines the quantity of drive energy to be mobilized in relation to the path-time to the object, or, in brief, the intensity of the object-directed processes. This immediately raises the question of how such computations or measurements take place in the psychical apparatus. How do they succeed or why do they fail? In other words, ultimately, how does the psychical apparatus *judge* the distance from the object or, more precisely, determine whether the drive object is in the right place, too close or too distant in psycho-geometric space?

Notes on the Formation of Judgement

As a preliminary to my discussion of the formation of judgement, let me say that the emphasis in my argument will fall on the idea of *judging as referencing*. The decision whether something is large or small, close or distant, good or bad, right or wrong, neurotic or psychotic, progressive or regressive can be made only in comparison with a scale or standard of some kind. After all, a thing can never be large in itself, but is large only in relation to something smaller. Precisely in this sense, Freud states in his conception of the psychical apparatus that *judging* consists in a *comparison* or *referencing* which becomes possible through the "simultaneous cathexis of a wishful complex and a perceptual complex"; and it is precisely the discrepancies occurring that constitute the stimulus to continue the psychic processes, whereas identity (of wish and perception) terminates the thought process (1895, p. 328) or triggers discharge. Freud showed that, with the onset of the reality principle, a "functional differentiation", or "split", arose within the psychic organization:

> With the introduction of the reality principle one species of thought-activity was split off; it was kept free from reality-testing and remained subordinated to the pleasure principle alone. This activity is *phantasying*, which begins already in children's play, and later, continued as *day-dreaming*, abandons dependence on real objects (1911, p. 222).

In the process of judgement, the structural level of fantasies, on which, on the one hand, old, earlier wishes are activated and, on the other, new ones are formed (e.g. daydreaming), is 'referenced' to the structural level of reality, on which current perceptions are registered and also earlier ones are reactivated (remembered)—that is to say, the two levels are compared with each other, and it is this comparison that makes it possible to decide whether something perceived is inside or outside, and whether the factual situation of the external world does or does not conform to the demands or wishes of the internal world.

However, this comparison is highly susceptible to disturbance. It is only too easy for the seemingly immovable markers of the reality level to be displaced in favor of unconscious wishes or urgent current need situations, or on account of neurotic anxieties and conflicts. Freud described this process in his writings on 'Neurosis and psychosis' (1924a, 1924c). Whereas in psychosis the relation to reality is severely impaired or lost (the internal world rules), this relation is preserved in neurosis, but is subject in *certain areas* to specific distortions—as it were, shifting of the markers for judging the external world due to the breaking through of unconscious fantasies and tendencies to the organizational level of reality perception. In other words, the neurotic miscomputation of the psycho-geometric locus of the object arises because, in the areas of infantile conflicts, the structural level of reality testing is inadequately formed or in part regressively deactivated, so that the object is, as it were, perceived on that level from an infantile perspective: psychic reality is then *reality pure and simple*.

The Psychoanalysis of Aggression

The foregoing considerations on the formation of judgement were necessary in order for us to proceed far enough with the reconceptualization of aggression and to facilitate understanding of the field that is most important for psychoanalysis, namely that of 'neurotic aggression'. After all, hardly anyone will consider there to be any problem in aggression as 'appropriate' behavior (i.e. appropriate as seen from outside), for example, in response to a danger; it is more likely that the *absence* of aggressive self-defense in such a situation would give an analyst food for thought. It is interesting in this connection to note how Freud relates the opposition of flight and attack to the structural maturity of the individual:

This reaction to the perception of danger now introduces an attempt at flight, which can have a life-saving effect till one has grown strong enough to meet the dangers of the external world in a more active fashion—even aggressively, perhaps (1926, p. 202).

In the case of real danger, aggression is an expression of a stable psychic structure, the deciding element no doubt being correct appreciation of the quantitative factor of the danger in relation to the subject's own capacity for defense. Conversely, a problem is presented by (manifestly) 'inappropriate aggression', which I here connect with a 'miscomputation'—an incorrect appreciation—of the distance of the object in relation to a current need, a misjudgment in the central question of closeness/distance regulation in psycho-geometric space. Since it is structures that compute, control and regulate the intensity of drive excitation, it is the infantile fantasies represented through these structures that are activated by the drive tendencies prevailing at any given time, and that trigger aggressive behavior unless they are modulated and corrected by a structural network (e.g. that of the reality principle) having a solid foundation.

The Transference Object

Fantasy is the crucial factor in the 'transference', which, in formal terms, leads to a neurotically distorted perception of the psycho-geometric locus of the object. Where the infantile neurosis operates, the reality principle is impaired, and the complex processes of mediation between the internal and external worlds that regulate action and affect are fragile. The infantile wish of the adult patient places the object in the transference position of a parent figure, who is either perceived as too close (e.g. in symbiotic entanglement) or experienced as too distant and rejecting with regard to a drive tendency (e.g. in the Oedipus complex). Consequently, the psycho-geometric locus of the (real) object in the neurotic perception does not fit the subject's current (infantile) need situation. The subject's behavior towards objects (wife, employer, analyst etc.) then no longer constitutes an appropriate reaction of mediation between the drive's need or desire and the possibilities of satisfaction in relation to the real situation, but instead corresponds to a continued anticipation of being overwhelmed or of not being satisfied; the (passive) fantasy of being overwhelmed leads to a primarily 'defensive aggression', while the (active) fantasy of not being satisfied tends to result more in 'persecutory aggression'—that is, an intensification of the drive tendency for the purpose of reaching and overwhelming the object. The inappropriate intensity of the neurotic reaction thus results from the fact that, first, the assessment of the path-time to the real object is perceived, or computed, in distorted form (reduced or increased) in accordance with the infantile fantasy, and, second, that the mobilization of quantities of drive energy for putting the subject's own (drive) tendencies into effect is increased on account of the anticipation of being overwhelmed or of not being satisfied. These two factors together are expressed in an intensification of the relevant drive tendency and its aggressive expression in the form of action and/or affect. In addition, the manifestation of a neurotic conflict in the present is always accompanied by a regression, and regressions entail the deactivation of the structures that inhibit and regulate the drive process: this is another element in the phenomenon whereby the increase in the intensity of a drive tendency becomes disproportionate, leading in this case to aggression.

Clinical Example

Mr. M, a lawyer in his late thirties, came to me for analysis (four sessions a week on the couch) owing to depressive mood changes and difficulties in his personal relationships. At first, and for a long time, he would be very polite and reserved, and sometimes also cool, usually reacting to my interventions with indifference or rejection. Mr. M had been born in an eastern European country and, according to his own account, spent his first nine years in poverty. He had few memories of this phase of his childhood. His family had then emigrated to Austria, where he had been able to attend high school and university. Although his intelligence was above average, his career in his law firm had brought him only mediocre professional success, apparently because of his difficult relationships with his colleagues. Mr. M reported that his colleagues considered him cranky. He collected used sheets of paper and printed matter left blank on the back and took them home from the office by the sackful, where he later used them to draft out his correspondence. He was often the last to leave the office at night, and would then go through all the rooms turning off desk lamps and computers so as not to waste electricity— something that had already given rise to violent conflicts with some of his colleagues. At the end of a meeting, he would sometimes also fill his briefcase with left-over sandwiches or cakes from the buffet and take them home. For Mr. M himself, this behavior was only slightly ego-dystonic; his only worry was that others might see him doing it, which he would find embarrassing because he might then be thought to be poorly off.

Mr. M had gradually become more open and discovered the analysis to be an important 'source of life' for him. When he obtained a surprise promotion in the third year of his analysis, he was convinced that it was connected with our work. He now developed a kind of ardent enthusiasm for the analysis; he turned my comments over and over and back and forth in order, as he put it, to make them analytically useful for himself in every respect, but, rather than linking them to his associations, he tended, in so doing, to resolve them into insignificant details. He quickly became dissatisfied if I did not react to what he said quickly or 'substantively' enough. After the sessions with him I often felt exhausted, as if after a pointless struggle. A greed for my interpretations became evident, and contrasted starkly with his capacity for truly absorbing and digesting them. With the approach of a long holiday break, Mr. M got into a state of permanent irritation; again and again he would accuse me of fetching him from the waiting room late, or he would find our sessions insufficiently productive, and one Friday evening he telephoned me in a break between two sessions and announced that he had to have one or two sessions over the weekend. I told him that I was unfortunately unable to arrange this, but that we would talk about it on Monday.

Mr. M came along on Monday in a thoroughly black mood. He'd had a wretched weekend. Finding his refrigerator empty, he had 'had to manage with his emergency reserves: dried milk and rice'. He'd had a headache and had made no progress with the draft of a new project he was supposed to present shortly. While sitting at the computer in a state of torment, he had brooded over why I had been unable to see him—whether I simply wanted to sit out my sessions with him inflexibly, or whether (a less unpleasant thought) I had perhaps had to attend a weekend conference. This had suggested to him the idea of searching for the programs of the psychoanalytic associations on the internet, but again and again he had had trouble doing so; his 'shitty old computer' had not worked and he had become absolutely enraged, but had not wanted to give up. 'I pursued you with absolutely furious energy, but every time you crashed out on me again!' he said. 'I damn well wanted to know where you were over this shitty weekend. I needed a session, and you weren't there!'

I told him that he had literally felt as though he were starving.

Mr. M replied, 'Fortunately I have my own reserves. I made myself a rice pudding with the dried milk, and then ate so much of it that I felt quite sick. I did not want to go out. I was so fixated on the idea of having to see you that I could not have gone anywhere else'.

I said that he had instead chased after me on the internet.

Mr. M confirmed this, saying that he could not really understand why he had crashed out of the program again and again just at the point when he could have clicked on the list of events. And when he finally did have the list, oddly enough he had lost himself in details of all kinds. In the end he got so angry that he had simply switched off the computer altogether, because he had already consumed so much electricity, and all for nothing, for absolutely nothing.

At this point I was able to start showing him his ambivalence, his gigantic hunger for getting something from me and his strategies for defending against it at the same time, which caused him to tear what I gave him into pieces and make it unusable rather than absorbing and digesting it and thereby feeding on it in such a way that he felt that he had enough to tide him over the weekend. Over a number of sessions, we were able to develop the idea that, out of fear of becoming dependent on me as a 'source of nourishment', but of not having me at his disposal when he needed me, he preferred not to accept what I gave him, but in the process became more and more hungry and desperate. In the end he would fill himself up with his own reserves (dried milk) until he felt quite sick, or with 'that furious energy of pursuit' that briefly gave him a feeling of strength and power, in the process trying to secure from me what I had not given him of my own accord (information on how I was spending my weekend)—but he would then, in turn, sabotage this effort by constantly causing his computer to crash because he could not bear me to be so 'important'. All he then had, in the end, was the feeling of having used up his already exiguous energy, thus exacerbating his distress even further.

Much could be said about this long and difficult phase in Mr. M's analysis, which was characterized by anxiety, envy and greed. However, in the present context I wish to concentrate on the 'furious energy of pursuit' with which he chased after me, whether at the beginning of the session when I allegedly did not fetch him from the waiting room in time, or when he telephoned on the Friday, or on the internet over the weekend. Threatened in his fantasy he experienced a surge of his self-preservative drives swelling up inside him like in a real 'danger to his survival'—a feeling of starvation in anticipation of the forthcoming holidays. In the transference I, as the feeding object, was in the process of 'going away' and, on the unconscious level, even when I was there, I was 'not close and available enough', which imperiled him and made him furious. Understanding his aggression as a neurotically stirred self-preservative need that was intensified in anticipation of remaining dangerously unfulfilled (not as the expression of an aggressive drive in its own right), I could stay in empathic contact with the patient and formulate interpretations that corresponded in a deeper sense to the fantasies and anxieties of his experiential world, rather than interpreting the aggression of which he himself was perfectly conscious (along the lines of: 'you are furious because I did not give you an extra session'). In other words, I concentrated my interpretations not on the aggressive affects (rage, envy, greed), but on his intensified lethic needs—his survival anxiety—which made the "furious energy" of his his aggressive feelings more easily understandable for him.

We have a similar experience with patients who, for example, within a positive oedipal transference love, become aggressive because they (partly unconsciously) come to feel that we are rejecting their love, that their love is something terribly shameful or that we are laughing at them behind their backs. The annoyance they develop in consequence, which sometimes tends to involve us, too, in a sadistic cut-and-thrust, is an expression of an intensification of their sexual desire, which is unconsciously struggling against the prohibition of incest transferred to the here-and-now. That is to say, the patient experiences us as 'unattainable' (far away) for his/her tendencies; his/her libidinal-aggressive affect pursues us in order to achieve its aim after all. It seems to me that in such situations an interpretation of this kind of aggression—for example, "you are angry with me because… and you want to punish me for it"—takes account only of the manifest behavior, disregarding the underlying intensified libidinal strivings of the patient, who is in reality not 'angry' with his/her analyst but 'loves' him/her in the transference, and in fact wishes not to 'punish' him/her but to 'win him/her back'; and, indeed, the patient's defiant 'not-any-more-with-me-you-don't' is surely very often intended as a summons to us to concern ourselves more intensively with our patient. The interpretation of aggression as such, as a rule, makes the patient feel bad or accused or ashamed (Meerwein, 1973). If our interpretation focuses on the patient's love, which, in the transference, feels disturbed and wounded in accordance with the infantile pattern and therefore leads to aggressive feelings, or which is expressed in the frustration or tormenting of objects along the lines of a sadomasochistic primal-scene interpretation, this will preserve, or open up, access for the patient to his/her primarily libidinal tendency and at the same time offer him/her insight into an internal process that takes place in a similar way in other situations, in which it can then also be better mastered.

The Narcissistic Grandiose Self

Just as the neurotic misjudgment of the psycho-geometric locus of the *object* can be understood as the trigger of intensified drive-related behavior, as described in the previous section, so an associated neurotic misjudgment of the psycho-geometric locus of the *subject* can give rise to the need for intensification of drive tendencies, and hence aggression. Let us take the 'narcissistic grandiose self' as an example. All the problems of narcissistically grandiose personalities arise in relation to objects (which is why some also withdraw into splendid isolation, in order to escape the permanent offenses inflicted by the outside world). The term 'grandiose self' or, alternatively, 'inflated self' shows that a spatial category is involved in this case, too, namely 'volume'. Because the volume of the self is increased in the narcissistically distorted self-perception, sometimes to positively gigantic (godlike) proportions, the subject literally finds him/herself constantly bumping into things: the self is too big to proceed unmolested along the crooked paths of everyday interpersonal intercourse. Since it needs and demands more space in his/her self-perception than the real and transference objects are prepared to grant it, it believes itself to be constantly attacked or penetrated. If the object comes too close to it, it feels assaulted and wounded, and hence justified in angrily defending its position. And if the object is experienced as having gone so far as to penetrate into the sphere of the narcissistic subject's self, it must be destroyed like a foreign body. Because of the misappreciation of its own size and, in consequence, the fact that the object has approached closer than the minimum permissible distance, the subject feels permanently threatened and cornered by the object 'as the other', and, in the process, sometimes also imagines itself reduced to the tiniest possible proportions. The aggression of a narcissistic patient is therefore either 'grandiose-expansive' or 'defensive'—defending mainly against the perception of his/her own needs and desires, which unavoidably summon the object on to the scene. Only if the object allows itself to be incorporated into the grandiose self in the form of a 'selfobject' (and thereby to be eliminated as such) is the closeness/distance problem, which is responsible for his/her increased vulnerability, and hence his/her propensity to defend him/herself aggressively, disposed of.

Clinical Example

Ms D, an architect in her early forties, had been in analysis with me for four years (five sessions a week on the couch). She was married, but mostly lived alone, as her husband was in charge of projects in the Third

World for a major multinational company and often had to work for months at a time in the field. Ms D claimed to have adapted well to this situation. She had come to me because she could not decide whether she wanted to have a child while she still could, and also because she sometimes felt lonely—something she attributed to her constant tendency to withdraw from others.

As the analysis progressed, it, too, became increasingly characterized by these tendencies to retreat. If she had—surprisingly—responded with interest to one of my interpretations, she would often skip the next session or, if she did come, she would cast doubt on what we had discussed the previous day. She also felt that all I wanted to do with my interpretations was to show her how stupid she really was. She reproached herself for not having thought of what I had contributed, and concluded again and again that she would have done better not to say anything at all. Free association was 'much too dangerous' for her because an ill-considered remark on her part might put me on the track of things she did not want to talk about. She remained silent for much of the time.

Her great sensitivity and readiness to take offense often had a paralyzing effect on me, and I realized that with her I was particularly reticent and careful with my interventions. I reflected that, as a result, I was at the same time allowing her to control me, thereby indirectly confirming the 'dangerousness' of the thoughts and fantasies which she feared. My attempts to interpret to her that she was trying, by her withdrawal maneuvers, to keep me in check and to nullify my interventions were met with a wall of silence. A great deal of aggression was in the air—aggression of the quiet variety, which to address was often difficult for me because it seemed to be so remote from her consciousness; when I did address it, she felt herself to be unjustly accused (counterattacked), as she had, after all, 'done nothing', and she would withdraw masochistically into her own world. I nevertheless continued to point out this dynamic to her in our sessions whenever this seemed to me to be possible.

One day she told me that she had received an invitation to spend a weekend at some friends' house. She described in detail the various activities planned there and all the other people who were invited—but then ended with a mixture of resignation and indifference by declaring that she had turned the invitation down.

I said, 'It sounds as if this invitation was simply *too* enticing, and that is why it had to be turned down'.

After a moment's reflection, Ms D said, 'There is something in what you say'. But she then immediately explained that she must not accept that. After all, that would mean that she might need me, which would be an exaggeration. She then changed the subject, embarking on a detailed account of her annoyance with the person in charge of some building works she was having done because he preferred a different supplier for a certain construction material from the one she had suggested. After a short silence she said that I surely did not want to hear that but would rather have her stay with the previous subject.

> *A*: You think I don't want to hear about your annoyance.
> *P*: You are annoyed that I am not staying with the previous subject because you have made a particular point of it. That makes me appear in a bad light. But if I want to talk about something else, you think I am just avoiding the issue. I must always be very careful what I say. It is like walking across a minefield. One false move and the bomb goes off.
> *A*: You might blow up.
> *P*: I might put my foot in the bowl of fat[3]—and that would be another typical sign of my clumsiness.
> *A*: You might offend me.
> *P*: Of course you would not be offended. Nothing can offend you. That is curious. So if it turned out that I was the bowl of fat… [She stopped short with a laugh.] Well, of course I meant to say that you were the bowl of fat I might put my foot into…
> [She seemed confused and fell silent.]
> *A*: It does not seem at all clear which of us is the bowl of fat, but it seems hard to avoid that bowl of fat. Everything I or you say could

---

[3] Translator's note: A German expression meaning 'to put one's foot in it'.

be an insult. The offenses are scattered all around us, as if in a minefield, unpredictable and just below the surface, ready to explode at
any time.

P: Even the way you put all that together offends me. I feel stupid
because I have said something stupid. And if you make something
intelligent out of it, that feels to me like an insult. It is getting too
close to me. But then, it is always like that. In fact, everyone always
comes too close to me.

A: If I come too close to you, you feel threatened. If there is an enticing invitation, you have to refuse it. If there is 'something in' what I
say, which you might perhaps be able to use, it annoys you. And if I
put all that together in a way that makes sense, it offends you. There
are so many hurts on our path through this minefield. Perhaps these
hurts and offenses have something to do with all these enticing
things—with the terrible feeling they arouse in you: the wish for
more.

P: [In a whisper] I do not want to be dependent. Never and on no
one. That would be the worst possible thing for me. And, after all,
you would just drop me anyway…

Ms D's description of her problem and our dilemma is absolutely accurate: in fact, everyone always comes too close to her. She feels constantly
under attack, both by my interventions and, sometimes, even by my
silence, and is therefore constantly on the defensive. What she is defending against is her own neediness, her own desire, the activity of the drive
itself, which arouses a greed and a longing for the satisfying object in
her. This makes her furious, because she then feels small and dependent,
which offends her self-conception as an omnipotent self-sufficient
monad. Her innermost problem can therefore be described as follows:
when a demand—whether sexual or self-preservative—arises in her, she
wants to have the exciting or feeding object very close to her, but this
closeness immediately appears gigantic and threatens to overwhelm her
('everyone always comes too close'); she therefore repulses the object,
but then the object is no longer available, so that it becomes a 'bad'
object; it therefore has to be dropped, and while this frees her from her

demand, it leaves her in a state of dissatisfaction, which then feels as if *I* have disappointed and dropped her ('after all, you would just drop me anyway'). The drive activity within her arouses anxiety because it conjures up the situation of being overwhelmed, while her distancing herself also arouses anxiety because she is then afraid of 'losing' and/or 'forgetting' the desired object in space and time. In other words, the psycho-geometric locus of the object is at the same time always *both* too close *and* too distant. 'Gigantic' and 'tiny' are the precise perspective attributes of a self-image that, within this closeness/distance problem constellation, is moved now excessively close to the object and now excessively distant from it—and, when at its maximum distance, the object as such has finally disappeared altogether. My patient engages in a constant effort to compute my reactions in advance, to guess what I am going to say, and in this way she also, as it were, wants to incorporate me within herself—to eliminate me as an object in my own right, independent of herself, beside her. Her withdrawal into silence, disappearance into her fantasy world or staying away from our sessions thus at one and the same time corresponds both to her need for a powerful retaliatory measure (to exclude me) and to an intensified restorative self-cathexis. With regard to the technical difficulties of interpreting this pathology, then, it is not a matter of calling into question the aggression—which is a defensive measure aimed at maintaining narcissistic equilibrium—as such (this is experienced as a threat and often results in a regression), but, instead, of working towards a situation in which the patient is able to perceive his/her (sometimes gigantic) sense of neediness and to accept it within the transference relationship; acknowledging the fragility of the narcissistic self is strengthening the ego.

In the first clinical vignette the acute problem centered on the (persecutory) aggressive enhancement of a self-preservative drive excitation, and we can think of other examples focused on the fantasized disturbance or prevention of sexual tendencies; however, it is more difficult to recognize the dominant drive element in the defensive aggression of narcissistic personalities. Fantasies about the analytic situations concerned may occasionally be helpful here. If a patient tells me that he/she comes to me with all his/her brilliant thoughts and, in fact, expects me to deify him/her for it, I would regard the libidinal side of his/her narcissism as dominant owing to the object-relatedness thereby expressed (*'narcissisme de vie'*, Green, 1983); conversely, if another patient tells me that the analysis is like a solarium to which he/she simply goes regularly as if to get a tan, the absence of the human object (or its dead, machine-like quality) and the total focus on his/her own self is more likely to be a sign of an at least temporarily dominant lethic character to his/her narcissism (*'narcissisme négatif'*). Be that as it may (and, as a rule, we always observe mixtures of the two tendencies in variable proportions) I contend that in both cases aggression arises, in the case of a narcissistic grandiose self, because the psycho-geometric locus of the object fluctuates between the extremes of 'too close' and 'too distant', thus presenting a permanent threat, which must be met defensively, both to the necessary satisfaction of the drive and to the subject's own self-image.

Conclusion

The ideas put forward in this paper are directed against the conception of aggression as a primary drive on the level of the basic death drive or as an antagonist to the sexual drive. I suggest that *aggression should instead be understood as an intensification of one of the two (or both) primary drive tendencies*, expressed in actions, affects or affective actions. Owing to the complexity of drive processes (their multiple reversals and re-reversals, turning into their opposite etc.), it is often very difficult to determine whether the primary or dominant drive tendency is sexual or preservative. However, if we see aggression as the expression of an actual or imagined threat necessitating the intensification of a basic drive tendency, we shall be able, for the purpose of analyzing the aggression, to adopt a more subtly differentiated approach to the question of whether the tendencies involved are primarily those of the preservative or of the sexual drive.

While the conception of aggression I have developed is in some respects new, it is not entirely so. In accordance with this conception, it is perfectly possible to retain the idea of an inward-directed or an outward-directed aggression, precisely where it is indicative of an increase in intensity in one direction or the other. Why, then, am I opposed to the notion of an aggressive drive as the drive antagonist to the sexual drive if I, after all, consider that there is such a thing as inward-directed aggression, as postulated by Freud in primary masochism as the representative of the death drive?

I believe that we will analyze and interpret aggression differently if we do not conceive it as a primary drive expression, and hence assume 'a tendency towards the satisfaction of aggression', but instead first make the effort to identify the relevant drive tendency in the aggressive manifestations. In other words, the present conception assumes that it is not aggression as such that strives for satisfaction, but that it is the sexual drive or the preservative drive, which—for whatever (fantasy) reasons, but always for the purpose of attaining its aim—has undergone the intensification that is manifested in our patients' aggressiveness.

Also, I think it is necessary to lay stress once again on Freud's original concept of a self-preservative drive—or, more general, a preservative drive. Just as much as the sexual drives' urges, the tendencies of a preservative drives call for structuring interventions and, if neurotically or pathologically derailed, for interpretation and working through (of their excessive need for satisfaction). It has, in my view, been a persistent problem of psychoanalytic theory and clinical practice that the heavy shadow of Freud's death drive or aggressive drive has obscured the important position and significance of his original conception of a self-preservative drive and thereby removed it from the field of our analytic perception. Even if, as in my two vignettes, we work with a technique that induces us not to address aggression as such directly but instead to explore together with the patient *what* it is that has made him/her aggressive, and even if we do not particularly think of drive theory or even reject it, our thinking and perception are nevertheless traditionally steeped in the notion of the polarity of 'sexuality' and 'aggression', which may obscure the manifold tendencies of self- and object-preservation as psychologically significant formations requiring analysis.

References

Dollard, J. et al. (1939). *Frustration and Aggression.* New Haven: Yale Univ. Press.

Fonagy, P. et al. (1993). Aggression and the psychological self. *Int. J. Psycho-Anal.*, 74: 471-85.

Freud, S. (1895). A project for a scientific psychology. *S.E.* 1.

Freud, S. (1896). The aetiology of hysteria. *S.E.* 3.

Freud, S. (1905). Three Essays on the Theory of Sexuality. *S.E.* 7.

Freud, S. (1909). Analysis of a phobia in a five-year-old boy. *S.E.* 10.

Freud, S. (1911). Formulations on the two principles of mental functioning. *S.E.* 12.

Freud, S. (1915a). Instincts and their vicissitudes. *S.E.* 14.

Freud, S. (1915b). Repression. *S.E.* 14.

Freud, S. (1920). Beyond the Pleasure Principle. *S.E.* 18.

Freud, S. (1924a). Neurosis and psychosis. *S.E.* 19.

Freud, S. (1924b). The economic problem of masochism. *S.E.* 19.

Freud, S. (1924c). The loss of reality in neurosis and psychosis. *S.E.* 19.

Freud, S. (1926). The Question of Lay Analysis. *S.E.* 20.

Freud, S. (1933b). Why war? *S.E.* 22.

Freud, S. (1938). An Outline of Psycho-Analysis. *S.E.* 23.

Green, A. (1983). *Narcissisme de vie, narcissisme de mort.* Paris: Minuit.

Kernberg, O. F. (1976). *Object Relations Theory and Clinical Psychoanalysis.* New York: Jason Aronson.

Kernberg, O. F. (1992). *Aggression in Personality Disorders and Perversions.* New Haven: Yale Univ. Press.

Klein, M. (1932). *The Psycho-Analysis of Children.* Trans. A. Strachey. London: Hogarth Press, 1975.

Kohut, H. (1977). *The Restoration of the Self.* New York: Int. Univ. Press.

Laplanche, J. (1979). Le primat de l'autre en psychanalyse. In: *Travaux 1967-1992.* Paris: Flammarion, 1997.

Laplanche, J. & Pontalis, J.-B. (1973). *The Language of Psycho-Analysis.* Trans. D. Nicholson-Smith. London: Hogarth Press, 1973.

Meerwein, F. (1973). Zur Technik der sogenannten Aggressionsdeutungen. *Jahrbuch Psychoanal.*, Vol. 10. Berne: Huber, pp. 63-76.

Mitchell, S. A. (1993). Aggression and the endangered self. *Psychoanal. Q.*, 62: 351-82.

Ornstein, P. H. & Ornstein, A. (1990). Assertiveness, anger, rage, and destructive aggression: a perspective from the treatment process. In: *Rage, Power, and Aggression*, ed. R. A. Glick & S. P. Roose. New Haven: Yale Univ. Press.

Parens, H. (1979). *The Development of Aggression in Early Childhood*. Northvale, NJ: Jason Aronson.

Rizzuto, A.-M. et al. (1993). A revised theory of aggression. *Psychoanal. Rev.*, 80: 29-54.

Schmidt-Hellerau, C. (1995). Lebenstrieb & Todestrieb, Libido & Lethe. Ein formalisiertes konsistentes Modell der psychoanalytischen Trieb- und Strukturtheorie. Stuttgart: Verlag Internationale Psychoanalyse.

Schmidt-Hellerau, C. (1997). Libido and lethe. Fundamentals of a formal-ized conception of metapsychology. *Int. J. Psycho-Anal.*, 78: 683-97.

Schmidt-Hellerau, C. (2000). *Pulsion de vie, pulsion de mort. Libido et Léthé (French translation of Schmidt-Hellerau, 1995).* Trans. J. Étoré. Lausanne: Delachaux et Niestlé.

Schmidt-Hellerau, C. (2001). *Life Drive & Death Drive, Libido & Lethe. A Formalized Consistent Model of Psychoanalytic Drive and Structure Theory (English translation of Schmidt-Hellerau, 1995).* Trans. P. Slotkin. New York: Other Press.

Spitz, R. (1953). Aggression. In: *Drives, Affects, Behavior*, ed. R. M. Loewenstein. New York: Int. Univ. Press, pp. 126-38.

Spitz, R. (1969). Aggression and adaptation. *J. Nerv. Ment. Dis.*, 149: 81-90.

Stechler, G. & Halton, A. (1987). The emergence of assertion and aggres-sion during infancy: a psychoanalytic systems approach. *J. Amer. Psychoanal. Assn.*, 35: 821-38.

Stern, M. (1974). Das Problem der Aggression. Bemerkungen über Trieb, Trauma und Tod. *Psyche*, 28: 495-507.

Winnicott, D. W. (1984). *Deprivation and Delinquency.* London: Tavistock.

CHAPTER 4

Where Models Intersect

A Metapsychological Approach[*]

Current scientific interest in how the mind works creates a major challenge for psychoanalysis. Here I propose metapsychology as a bridging concept for an interdisciplinary dialogue. I present a new framework on a micro-structural level, within which different psychic representations are hierarchically organized. This framework permits a detailed comparison with Alexander Luria's (1973) neuropsychological model of the working brain (including recent theories of affect), and makes it possible to deline-ate the similarities as well as the differences between the psychoanalytic model of the mind and the neuropsychological model of the brain.

Psychoanalysis can consider itself lucky: there is a tremendous interest at present in how the mind works throughout academic disciplines and popular culture. Books promising to provide answers about this intri-guing topic approach the top of nonfiction bestseller lists. One might think that the time for psychoanalysis has finally arrived! However, the authors of the most discussed of these exciting works are neurologists, neuroscientists, cognitive psychologists, and philosophers; psychoana-lysts are rather the exception amongst those who take up telling us what is basic and what is essential in our mental life and activity. This is startling, because the exploration of how the mind works is the very

[*] (2002). Psychoanalytic Quarterly, 71(3):503-544

heart of psychoanalysis. Are we missing the chance to share what we can contribute to this joint effort in researching mental processes?

I want to begin by emphasizing that every substantial answer to the question of how the mind works is a theory. More or less sophisticated and elaborate though it may be, it is still a theory in that it is a construction embracing conclusions and speculations, partly derived from or related to a number of observations or experiential "facts". These facts have been interpreted within the framework of a specific vantage point, synthesized on a different and gradually more abstract level of thinking to a body of theses (Rubinstein 1967), which is designed to provide a more or less plausible explanation of its subject: the mind in part or as a whole. Up to this very day, mind and brain are still much too complex to be fully understood at the level of the detailed functioning of every component and in their many functional interactions.

Hence, there is a limited amount of clinical or experimental data available, upon which is based an interpretation of that data. Data from neuroscientific research or from experiments in the labs of cognitive psychologists seems to be regarded as "harder" or more "truth-worthy"—and therefore "better"—than data from our clinical psychoanalytic work with patients on the couch. But whatever opinion we have about it, the so-called better (experimental) data does not necessarily make for better theories; it does not even generate theories that are more "objective". Green (1999) pointed out that "although scientists spend most of their time listening to facts, which obey the exigencies of scientific methodology, when they come to theory, there is as much disagreement, controversy, and room for divergent interpretations, as between psychoanalysts" (p. 40). So it is not the data itself (as proven as that may be), but rather, it is the interpretation of the data, i.e., the way we understand it in the context of all we have understood before or anew, that makes up a specific theory—as well as its inherent limitations.[1]

---

[1] The fact that these interpretations are mental products, like many others (e.g., stories, fantasies, mathematical operations), each valuable for a different purpose, lends a disillusioning quality to them. We tend to think of theories as a kind of truth—although the history of theories should have taught us differently. Freud (1937) was courageous

According to this perspective, we can view metapsychology as a comprehensive theory of the mind, outlined in a rough but amazingly differentiated way by Freud, and enriched by many contributions from other psychoanalysts since his time. Furthermore, we can work with this theory creatively, according to laws of reason and logic. Such a scientific approach to metapsychology will not be "biographically" concerned with Freud (e.g., what he himself meant by a certain concept), or historically with the science of the nineteenth century (e.g., the lack of neuroscientific knowledge that has since come to light), but rather with what this theory in itself affords today—what it helps to conceptualize and what it does not. Where the theory fails to fit theoretical demands or to prove clinical validity, it can be rethought and modified.

But how can metapsychology be used today? This paper is an attempt to speak to this question. I will put forward a different reading and understanding of some of our basic psychoanalytic concepts, which I have extensively elaborated elsewhere (Schmidt-Hellerau 2001). For the purposes of this paper, I will focus mainly on one frame of reference that I have introduced into Freud's "psychic apparatus": the DPM (Drive-Perceptual-Motor) system. It is important to keep in mind that this is just one of four integrated frameworks, which together—and only together—form what I consider a psychoanalytic model of the mind.

I will then summarize Alexander Luria's (1973) model of the brain, comparing it step by step with the different layers of the DPM system. Here again, we need to be aware of the fact that Luria's model of the working brain is a neuroanatomical presentation; other approaches (e.g., neurophysiological or neurochemical) would need to be included in a more comprehensive discussion. Yet to start with a limited sector in both areas allows for a more detailed comparison. It is fascinating to discover the congruity of the two models—and intriguing, once one has made this discovery, to further reflect on the similarities and differences between the psychoanalytic model of the mind and the neuropsychological model of the brain.

---

enough to recognize this, noting that "without metapsychological speculation and theorizing—I had almost said 'phantasying'—we shall not get another step forward" (p. 225).

A Formalized Conception of Metapsychology

Though simple in its basic functions, Freud's original concept of the psychic apparatus was amazingly rich and differentiated, and remains open to further developments even today. In my revision of metapsychology (Schmidt-Hellerau 1995a, 2001), I chose a formalized way of rethinking and reformulating this model of the mind. My interest lay more in the *how* of the theoretical argument's structure than in its detailed *what*, its content. As previously summarized (Schmidt-Hellerau 1997), I started out with Freud's basic assumptions that: (a) there are two antagonistic drives, and (b) there is a regulating principle that works to maintain the dynamic stability of the whole system.

The antagonistic drives (the sexual and self-preservative drive[2] in Freud's first drive theory, as well as the life drive and death drive in his later version) can be viewed as vectors, like forces "driving" virtually endlessly, each in just one direction. Libido is the energy assigned to the sexual or life drive. Lethe is the energy term that I have introduced (Schmidt-Hellerau 2001) to designate the preservative or death drive. The libidinal and lethic strivings of the two primal drives therefore lead to libidinal and lethic cathexes of certain structures at which the increase of drive energy is subjected to the regulating measures of a structure.

The basic regulating principle is the pleasure principle, tending toward immediate homeostatic measures ("discharge") whenever any increase of tension within the system psyche is detected. More complex regulating principles (e.g., the principle of constancy [Freud 1950], the reality principle [Freud 1911]) develop only gradually via a series of failed and successful interactions with the environment. In these interactions, all sorts of objects provide support (e.g., the present mother) and hindrance (e.g., the absent mother) to drive satisfaction or the dynamic stability of the whole system. The growing capacity to memorize these interactions is reflected in the building up of self and object

---

[2] In this paper, the original Strachey translation of Trieb as instinct is being corrected to drive, Freud's notion *self-preservative drive* is—in adaptation to my revised drive theory and when appropriate—corrected to *preservative drive*.

representations (via identification and the internalization of these complex interactions), which contain the regulating measures of external auxiliary objects. That is to say, these more adaptive regulating principles are the result of structural development within the psychic apparatus.

Use of the concept of structure here includes (on a micro level) partial or whole self and object representations, for example, as well as the whole network of affectively related self and object representations, and even (on a macro level) the organization of these microstructures within the systems of the Ucs., Pcs., and Cs., or the id, superego, and ego. Structure activity on a micro and macro level consists of the regulation of psychic processes.[3] It is the libidinal and lethic drive activity that activates the regulating principles within the structures, and it is the regulating measure of the structures that controls and initiates further drive activity (e.g., of the antagonistic type)—all in order to maintain a dynamic equilibrium state of the system psyche, a state that guarantees its best condition of functioning.

Within this perspective, when we say that the sexual drive (vector) is directed outward (i.e., toward the external love object), and the self-preservative drive (vector) is directed inward (i.e., toward preservation of the self), we understand the notions of outward and inward as opposites, like life and death, waking and sleeping, drive and repression,[4] yes and no, positive and

---

[3] Gill (1963) introduced the term macrostructure for the agencies of the id, ego, and superego. He used the term microstructure for ideas and memories, indicating that these represent relatively stable organizations within the macrostructure and are subordinate to it. My use of macrostructure is broader, in that it includes the systems Ucs., Pcs., and Cs. as macro-organizers of mental activity. I use microstructure to refer to elements of psychic activity that form the building blocks of the macrostructures.

[4] If we focus exclusively on drive activity as a unidirectional movement within the system, we can easily see that the general concept of repression—by definition, a movement in opposition to an actual drive activity—can be formally defined as the activity of the antagonistic drive, in opposition to whichever drive is actively striving for satisfaction at any given moment. In this way, the drive-repression theory is reformulated within the basic notion of the dual antagonistic drive theory; for example, the symptom, defined as a compromise between drive and repression, can be understood as a compromise between the two opposing drives (Schmidt-Hellerau 1995a, 2001).

negative, or, most generally, plus and minus. To think in these terms means to abstract from the experienceable meanings of sexuality or self-preservation—that is, from the phenomenological side of what we theoretically address when we speak of a drive activity in a specific moment. We then focus only on the opposing (+/−) directionality of the drives.[5]

Thus, drive and structure are the two axiomatic concepts that generate the entire psychoanalytic model of the mind, guaranteeing its dynamics (the drives) as well as its stability (the structures with their regulating principles). Each psychic unit can be said to involve the basic interaction between drives and structures—or, in a more concrete way, each psychic activity involves the regulating activity of a network of structures, as well as the more or less balanced force of both drives (or of drives and repression).

The Micro Level of Organization

Freud (1915a, 1915b) elaborated his drive conception in order to further specify the relationship between the notions of drive and its different representations. Because representations—i.e., the object that represents a particular drive's striving—are here conceptualized as structures, his 1915 papers can be understood as elaborating the interaction between drive and structure. In order to organize these various elements of Freud's more differentiated drive conception in an easily comprehensible way, I have devised a framework that clearly displays the relationships between all of them. A good starting point for this endeav-

---

[5] Due to my strictly formalized reading of metapsychological concepts, I take this (-) directionality of the death drive not in a qualitative sense—that is, something "bad" that is aggressive or destructive—but as an active, inward orientation of a drive tendency, one that we all know from the experience of sleep (called "the brother of death"). In this sense I disconnect the death drive from aggression as its expression and/or energy term, which Freud only reluctantly assigned to it; instead, I focus on his description of the *silent* work of the death drive, its quiescent strivings, and for these I use the term lethe. In the same way that the term libido is used for the energetic expression of sexual and life drives, I propose to use lethe as the energy term of both the self-preservative and the death drives (Schmidt-Hellerau 1995a, 1997, 2001).

or proved to be Freud's (1900) basic sketch of the psychic apparatus (p. 537), in which he distinguished between a sensory or perceptual (Pcpt.) and a motor (M) end. This sketch is reproduced below as Diagram 1.

DIAGRAM 1

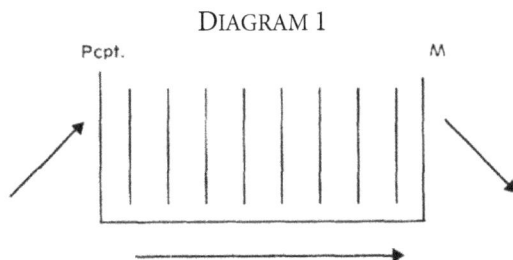

But the system psyche has to deal not only with sensory stimuli coming from the Pcpt., but also—and most of all—with endogenous drive stimuli. Therefore, I have added to this sketch a drive system, the D-system, in accordance with the theoretical assumptions of Freud's (1950) A Project for a Scientific Psychology. If we now focus on the mnemic representations of the perceptual and motor systems accumulating as a consequence of the activity of sensory stimuli from outside, as well as of drive stimuli from within (cathexis), we can connect these three part-systems as follows: the drive system (D) functions as an overall, antagonistically organized energizer of the whole psychic apparatus; the perceptual system (P) works as the receptor side of the psychic apparatus; and the motor system (M) functions as its cffcctor side. This DPM (Drive-Perceptual-Motor) association thus incorporates the basic model, which represents each psychic unit or process, as portrayed below in Diagram 2.

DIAGRAM 2

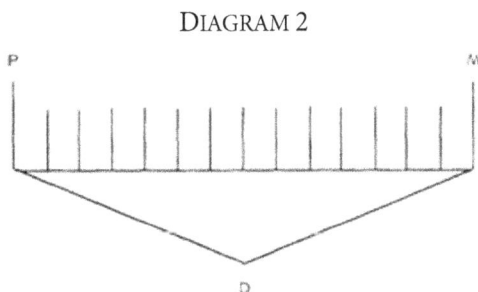

After completing a detailed analysis of Freud's 1915 papers (see Schmidt-Hellerau 2001, pp. 131-141), I introduced into this basic diagram the different elements of Freud's more comprehensive drive conception. The D (drive) system contains the sexual and preservative drives (also conceptualized as the life and death drives in Freud's writings since 1920). Within the P (perceptual) and M (motor) systems, three developmentally organized steps can be established. On the perceptual side, at the bottom (P1) lie the drive sources, the somatic representations (from which arise the component drives).[6] At the next level up (P2) are the self and object representations; and the highest, most sophisticated level (P3) is the realm of the thing representations. On the motor side of the diagram, the bottom tier (M1) holds the drive aims, with the action representations (of the specific actions); above this level (M2) are the affect representations[7]; and on the third level (M3) are the word representations. This scheme is portrayed in Diagram 3.

---

[6] The fact that the issue of the missing drive sources for the second drive could never be satisfactorily resolved has much to do with Freud's decision to interpret the death drive as the aggressive drive. However, it seems important not to obliterate the concept of the preservative drive. Therefore, in order to fill this old gap, I have introduced the concept of the biogenic zones (representations of the inner organs) as drive sources of the preservative drive—corresponding to the erotogenic zones as drive sources of the sexual drive (see Schmidt-Hellerau 2001); the notion of the somatic representations comprises both the biogenic and erotogenic zones.

[7] Solms and Nersessian (1999) described Freud's concept of affect—and related "felt emotions"—as: (1) a form of perception or a perceptual modality; (2) a motor pattern of discharge; (3) a memory aspect; and (4) an inhibitory or executive aspect. To regard affect as a perceptual modality could lead one to place affect on the perceptual side (P) of the DPM system. However, as each psychic activity (e.g., motor activity) can and does tend to be subject to conscious perception, the attribute of consciousness (here concerning a different framework, the topographic theory) does not seem to be an appropriate criterion for differentiation. In A Project for a Scientific Psychology (1950), Freud dealt with the perception of motor discharge by feeding it back to the ψ-system and giving it a motor representation in the ψ-pallium. Therefore, I choose to focus on the motor or effector side of the DPM system, placing affect on M2. As Damasio (1999a) stated, "an anatomical affect-related 'organ'... is, in effect, an 'action' organ that also 'senses', inasmuch as sensing is needed to control action" (p. 39). The memory aspect of affect is expressed in its being conceptualized as a representation, a re-evocable pattern formation, ingrained in a structure. The inhibitory or executive aspects here are viewed as part of the general function of the structure, not relating exclusively to affects.

In Diagram 3, each box represents a structure, and each dart a drive. The drive or D system itself is conceptualized as a structure from which basic drive activity emanates; from its lowest level, the activity of life and death drives is initiated. They correspond in their antagonistic orientations mentioned above to a movement outward or inward, to waking or sleeping, or to a general motion of yes or no, positive or negative, plus or minus. On its next level (the clinically most relevant one), the activity of the sexual and preservative drives comes into play, impinging libidinal or lethic demands on the structures within the P-M tiers—be this in the form of a particular drive activity or its repression. The boxes within the P and M systems contain the structures of various representations and subrepresentations. Several representations within each box, as well as in boxes on different tiers of the P-M systems, might be activated at the same time or succeedingly, either in the function of a drive (a plus-activation) or a defense against such a drive activity (a minus-activation).

DIAGRAM 3

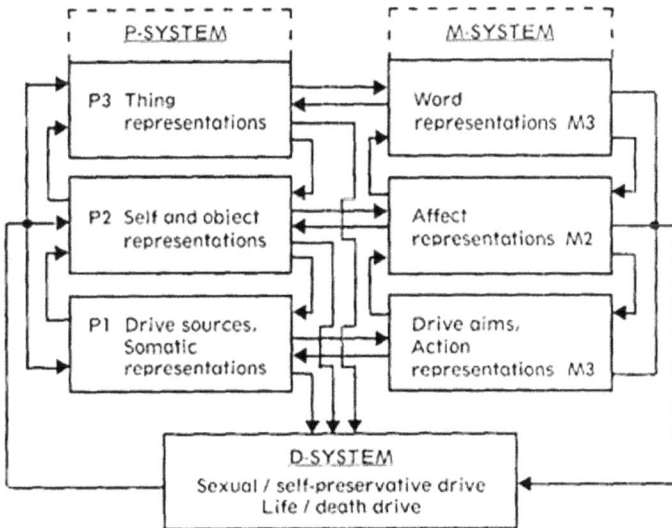

The darts also indicate the conception of drive circuits between two or more boxes, representing the microprocesses we imagine when a conflict is negotiated or a dream is elaborated.[8]

Viewed as a hierarchical order, this diagram depicts psychic progression via developmentally achieved steps, and conversely, regression and the various forms it may take. For instance, in the psychic apparatus of a newborn infant, a stimulus from D, the self-preservative drive (e.g., hunger) might arise, activating P1, a biogenic zone (e.g., the stomach), and seeking discharge/expression with M1 motor actions (e.g., screaming, wriggling)—thus completing a full DPM circuit. Later in the infant's development, the same stimulus, D, affects not only the biogenic zones (P1), but also P2, the associated object representation (e.g., the mother), and instead of or concomitant with its motor actions (M1), an associated affect (M2) is triggered—which might result in the infant's desire, despite hunger, to be fed only by the affectively meaningful object (P2-M2, the beloved mother).

Here the circuit involves the DPM system in a more complex way, indicating that the P2-M2 association affords an increase in regulating measures, which allows for a temporal delay of drive satisfaction.[9] Still later, there will be many more strategies—including those of P3 and M3—for picturing, thinking about, and discussing the very same drive stimulus of hunger, thus permitting the possibility of delaying satisfaction for even a very long time, if necessary. The developmental progression briefly outlined here simultaneously portrays a scheme of the major steps of regression—that is, from talking about an affect (M3), to acting upon it (M2), to acting anything in order to avoid the affect (M1).

---

[8] Schore (1997) emphasized the value of the two concepts of drive and representation: "Recent psychobiological and neurobiological studies thus strongly indicate that the concept of drive, devalued over the last twenty years, must be reintroduced as a central construct of psychoanalytic theory" (p.827, italics in original). Schore also found the psychoanalytic concept of mental representation to function as a "biological regulator" (p. 828), and he again acknowledged the fields of psychology and neurobiology as having provided the basis for this conclusion.

[9] Kernberg (1980) described "units of self and object representations (and the affect dispositions linking them) [as] the building blocks on which further developments of internalized object and self representations, and later on, the overall tripartite structure (ego, superego, and id), rest" (p. 17).

I have noted above that each psychic unit involves an interaction between drives and structures. To elaborate, each complete psychic unit can be conceptualized as a DPM unit, involving drive activity and at least one of the tiers of the P and M parts of this system. For instance, the simple schema of a wish ("I want strawberries"/"I love O") can be understood as an association of memory traces or structures, which is activated by a drive stimulus, D, and includes the cathexis of an object representation, P, and an action or affect representation, M. Psychic representations of objects are not perceived as mere copies of their perceptual realities, but as subjectively tinged by the individual's needs, desires, or fears. This applies to virtually all representations, including those that incorporate memories (complex representations), all of which contain subjective elements of fantasy and thought processes.

This diagram also clearly depicts the various ways in which a drive stimulus can activate, connect, displace, bypass, exchange, or reverse any of these different representations—thus manifesting forms of drive vicissitudes or defense mechanisms—both within the boxes of the diagram and between them, in infinite variations. Freud described these processes many times, e.g., when elaborating on the mechanism of paranoia (1911, p. 63ff). In this passage, Freud noted that an originally homosexual proposition, "I [a man] love him," had been turned into one of the following conscious perceptions: "I do not love him—I hate him, because he persecutes me," or "I do not love him—I love her, because she loves me," or "It is not I who loves the man—she loves him," or "I do not love at all—I do not love anyone." In viewing these shifts according to the diagram, we see that the homosexual conflict has led at the level of P2 to a displacement or exchange from the self-representation of "I" (love him), to an object representation of "she" (loves him), and from the original object representation of "him," to "her" and/or to the complete denial of "not anyone." Concurrently, on the level of M2, the original affect representation, "love," is turned into "hate," followed by regression to an action representation on M1—"he persecutes me," or to denial—"I do not love at all." These relatively simple examples of drive vicissitudes at the level of self and object representations (P2) and of affect (M2) are representative of a full range of defense mechanisms, which might be different on all tiers of the P-M systems.[10] Freud (1915a) described these processes according to his metapsychological plan:

> Clinical observation ... shows us that besides the idea, some other element representing the drive ... undergoes vicissitudes of repression which may be quite different from those undergone by the idea.... This other element of the psychical representative ... finds expression ... in processes which are sensed as affects. [p. 152, italics added]

The DPM system, which I introduced to complement Freud's model of the mind, thus provides a framework for detailed reflection on the basic elements of all sorts of psychic activity. Its different components on the three tiers of the P and M systems (including self and object representations) can be seen as the molecules or constituents of more complex or global units, called "the self" or "the object." These latter configurations are highly sophisticated; according to particular, actual circumstances, they are specifically selected pattern formations that integrate or combine a whole variety of processes within the DPM system onto a higher level within the hierarchy. For those more integrated units, the self and the object, I have outlined a different framework, called the subject-object track (Schmidt-Hellerau 2001).

The subject-object track organizes self configurations on different levels, starting with the very first and primitive ones at the bottom (e.g., the helpless, infantile self), and reaching up to mature, more developed ones at the top (e.g., the self as spouse, as parent, the professional self, the political self). The same applies to object configurations. While each momentary combination of a self or an object configuration derives all its constituents from the DPM system, the units of self and object can interact or relate on different levels of the maturity scale. (For example, in the transference, an infantile self may relate to an adult/parental object, or vice versa.) The possibility of fluid shifts on the maturity scales of the subject-object track allows for an infinite number of specific combinations within self-object relationships. Although

---

[10] For examples of exchange, displacement, reversal, and so forth on the level of word and thing representations (M3-P3), see Freud (1901).

clinical psychoanalysis usually deals primarily with these global and complex units of self and object, periods of detailed analysis may focus on the generation of a specific affect (M2) or a specific wording (M3), or the roles and handling of certain thing representations (P3).

Both the DPM system and the subject-object track can be introduced into Freud's scheme of the psychic apparatus, thus providing two supplemental frameworks to facilitate more precise reflection about how the mind works, as illustrated in Diagram 4.

DIAGRAM 4

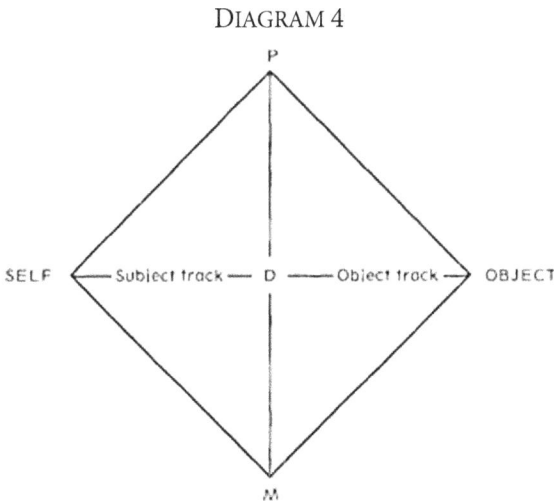

Diagram 4 shows the two frameworks arranged crosswise from above. The subject-object track reaches down to the D system, interacting with all the elements constituting the self and object configurations (from the most primitive to the most mature) from the three tiers of the P and M systems (see also the complete view of the model from the outside, depicted in Diagram 5).

The Macro Level of Organization

Starting with his sketch in the seventh chapter of The Interpretation of Dreams, Freud (1900) focused on the states of psychic processes, rather than on their different elements, dividing them according to their designation as conscious, preconscious, or unconscious. Thus, he developed his first model of the mind, the topographic theory, with its three macrostructural units: the systems Ucs., Pcs., and Cs. If we envision this framework as horizontally organized, we picture each of its systems stretched out in the sense of a layer: a huge unconscious stratum at the bottom, a thin conscious one on top, and the preconscious one lying somewhere in between.

Freud's (1923) second model of the psychic apparatus divided the mind differently, but partially overlapped with his earlier topographic model. He now differentiated three structural units—the id, superego, and ego—and focused more on the functions and contributions of each to the working of the model as a whole. This second theory might be envisioned as a vertical framework, since all three macrostructures cut through the three layers of the topographical model. That is to say, the ego, the superego, and the id all participate in, have access to, and display features of the Ucs., Pcs., and Cs. (However, the id's access to consciousness is rather limited—to situations such as psychotic states, for example [Freud 1915b, p. 197].) Although most analysts are more comfortable using Freud's second, more elaborated structural theory, the topographic model has never been abandoned, and some even prefer it to the former. Since the two models focus on different aspects of the mind's functioning, we can keep and use both as complementary organizational frameworks for our thinking about psychic processes.

In focusing on the second structural theory, it becomes clear that the newly created structures of 1923, the id, superego, and ego, not only overlap with parts of the systems Ucs., Pcs., and Cs., but also with each other; thus, they are outlined with rather fluid perimeters. Freud (1933) noted that "the ego is after all only a portion of the id" (p. 76); he also assumed "the existence of a grade in the ego, which may be called the 'ego ideal' or 'super-ego'" (1923b, p.28). He further stated that: "the ego forms its super-ego out of the id" (1923, p. 38), and pointed out that "the super-ego merges into the id" (1933, p. 79). Given his conceptualization of the ego as part of the id, and the superego as a part of the ego that merges into the id, Freud viewed the whole psychic apparatus as developing out of the id as its center. This deep entanglement of the structural units, their reaching out into each other's domains, is a major component of Freud's (1933) conception of how the mind works:

> We cannot do justice to the characteristics of the mind by linear outlines like those in a drawing or in primitive painting, but rather by areas of color melting into one another as they are presented by modern artists. After making the separation, we must allow what we have separated to merge together once more. [p. 79]

In this poetic formulation, Freud revealed his keen grasp of the functioning of the complex systems of mind and brain—which fits amazingly well with contemporary paradigms in neuroscience.

It is interesting to note that the areas of overlap of the three component psychic structures occur as a consequence of the interwoven processes of (primary and secondary) identifications and object cathexes (especially during the developmental time of the oedipal complex), which have a major impact on the formation of all three macrostructures. As we are aware, identification is a "process whereby the subject assimilates an aspect, property, or attribute of the other and is transformed, wholly or partially, after the model the other provides" (Laplanche and Pontalis 1967, p. 205). This general definition is compatible with the process of structure formation, and the generation of a new or the modification of an already established self or object representation, containing or carrying out the regulating measure of that very object (see Schmidt-Hellerau 2001). That is to say, any object cathexis and identification has an immediate and often lasting effect, stored in the structure of a self or object representation (P2). According to Freud 1923, 1933), all three macrostructures are informed by these processes, because the self and object representations that have been built up via object cathexes and/or modified by identifications—presumably with associated affects—become crucial elements of the id, superego, and ego. Thus, the P2-M2 tiers of the DPM system are the primary realm of overlap, where the three structures "merge together"—where the colors of an individual's mind melt and blend in a particular way to create the many unique pictures our patients present to us. Diagram 5 depicts a complete, three-dimensional view of the psychoanalytic model of the mind.

DIAGRAM 5

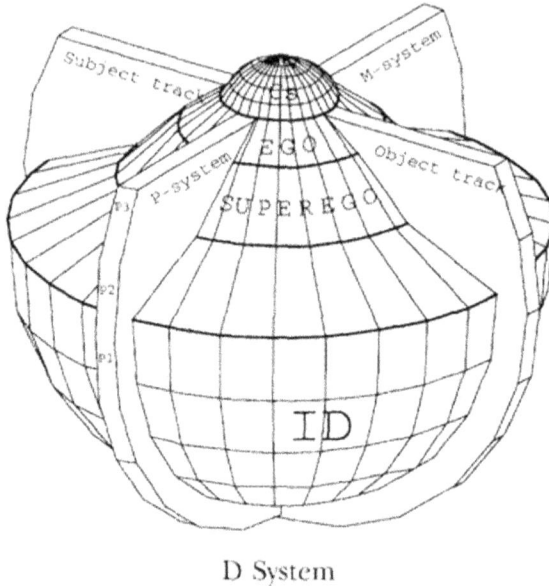

D System

Now we have four different frameworks within the model of the mind, two concerning the macro level and two the micro level of psychic organization: (1) the topographical (dealing with the different states of the Ucs., Pcs., and Cs.—to be added to the inside of the diagram as these layers described above); (2) the structural (dealing with the different functions of the id, super-ego, and ego); (3) the subject-object track (dealing with the distinct developmentally organized units of self and object); and (4) the DPM system (dealing with the drive representations).

An important point here is that each framework displays just one specific, and thus limited, perspective of any psychic process.

With any psychic phenomenon, event, or activity we can: (1) wonder about its state of consciousness; (2) describe it as controlled by or under the guiding functional principle of one of the three structures of id, superego, or ego; (3) focus on it as part of or linked to the unit of self or object; and/or (4) become interested in the specific involvement of its different elements, the drive representations. Thus, if we choose to conduct research on, for example, affect, perception, memory, dreams, or any other aspect of mental life, it may be advantageous for us to be clear about the specific framework on which we are primarily focusing. According to a psychoanalytic perspective, all those aspects of mental life (affect, perception, memory, and dreams) can be understood within all these frameworks, wherein each is viewed according to a different perspective.

To elaborate with an example, the fact that an affect or a specific perception can be conscious as well as unconscious (in a dynamic or descriptive way) does not tell us anything about the processes that generate affects or are involved in perception. In my view, these latter processes must be explored separately from those that are responsible for consciousness and unconsciousness (especially in the dynamic sense of these terms). It seems to me that the DPM system is an especially suitable framework for comparison of psychoanalytic concepts with the workings of the brain, because it differentiates psychic phenomena on a micro level according to those functions (perception of different sensory inputs, motor programs, affects, speech, and so on), which are already well explored in neuroscience.

Mind and Brain: Two Models Compared

An argument against the old metapsychological model of the mind that has been made repeatedly is the assumption that Freud's ideas were deeply influenced by the neuroscientific knowledge available at the end of the nineteenth century, which now, more than hundred years later, is regarded as widely outdated. One way of trying to escape this criticism has been to deny the importance to psychoanalysis of neurobiology and neuroscience, and instead to emphasize its autonomous position as a science or discipline of its own. However, as Kandel (1999) stated, exactly this reservation about (neuro)science has led to a decline in the scientific development of psycho-analysis, and in its influence on neighbor disciplines—most of all, psychiatry. "This decline is regrettable, since psychoanalysis still represents the most coherent and intellectually satisfying view of the mind" (p. 505).

While I completely agree with this point of view, an interesting aspect of this statement in the present context is the acknowledgment that "the most coherent and intellectually satisfying view of the mind" was formulated before and without the richer knowledge of neuroscience that is available to us at the beginning of the twenty-first century. This confirms what I emphasized earlier: that (neuroscientific) facts do not make the (metapsychological) theory. I agree with Kandel that it is important for psychoanalysis to enter into a genuine dialogue with neuroscience—and vice versa—but as individuals, we might decide to try different ways of doing so, and ultimately select different courses of action. One way is to hold on to Freud's basic theoretical assumptions—to reexamine and possibly modify them, and in so doing, to seek a monistic answer to the question of how mind and brain are related (Kandel 1998; Opatow 1999; Rubinstein 1965). If we choose this approach, then we might be asked to show, on a theoretical plan, how the psychoanalytic model of the mind's functioning could correspond to any model of the brain's functioning.

The work of Alexander Luria (who lived from 1902 to 1977) provides us with an opportunity for such a comparative investigation. Luria studied the social sciences, psychology, and later medicine, and was in his youth very interested in psychoanalysis. He wrote papers based on psychoanalytic ideas, planned to work on an objective approach to psychoanalysis, and even founded a small psychoanalytic association (which was greatly welcomed by Freud, according to a letter he wrote to Luria in 1922). As a medical officer during the war, Luria started to specialize in the diagnosis and treatment of brain lesions, which eventually led him to establish the new science of neuropsychology. His work in this regard is still highly appreciated today. I will focus here on his book entitled The Working Brain: An Introduction to Neuropsychology (1973), which represents an extraordinarily comprehensive attempt to conceptualize the brain as a functional whole.

In Luria's general understanding of the brain's functioning, as well as in the specifics of his model, we can identify an amazing number of parallels to a metapsychological model—out of which I will highlight only a few, comparing them with aspects of the DPM system, and also briefly pointing out some connections to Freud's structural model.[11]

As an initial general paradigm, Luria conceptualized all forms of psychic activity as "complex functional systems." Psychic activity cannot be localized in specific areas of the brain, "but must be organized in systems of concertedly working zones, each of which performs its role in complex functional systems, and which may be located in completely different and often far distant areas of the brain" (1973, p. 31, italics in original). This general statement corresponds to my proposition that each psychic unit is conceptualized as a DPM unit—that is, a process involving a full circuit through the drive system, the perceptual system, and the motor system, including the respective representations of these systems on the three related tiers. Each system performs its specific role, providing a necessary contribution to the dynamic complexity it describes.

As a second, more specific paradigm, Luria (1973) then postulated that there are:

> … three principal functional units of the brain whose participation is necessary for any type of mental activity …. [These are] a unit for regulating tone or waking, a unit for obtaining, processing, and storing information arriving from the outside world, and a unit for programming, regulating and verifying mental activity." [p. 43, italics in original]

Essential to these units is their arrangement in a hierarchical order, as well as the fact that they are subdivided into three layers or cortical zones. As we will see below, this statement accords with my conception of the DPM system.

---

[11] I first published this comparison in Schmidt-Hellerau 1995a. Kaplan-Solms and Solms (2000) later undertook a similar comparison and arrived in part at the same conclusions I had suggested; however, they focused more on a correlation between "the psychic sequence of conscious and unconscious mental events on the one hand, and the material sequence of physical brain events on the other" (p. 251).

The Unit for Regulating Tone or Waking, in Comparison with the D System

The performance of any psychic process is basically dependent on an optimal cortical tone in which excitation and inhibition are more or less balanced. This basic regulation of the cortical tone is organized in the subcortical and brain stem areas, especially by the reticular formation. The reticular formation, which has an ascending and a descending part, links the brain stem, hypothalamus, the lower structures of the mesencephalon, thalamic nuclei, the caudate body, and the higher nervous structures of the neocortex and archicortex. Via the ascendant track, the lower subcortex and brain stem structures of the reticular formation are able to influence, maintain, and regulate the tone of higher cortical structures, and conversely, via the descendant track, these higher cortical structures exert a regulating influence on the lower subcortex and brain stem structures of the reticular formation.

> With the discovery of the reticular formation, a new principle was thus introduced: the vertical organization of all structures of the brain. This put an end to that long period during which the attention of scientists attempting to discover the nervous mechanisms of mental processes was concentrated entirely on the cortex, the work of whose systems was deemed to be independent of the lower or deeper structures. With the description of the reticular formation, the first functional unit of the brain was discovered—an apparatus maintaining cortical tone and the waking state, and regulating these states in accordance with the actual demands confronting the organism. [Luria 1973, p. 46, italics in original]

Stimulation of the reticular formation affects the perceptual and motor systems, as well as the general cortical processes. Its nonspecific background effects concern the regulation of sleep and waking. However, the reticular formation also stimulates specific effects arising from three sources. The first source is made up of the basic processes responsible for the organism's homeostasis—respiratory and digestive processes, sugar and protein metabolism, internal secretion, and so on. In Luria's (1973) words:

More complex forms of this type of activation are connected with ...
behavioral systems ... known as systems of instinctive... food-getting
and sexual behaviour.... Naturally, in order to evoke these complex,
instinctive forms of behaviour, a highly selective, specific activation is
necessary, and the biologically specific forms of this food-getting or
sexual activation are the responsibility of the higher nuclei of the
mesencephalic, diencephalic, and limbic reticular formation. Many recent experiments.... show conclusively that highly specific nuclei of the
reticular formation, stimulation of which can lead either to activation
or to blocking of various complex forms of instinctive behaviour, are
located in these structures of the brain stem and archicortex. [p. 53,
italics added]

Within this description of the reticular formation as the vertical organizer of the activities of all structures of the brain, we can clearly
recognize the features of the D system. Within the psychoanalytic model
of the mind, in addition to the concept of structure, it is important to
realize that the concept of the drives is axiomatic; the drives are defined
as the activating force of any psychic activity. The whole psychic apparatus is constructed according to this basic assumption, that nothing
works without its being stimulated and infused by the drives. It is interesting to note that Luria's explanation of the working of the reticular
formation fits well with this general notion of the drive system as composed of two antagonistic drives.[12] In its basic nonspecific effects, Luria's
paradigm confirms the notion of the primal drives, namely, the life drive
(waking) and the death drive (sleeping), whereas the first source of the
specific effects concerns the sexual and the self-preservative drives. Also,
Luria's statement that stimulation of the reticular formation (D) has an
activating effect on the perceptual system (P), on the motor system (M),

---

[12] Freud (1950) had tentatively suggested that the primary brain fits pretty well with our
characterization of the system ψ .... Now the derivation and original biological significance of the primary brain are not known to anatomists; according to our theory, it
would, to put it plainly, be a *sympathetic ganglion*. Here is a first possibility of testing
our theory upon factual material. [p. 303, italics in original]

and in general on the cortical processes, is in perfect accordance with my proposition that every psychic unit involves all three parts of the DPM system.

The second source of the reticular formation's activation are the processes of stimuli coming from the outside world—that is, the "inflow of excitation from the sense organs" (Luria 1973, p. 55)—corresponding in my model to the small control loop of the D-P1 connection, within which the drives (D) stimulate the somatic representations (P 1) and vice versa.

The third source of activation of the reticular formation (and according to Luria, the most interesting one) concerns higher mental functions, such as intentions, plans, and programs that require language or internal speech. In Luria's words, "the fulfillment of a plan or the achievement of a goal requires a certain amount of energy, and they are possible only if a certain level of activity can be maintained" (p. 57). Here the descending track of the reticular formation plays a crucial role:

> These descending fibres, running from the prefrontal (orbital and medial frontal) cortex to nuclei of the thalamus and brain stems form a system by means of which the higher levels of the cortex, participating directly in the formation of intentions and plans, recruit the lower systems of the reticular formation of the thalamus and brain stem, thereby modulating their work and making possible the most complex forms of conscious activity. [pp. 58-60, italics in original]

Here once more, we see how higher mental functions that are psychoanalytically ascribed to the ego require basic drive energy, and how a constant exchange of information and mutual adjustment takes place between the lower and higher structures of the brain, comparable to that between the id and the ego (see Schmidt-Hellerau 2001). Thus, Luria's first unit of the brain fits well with the metapsychological concept of a drive system (D)—which is, as is well known, thought to be rooted in and to form a major part of the Ucs. or the id, and which plays an essential role in all psychic activity. I do not mean to limit the drive system to the reticular formation (other factors, such as hormonal influences, might play important roles); however, within the model outlined by Luria, the first unit of the brain functions in a way that correlates to what I ascribe to the D system.

The Unit for Obtaining, Processing, and Storing Information, in Comparison with the P System

The second functional unit of the brain works with the "lateral regions of the neocortex … including the visual (occipital), auditory (temporal), and general sensory (parietal) regions" (Luria 1973, p. 67, italics in original). This unit is responsible for the reception, analysis, synthesis (associative recombination), and storage of all kinds of information from the outside world. As Luria noted:

> Human gnostic activity never takes place with respect to one single iso-lated modality (vision, hearing, touch); the perception—and still more, the representation—of any object is a complex procedure, the result of polymodal activity, originally expanded in character, later concentrated and condensed. Naturally, therefore, it must rely on the combined working of a complete system of cortical zones. [p. 72]

In terms of the DPM system, this represents a clear focus on the percep-tual side (P1, P2, and P3).

The first and most basic zones of this unit, represented in the DPM sys-tem as P1, comprise "the primary or projection areas of the cortex" (p. 68). Here all incoming sensory information is analyzed according to its very specific properties—thus allowing a precise distinction to be drawn be-tween the different drive sources, as they would be called by psychoanalysts (i.e., zones), and the specifics of their sensoric stimulation.

The secondary (or gnostic) cortical zones, which are superimposed over the first, basic zones, work with "cells, whose degree of modal specificity is much lower, and whose composition includes many more associative neurons with short axons, enabling incoming excitation to be combined into the necessary functional patterns, and they thus subserve a synthetic function" (p. 68). In relating these secondary or gnostic cortical zones to what we have described as the specifics of P2, the self and object representations, it is fascinating to find that the experimental stimulation of these secondary zones leads to

> … recognizable visual hallucinations (images of flowers, animals, familiar persons and so on). Sometimes such stimulation caused the appearance of a complex sequence: the patient saw his friend approaching and beckoning him with his hand and so on. These hallucinations, it must be noted, were not restricted to a certain part of the visual field, and they were meaningful rather than topical in character. These hallucinations naturally reflected the subject's previous visual experience, and consequently, stimulation of the secondary visual cortical zones activated traces of those integral visual images which were stored in this part of the human cortex. [Luria 1973, p. 115, italics added]

The tertiary zones of Luria's second functional unit reveal an overlap of "the cortical ends of the various analysers" (p. 73), and comprise a big area between the occipital, temporal, and postcentral cortex, including the inferior parietal region. As Luria elaborated:

> This work of the tertiary zones of the posterior cortical regions is thus essential, not only for the successful integration of information reaching man through his visual system, but also for the transition from direct, visually represented syntheses to the level of symbolic processes—or operations with word meanings, with complex grammatical and logical structures, with systems of numbers and abstract relationships. It is because of this that the tertiary zones of the posterior cortical region play an essential role in the conversion of concrete perception into abstract thinking, which always proceeds in the form of internal schemes, and for the memorizing of organized experience or, in other words, not only for the reception and coding of information, but also for its storage. [p. 74, italics in original]

Obviously, these tertiary zones provide human beings with the capacity for logic, abstraction, and generalized thinking—a very sophisticated capacity, and one that I assigned to the P3 tier (or more inclusively, to the P3-M3 tier) of the D-P-M system, operating on the level of thing representations and word representations.

The Unit for Programming, Regulating, and Verifying Mental Activity, in Comparison with the M System

In describing the third functional unit of the brain, Luria (1973) ultimately approached the "organization of conscious activity" (p. 79). The first major group of this unit is the motor system, placed in the anterior regions of the hemispheres, including the primary (projection) motor cortex, the great pyramidal tract, and the extrapyramidal system. This unit corresponds to M1, where I have placed the action representations. Here Luria emphasizes an interesting organizational principle:

> The main difference now is that, whereas in the second, afferent system of the brain, the processes go from the primary to the secondary and tertiary zones, in the third, efferent system, the processes run in a descending direction, starting at the highest levels of the tertiary and secondary zones, where the motor plans and programmes are formed, and then passing through the structures of the primary motor area, which sends the prepared motor impulses to the periphery. [p. 82]

This characterization of the second unit as an afferent system and the third as an efferent one is in accordance with my characterization of the P system as a receptor system and the M system as an effector one. The opposite directionality of its neural processes—upward in the afferent system, downward in the efferent—corresponds to the metapsychological concept of psychic processes as forming complete DPM circuits (at the micro level), or to the ego and the id's having mutual influence on each other (macro level).[13] While Luria's first

---

[13] Freud's (1900) idea of the motor system as effecting "discharge" of drive energy (an "outward" direction) obscured his conception of psychic processes as circuits, although these were indicated in his diagram (p. 541). Here he described a multitude of processes, such as, for example, an energetic back-and-forth movement of cathexis between the

level of the third unit of the brain corresponds to the first tier of the M system, the next level (M2), where I placed the affect representations, is without parallel in Luria's model. Unfortunately, Luria died before he could put into action his plan to research brain systems that generate affect.[14] As this essential piece is missing in his model, I will draw on information from other sources.

Turning first to Iversen, Kupfermann, and Kandel (2000), We find a three-part model describing the neuronal organization of affect, involving lower, medial, and higher structures—each with reciprocal influences on the others, and with the amygdala occupying a central position[15]:

> The amygdala appears to be involved in mediating both the unconscious emotional state and conscious feeling. Consistent with this dual function of emotion, the amygdala has two projections. Many of the autonomic expressions of emotional states are mediated by the amygdala through its connections to the hypothalamus and the autonomic nervous system. The influence of the amygdala on conscious feeling is

---

Ucs. and Pcs.—a process that may ultimately lead to the weaving of a fantasy, a dream, or any other chain of thought.

[14] Affect is here used as a general term, embracing an emotional state (which may include physical sensations), as well as a feeling state (mental sensations). Many studies distinguish between the unconscious part of an affect, an emotion, ascribed to subcortical structures like the brain stem, the hypothalamus, and the amygdala, and the conscious perception of a feeling, involving higher cortical structures, the cingulate cortex, and the frontal lobes (Iversen, Kupfermann, and Kandel 2000, p. 982). Since I am not specifically concerned here with the distinction between unconscious and conscious psychic events, or with the bodily as opposed to the mental expression of affects (because every representation within the PM system is conceptualized as subject to unconscious as well as conscious experience, and to being expressed physically as well as psychically), I will here neglect this dimension of the research and treat affects as a whole, coherent entity. But we must keep in mind that the lower brain structures and their interactions with higher ones are crucial in determining the specific shape of a variety of affects and their state of consciousness. In this regard, see especially the rich work of Panksepp (1998, 1999).

[15] Damasio (1999b) distinguished: … three stages of processing along a continuum: a state of emotion, which can be triggered and executed nonconsciously; a state of feeling, which can be represented nonconsciously; and a state of feeling made conscious, i.e., known to the organism having both emotion and feeling. [p. 37, italics in original]

mediated by its projections to the cingulate gyrus and prefrontal cortex
…. As one might expect from its dual role, the output of the amygdala
influences both the autonomic and cognitive components of emotion.
[p. 992]

The central position of the amygdala, with its connections to lower and
higher brain structures, has its counterpart in my model in the position
of affect representations, on the middle tier (M2) of the effector side of
the DPM system. Damasio (1999b), LeDoux (1996), and Schacter (1996)
agree that the amygdala has been "found to play an important role in
emotional memory" (Schacter 1996, p. 214, italics added), which corresponds to the metapsychological concept of affect representations in
M2, insofar as something that is represented is stored in the form of a
memory trace. Damasio (1999b) elaborated on this notion of representation of affect, stating that different emotions display different patterns:

> The substrate for the representation of emotions is a collection of neu-
> ral dispositions in a number of brain regions, located largely in
> subcortical nuclei of the brain stem, hypothalamus, basal forebrain, and
> amygdala. In keeping with their dispositional status, these representa-
> tions are implicit, dormant, and not available to consciousness. They
> exist, rather, as potential patterns of activity arising within neuron en-
> sembles. Once these dispositions are activated, a number of
> consequences ensue. On the one hand, the pattern of activation repre
> sents, within the brain, a particular emotion as neural "object". On the
> other, the pattern of activation generates explicit responses that modify
> both the state of the body proper and the state of other brain regions.
> By so doing, the responses create an emotional state. [p. 79]

This concept of representation of emotions, which are at times dormant
and need to be activated in order to elicit an emotional state available to
consciousness, fits with Freud's general statements about repression of
affect.[16] It also matches the concept of different forms of defense operations,

---

[16] The old discussion about whether, according to Freud, an affect is always conscious,

such as the displacing, bypassing, reversing, or exchanging of such patterns or affect representations (assuming the structurally established existence of such patterns as a precondition). Applying my model, this process may occur on each tier of the PM systems, as well as on M2.

While the interaction of the amygdala with lower brain structures, especially the brain stem, corresponds to my view of a general influence of the D system on all processes within the P-M systems, the amygdala's links to the neocortex, especially the frontal lobes, corresponds to the connections between M2 and the position of word representations in M3. It is by means of these connections to the neocortex (that is, the temporal, frontal, and association cortices) that emotional learning and the cognitive interpretation of emotional states take place (Iversen, Kupfermann, and Kandel 2000). Damasio highlighted this most sophisticated level of affect by arguing that "the feeling state, the experience of emotion, is essentially a story that the brain constructs to explain bodily reactions" (Iversen, Kupfermann, and Kandel 2000, p. 985, italics added). To tell a story means to proceed to the position of word representation—that is, to connect M2 with M3.[17]

The omission of the designated position of affect in Luria's model might have resulted in his dividing this third unit of the brain into only two, rather than three, major groups (in his second unit of the brain, he identified three layers). This second major group, now roughly corresponding to my third tier of the M system, concerns the frontal lobes or prefrontal divisions of the brain:

---

or whether it makes sense to talk of unconscious affects, could be linked to the differentiation between the contribution of lower and higher brain structures to (unconscious) emotional and (conscious) feeling states. Freud (1915b) suggested that:

Strictly speaking ... there are no unconscious affects as there are unconscious ideas. But there may very well be in the system Ucs. affective structures which, like others, become conscious. The whole difference arises from the fact that ideas are cathexes—basically of memory-traces—whilst affects and emotions correspond to processes of discharge, the final manifestations of which are perceived as feelings. [p. 178, italics added]

[17] As LeDoux (1996) showed, this higher level of affect elaboration can be (momentarily) excluded—e.g., in a fear reaction requiring quick action—via bypassing the "high road" of the (sensory) cortex and activating the direct subcortical pathway between the sensory thalamus and the amygdala. The advantage of the short road is speed, while its disadvantage is a lack of cognitive precision regarding the stimulus.

It is these portions of the brain, belonging to the tertiary zones of the cortex, which play a decisive role in the formation of intentions and programmes, and in the regulation and verification of the most complex forms of human behaviour. [Luria 1973, p. 84]

To perform these complicated functions, the frontal and prefrontal regions of the brain, which have a reciprocal connection with the reticular formation that guarantees mutual adjustment to the required energy levels, must receive, synthesize, and organize complex afferent impulses from all parts of the brain. These regions are essential for the accomplishment of most higher mental processes—e.g., all activities relating to speech—and in this regard correspond to the position of word representations on M3 in my model. This part of the brain also controls purposeful behavior and movements, represses reactions to irrelevant stimuli, orients with respect to present and future, and is involved in all complex intellectual operations and the "state of increased activation which accompanies all forms of conscious activity" (Luria 1973, p. 95).

This description parallels what Freud (1923) attributed to the macro-structure ego:

We have formed the idea that in each individual, there is a coherent organization of mental processes; and we call this his ego. It is to this ego that consciousness is attached; the ego controls the approaches to motility that is, to the discharge of excitations into the external world; it is the mental agency which supervises all its own constituent processes, and which goes to sleep at night, though even then it exercises the censorship on dreams. From this ego proceed the repressions, too, by means of which it is sought to exclude certain trends in the mind not merely from consciousness but also from other forms of effectiveness and activity. [p. 17, italics in original][18]

---

[18] The fact that the prefrontal regions of the cortex do not mature before the age of four to seven years fits with the psychoanalytic view of a relatively late ego maturation at about the same time.

In comparing Luria's description of the functioning of the prefrontal and frontal lobes with Freud's description of the ego's functions, we should keep in mind that neither the ego nor the frontal lobes, nor any other unit of the mind or brain, can work on its own. I have conceptualized each psychic unit as a process involving all three parts of the DPM systems, with various complex processes occurring on each tier of each of its parts—not only on a micro level, but also on a macro level of psychic organization. Even if we focus on just one structure—e.g., the ego—it makes sense to think of the work of this one macrostructure in terms of its interaction with and inter-dependence on the two other structures. And in regard to the brain's functioning, Luria emphasized exactly this:

> It would be a mistake to imagine that each of these units can carry out a certain form of activity completely independently …. It will be clear from what has been said already regarding the systemic structure of complex psychological processes that this is not so. Each form of conscious activity is always a complex functional system and takes place through the com-bined working of all three brain units, each of which makes its own contribution. The well-established facts of modern psychology provide a solid basis for this view. [1973, p. 99, italics in original]

To summarize and briefly review this comparison of the metapsychological model of the mind with Luria's neuropsychological model of the brain on a visual plan, I have integrated the different positions (now without specifications) into Diagram 6 below.

DIAGRAM 6

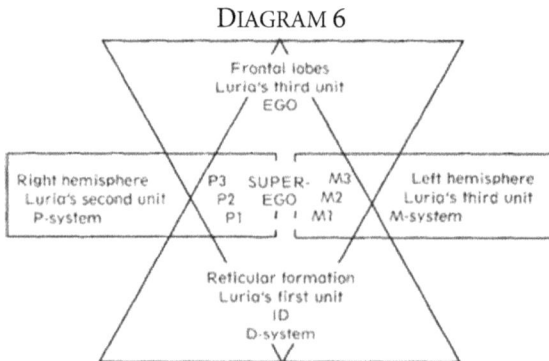

The first line in each section of this diagram specifies the part of the brain most involved in a specific function; the second line accounts for Luria's units of the brain; and the third line applies to the metapsychological units on a macro or micro level of mental organization. Although I have not touched on the superego in my discussion of Luria's model, it seems appropriate to include it here in the area of overlap of the P2-M2 representations. The two superimposed triangles, oriented in opposite directions, indicate the mutual influence of id and ego, with different proportions on each side—both influencing and being influenced by the superego or the shared tiers of the P-M systems respectively.

The Somatic and the Psychic Representations

The comparison of parts of my model of the mind—in particular, the D-P-M system—with Luria's model of the working brain suggests a concrete bridge from the mental to the physical and vice versa. However, we should remember that, although Luria discussed real brain structures—similar to the way in which we are discussing real psychic elements (affect, object and action representations, and so forth)—his model was as abstract as mine is. His outline focused on the interaction of major brain structures, leaving out hormonal, immunologic, and other systemic influences on the brain's functions (which most likely also impact psychic processes in terms of what I conceptualize as the DPM system). It is only by means of the collaboration of all these well-orchestrated systems that the working brain can be comprehensively described. Similarly, the DPM system alone provides only one framework, the micro level of psychic units. These latter are conceptualized as the building blocks, in various combinations, of the more complex configurations of the self and object, and the relations between them, as organized on the subject-object track. Furthermore, self and object are drawn into the primary or secondary process modes of the systems Ucs. or Pcs./Cs., and they are organized by or contribute to the specific functions of the macrostructures of the ego, superego, and id. That is to say, on the one hand, the connection between the two models can be taken quite concretely; on the other hand, we need to keep in mind that the models capture only part of the total picture.

In order to focus in greater depth on the differences and relationships between the mental and the physical, I will reach back more than hundred years to a brief essay by Freud entitled "Some Points for a Comparative Study of Organic and Hysterical Motor Paralyses" (1893). I find this essay fascinating because it allows us to follow the evolution of a new way of thinking, for which Freud, only three years later, created the notion of metapsychology (see also Schmidt-Hellerau, 1995b). Here we meet Freud as a competent neuroanatomist, a keen observer of psychic phenomena, and a clear thinker and theoretician, presenting a "line of thought that might lead to a conception" (p. 169, italics added) of psychic organization, as differentiated from a somatic organization.

Freud begins this essay by describing "two kinds of motor paralysis—periphero-spinal (or bulbar) paralysis and cerebral paralysis" (p. 160, italics in original). In the former, "the periphery is, so to say, projected upon the grey matter of the cord, point by point" (p. 161), which leads Freud to propose the term "projection paralysis" to describe it. Cerebral paralysis is seen to arise from lesions in higher parts of the cortex, with the periphery represented by groups of lesions; this is why Freud suggests calling it "representation paralysis." Because of this complex representation of the periphery, cerebral paralysis affects larger portions of the body (paralysis en masse), often in specific combinations of various body parts—e.g., an arm together with parts of the face and a leg. Furthermore, there is a specific order observable in such cases, namely, that "the distal segments always suffer more than the proximal ones; for instance, the hand is more paralysed than the shoulder" (Freud 1893, p. 161)—never the other way round.

Acknowledging the capacity of hysteria to simulate a whole variety of nervous disorders, Freud at first states that hysterical paralysis always simulates representation paralysis, never projection paralysis.[19] Closer examination reveals that hysterical paralysis:

---

[19] Freud (1893) limited his discussion of hysterical paralysis in this essay to flaccid hysterical paralyses (p. 162).

… is not bound by the rule, which applies regularly to the organic cerebral paralyses, that the distal segment is always more affected than the proximal one. In hysteria, the shoulder or the thigh may be more paralyzed than the hand or the foot. Movements may appear in the fingers while the proximal segment is still absolutely inert. [p. 162]

Taking into account observations that clearly differentiate organic from hysterical paralyses, Freud (1893) points out that hysterical paralysis "behaves as though anatomy did not exist or as though it had no knowledge of it" (p. 169, italics added).

Hysteria is ignorant of the distribution of the nerves, and that is why it does not simulate periphero-spinal or projection paralyses. It has no knowledge of the optic chiasma, and consequently it does not produce hemianopsia. It takes the organs in the ordinary, popular sense of the names they bear: the leg is the leg as far up as its insertion into the hip, the arm is the upper limb as it is visible under the clothing. There is no reason for adding paralysis of the face to paralysis of the arm. [p. 169]

Exactly at this point, Freud makes an important step, stating that "hysterical paralysis is also a representation paralysis, but with a special kind of representation" (p. 163, italics added). The representation he might have had in mind (although he did not refer to it as such) is the psychic representation of the body. (This would correspond to the somatic representations in P1, according to the metapsychological DPM system.) In contrast to the organic representation of the body in the brain, which depends on neuroanatomical factors (as has been empirically proven), psychic representation of hysterical paralysis reflects, according to Freud (1893), "the everyday, popular conception of the organs and of the body in general … our tactile and above all our visual perceptions" (p. 170). The physical lesion that causes cerebral paralysis corresponds to the "alteration of the conception, the idea, of the arm" in hysterical paralysis (p. 170, italics in original).

Considered psychologically, the paralysis of the arm consists in the fact that the conception of the arm cannot enter into association with the other ideas constituting the ego of which the subject's body forms an important part. The lesion would therefore be the abolition of the associative accessibility of the conception of the arm. The arm behaves as though it did not exist for the play of associations. There is no doubt that if the material conditions corresponding to the conception of the arm are profoundly altered, the conception will also be lost. But I have to show that it can be inaccessible without being destroyed and without its material substratum (the nervous tissue of the corresponding region of the cortex) being damaged. [p. 170, italics in original]

As we know, Freud here came to the conclusion that "the paralysed organ or the lost function is involved in a subconscious association" (p. 171, italics in original), and I will not further delve into Freud's elaboration of what in the Ucs. causes this exclusion of the psychic representation of the arm from associative processes, since that is not my point here.[20] Rather, I want to focus on the theoretical implications of Freud's reflections on these different forms of paralyses.

In describing the two organic paralyses, projection and representation paralysis, Freud notes that on a strictly neuroanatomical basis, "there is a change in arrangement at the connecting point between the two sections of the motor system" (p. 161, italics added). Then, in analyzing the characteristics of hysterical paralysis, he revealed another "change in arrangement"—this one obviously located "at the connecting point" between the somatic and the psychic. The striking factor in hysterical paralysis is, after all, that the organ, e.g., the arm, is paralyzed, although no physical lesion can be found within the neural tissue— hence, the arm should move. And this can only mean that we have to envision another level of organization in the brain, the level of psychic representations, which is—at least at times—hierarchically superordinate to the organization of somatic processes.

---

[20] Freud (1893) proposed that "the conception of the arm is involved in an association with a large quota of affect" (p. 171), and that when "the subject is unable or unwilling to get rid of this surplus, the memory of the impression attains the importance of a trauma and becomes the cause of permanent hysterical symptoms" (p. 172).

It is at this point that we cannot limit ourselves to a conception within the DPM system, within which the arm is thought to be represented in P1. Although the psychic representation of the arm in P1 might be excluded, bypassed, repressed, or otherwise discounted, the reasons for this relate to factors described by other frameworks of the model of the mind. Thus, we will have to consider another "change in arrangement"—from the DPM system to the subject-object track—because the arm is part of the more complex psychic unit of the self, and this self is obviously caught up in a conflict with a specific object. Since the decisive factors of this conflict are unconscious, we will also have to include a change in arrangement that takes into account a shift to the specific working modes of the Ucs., and yet another one addressing the specific interactions between the structures of ego, super-ego, and id. That is to say, hysterical paralysis is based on an unconscious fantasy, including wishes and their related anxieties and defenses, the elaboration of which is the result of complex dynamic negotiations in different areas of the four frameworks, as well as among all of them.

The "changes in arrangement" occurring at the connecting points between the different levels of somatic organization and the levels of psychic representations are infinitely variable. They may be considerable, as in the infantile cloacal conception of impregnation, pregnancy, and birth; at other times, they might involve merely the slight but crucial difference between the anatomical and the psychological conceptions expressed as arm and sleeve. Such differences express individually shaped changes in the arrangement of our psychic conception of the body, as compared to our physical conception. The idea of a dynamic interaction among all four frameworks on the psychological plan, combined with an at least equally complex dynamic interaction between different levels of physiological organization, contributes to the difficulty of figuring out how mind and brain work together. Nevertheless, this task is ultimately not an impossible one.

Concluding Remarks

We have seen that there are substantial links between the metapsychological model of the mind and Luria's (1973) model of the working brain. This comparison provides one paradigm for how we may relate psychoanalytic concepts to the neuroscientific understanding of different structures and functional units of the brain. Various authors have opened similar discussions (Reiser 1994; Shevrin et al. 1996; Solms 1997), and further exploration certainly lies ahead.

A problem we must confront in building bridges between psychoanalysis and neuroscience is that we talk on both sides of highly complex processes. The DPM system provides a framework on the psychological side that allows us to break down this level of complexity, because it differentiates between various mental representations, all of which function as building blocks of each psychic microelement. With its depiction of this relatively detailed, "microscopic" view of the psychic elements, the DPM system can serve as an avenue connecting us to data collected in neurobiology, brain research, and neuropsychology.

Appreciating similarities between the metapsychological model of the mind and Luria's neuropsychological model of the brain should not lead us to ignore the differences between them. As Freud's comparative study between organic and hysterical paralyses demonstrated, unconscious conceptions (psychic representations) can have an enormous impact on the body, one that overrules even the unimpaired functions of the brain.[21] The subtle challenge posed by Freud's early essay (1893)— one with which we still grapple today—is that (at least at times) it placed the level of psychic organization above the physical one, that is, in a hierarchically superordinate position.

Psychoanalysis has repeatedly been asked to adapt its concepts, and even to prove them, according to the findings of neuroscience and cognitive psychology, and we should certainly be open to learning from these disciplines and others. But psychoanalysis can also call on neuroscience in a reciprocal way, asking that it consider specific research strategies that take into account the psychoanalytic understanding of mental processes, developed and collected now for more than a century. Metapsychology, when

---

[21] It is worthwhile to note here that Kaplan-Solms and Solms (2000) took their research in the opposite direction, exploring the influence of the impaired brain on psychic functioning.

described on an abstract, formalized level (Schmidt-Hellerau 1995a, 1995b, 2001), provides suitable bridging concepts that can facilitate our communication and mutual understanding in this endeavor. For the neuroscientist, it may be hard to accept the idea that a simple, everyday conception of the arm—as a piece of the body defined by the sleeve—occupies a hierarchically superordinate, and therefore more powerful, position in the brain than its sophisticated and complex, neuronally organized counterpart. But for scientific research to accept this idea as a working hypothesis poses an exciting challenge for the future.

References

Damasio, A. (1999a). Commentary on Jaak Panksepp: emotions as viewed by psychoanalysis and neuroscience: an exercise in consilience. Neuro-Psychoanalysis, 1:38-39.

Damasio, A. (1999b). The Feeling of What Happens: Body and Emotion in the Making of Consciousness. New York/San Diego, CA/London: Harcourt Brace.

Freud, S. (1893). Some points for a comparative study of organic and hysterical motor paralyses. S.E., 1.

Freud, S. (1900). The interpretation of dreams. S.E., 4-5.

Freud, S. (1901). The psychopathology of everyday life. S.E., 6.

Freud, S. (1911). Psycho-analytic notes on an autobiographical account of a case of paranoia (dementia paranoides). S.E., 12.

Freud, S. (1915a). Repression. S.E., 14.

Freud, S. (1915b). The unconscious. S.E., 14.

Freud, S. (1923). The ego and the id. S.E., 19.

Freud, S. (1933). New introductory lectures on psycho-analysis. S.E., 22.

Freud, S. (1937). Analysis terminable and interminable. S.E., 23.

Freud, S. (1950). A project for a scientific psychology. S.E., 1.

Gill, M. (1963). Topography and systems in psychoanalytic theory. Psychol. Issues, 3, Monograph 10.

Green, A. (1999). Consilience and rigour: commentary to Jaak Panksepp, "Emotions as viewed by psychoanalysis and neuroscience: an exercise in consilience." Neuro-Psychoanal., 1:40-44.

Iversen, S., Kupfermann, I. & Kandel, E. R. (2000). Emotional states and feelings. In Principles of Neural Science, ed. E. R. Kandel, J. H. Schwartz & T. M. Jessell. New York/St. Louis, MO/San Francisco, CA: McGraw Hill, pp. 982-997.

Kandel, E. R. (1998). A new intellectual framework for psychiatry. Am. J. Psychiatry, 155:457-469.

Kandel, E. R. (1999). Biology and the future of psychoanalysis: a new intellectual framework for psychiatry revisited. Am. J. Psychiatry, 156:505-524.

Kaplan-Solms, K. & Solms, M. (2000). Clinical Studies in Neuro-Psychoanalysis: Introduction to a Depth Neuropsychology. London: Karnac.

Kernberg, O. F. (1980). Internal World and External Reality: Object Relations Theory Applied. London: Mark Paterson, 1985.

Laplanche, J. & Pontalis, J.-B. (1967). The Language of Psycho-Analysis, trans. D. Nicholson-Smith. New York: Norton, 1973.

LeDoux, J. (1996). The Emotional Brain: The Mysterious Underpinnings of Emotional Life. New York: Touchstone.

Luria, A. R. (1973). The Working Brain: An Introduction to Neuropsychology, trans. B. Haigh. New York: Basic Books.

Opatow, B. (1999). Affect and the integration problem of mind and brain. Neuro-Psychoanal., 1:97-110.

Panksepp, J. (1998). Affective Neuroscience: The Foundations of Human and Animal Emotions. New York/Oxford, England: Oxford Univ. Press.

Panksepp, J. (1999). Emotions as viewed by psychoanalysis and neuroscience: an exercise in consilience. Neuro-Psychoanal., 1:15-38.

Reiser, M. F. (1994). Memory in Mind and Brain: What Dream Imagery Reveals. New Haven, CT/London: Yale Univ. Press.

Rubinstein, B. (1965). Psychoanalytic theory and the mind-body problem. In Psychoanalysis and Current Biological Thought, ed. N. S. Greenfield & W. C. Lewis. Madison, WI: Univ. of Wisconsin Press, pp. 35-56.

Rubinstein, B. (1967). Explanation and mere description: a metascientific examination of certain aspects of the psychoanalytic theory of motivation. In Motives and Thought: Psychoanalytic Essays in Honor of David Rapaport, ed. R. Holt. New York: Int. Univ. Press, pp. 18-78.

Schacter, D. L. (1996). Searching for Memory: The Brain, the Mind, and the Past. New York: Basic Books.

Schmidt-Hellerau, C. (1995a). Lebenstrieb und Todestrieb, Libido und Lethe: Ein formalisiertes konsistentes Modell der psychoanalytischen Trieb und Strukturtheorie. Stuttgart, Germany: Verlag Internationale Psychoanalyse.

Schmidt-Hellerau, C. (1995b). Die Geburt der Metapsychologie: Zur Aktualität des "Entwurfs einer Psychologie" (1895). Psyche, 49:1156-1195.

Schmidt-Hellerau, C. (1997). Libido and lethe: fundamentals of a formalised conception of metapsychology. Int. J. Psycho-Anal., 78:683-697.

Schmidt-Hellerau, C. (2001). Life Drive & Death Drive—Libido & Lethe: A Formalized Consistent Model of Psychoanalytic Drive and Structure Theory. New York: Other Press.

Schmidt-Hellerau, C. (2002). Why aggression? Metapsychological, clinical, and technical considerations. Int. J. Psycho-Anal., 83: 1269-1289.

Schore, A. N. (1997). A century after Freud's project: is a rapprochement between psychoanalysis and neurobiology at hand? J. Amer. Psychoanal. Assn., 45:807-840.

Shevrin, H. (1999). Commentary to Jaak Panksepp, "Emotions as viewed by psychoanalysis and neuroscience: an exercise in consilience." Neuro-Psychoanal., 1:55-60.

Shevrin, H., Bond, J. A., Brakel, L. A., Hertel, R. K. & Williams, W. J. (1996). Conscious and Unconscious Processes: Psychodynamic, Cognitive, and Neurophysiological Convergences. New York: Guilford.

Solms, M. (1997). The Neuropsychology of Dreams: A Clinico-Anatomical Study. Mahwah, NJ: Lawrence Erlbaum.

Solms, M. & Nersessian, E. (1999). Freud's theory of affect: questions for neuroscience. Neuro-Psychoanal., 1:5-14.

CHAPTER 5

We are Driven[*]

Is metapsychology out—or in again? Is it a millstone tied around our necks—or is it an intriguing Freudian witch whom we can even dance with? Is the concept of drives an outmoded oddity—or an indispensable companion, inspiring our understanding of the patient's material and even opening new windows for further development? Can we proceed with the concept of structures and object relationships alone—or do we need the concept of drives in order to understand what these object relationships are all about? I clearly opt for the second option in each of these pairs of alternatives. Reflecting on the sophisticated metapsychology debate that unsettled psychoanalysis in the United States for many years, I review some of the most frequently quoted objections to the concept of drives. Further, I offer an introduction to modern drive theory with the new duality of sexual and preservative drives, as well as a different concept of aggression, and explain how drives relate to structures—specifically, to the representations of self and object.

[*] (2005). Psychoanalytic Quarterly, 74(4):989-1028
A shorter version of this paper was given as the *Academic Lecture* on February 24, 2005 at the Boston Psychoanalytic Society and Institute. I dedicate this paper to my first psychoanalytic colleague and friend in Boston, Ellen Blumenthal, MD. Acknowledgments: For their helpful and informative comments about previous versions of this article, I thank Drs. Ellen Blumenthal, Fred Busch, Anne Erreich, Axel Hoffer, Daniel Jacobs, Anton Kris, Melinda Kulish, Bonnie Smolen, Barbara Stimmel, Pamela Wine, and Peter Wohlauer.

Bill sits in the library and works on his paper. He is staring into the open air, trying to formulate his argument, when suddenly another student walks by. He had briefly noticed her in the previous class, before a huge guy had placed himself in between them and barred his view. Now he can see that she wears one of those short, tight T-shirts that leave room to air the belly button—she has a cute little diamond sitting on top of hers. She looks smashing. Bill follows her with his eyes as she goes to the back of the room and sits down. This is his dream girl! Bill starts fantasizing about going over and introducing himself. He could say: "Are you also working on …?" Silly! Maybe, instead, something fancy like "Julia Roberts would fade next to you"—even more silly! Or "What about dinner at 8:00?" He wonders what she's reading. To whom is she talking now? Is this her boyfriend? Certainly not—that nerd! She seems to be a little older than he—but so what, times have changed. He could take his father's car and drive her to this nice little fish restaurant on the coast.… At this point, Bill finds himself getting up, and sort of unpurposefully strolling toward the back of the room. His heart is pounding. He has not yet made up his mind what to say; he knows that something will come to him. She looks at him just a moment before he reaches her desk. She smiles, and he smiles, too. "Hi," he says. "I'm Bill. I saw you this morning in philosophy class, and you look—like my analyst!"

The Debate about Drive Theory

What is most specific and unique in the psychoanalytic approach to mental life is our understanding that man is *unconsciously driven* to perceive, think, feel, relate, act, interact, and react to his objects and his environment in a particular—and sometimes quite unexpected—way. Interestingly enough, though, this foundation of psychoanalysis—*the driven nature in the dynamics of our unconscious mental life*—has been questioned and discredited in American psychoanalytic discourse throughout the last three to four decades. The debate was intense, with revolutionary components; the arguments put forth were smart and inspired by the exciting idea of stepping out of our nineteenth-century scientific clogs and moving on to today's twenty-first-century thinking and relating.

As sophisticated as the level of dispute was, however, only a few of us may remember in detail how the arguments raised for and against our most basic psychoanalytic concepts have been convincing us during those years. Instead, what we seem to have been left with in the aftermath of this battle are slogan like headlines of some of the most prominent articles published in this debate, evidenced by the following examples. Question: "Two theories or one?" (George Klein 1973). Answer: "Metapsychology is not psychology" (Gill 1976); therefore, one theory—clinical theory—is enough (Gill 1977, p. 582). Question: "Drive or wish?" (Holt 1976), and the answer, given in the same source, is: "Drive is dead, long live wish!" (p. 194). Question: "Metapsychology—who needs it?" (Meissner 1981), posed with the rhetorical impact that seeks the answer: "Nobody!" And finally: "Does metapsychology still exist?" (Modell 1981), to which the implied answer seems to be "No!"

It is striking to note the discrepancy between the scientific level of these articles and the simple, campaign like quality of their principal statements, which were capable of bringing about a mass movement that resulted in a widespread belief in "the actual death of metapsychology" (Holt 1985, p. 289). Regardless of how subtle and differentiated the scientific examinations of metapsychological concepts were, the resulting proclamations were rather blunt, e.g., that metapsychology, and drive theory in particular, are "worthless" (p. 292), "untenably mechanistic" (Holt 1976, p. 163), "indefensible: philosophically shaky, factually mistaken … often clinically misleading," and that we "must give it up" (p. 179). In reviewing the literature, Modell (1990) comes to the conclusion that "the term instinct or drive no longer exists" (p. 184).

Had Freud heard of Bill's adventure in the library, described above, he most likely would have thought that Bill was *driven by infantile sexual urges* as they had more recently resurfaced in Bill's analysis within a classical oedipal context. Of course, Bill's experiences and associations are not always that manifestly sexual and oedipal. He talks about a million things in his analytic sessions, winding his way through this and that, telling his analyst that he plans *x* and *y*, that he competes with the one and is smitten with the other, and broods over why he cannot do anything and always fails with his projects, and so on. In his analysis, he has opened the picture book of his early sexual fantasies, and now he is elaborating them with the help of whatever is available in the moment: contemporary science, politics, and literature, the events of his daily life, and in particular with his observations regarding his analyst. In many different ways, he talks about how he thinks he eventually *can* win over the love of his life, and how he defends himself against the scary aspects of such a victory.

Thus, if we consider the trajectory of Bill's associations in a single session and over the weeks, we might discover that, currently, his thoughts are *driven by unconscious sexual strivings toward his dream girl, his analyst, his mother*—and the struggles to resolve the conflicts he has about them. So we might then wonder: Has the explanatory power of Freud's drive concept really faded or been proven wrong? "Has sexuality anything to do with psychoanalysis?" (Green 1995). Has man's unconscious (as distinct from our thinking about it) become more sophisticated since the early days when Freud (1908) captured infantile sexual theories and their ongoing impact on mental life? In short, do people still experience this "old-fashioned" oedipal conflict, after all we have learned about it, leading to its status as part of our Western popular culture? What *else*'s new?

It is true that Freud's metapsychological papers lead us in innumerable ways into a jungle of concepts that he developed, questioned, and recast many times throughout his life. No wonder we trip over logical breaks, puzzling contradictions, and serious inconsistencies within his model of the mind. How to deal with the situation? Certainly, we can trace the mistaken arguments, point out where he was wrong, and cut out these elements. However, we can also "make Freud work" (as French psychoanalysts might say): we can take contradictions, logical gaps, inconsistencies, and so on as a stimulus and challenge to our reflections, and try to further develop these concepts under scrutiny, thus improving the model as a whole. I have found doing this to be an exciting metapsychological journey (Schmidt-Hellerau 1997, 2001), one that I cannot summarize here. However, I want to offer a fresh look at the theoretical and clinical value and necessity of Freud's concept of *drive*, and to show how we can relate it to psychic structure in general, and to the structures of *self* and *object* in particular.

I do not mean to say that Freud is all we need. So many important contributions have been made in the past hundred years that we cannot even think of psychoanalysis in a "purely" Freudian way anymore—nor do we want to. Nevertheless, reassessing the creative potential of his basic concepts and transferring them into modern drive theory will enable us to integrate essential parts of our contemporary psychoanalytic knowledge in a comprehensive way, and, from there, to explore new areas of the mind—thus invigorating our cause quite a bit. It is my experience that many colleagues find it hard to engage in and relate to theoretical papers on an abstract metapsychological level; and that is why I will here muse on this seemingly outmoded concept—*drive*—in order to show why I think we have an absolute need for it in our theoretical *and* clinical thinking.

Confusing Drive and Structure

English-speaking psychoanalysis has been largely shaped by Strachey's translation of Freud's term *Trieb* as *instinct*. However, Freud distinguished precisely between *drive* (Trieb) and instinct *(Instinkt)*, and used the latter term only six times in all of his works. *Instinct* for him meant an "inherited mental formation" (Freud 1915a, p. 195), and such a formation, whether completely inherited (e.g., the famous egg-rolling movement of the grey-lag goose [Lorenz 1981]) or partly inherited and partly acquired, is a complex structural unit, a *fixed* action *pattern* (Tinbergen 1951). The psychoanalytic notion of *Trieb* or *drive*, in contrast, designates merely "a pressure that is relatively *indeterminate* both as regards the behavior it induces and as regards the satisfying object" (Laplanche and Pontalis 1967, p. 214, italics added). According to Freud's (1915b) conception, the drive originates in a bodily need and aims toward an object "through which the drive is able to achieve its aim" (p. 122), namely, satisfaction. Satisfaction can be achieved with many different actions and diverse objects; satisfaction is not built in, but is learned and created via interaction with meaningful objects. Thus, the drive is defined simply as a *directed movement*: from the subject (its somatopsychic needs and wishes) to the object (which provides satisfaction).

167

Considering this definition, the use of the term *instinct* instead of *drive* in Strachey's translation was confusing.[1] It seems to have contributed to the fallacy that the terms *drive* and *motivation* are equivalent (Strachey occasionally translated *Triebkraft* as *motive force*, for example). George Klein (1967) explicitly urged that we "speak about motivation in terms of properties of a *behavioral unit of ideation, affect, and action*, and not about' drive'" (p. 84). Thus, even though the notion of *motivation* is not a fixed action pattern, it is clearly a *specific* pattern, a *structure* containing *ideation, affect, and action*—it is not simply a push toward something. (See also Kernberg 1980.) The same principle applies for Holt's claim that *drive* can be replaced by *wish* because every wish is structured by the configuration "*S* wants *O*," which is a specific configuration of a Self (representation), an Object (representation), and an affect/action (representation).

Hence, all three notions—*instinct, motivation,* and *wish*—designate quite complex structure formations, while the notion of *drive* merely stands for the directed movement that will energize these structures (wishes).[2] This distinction must be appreciated, first of all. One can certainly understand that psychoanalysts wanted to get rid of the ethological term *instinct*, which must have felt at odds with human psychic life; however, the suggested replacements do not capture what Freud

---

[1] The gravity of this difference is acknowledged in plans to revise the Standard Edition under the leadership of Mark Solms; in this new edition, instinct will be replaced by drive (Solms 2005). In the remainder of this paper, I will consistently use the notion of drive instead of instinct.

[2] The same applies to Brenner's (1982) distinction between drive, an "impersonal and general" concept, and drive derivative, a synonym of drive representation or drive representative. The latter is for him a personal and specific (clinical) concept: "A drive derivative is a wish for gratification.... A drive derivative is unique, individual, and specific. The concept of drive, on the contrary, is a generalization about drive derivatives, based on many individual observations and inferences" (p. 26, italics added). In my view, Brenner's drive derivative—a wish—is a structure, and here I agree. However, the term drive derivative seems to make the wish a part of the drive, which might also end up mingling drive with structure. It is interesting that Freud used the term derivative with regard to the unconscious (Laplanche and Pontalis 1967, p. 116)—in speaking of the derivates of the repressed, which again are unconscious wishes, hence structures cathected by drives.

conceptualized by the notion of *drive*. Instead, these replacements went on *mingling drive with structure*, which eventually created a serious problem for psychoanalytic thinking and development.

This is why I wish to propose two short definitions of *drive* and *structure* at the beginning of this discussion: they make clear how I will use them here and how they can advantageously be used in general. First, the term *drive* designates a one-directional movement of psychic energy, a force that has its starting point in a bodily need (and how it becomes represented) and "drives" (virtually endlessly) in one direction until it finally reaches the required object of satisfaction or its mental representation. Its conception can be best pictured as an *arrow*.

Structure is used here in its most common meaning as any unit within which the parts or elements are organized, arranged, or interrelated in a specific way. Its conception can be nicely pictured as a *snowflake*. We conceptualize the mind as a functional organization of structures on different levels of complexity: thus, a *wish* as described above is a relatively small and clearly circumscribed (micro-)structure; while the *superego*, on the other hand, is a big and very complex (macro-)structure. The *representations of self and object* that I will focus on in particular are two rather complex structures of the mind, harboring and elaborating to varying degrees the wishes, as well as interacting with and being part of the superego.

Given these two definitions, I conceptualize the interaction between drive and structure as follows: whatever we experience, store, and create in our minds is represented as a structure, and what activates or energizes these structures are the drives. Without the drives' energy, these structures exist but are *inactive*. It is only their cathexis from the drives that makes these structures effective.[3] Thus, the structure can be compared to a light bulb that requires the switching on of electrical energy in order to light up.

I am not concerned with the question of whether these definitions

---

[3] We are used to conceptualizing these cathexes as a mixture of both the primal drives' energies, but for clarity, we might here think of one or the other drive as taking the leading role.

match exactly what Freud once said, wrote, or meant to state; this would be of historical or biographical interest, but is not my point here. Instead, I want to assert that distinguishing between the notions of drive and structure in this clearly defined way is in accordance with Freud's thinking in general, and helps us reassess the function of modern drive theory in our understanding of how the mind works.

The whole metapsychological model of the mind is based upon these two concepts, *drive* and *structure*—it is a "drive/structure model" (Greenberg and Mitchell 1983); the drives provide the model's dynamics, and the structure provides its stability. Of course, drive and structure are not real things; they are comprehensive constructs that we have invented in order to build a theory—and theories, too, are inventions, created to fill the gap between what we know as a fact and what we do not know but want to know. For example, as long as man did not understand how a thunderstorm came about, he made up theories about it (gods banging clouds together, etc.). Since we now know how thunderstorms come about, we no longer have a theory about them, but simply the description of the processes resulting in a thunderstorm. That is to say, theories create hypotheses about what we do not know—e.g., how the mind works. Consequently, they are always speculative, even though they usually convey a consistent set of those hypotheses thought to be the most plausible at a specific time, considering all the facts that we *do* know. That is why a theoretical creation is not wild or totally free. However, it could still be called a fiction because it extends beyond knowable facts, and it is particularly this extension, these *ideas beyond the knowable* that push and guide our inquiry and research. It follows that theories cannot be "true"; they can only be more or less, or not at all, heuristically fruitful.

Considering this, metapsychology can be viewed as an indispensable *theoretical model* about *how the mind works in general*. It is not about the *specifics* of how a person experiences his/her individual life. Even though these are two different ways of looking at psychic processes, they relate to each other in a dialectical movement that we have to grapple with (Smith 2003a). Rising to this very challenge to our thinking is what makes psychoanalysis a profession—that is, in comparison to the helpful support and suggestions that a patient might receive from family or friends (Busch and Schmidt-Hellerau 2004). I believe that, in order to optimally treat a patient, we need to think about both: the patient's individual history and the specifics of his/her personal experience, on the one side, and the general principles of mental functioning that come into play while processing and creating this kind of experience, on the other side.

Drive: A Border Concept

There are two reasons to focus on drive theory: first, because it is a central concept, at the heart of metapsychology—the basis of what we understand by the dynamic moment of psychic processes; and, second, because it has been much more discredited than the notion of structure—thus, "the debate about metapsychology can be reduced to debate over drive theory" (Opatow 1989, pp. 647). Holt (1976), one of drive theory's sharpest critics, has actually felt quite torn about it:

> What is loosely known as the theory of instincts includes both a number of *Freud's most important and lasting insights* and some of *his most regrettable theoretical failings*. It badly needs fundamental revision; but the process must be both *radical* and *conservative*—what is *not good* must be *extirpated at the root*, but what is *good* must be *retained*. [p. 158, italics added]

Holt wishes to preserve the insights of psychoanalytic drive theory, but he ends up claiming that "nothing less than discarding the concept of drive or instinct will do" (p. 159). Here we might wonder: How can we preserve the "most important insights" if we extirpate at the root the very concept they are based upon? And: What else could replace the notion of *drive* once it is given up? George Klein's (1967) suggestion to instead use the term *peremptory ideation* has not generally felt practical or appealing to most of our colleagues; our discussions show that this term has not become part of our psychoanalytic vocabulary. A convincing replacement for this important concept has not come up. Twenty-three years after Klein proposed this term, and in the wake of further developments in this long-lingering dispute on metapsychology, Modell (1990) still emphasizes the "need to find a viable substitute for instinct theory" (p. 195).

Basically, we are free to name a theoretical concept whatever we might choose—yet there seem to be some requirements to do so successfully. There is something about the *parsimony* and *simplicity* of theory in general, and its notions in particular, that seems to determine whether a theory works or not. The term *drive* has this comprehensive simplicity: It captures the essentials that we want to address with it, and it is placed at the border between (abstract) theory and (concrete) experience. We can define the notion of *drive* as a metapsychological concept concerning the direction of the dynamic movement of psychic processes, *and* we can experience ourselves as *being driven* to do something. I think we are actually quite lucky to have this notion of drive at our disposal because it plays on both levels, the level of our theoretical thinking and the level of our (the patient's) personal experience. Critics certainly do not deny the existence of that feeling—man's being driven to a specific goal; they have objected only to the theoretical side of this notion. So let us have a closer look at the latter.

It is my sense that Freud was fully aware of and appreciated the fact that the notion of drive allows for this double use, in the sense of an abstract concept and of an experience-near quality or psychic phenomenon. Yet in his famous, often quoted definition of drive, Freud (1915b) points to still another link that is made possible with this notion, the link between the physiological and the psychological.

If we now apply ourselves to considering mental life from a *biological*[4] point of view, a "drive" appears to us as a concept on the border[5] between

---

[4] Strachey added italics to the word biological here, but it was not emphasized in Freud's original German text, and I do not believe that such an emphasis was intended by Freud.

[5] Strachey translated Grenze as frontier—however, I would replace it here with the more usual term border.

the mental and the somatic, as the psychical representative of the stimuli originating from within the organism and reaching the mind, as a measure of the demand made upon the mind for work in consequence of its connection with the body. [p. 121]

This and similar statements led to an extensive debate about whether the notion of drive is actually a rather biological or a purely psychological concept. In order to understand this idea of a "concept on the border" or *border concept (Grenzbegriff)*, let us think of the border between the United States and Canada. Is this border American or is it Canadian? The answer is: It is neither American nor Canadian. It is an international agreement about the size or endings of each one's territory. Best to explain that it is a thin line on a map, dependent on two signatures on a contract—which can be changed. In most areas, you cannot even see it, and in that respect, it is also virtual. Now the same applies for the *drive as a border concept between the psychic and the somatic*: It is neither psychological nor biological. It is an intellectual agreement, a theoretical construct, something that does not exist in reality in a material sense, but is a notion we find helpful in *thinking* about psychic phenomena as different from *and* connected with somatic phenomena.

Thus, the metapsychological concept of drive—and, I suggest, all metapsychology—is an abstract mental construct, a concept (and a model) at the border between biology and psychology, dividing and linking both. That is why a question like "Is there such a thing as a *death drive?*" (which is usually answered with "no") represents a failure in thinking; the questions can only be "Are there phenomena that we can unite by a notion to be defined and called the *death drive?*" and "Does it make sense, or is it heuristically fruitful, to make use of such a concept?"

An intriguing question, then, is how this border concept of drive divides and links biology and psychology. Freud (1910), informed by Darwin, started out with two categories of basic or primal drives:

[There are] … *drives which subserve sexuality*, the attainment of sexual pleasure, *and those other drives, which have as their aim the self-preservation of the individual*—the ego-drives. As the poet has said, all the organic drives that operate in our mind may be classified as "*hunger*" or "*love*". [p. 213, italics added]

In fact, we cannot ignore the demands of the body for food and sex; they powerfully affect and besiege our minds with images, thoughts, impulses, and feelings—in particular, when something interferes with their satisfaction—and we would be lying if we did not admit that we have all at times felt strongly *driven* to promptly go for the one or the other. Thus, Freud's first drive theory made much sense; it implicitly divided all mental activity according to one of the two somatopsychic functions, self-preservation and sexuality (both applied in the broadest sense of these terms).

Given the important position of these two primal drives, reemphasized by Freud throughout the first twenty years of his writings, I am intrigued by the fact that he elaborated on only one of them, the sexual drive. The self-preservative or ego drive (as he occasionally called it after 1910) merely followed along in the shadow of sexuality. In 1920, when Freud started to revise his metapsychology, he unfortunately merged sexuality *and* self-preservation into his new *life drive*, and declared a *death or aggressive drive* to be its antagonist. Since then, with Freud, we have all—even those who have turned away from drive theory altogether—considered sexuality and aggression as *the two basic primal drives* or motivating factors in mental life. As a consequence of this shift, self-preservation—or the *preservative drive*, as I have suggested (Schmidt-Hellerau 2005a)—became a blind spot in our psychoanalytic perception. It is not that we did not notice, for example, the attachment and separation issues of a clinging patient who does not feel safe without his analyst, or the anxieties of the hypochondriacal patient who is convinced she will shortly die, or the worries of the obsessional compulsive patient who needs to constantly clean everything, including himself, in order to rid himself of dangerous germs. It is only that we were used to understanding these problems as conflicts around sexuality and aggression, and no doubt these *are* important factors in what makes our patients suffer.

However, it seems to me that, while translating such patients' pain into sexual and aggressive issues, we may have failed to appreciate how much these patients are unconsciously *scared to death*, how much they *struggle to survive*, how much they are basically *driven* to do all they feel is necessary *to preserve themselves* and/or their objects. The three examples of patients above are amongst the louder ones—yet I also wonder: Do we notice the softer voices that speak of these needs or the neglects of self and object preservation in our day-to-day clinical work? If we included in our thinking and listening the concept of a preservative drive as a basic and primal force of the mind, wouldn't this open our ears to the more subtle associations that communicate the patient's self and object-preservative concerns—which are sometimes the major cause of the patient's inhibitions and depressions, and can even constitute the main trajectory of all his/her neurotic derailments?

I agree with Smith (2005a) about the need to differentiate between the uses of *drive* in metapsychology and in clinical work. He draws a distinction between drives and drive derivatives or wishes as being on different levels of abstraction, and questions whether it is possible for "the material that the analyst observes in the hour [to be] a kind of window through which the drives can be seen quite directly" (p. 344). I think the distinctions between levels of abstractions (see Schmidt-Hellerau 2001, pp. 10-17) relate mainly to the purpose of our psychoanalytic discourse—whether we talk about drives within a metapsychological framework (their definition, their function, contribution to structure building, and so on), or whether we talk about the concrete clinical phenomena that we have captured and conceptualized (on a metapsychological level) as drives (e.g., the patient's unconscious and conscious *urges*). Keeping this in mind, I would feel comfortable in saying that we can observe the workings of the drives, drive activity, the ideational expression of the drives, or drive derivatives in the analytic hour; to state this differently, if we had not developed the *concept* of drives, we would not be able to observe drive *derivatives* either.

To hold on to and to reorganize drive theory—to decide which drives we postulate as primary—is not just a matter of theory; it is a matter of practical work. I will not discuss Freud's 1920 theory of life drive and death drive here[6] I want to highlight the sexual and preservative drives

---

[6] For a more detailed discussion of Freud's second drive theory, see Schmidt-Hellerau

as primal, and also to explain my conceptualization of aggression, these three influences being the most relevant for our daily clinical work. Recently, I have elaborated on some ideational and affective expressions of self and object-preservative strivings (Schmidt-Hellerau 2005a), and I would like now to focus on the preservative drive (or what we could call a *partial drive*, hunger), in order to demonstrate the important role of our concept of drive in psychic processes occurring at the border between soma and psyche.

Hunger: Part of the Preservative Drive

Hunger occurs as a *feeling* when an indefinite number of somatic incidents come together—for instance, the blood sugar level and/ or the body temperature decreases, receptors in the stomach signal empty contractions, and so on. The whole ensemble of known (and still unknown) somatic processes that stir up our feeling of hunger can be bundled and conceptualized, according to a metapsychological scheme, as a partial drive for self-preservation. What makes hunger *psychoanalytically* interesting is the fact that it drives us to a potentially endless number of fantasies, thoughts, feelings, and behaviors that actually fill a substantial part of our daily mental life. In the simplest example, when we are hungry, something like a sandwich pops up on our mental screen, we go and get it, eat it, and that's it. But the process becomes more complicated if we want a specific food and have to find out where and how to get it; this already affords a lot more mental activity. Or, think of a situation in which we are prevented from getting something to eat, perhaps because we are sitting in the middle of a two-hour conference; then—sometimes even without realizing that we are getting hungry—we might find ourselves distracted: all of a sudden we feel annoyed to see our neighbor slowly chewing something, or we might lose ourselves in musing about whom we want to invite for the next Thanksgiving party, even though it is only April. These are a few examples of how a conscious or preconscious sense of hunger *drives* us to all sorts of ideas and activities that we would not have had if we had not

---

1997, 2001, 2005b, 2006.

been hungry. There is nothing neurotic about this, but much psychic activity is involved.

The most obvious examples of the *psychopathological sides of hunger* are, certainly, eating disorders, hypochondria, or psychosomatic disorders centering around the stomach. Patients with these problems are unremittingly, and at times completely, preoccupied with obsessing and puzzling about their food intake and digestion; they have lots of strong feelings around these concerns and need to do something about them. They are literally *driven* to rally all their psychic activities around these issues because, in the end, such issues are all about dealing on a more or less unconscious level with self-preservation and the warding off of an imagined fear of threatening death.

Certainly, much more often, we have a neurotic patient on the couch who is freely associating. For instance, a patient named Amy tells me about this wonderful little Italian delicacy store that she discovered yesterday after our session. Even though she had planned to go directly to the library, she eventually found herself in the middle of a discussion with the shopkeeper about a specific combination of vegetables. Of course, once again, she bought much too much; she is always so uncertain about whether she'll have enough or not…. Then she indulges in telling me how she was later preparing these vegetables with a rack of lamb, and all the herbs she used according to a new recipe from the *New York Times Magazine*; more details follow. Amy pauses, and then tells me how afraid she was of ruining the dinner, of the risk entailed in preparing it in a totally new way. She so wanted to surprise and please her husband. Everything actually turned out quite well: the meat had this spicy crust on the outside and was as pink inside as it should be, the vegetables matched amazingly well (she had not been sure about that), and they had a French baguette with it and some Chianti…. I sit and listen to her somewhat anxious and defensive voice, and I wonder: Why is she telling me this, why does *this* come up, and why does she sound so worried about it?

Here an analyst might have all sorts of ideas, depending on where the psychoanalytic process is at this point, where the previous session stopped, and where his/her countertransference feelings go. Maybe the patient wants to tell her analyst that she can make use of something new she has learned in the analysis, "a new recipe," and with this, she tells her analyst that "your food was good, I liked it, I could digest it and make use of it." Or, on the contrary, she might be saying that she has no need of food from the analyst (interpretations), but can prepare much better food on her own by using a magazine. Or, on a competitive road, she might want to emphasize that her food is certainly better than anything the analyst might ever cook. Or, the patient might aim to project her deprived feeling of not getting what she assumes her analyst gives to someone else by trying to make her analyst envious that it is her husband who got to eat this perfect meal, not the analyst herself. And so on.

In this specific case of my session with Amy, I felt admiration for the perfect meal. She displayed it to me as it might have existed in a cookbook—no criticism was possible. However, considering her anxious and defensive voice, my sense was that, while wanting to be the perfect cook (competing with me, as well as seeking my admiration for how well she had done), Amy was also afraid of some criticism coming from me— e.g., that her meal might not have been so perfect, or that she should have instead gone to the library and worked. What she had accomplished felt to her to be on shaky ground, for reasons that we would need to learn more about. Then my thoughts went to her worries of never having enough—to survive? Something essential was missing— something that made her afraid of the insatiable other, whose hunger threatened to engulf her. She needed to have and to give me a lot, yet she was not sure whether it would ever be good enough, whether I would ever be satisfied.

Without elaborating further here on what emerged in this hour, let me clarify that my point is that Amy's food talk is associative material; it fills out her analytic hour, it is psychologically complex and meaningful, and it is designed to tell me something important. So the question with her—as with all analysands' associations—is always: What *drives the patient to have these food associations* and not others?

Before we explore this question further, another objection related to the concept of drive must be addressed.

Reductionism

The standard argument that follows here is one of the strongest-felt objections and one of the most often heard: Psychoanalytic drive theory is reductionistic. It reduces the whole variety and diversity of individual thoughts to just two basic drives—and this is impossible. Holt, correctly pointing out that Freud "made it explicit in several contexts (1905, 1911) that all motivation originated in bodily stimuli" (Holt 1976, p. 165), strongly objects to this point of view: "I do not hesitate to say that it is impossible to demonstrate any relevant somatic stimulation connected with the vast majority of human motives" (p. 165).

However, as the brain is part of the body and constantly provides somatic stimuli to which we react on a mental, psychological level, all human motives are connected to the somatic. Further, would Holt's (1976) assertion have been different if it had been based on the sexual and the preservative instead of an aggressive drive?

> It is clinically obvious that sex and aggression in their many manifestations are overridingly important; but fear, anxiety, dependence, self-esteem, curiosity, and group belongingness (to name only an obvious handful) cannot validly be reduced to sex and aggression, and are motivational themes the therapist cannot afford to ignore. [Holt 1976, p. 169]

As Amy's session exemplifies, feelings of fear, dependence, self-esteem, curiosity, and so on do come up in the context of food concerns. So the aim is not to *reduce* all her feelings and fantasies by saying something like: Amy is just hungry—or Amy thinks her husband/analyst is hungry (which would already be an intriguing difference). Rather, we might see how many feelings—how many worries, hopes, and pleasures, how many activities, interactions, and ambitions—emerge around *her being driven* to enter this delicacy store, to prepare this dinner, and to tell me about it. Feeding themes like these might indicate a deep unconscious greed, a sense of starving—or of having previously exploited, eaten up, or taken too much from the analyst, who then needs to be refilled. Thus, the notion of a self and object-preservative drive does not *reduce*; rather, it *widens* our access to the clinical material, *and* it provides a comprehensive concept within which all the single events the patient relates (the many feelings, thoughts, fantasies, and actions) make *meaning* as part of the patient's *striving for a specific, still unconscious goal.*

But there is more to it than this. Obviously Amy's material presents the need side of hunger in a rather concrete, literal sense. However, a patient does not have to talk about *food* to communicate a deep, threatening, and insatiable hunger. Instead, she might talk about many other things: swallowing up books, not being able to stop watching TV, wanting more and more interpretations from her analyst, endlessly increasing the preliminary research data for a paper she plans to write, or in many other ways. All these greed themes might be stimulated by self-preservative needs, indicating the patient's need to engulf everything as if it were food and would ensure her survival. The case of a workaholic student who displays some sort of "intellectual obesity" is clearly different from that of another student with a mature, creative, and productive way of studying. However, the same issues (piling up books, amassing data and knowledge by reading and researching, a yearning for interpretations, and so forth) might have a more phallic ("showing off") or erotically exciting ("being stimulated by and excited about it") unconscious meaning for a third student.

Here it is important to realize that *it makes a difference* whether a striving for some sort of incorporation is primarily *self-preservative* or *sexual.* The mere object (e.g., books), and the (inter-)action with it (e.g., accumulating them), does not tell us what function they serve for the patient. What drive theory helps us to capture is the general trajectory of the patient's strivings that provide an understanding of *the unconscious meaning* of the issues at stake, of *what moves the patient in doing these things, what drives her to bring them up*—how does she use or abuse them, what is she struggling with, and what does this behavior aim for in a particular moment of a cure? And, last but not least: Is all that occurs in a particular moment *pressing for* satisfaction, or *repressing* satisfaction?

Holt (1976) elaborates on his interpretation of Freud's views in furthering the reductionism argument:

> Another curious feature of Freud's various versions of his theory of in-
> stinctual drives is his strong preference for only two fundamental
> motives, to which all others could be reduced.... It was as if his convic-
> tion about the central importance of *conflict* forced him always to
> postulate an opposed duality of basic drives. [p. 169, italics in original]

Holt is right in that Freud's conflict theory and his understanding of the
dynamics between drive and repression are essentially based on the antagonism of two primal drives (Freud 1910, 1925). To me, however, this
hypothesis is less "curious" than heuristically fruitful. Green (1999), who
admits that there is no longer "a consensus on the hypothesis of a primal
conflict setting two major groups of drives in conflict with each other" (p.
82), reminds us that "the thesis of fundamental drive conflict corresponds
in Freud to an exigency, that is to say, of explaining the fact that the conflict
can be repeated, displaced, transposed and that its permanence resists all
the transformations of the psychical apparatus" (p. 83). Even though we
certainly can observe, describe, and analyze conflict in various ways (Smith
2003a[7]), I am not sure that these differences necessarily preclude or contradict its conceptualization with regard to the basic drives' antagonism. We
might look at the same issue from different perspectives, or use different
languages to talk about it, or use drive conflict in a more or less restrictive
way. For instance, Smith (2003b) suggests that the erotic and aggressive
drives are never in conflict unless one is defending against the other. I
would agree with respect to sexuality and aggression. However, our view
might change if we consider preservative and sexual drives as primary. I
have recently proposed (Schmidt-Hellerau 2005a) that we can think of
conflict as *monolithic* or *binary*, depending on whether only one of the
sexual and the preservative drives, or both, are involved, and that conflict
always plays out as a struggle between the objects of these primal drives.

---

[7] This might also apply to those who do not consider conflict theory as central
to psychoanalysis any longer. Smith (2003b) suggests that "many theorists who would
emphasize alternatives to conflict theory may be speaking of aspects of experience that
are not mutually exclusive from, but may quite compatibly exist within, a conflictual
view of the mind at different levels of generalization". (p. 91)

This latter perspective leads to some exemplary questions about the predominance of wish and defense: Is a patient who indulges in chocolate-eating orgies, or who feels sickly and in need of a doctor, expressing a *wish* to be taken care of (based on an unconscious fantasy of being endangered in her survival), and thus conveying self-preservative drive activities striving for satisfaction; or is that same patient expressing a (regressive) *defense* against the arousal of sexual wishes toward her analyst? Further, does a patient *defend* against self-preservative wishes to be taken care of by her analyst by engaging in promiscuous sexual adventures, or are these enactments to be understood as an untamed expression of her sexual drives—i.e., a provocative revenge for not being accepted as her analyst's love object?

I think that relating conflict to the two primal drives is tremendously stimulating in terms of our clinical reflections on the patient's material. So we might consider: Isn't it interesting, doesn't it make a difference, and what does it mean that Amy chooses *food* and not some sort of *erotic* item to reach out for, appeal to, compete with, or please her husband (and me in the transference)? Does Amy prefer to step into her kitchen, rather than exploring new and exciting sources (research materials) in the library, because she has a conflict about her progress in analysis, based on an unconscious or conscious idea/sense that her mother-analyst needs to be relentlessly object-preservative, needs to be constantly required as the helpful (overprotective) caretaker who cannot let go? Or does the patient employ thoughts and activities about food as an unconscious or preconscious defense against her sexual wishes and fantasies? Or is this choice a compromise in that, by cooking for her husband (a success story for her analyst), Amy makes up for enacting an unconscious castration fantasy that her husband will be too tired after dinner for sex (i.e., the analyst would feel disappointed that the patient has made no progress in her work)? Or—quite the opposite—does Amy use the food (talk) as some sort of seductive, erotic foreplay, as an introduction to her sexual longings?

There are many clinically relevant questions that come up if we are holding in mind, in general, the concept of two opposing primal drives, and—as always—the patient's associations, together with the analyst's countertransference understanding, will help us figure out which way to go. All of this demonstrates that drive theory is quite the opposite of reductionism. The reductionism argument actually stands the heuristics of the notion of drive on its head (in a rhetorically effective, yet misleading way), and we can easily turn it back on its feet by noting: Isn't it fascinating to observe these virtually endless ramifications (displacements, reversals, amplifications, and so forth) that emerge when a basic drive's need (which is never felt to be satisfied, nor could it be given up) is psychically activated, stimulating the patient to be creative in her thinking and communications?

One might view the patient's associations in relation to the drive as like a tree's innumerable branches, with leaves and blossoms that all spring from one basic trunk. To appreciate the beauty of the top of the tree does not mean reducing it to its trunk—just as we cannot and should not ignore the trunk out of which this individual tree's variety of branching grows, for without this trunk, there would be no branching. Let me elaborate this tree metaphor a little further: below ground, there is another "treetop," the branching of roots, which we can compare to the somatic processes that we presuppose for the border concept drive. This image conveys the whole complexity of physiological processes (integration of brain stem, midbrain, and higher cortical functions, as well as their interaction with bodily organs, and with neurophysiological, neurohormonal, and immunological processes) that come together into something like the *somatic side of hunger*—which leads to another complexity, the *psychic side of hunger*, with all its ramifications of fantasies, thoughts, feelings, and actions mentioned above.

If we always had to talk of all the details implied in a particular experience, we would never come to an end of the discussion. And this is one important function of the theoretical concept of drive: it allows us to conceive of the general trajectory. For instance, it is practical and helpful for us to conceptualize a simple notion—e.g., hunger—as part of a more general and comprehensive concept—e.g., the *preservative drive*, when we think about hunger-related issues in a psychoanalytic context.

Drive Energy

Many papers have been published about the concept of psychic energy (e.g., Applegarth 1971; Gill 1977; Rosenblatt and Thickstun 1970; Swanson 1977), which postulate that this concept distorts the logico-philosophical requirements of conceptualizing the mind–body relationship, is scientifically untenable, and at odds with all laws of physics and thermodynamics, as well as clinically "useless" and "irrelevant to the explanation and understanding of human behavior" (Swanson 1977, p. 603). Therefore, we might wonder, can't we do without the concept of psychic energy?

The most important argument concerns the nature of psychic energy—what this energy *is*. Rosenblatt and Thickstun (1970) assert that the concept of psychic energy is based on a mind–body *dualism*: "Drive energies are biological in origin but are somehow translated into psychic representations, neither biological nor chemical in nature, but instead 'psychic'—and this is the 'energy' with which psychoanalysis deals" (p. 269). What is being criticized here is the implication of a mysterious jump from physiological (measurable) energy into some sort of psychic (immeasurable) energy. However, psychic energy is a metapsychological notion, and thus a *border concept*, like *drive, neither biological nor psychological*—it is a tool that helps us think about some of the occurrences within psychic processes.

Holt (1976) disputes this:

> Psychic energy lacks any explanatory power and is merely a set of descriptive metaphors. They owe their survival not to enhancing our understanding or providing any new insights into the detailed workings of behavior, thought, and affect, but to their rich literary suggestiveness. [p. 171]

I would not discredit "literary suggestiveness"; it speaks to the fact that this concept captures *something essential*—some way of being *energized* (or not) that we all know from our own experience. Freud accounted for this specific feeling by making *energy* an important and integral part of his

184

drive concept. The drive provides the *direction*, the *movement*, and the energy is *what* is directed, the "*something*"—a specific *quantity*—that is invested in, for example, an object (its representation), an activity, a feeling, and so forth. Of course, there is no physical measure of this quantity; however, it is pragmatically and theoretically important to think of quantitative differences of energy, because these differences correspond to our experiences of *more* or *less*—a constant concomitant of *all* our psychic activities. There is always some sort of *quantity* implied when we talk of *strong* or *weak* beliefs, when we have a *powerful* or a *subtle* feeling, are *heavily* or *only peripherally* involved, or show a *strong* or a *lack of* interest, to give a few examples. Thus, *quantities* determine our psychic presence and experience to a considerable degree, and that needs to be addressed in the corresponding theoretical construct.

Also, quantities affect our psychic equilibrium. The assumption is that all living beings, including humans, try to stay within a certain range of dynamic stability (homeostasis), physiologically as well as psychologically. If there is "too much" or "too little" on one or the other side, our system is thrown out of balance (perceived as unpleasure expressed in different degrees of anxiety). For instance, the concept of psychic trauma is based on this quantitative measure, metapsychologically spoken: a "too much" or a "too little" of an impact in relation to the structural capacity to balance it (or, experientially spoken, an over- or understimulation that is severely shocking or depriving for a person in relation to his or her need for stability). In consequence of this basic idea of homeostasis, we assume that a quantitative imbalance will set off reactions—for instance, defenses—as coping mechanisms. That is to say, not only do we have to deal with the *dynamics* of psychic conflicts, the shifts between the two antagonistic drives, but we also have to deal with *energy quantities*, that is, different degrees of *intensity*, a specific "more or less" amount of energy marshaled in order to defend one position or to strive for another. As Opatow (1989) put it: "'Psychic energy' would be a measure of the *intensity* of this activity" (p. 647, italics added).

Rethinking Aggression

These principles allow us to rethink our conceptualization of aggression. As I have elaborated elsewhere (Schmidt-Hellerau 2002), I doubt that it is wise to think of aggression as a primal drive or as a motivating factor *in itself.* While sexuality is about having sex, and self-preservation is about preserving oneself (thus, they are primal drives, not reducible to anything else), aggression is not about aggression per se, but is always about something else—namely, about survival or sexuality, or about overcoming or defeating any interference, real or imagined, to the goals of those two primal drives. In order to succeed, we will increase our efforts as expressed by the energy quantities invested in our strivings. That is to say, what we experience as *aggression is the expression of intensified sexual or preservative drive activity.*[8]

The rationale for this is: A drive is defined as a movement from the (somatopsychic) source of the subject's need/desire to the object of satisfaction; if satisfaction is not achieved, then unpleasure persists; thus, the goal of getting to the required object is a decisive determinant of any drive activity. How can the mental apparatus successfully meet this requirement?

Within each object relationship, the regulation of *closeness* and *distance* is crucial. However, to be in a psychological sense *near* or *distant* is not just a matter of inches or meters. As long as a small child feels safe and secure, mother is close enough if she is somewhere in the house; if the same child is hungry or scared, mother is much too far away if she is only in the next room. In this sense, closeness and distance are drive-related categories. It is the momentary need/desire—be it stirred up

---

[8] How shall we consider the intensity of a drive's activity—since that intensity is a function of *quantity* and speed, the latter of these being a function of time and distance? As an illustration, we might think of a series of actions: You can touch a man, push, hit, knock him down, or kill him. The differences among these actions are determined by the energy quantities and by the speed with which they occur—that is, the time within which the hand or its projectile makes its way to the object (e.g., the bigger the rock and the higher its speed, the greater the intensity with which it hits its target), as well as the distance between the point at which the energy is initiated and the object.

186

from the inside or from the outside—that determines whether the distance to the object of satisfaction is *just right, too little*, or *too big*. Obviously, this is something very complex to measure. I believe that our minds are constantly calculating and anticipating the appropriate intensity afforded in order to *reach*, to *frighten off*, to *flee*, or to *destroy* the relevant object.

During the child's development, these complex processes of computation are learned and stored—like the child's purposeful grasping movements, which first miss the desired object, then knock it down; and only bit by bit does the child learn to evaluate how far the arm has to reach out in order to pick up the object, how quickly this has to happen in order to catch it if it is moving, and how strongly the hand has to hold it in order to keep it without either losing or squeezing it. Computations of this kind are the basis for activating the necessary energy quantities and setting the desired speed in relation to any specific action. They are learned and stored in our mental structures, and, as mature or immature as these structures may be, they are used in order to *anticipate* the appropriate intensity of any striving. Thus, if the drive object is far away, more energy is put up in order to reach it than if it is close by.

However, in states of psychopathology or neurotic conflict, these anticipatory processes fail. A regressed patient in analysis might react like a child who is afraid that the libidinal object is absent-minded or withdrawing, while she, the analyst, is actually quite with him; thus, he might angrily raise his voice in order to reach her; or he might feel threatened in thinking the analyst came too close, and he might need to preserve himself by furiously pushing her away.

What I am suggesting here is that we do not get angry or aggressive merely in order to enjoy our aggression. But we do get increasingly angry and aggressive if we are hungry and prevented from eating—or, more generally, if our self-preservation, our survival, is (or is neurotically feared to be) attacked or endangered; and we do get enraged and aggressive if our loved one is flirting with someone else. Greed/envy and jealousy arc the classical motivations for murder. Or, with regard to narcissism (which may concern both our libidinal and preservative investments in ourselves), we might get angry if our cherished ideas, or we ourselves, seem to be victims of ridicule, depreciation, or questioning. Thus, what is correctly perceived as aggression is an activity of this intensity that is put up in order to defend, regulate, or overcome the distance to the object of the individual's preservative and sexual strivings. And that is why I suggest staying with the sexual and preservative drives as primal, and why I define aggression as the expression of an *intensification* of either or both of them.

It is interesting to note that Brenner's (1982) argument against Freud's conceptualization of drives as "somatopsychic or frontier phenomena in mental life" stands or falls with the conceptualization of aggression:

> It is not until one turns from libido theory to the theory of aggression that the evidence against the frontier concept of drives becomes irrefutable. As long as libido was the only drive, i.e., before 1920, it could be argued that the frontier concept was tenable. [Brenner 1982, p. 15]

Of course, there were always two drives evident in Freud's thinking, even though he focused on just one of them. Nevertheless, I agree with Brenner's statement that what is "fundamental to Freud's concept of a drive is that it is something somatopsychic.... The source of a drive, Freud believed, is a somatic process, e.g., excitation of nerve endings in an erogenous zone, in the case of libido" (p. 16). Psychoanalysis has always struggled with the paucity of equivalent sources for aggression—and that is precisely where and why Brenner departs from the drive as a "frontier concept." However, if we conceptualize aggression as an intensified expression of the sexual and preservative drives, and postulate that the sources of the preservative drive are, as I have called them, the *biogenic zones* (that is, primarily, all the inner organs necessary for self-preservation—the stomach for hunger, the lungs for breathing, etc., and, further, the whole body with its requirements for integrity, analogous to the whole skin as an erotogenic zone for the sexual drive[9]), then we have the sources of both primal drives, the erotogenic and the biogenic zones,

---

[9] For further elaboration of these ideas, see Schmidt-Hellerau 2001

and their link to aggression. And, therefore, we can consistently stay with the conceptualization of drives as somatopsychic and as *frontier concepts* or *border concepts* between the body and the mind.

The clinical implications of this shift in our conceptualization of aggression seem meaningful to me, for if we think of aggression as a primal drive or an irreducible motivation, we will search for it as an *entity in itself*. We will then think about a gentle, passive patient by wondering, "But what about his aggression?" Or we will assume that he defends against or represses his aggression by being concerned about his objects, including the analyst. We may talk about his aggressive fantasies as if they are all he needs to acknowledge. Yet if we conceptualize aggression as an *intensification of the sexual or the preservative drive's strivings*, we will always wonder where his aggression comes from, *what it is about*.

For example, a patient who is angry with me before a vacation break is not angry or aggressive because he exercises his aggressive drive or because he is motivated to be aggressive as such. He is angry because he feels threatened in his self-preservation and survival (Schmidt-Hellerau 2002, pp. 1280-1282), or because he feels defeated in his loving and sexual demands, and he therefore *intensifies his efforts to get through to me*— because the announcement of my vacation has already distanced me in his mind. What I would interpret to this patient and would want him to know is not only that he is aggressive (i.e., he has hostile fantasies)—often, the patient will know this quite well—but also that he feels so threatened in his safety, or challenged in his love, by my leaving that he wants to fight off this danger. With this interpretation, I show him that I am still with him, that I heard him, that he (his fear, his love) has reached me.

As is well known, the energy term for the sexual drive is *libido*; and all the investments along this line are called *libidinal*—thus, we assume that we create internally what we call a *libidinal object*.[10] Freud's incapacity to

---

[10] It is worthwhile noting that the term object is not limited to the real person out there. The representation of this person, the object representation, is a structure of our minds that can be the object of drive activity, e.g., when we think of or fantasize about a person. Green (1999) emphasizes this capacity of "transforming structures into an object" as the "objectalizing function" of the life drive (p. 85).

find a suitable and convincing energy term for his self-preservative drive probably contributed to his eventually forgetting about it altogether, once he had subsumed it under the heading of Eros. In order to close this conceptual gap, I have suggested *lethe* as the long-missing energy term for the concept of a preservative drive (Schmidt-Hellerau 1997, 2005a). *Lethe* is a term borrowed from Greek mythology, meaning *forgetting*; thus, it fits the comparatively more inward-directed, silent, digestive, and quieting tendencies that I would assign to the functions of the preservative drive. This energy term enables us to call investments that predominantly originate from the preservative drive *lethic investments* and its objects *lethic objects*.

Differentiating between libidinal and lethic investments allows us to more clearly recognize whether the patient is relating to the analyst in the transference as an early caretaker or as an infantile love object. For instance, in the case of Amy, discussed above, we might ask: Do the patient's associations show a predilection for more *libidinal* or more *lethic* issues? Does Amy show a conflict between, or an unconscious confusion in, her object relations; that is, is her husband/analyst viewed as a *libidinal* or love object, or rather as a *lethic* or preservative object— that is, a nurturing object, or an object to be nurtured? In short, are her conflicts or confusions related to *love* or *care?* This example highlights the fact that to call all relatedness *libidinal* blurs the distinction between *preservative needs* and *erotic desires*.

Self and Object—with or without Drives

The relation to the object is central to psychoanalytic thinking. For Freud (1915a), it is the object "through which the drive is able to achieve its aim" (p. 122). The object may change, and the same object may serve "several drives simultaneously" (p. 123), yet without an object, there is no satisfaction. Thus, the infant is related to the object via his/her drives—an assumption that makes Freud's drive theory basically an object relations theory.

The paradigmatic situation to describe the onset of this relationship is that of the *hungry baby*. This situation provides a detailed model of how Freud envisioned structural development in general, and the emergence of *self* and *object* in particular (Freud 1895, 1900, 1911), and how drives and structures interact. The general scheme says that when the infant is hungry (when a self-preservative drive stirs up a need for food), he/she screams and kicks, mother comes, understands the baby's needs, feeding takes place, and the hunger subsides—satisfaction is achieved, and the baby is, as it were, "safe". According to Freud, the repetition of this same course of events leads to a *memory trace* within which all the essential elements of this experience are associated: the (partial) *drive* stimulus (hunger), the *perception* of the need-satisfying object (mother), and the specifics of the *motoric* action (screaming, sucking, burping). *A first mental structure has been formed.*[11]

> As a result of this link that has thus been established, next time this need arises a psychical impulse will at once emerge which will seek to re-cathect the mnemic image of the perception and to re-evoke the perception itself, that is to say, to re-establish the situation of the original satisfaction. An impulse of this kind is what we call a wish. [Freud 1900, p. 565]

From then on, the drives will be capable of activating representations of the emerging self with object, thus eliciting *the wish to be with the object.* It is an impressive though often discounted fact that most ideas on structure formation and the emergence of self and object representations, including a number of contemporary contributions, make use of

---

[11] The first representations of self and object can be conceptualized as being more physical, or at least psychophysiological, since self and object are not yet clearly differentiated (Jacobson 1964, p. 40). Milrod (2002) states: "The development of the self representation resembles that of the object representation. Both arise simultaneously as islands of awareness that appear with distress and vanish with satisfaction. Anything which makes the infant aware of the outer world or non-self, makes him simultaneously aware of aspects of the self" (p. 12). Further, we can focus on the affective shift between distress and satisfaction, and call this a unit of "self and object representation (and the affectd dispositions linking them)" (Kernberg 1980, p. 17).

this very same example, which Freud outlined in his "Project" (1895) and in the seventh chapter of *The Interpretation of Dreams* (1900). This proves that what Freud conceptualized as a drive activity is by no means regarded as irrelevant. For example, Lichtenberg (2003) envisions the emergence of the neonate's "sense of self" as triggered by the infant's "internally derived needs" (p. 499), namely, hunger and the mother's feeding response. He relates the emergence of the sense of self to the same experience stimulated by hunger; but he does not conceptualize this as drive activity, that is, as part of a self-preservative drive (hunger), calling it instead a *need*.

In fact, *need* seems much closer to our psychic experience, and Freud (1915a) actually once thought that it might be a "better term for a drive stimulus" (p. 118). So why didn't he, or why shouldn't we, definitively replace the "old-fashioned" notion of *drive* with *need?* I think that a risk of doing so lies in what language insinuates: the term *need* evokes the idea of an individual as a *passive recipient*, as someone whose needs have to be met by the object, while the notion of *drives* focuses on the sub-ject's *active* side, his or her being *driven* to cry out and to *go for* what he/she needs—part of man's ceaseless *strivings*, his/her part of the game, his/ her contributions to life and neurosis. As both notions address important yet different aspects, I would suggest keeping *drive* as the general notion, using *need* for the preservative, and *desire* for the sexual strivings. The term *drive* would thus address the two basic movements toward the satisfying object, while *need* and *desire* would specify the character and function of those strivings.

Fonagy et al. (2003) hold on to the active side of man. Their notion of the *self as agent* acknowledges agency—yet drives are not part of their vocabulary. Fonagy et al.'s *agentive self* is very different from what we understand by a *driven self*, since the latter includes not only a more primitive state of mind (with an ongoing impact on adult mental func-tioning), but also—most important in psychoanalysis—the unconscious side of man's being driven. Fonagy et al. suggest that "sometime during their second year, infants develop an *understanding of agency* that is already mentalistic: they start to understand that they are *intentional agents whose actions are caused by prior states of mind, such as desires*"

(p. 421, italics added). Such an "understanding of agency" implies self-reflection, the awareness of a succession between "prior states of mind, such as desires" (which traditionally are ascribed to the sexual drives) and their translation into subsequent "intentional" acts.

Thus, the *self as agent* is to a large extent a conscious configuration, a structure within the ego. By contrast, a *driven self* is a self that is, indeed, driven—e.g., by hunger or sex—regardless of whether or not this self can already act specifically and successfully on this need/desire (the maturity aspect), and whether it knows about its being driven or not (the aspect of unconscious mental activity). *Driven self* speaks to a self as a structure within the id, superego, or ego that is activated and then *urges* man to *act* in some way.

I find Fonagy et al.'s minute elaboration of developmental steps, and, in particular, their concept of mentalization (Fonagy et al. 2002), very instructive—and in fact easily compatible with drive theory. Without the psychoanalytic concept of drives, however, their theory would risk losing its focus on and access to the dynamic unconscious processes that are unique to the psychoanalytic approach to mental life.[12]

I think that one important explanation for the widespread dissatisfaction with drive theory among analysts in the United States is that it is part of the (indirect) response to Freud's unfortunate decision to drop his notion of the self-preservative drive by merging it with Eros when he introduced aggression as a new primal drive in 1920. To construe all the infant's and adult's daily activities and interactions as the expression of

---

[12] From a structural point of view, Smith (2005a) correctly emphasizes the importance of agency in our model of the mind: "If the desire for care and the excitement of sex can be collapsed so directly into a conflict between drives, might it be more difficult to find the patient's agency in the creation of his or her own experience?" (p. 345). Smith (2005b) sees compromise formation as made up of competing wishes, defenses, self-punishments, and painful affect, all negotiated by the person as agent. However, if we view agency as the ego's capacity to negotiate between the demands from the id, the superego, and the outside world, we then see the ego (a structure) as the locus of compromise formation; from this standpoint, drive theory tells us only with what energy these macrostructures work and what they have to negotiate in a particular moment, and it does not tell us about the capacity of the ego to exercise agency (choices, decision making, and so on).

an aggressive or sexual drive or their conflicts felt artificial, odd, or unconvincing. I wonder how psychoanalysis would have developed if Freud had stayed with and further explored his first self-preservative drive?

We can understand much of an infant's needs and a lot of our daily activities and interactions as being basically *preservative*: not only are we driven to preserve ourselves, we are also driven to preserve our objects (Schmidt-Hellerau 2005a). Greenberg and Mitchell (1983) emphasize this very point (even though not as a drive activity) in reference to the early work of Sullivan:

> The expression by the infant of his need calls out a reciprocal and complementary need impelling the caretaker to care for the infant's needs. The cry of the hungry baby arouses a tender feeling in the mother, accompanying the physical engorgement of the breasts with milk. *The baby needs to be fed; the mother needs to nurse.* [p. 92, italics added]

Sullivan and Fairbairn—at the foundation of contemporary relational psychoanalysis—declared classical drive theory to be wrong and instead shifted the emphasis to the object. While I would agree that the need is on both sides, baby's and mother's, I would disagree that our interest in object relations requires us to obliterate drive theory. In fact, there was a lingering sense in those who early on opposed Freud's drive theory that psychoanalysis does not work without it. Despite decisively criticizing the notion of *libido*, Fairbairn retained it as part of his thinking, and Greenberg (1991)—even though reluctantly—holds on to the notion of *drive*, suggesting two new drives, a *safety drive* and an *effectance drive*. Speculating that Freud was not interested in his self-preservative drive because it was "too peremptory" (p. 104), Greenberg seems to encompass similar territory with his *safety drive*. Yet, in defining his drives as purely *psychological* and emphasizing that "the somatic is external to the mind" (p. 117), Greenberg chooses to abandon Freud's "somatic strategy," arguing that "for a somatic stimulus to be a stimulus it must first be the object of experience"; it must be "interpreted by a mind whose purpose is to interpret sensory data" (p. 117).

I would wonder what this "interpreter" is made of and how it developed the the knowledge and capacity to interpret the body and its sensory data or its demands. However, more than about these theoretical or philosophical questions. I would be concerned about splitting the psyche off from the somatic (Greenberg 1991, p. 117); such a declaration might lead to an illusion about the mind's freedom and independence from basic physiological processes, thus considerably limiting our perspective on the whole range of preservative and sexual issues that emerge from the body's demands and that are part of our psychic fabric. According to the tree metaphor mentioned earlier, this view would turn the drive into a tree without roots.

In the end, though, Greenberg's notion of drive as a "directedness that governs human behavior" (p. 118) does not look as dissimilar from Freud's view as he suggests. While not wanting to blur the differences between the conceptualizations mentioned above and classical drive theory, I find it intriguing that in one way or the other, the former all contain and preserve what the latter is about, thus strongly indicating that the *drive is not dead*; on the contrary, *the drive lives on*.

Freud defined the drives as a border concept between the biological and the psychological, and he built his model of the mind with just these two concepts, drive and structure, stating that drives activate ideas in order to effectively reach their aims. It follows that our ideas are merely the expressions of our drives (Freud 1910). This is actually quite a radical statement; it says that our bodily requirements are always part of the game, and whenever *any* idea pops up on the mind's inner screen, we can assume that a drive activated it. All psychic processes, the endless chain of our thoughts, associations, and feelings, express the dynamic movements between our various partial drives as represented by the structures they energize. To highlight this point, I should note that this conception implies that *the drives are the only energizers of mental structures and functions—and, therefore, they are indispensable.*

From here, it seems possible to respond in a heuristically fruitful way to a crucial question that we cannot avoid in any model of how the mind works: Why is *this* structure (fantasy, memory trace, representation), in this specific moment, activated—or created—and not any other? And why does it lead to *this* next association—and not to any other? I think the only conclusive way to conceptualize and explain the specificity of *what comes to mind*, and the specific, consecutive, dynamic movement within our thought processes, is to note that *these ideas want to get us somewhere*; they express an ongoing drive activity. We often do not know at first what a specific drive activity is aiming for. It activates ideas in displacements, condensations, and other roundabout ways, including the whole range of defenses that interfere with the specifics of the dynamics between primary and secondary thought processes (Freud 1915b). Most often, the drive activity involves a slow sort of dreamlike elaboration of its final goal. However, without these strivings, without this dynamic interaction between the two basic antagonistic drives that create the psychic processes, we would be stuck with one idea and not get any further.

Also, the fact that an object representation—e.g., "Daddy"—is activated does not tell us what that particular representation means in this moment. "Daddy" might represent either a (lethic) wish for protection or a (libidinal) wish for love—to mention just two basic possibilities. Only if and when we refer back to the seemingly major ongoing drive activity is its specific meaning revealed. (We are usually not aware that this is what we are doing, metapsychologically speaking, when we try to understand what the patient's material *is all about*.) It follows, then, that in order to know what we want, what we need or desire, we have to have "thoughts" with which to represent it. And in order to understand what these thoughts and ideas *mean*, we have to learn about the specific drive activities that stirred them up.

I would say that, *from birth to death, we are driven*. At the beginning of life, there is no "knowledge" about the "what for" of our drives' aims, and, later on, we do not realize that these many "whats" we have come to know about are what we are "driven to." *Yet at every instant, we are where our drives take us.*

"Where am I?" my patient Amy wonders, lying on the couch. "It's funny—I just saw myself in the kitchen, pulling the rack of lamb out of the oven. I was so excited! It looked perfect and it smelled delicious. My heart was beating when I made the first cut. And I had this thought: I wished that *you* could see it; I wished you would have dinner with me tonight."

Concluding Remarks

It is interesting to note that, amongst all metapsychological concepts, it is Freud's drive theory that has been most fiercely disputed. I wonder whether the rejection of drive theory indicates that we are still wrestling with the second (biological) and the third (psychological) of the big blows to human narcissism that Freud (1917) pointed out so clearly. We seem to be still reluctant to learn Darwin's lesson—that "man is not a being different from animals," but is an "animal descent" (Freud 1917, p. 141)—actually, a mutation of the monkey. This reluctance became apparent in June 2000, when Craig Venter and Francis Collins's announcement that the human genome is 98.4 percent identical with the chimpanzee's genome produced worldwide amazement. Of course, it is hard to think of ourselves as being driven in the same way that a monkey is. However, to obliterate drive theory from our psychoanalytic thinking seems to send us back to a period *before* Darwin. If 98.4 percent of our human genome propels a potential in mankind to act like a beast, then we need to learn as much as we can about this aspect of our motivations, which requires acknowledgment of our drives as rooted in the body in the first place.

It is no doubt clear that I strongly advocate staying in touch with and building on our classical psychoanalytic model of the mind, based on Freud's metapsychology of *drive* and *structure*, elaborated since his time in many valuable contributions. While modern research has provided a lot of new data about structure formation that we can integrate into our thinking, I find that an open interest in what seems to me so specific for psychoanalysis—the drives' impact on structure—is missing from our discourse. I believe that our understanding of drive activity is most vital and essential for understanding dynamic processes in psychoanalysis. A psychoanalytic model of the mind without drives is like a house without people who live in it, who use and invest in its equipment in a specifically meaningful way. Without the concept of drives, it seems to me, our psychoanalytic understanding goes rather flat; it loses its depth, its connection to unconscious strivings and fantasies and to vital bodily needs, its dynamics, and its directedness. Therefore, I propose to turn our attention to modern drive theory, with its antagonism based on preservative and sexual drives, and to restart psychoanalytic research in this fascinating area of mental life.

Also, it is worth noting that, while many analysts seem to be uncomfortable with the supposedly old-fashioned notion of *drive*, modern neuroscience has no problem in employing it. See, for example, the following excerpt from a book entitled *Principles of Neural Science*:

> The issues that surround drive states relate to survival. Activities that enhance immediate survival, such as eating or drinking, or those that ensure long-term survival, such as sexual behavior or caring for offspring, are pleasurable and there is a great natural urge to repeat these behaviors. Drive states steer behavior towards specific positive goals and away from negative ones. In addition, drive states require organization of individual behaviors into a goal-oriented sequence. Attainment of the goal decreases the intensity of the drive state and thus the motivated behavior ceases. A hungry cat is ever alert for the occasional mouse, ready to pounce when it comes into sight. Once satiated, the cat will not pounce again for some time. Finally, drive states have general effects; they increase our general level of arousal and thereby enhance our ability to act.
>
> Drive states therefore serve three functions: they direct behavior toward or away from a specific goal; they organize individual behaviors into a coherent, goal-oriented sequence; and they increase general alertness, energizing the individual to act. [Kupfermann, Kandel, and Iversen 2000, p. 999]

If we consider psychoanalytic drive theory as I have outlined it in this article—that is, with self and object preservation as well as sexuality as primal drives—then it is striking how much commonality we find between neuroscientific principles, as outlined above, and psychoanalytic drive theory. Therefore, I want to encourage a new interest in our metapsychological model of psychic functioning. The harsh repulsion of metapsychology has deprived many of its adherents of a uniquely elaborated conception of psychic processes, one that Kandel (1999)—despite all criticism—calls "the most coherent and intellectually satisfying view of the mind" (p. 505). Its foundations were laid more than one hundred years ago, and they have been elaborately developed and expanded ever since—yet there still remains a lot to be discovered.

References

Applegarth, A. (1971). Comments on aspects of the theory of psychic energy. *J. Amer. Psychoanal. Assn.*, 19: 379-416.

Brenner, C. (1982). *The Mind in Conflict.* Madison, CT: Int. Univ. Press.

Busch, F. & Schmidt-Hellerau, C. (2004). How can we know what we need to know? Reflections on clinical judgment formation. *J. Amer. Psychoanal. Assn.*, 52: 689-707.

Fonagy, P., Gergely, G., Jurist, E. L. & Target, M. (2002). *Affect Regulation, Mentalization, and the Development of the Self.* New York: Other Press.

Fonagy, P., Target, M., Gergely, G., Allen, J. G. & Bateman, A. W. (2003). The developmental roots of borderline personality disorder in early attachment relationships: a theory and some evidence. *Psychoanal. Inq.*, 23: 412-459.

Freud, S. (1895). A project for a scientific psychology. *Standard Edition*, 1.

Freud, S. (1900). The interpretation of dreams. *Standard Edition*, 4/5.

Freud, S. (1905). Three essays on the theory of sexuality. *Standard Edition*, 7.

Freud, S. (1908). On the sexual theories of children. *Standard Edition*, 9.

Freud, S. (1910). The psycho-analytic view of psychogenic disturbance of vision. *Standard Edition*, 11.

Freud, S. (1911). Formulations on the two principles of mental functioning. *Standard Edition*, 12.

Freud, S. (1915a). Instincts and their vicissitudes. *Standard Edition*, 14.

Freud, S. (1915b). The unconscious. *Standard Edition*, 14.

Freud, S. (1917). A difficulty in psycho-analysis. *Standard Edition*, 17.

Freud, S. (1920). Beyond the pleasure principle. *Standard Edition*, 18.

Freud, S. (1925). The resistances to psycho-analysis. *Standard Edition*, 19.

Gill, M. M. (1976). Metapsychology is not psychology. In *Psychology Versus Metapsychology: Psychoanalytic Essays in Memory of George S. Klein*, ed. M. Gill & P. S. Holzman. New York: Int. Univ. Press, pp. 71-105.

Gill, M. M. (1977). Psychic energy reconsidered: discussion. *J. Amer. Psychoanal. Assn.*, 25: 581-597.

Green, A. (1995). Has sexuality anything to do with psychoanalysis? *Int. J. Psycho-Anal.*, 76: 871-883.

Green, A. (1999). *The Work of the Negative*. London: Free Assn. Books.

Greenberg, J. (1991). *Oedipus and Beyond: A Clinical Theory*. Cambridge, MA: Harvard Univ. Press.

Greenberg, J. R. & Mitchell, S. A. (1983). *Object Relations in Psychoanalytic Theory*. Cambridge, MA: Harvard Univ. Press.

Holt, R. (1976). Drive or wish? A reconsideration of the psychoanalytic theory of motivation. In *Psychology Versus Metapsychology: Psychoanalytic Essays in Memory of George S. Klein*, ed. M. Gill & P. S. Holzman. New York: Int. Univ. Press, pp. 158-197.

Holt, R. (1985). The current status of psychoanalytic theory. *Psychoanal. Psychol.*, 2: 289-315.

Jacobson, E. (1964). *The Self and the Object World*. New York: Int. Univ. Press.

Kandel, E. R. (1999). Biology and the future of psychoanalysis: a new intellectual framework for psychiatry revisited. *Am. J. Psychiatry*, 156: 505-524.

Kernberg, O. F. (1980). *Internal World and External Reality: Object Relations Theory Applied*. London: Mark Paterson, 1985.

Klein, G. S. (1967). Peremptory ideation: structure and force in motivated ideas. In *Motives and Thought: Psychoanalytic Essays in Honor of David Rapaport*, ed R. Holt. New York: Int. Univ. Press, pp. 78-128.

Klein, G. S. (1973). Two theories or one? *Bull. Mennin. Clinic.*, 37: 102-132.

Kupfermann, I., Kandel, E. R. & Iversen, S. (2000). Motivational and addictive states. In *Principles of Neural Science*, ed. E. R. Kandel, J. H. Schwartz & T. M. Jessell. New York: McGraw-Hill.

Laplanche, J. & Pontalis, J.-B. (1967). *The Language of Psycho-Analysis*, trans. D. Nicholson-Smith. London: Hogarth, 1983.

Lichtenberg, J. D. (2003). Communication in infancy. *Psychoanal. Inq.*, 23: 498-520.

Lorenz, K. (1981). *The Foundations of Ethology*. New York: Springer.

Meissner, W. W. (1981). Metapsychology—who needs it? *J. Amer. Psychoanal. Assn.*, 29: 921-938.

Milrod, D. (2002). The concept of the self and the self representation. *Neuro-Psychoanal.*, 4: 7-23.

Modell, A. (1981). Does metapsychology still exist? *Int. J. Psycho-Anal.*, 62: 391-402.

Modell, A. (1990). Some notes on object relations, "classical" theory, and the problem of instincts (drives). *Psychoanal. Inq.*, 10: 182-196.

Opatow, B. (1989). Drive theory and the metapsychology of experience. *Int. J. Psycho-Anal.*, 70: 645-660.

Rosenblatt, A. D. & Thickstun, J. T. (1970). A study of the concept of psychic energy. *Int. J. Psycho-Anal.*, 51: 265-277.

Schmidt-Hellerau, C. (1997). Libido and lethe: fundamentals of a formalised conception of metapsychology. *Int. J. Psycho-Anal.*, 78: 683-697.

Schmidt-Hellerau, C. (2001). *Libido and Lethe. A Formalized Consistent Model of Psychoanalytic Drive and Structure Theory*. New York: Other Press.

Schmidt-Hellerau, C. (2002). Why aggression? Metapsychological, clinical and technical considerations. *Int. J. Psycho-Anal.*, 83: 1269-1289.

Schmidt-Hellerau, C. (2005a). The other side of Oedipus. *Psychoanal. Q.*, 74: 187-217.

Schmidt-Hellerau, C. (2005b). Surviving in absence. On the preservative and death drive: their relation and clinical value with regard to trauma and severe psychopathology. Paper presented at the International Psychoanalytical Association Congress, Rio de Janeiro, Brazil, July 29.

Schmidt-Hellerau, C. (2006). Fighting with spoons: on caretaking rivalry between mothers and daughters. *Psychoanal. Inq.*, 26:32-55.

Smith, H. F. (2003a). Theory and practice: intimate partnership or false connection? *Psychoanal. Q.*, 72: 1-12.

Smith, H. F. (2003b). Conceptions of conflict in psychoanalytic theory and practice. *Psychoanal. Q.*, 72: 49-96.

Smith, H. F. (2005a). Dialogues on conflict: toward an integration of methods. *Psychoanal. Q.*, 74: 327-363.

Smith, H. F. (2005b). Personal communication.

Solms, M. (2005). Personal communication.

Swanson, D. R. (1977). A critique of psychic energy as an explanatory concept. *J. Amer. Psychoanal. Assn.*, 25: 603-633.

Tinbergen, N. (1951). *The Study of Instinct*. Oxford, England: Clarendon.

CHAPTER 6

Surviving in Absence

On the Preservative and Death Drives and their Clinical Utility[*]

This paper offers a new theoretical and clinical look at the death drive in connection with the preservative drive. I elaborate on the problems in Freud's Beyond the Pleasure Principle *(1920) and reformulate the transition between Freud's first drive theory and his second one within an implicit object relations theory. Simultaneously with this revised version of drive theory, I develop a structural theory for the realm of healthy self- and object preservation and for pathological or deadened self and object parts, including the devastating effects of trauma. Clinical material from an extended psychoanalysis shows how these concepts can help us understand these patients' absence and "deadness" and rethink the technical challenges they provide.*

It was many years into the analysis of Sam before I learned something about his early life. Sam had no memories of his childhood. He came to treatment because he was afraid of dropping out of his studies. He could not bring himself to do the things he needed to do. But he said he wanted to improve. In his first session, I tentatively connected two of the thoughts that he shared with me. Sam was interested. However, in our

[*] (2006). Psychoanalytic Quarterly, 75(4):1057-1095.
A shorter version of this paper was first presented on October 21, 2004, at the Finnish Psychoanalytical Society in Helsinki.

second meeting, he fundamentally doubted any value of what he had appreciated earlier. This became a general feature through many years of our analytic work together. There was a *strong negative therapeutic reaction* that threw us back, again and again, whenever we seemed to have gained any bit of new insight or experience of therapeutic progress. It often felt as if we walked one step ahead, followed by one or two steps backward.

For a long time, I knew next to nothing about Sam or his daily life. He talked reluctantly, and his communications were spare at best. Much was missing in what he did tell me. And Sam himself was missing. During the initial period when we worked on a once-a-week basis, Sam often came only to the second half of our session. When, after a year, we increased to twice a week (because he felt he had not made the progress he had hoped for), Sam regularly showed up for only one of these two weekly sessions. Despite this record of absence, we eventually agreed to try analysis, four times a week on the couch.

At that point, Sam brought me his first and only dream for years: *He dreamt he was with someone on a sailing boat, in the middle of the ocean, on his way to America, and there was a total calm, no wind at all, and he had no idea what to do or how to sail.* There were no associations to his dream, except that he thought that the dream made no sense. I associated this dream with our upcoming analytic journey, and I thought he was letting me know what lay ahead.

With the beginning of the analysis, Sam usually came to our four sessions each week, but remained silent for the first half of each. Sometimes he did not show up. However, he always paid for all sessions; this was never an issue. As he fully occupied his space in the analysis (being there or not, talking or not), eventually I took it that, with these absences and silences, he was bringing in a missing, absent, speechless part of his self. His *not being there* was *there*—somewhere in the analysis.

Then Sam stopped talking altogether. He came in on time, lay down, and kept silent till our time was over, when he would get up and leave. In many ways, I tried to get in touch with him. Nothing was successful. Thus, I mostly kept silent, too, feeling that we needed simply to endure, to survive the calm. We were both there, silently framed with four weekly sessions into some kind of still life, while something unshared went on in each of our minds. Yet even though there were only a few sentences or words that Sam spoke to me over a long period of time, I never lost hope: one day we would move forward.

Years later, I am still working with Sam, now in the fifteenth year of his analysis. Much has developed since, and much work remains to be done. Later in this article, I will expand on some difficulties in Sam's analysis and elaborate on how we can think about a specific pathology of mental functioning that we encounter in analyses in which *absence* is a major feature. I have wondered about how absence is represented in the minds of our patients, and what might prevent them from, or interfere with, retrieving the absent.

I want to explore some of these questions mostly by trying to recapture the theoretical and clinical value of two Freudian concepts that have not been present much in our general psychoanalytic discussions: the self-preservative drive and the death drive. I would stress that both concepts are indispensable, both to our understanding of how a human mind works *and* to the work of clinical psychoanalysis—not only with severely disturbed or traumatized patients, but with healthy neurotics as well.

The Consistency Crack in Freud's Drive Theory

In a footnote added in 1924 to his *Three Essays on the Theory of Sexuality* (1905), Freud noted: "The theory of the drives is the most important but at the same time the least complete portion of psychoanalytic theory" (p. 168). This might sound amazing, since only four years earlier, Freud had completely reformulated his drive theory (1920), and on the basis of this revision restructured his model of the mind (1923). Yet his observation was correct and shows—once again—Freud's enormous sensitivity to the logical breaks in his theoretical constructions. The introduction of his second drive theory constitutes a consistency crack in this "most important part" of his psychoanalytic theory, and this had a tremendous impact on how psychoanalysis developed throughout its first century.

I have worked for many years on the resolution of the problems

Freud left us with (Schmidt-Hellerau 1995, 1997, 2001, 2002b, 2003, 2005a, 2005b), because I believe that inconsistency in our model of the mind leads to inconsistencies in our clinical thinking. Our concepts influence our perception and understanding, and if we misconceptualize any part of psychic life, we will misperceive and misunderstand that aspect of a patient's material. Previously, I have reassessed Freud's concepts of aggression (2002b, 2005b) and self-preservation (2005a, 2005b, 2006a); here I want to suggest a solution for a lingering question regarding Freud's drive theory: how can we think about a death drive in relation to a preservative drive?

As I have elaborated elsewhere (Schmidt-Hellerau, 1995, 1997, 2001, 2002a), Freud constructed his model of the mind as a homeostatic (dynamically stable) system by postulating *two antagonistic drives* (first the sexual and self-preservative drives, and later the life and death drives) and *a regulating principle* (that is, principles of inertia, constancy, pleasure, reality, and so on). The drives' antagonistic aspect (opposites like *life* and *death* paralleling those of, e.g., *waking* and *sleeping, yes* and *no*, or *plus* and *minus*) was required as a means by which the regulating principles could maintain and reestablish homeostasis.[1] The regulating principles are situated in the structures of the mental apparatus; they vary, being modified through learning and adaptation, and they determine in each case what constitutes homeostasis at a certain level and point of time.[2]

---

[1] Freud's first description of how the mental apparatus maintains its equilibrium relied on a reflex model of discharge: an increase of any excitation leads the system to an immediate discharge (decrease) of this surplus. Yet, already in the "Project for a Scientific Psychology" (1950), written in 1895, he outlined a much more sophisticated version of this basic idea: that is that, in order to protect itself from over-excitation, the mental apparatus builds up structures whose long-term cathexis with energy (storage) allows for a regulation in which an increase on the plus side will be balanced by an activation on the minus side (Schmidt-Hellerau 1995). Examples are the pair of drive and repression, and Freud's understanding of the symptom (combining wish and defense) or the compromise formation—his whole idea of psychic conflict being based on the opposition between two primal antagonistic drives and their derivatives (Freud 1910, pp. 213ff.).

[2] Homeostasis does not require a 1:1 or 50:50 ratio. For instance, the newborn organism is balanced by an approximate ratio of 1:2 in sleeping and waking time, while the adult's

Freud (1915) defined the drive as departing from "sources of stimulation within the organism," and as exercising a "constant force" (p. 119), a pressure toward the object through which the aim —satisfaction—is reached. It is worth noting that *source, pressure, object*, and *aim* are all part of his elaborate conception of drive.

Freud had no problem with pointing out the sexual drive's sources, the *erotogenic zones* (mouth, anus, genitals, skin, eyes). However, he never came up with the sources of a self-preservative drive. According to the general definition of a source as "the somatic process which occurs in an organ or part of the body and whose stimulus is represented in mental life by a drive" (Freud 1915, p. 123), I have suggested appointing the inner organs (stomach, abdomen, lungs, bladder, etc.) as the *biogenic zones* of a self-preservative drive—eliciting the urge to eat, drink, breathe, urinate, defecate, sleep, etc. (Schmidt-Hellerau 1995, 2001). Thus, Freud's idea—that the drive originates in bodily stimuli and strives, dart like and virtually endlessly, until it meets the object of satisfaction—is generally applicable to both the sexual and self-preservative drives.

In 1920, Freud fundamentally changed this conception of drive by confusing the functions of drive and structure. Following are the eight flaws in his argument, as I see them:

1. In considering his clinical experience with patients who repeat *unpleasurable* experiences, Freud wondered if these phenomena point to something *beyond* the pleasure principle—thereby confusing the *feeling of unpleasure* with the *function* of the *pleasure principle*. However, according to all his previous definitions, the pleasure principle functions as a method to maintain a balanced state, and a neurotic state that *feels* unpleasurable (e.g., something like an attachment to *painful feelings* [Valenstein 1973]) *is* nevertheless a *familiar, hence balanced state*, thus within—and not beyond—the pleasure principle.

---

life is balanced by the reverse: sixteen hours of waking time and eight hours of sleep. What changes over a lifetime (and through psychoanalysis) is the homeostatic value (ratio) in the structures; what does not change is the activity of our drives, our basic urges (pressure), our being driven to fall asleep or to wake up.

2. The fact that the patient's unpleasurable experiences are endlessly repeated led Freud to postulate a *compulsion to repeat* that he then erroneously assigned to the drives. This was a misconception, because what Freud observed in his patients and what he described as *repeated* was not just a single drive activity. Rather, it represents the whole process of pressure and repression—the whole specific transferential reproduction of scenes, relational configurations, and so forth (Schmidt-Hellerau 2001, pp. 179ff.)—and thus the *regulation* of a complex psychic process.

    The complexity of what is repeated demonstrates that the *compulsion to repeat* is a *structural phenomenon;* it describes the function of the regulating principles in the structures that activate particular drive-excitations for the cathexes or anticathexes of certain representations, in an effort to maintain a previously (within the structures) established equilibrium.

3. This error is important because Freud assigned the compulsion to repeat, in particular, to the first primal drive (the death drive), and in the wake of this, he rewrote his general definition of the drives:

    > It seems, then, that a drive is an urge inherent in organic life to restore an earlier state of things which the living entity has been obliged to abandon under the pressure of external disturbing forces; that is, it is a kind of organic elasticity, or, to put it another way, the expression of the inertia inherent in organic life. [Freud 1920, p. 36, italics in original]

    Freud was right: the restoration of an earlier state of things is the function of the *inertia principle*, that is, a function of the structure. Memory of any "earlier state of things" lies in the structures of the mind and is not a quality of the drives. To define a drive as "an urge ... to restore an earlier state of things" casts it as a mysterious, intelligent entity (homunculus) that remembers what was. Instead, I would retain Freud's first definition, in which a drive links man's bodily needs to external objects, and can do nothing but *drive* until satisfaction is reached.[3]

    ---

    [3] This definition (based on Freud's 1915 essay) is scientifically clear and accessible for

From his new general definition of drives—which struck Freud himself as "strange" (1920, p. 36)—Freud concluded that, earlier than life, there was death; and, therefore, the first drive to restore an earlier state of things would be a death drive; and, consequently, the required antagonist needed to be called a life drive. This is an intriguing thought, and despite the crooked ways in which Freud got there, I am far from dismissive of this revised notion. On the contrary, I think that, with this step, Freud extended his grasp on the drives in a remarkable (though still obscure) way that I will try to illuminate later. But first I will continue briefly summarizing my critique of Freud's elaboration of the death drive.

4. In integrating his first into his second drive theory, Freud saw no problem with the sexual drives. He concluded: "They are the true life drives" (1920, p. 40). However, in trying to lump together his previous conception of the self-preservative drive (or ego drive) with the newly created death drive, he felt puzzled:

    > Seen in this light, the theoretical importance of the self-preservative drives … diminishes. They are component drives [of the death drive] whose function it is to assure that the organism shall follow its own path to death, and to ward off any possible ways of returning to inorganic existence other than those which are immanent in the organism itself. [1920, p. 39]

    This is an interesting statement, leaving enormous room for self-preservative activities within the general limits of genetic determination. However, to Freud, a self-preservative drive seemed to oppose, rather than to be on the same trajectory with, a death drive. Thus, he quickly dropped this possibility:

    > We were prepared at one stage [see Freud 1920, p. 39] to include the so-called self-preservative drives of the ego among the death drives; but we subsequently [p. 52] corrected ourselves on this point and withdrew it. [1920, p. 53]

---

neuropsychoanalytic investigation, but his 1920 revision loses this necessary stringency and is, in a phylogenetic sense, vaguely metaphorical.

At this point, Freud dissolved and mingled "the original opposition" between his sexual and self-preservative drives, now stressing "the libidinal character of the self-preservative drives" and calling Eros "the preserver of all things" (1920, p. 52). This then eased his way toward declaring the self-preservative drives as part of the life drives, an attribution that seemed all too obvious. Yet by subsuming both the self-preservative *and* the sexual drive under the umbrella of his life drive (Eros), Freud abandoned his first drive antagonism, which was basic to twenty-five years of theory development. This step should have concerned him with regard to its possible implications for his model of the mind. Yet instead, Freud struggled to determine what the characteristics of his newly created death drive might be.

5. As is well known, Freud spoke to this issue by seizing on the idea that *aggression* and *destruction* as found in *sadism* provided a representative of the death drive:

    > We started out from the great opposition between the life and death drives. Now object love itself presents us with a second example of a similar polarity—that between love (or affection) and hate (or aggressiveness). If only we could succeed in relating these two polarities to each other and in deriving one from the other! From the very first we recognized the presence nce of a sadistic component in the sexual drive …. But how can the sadistic instinct, whose aim it is to injure the object, be derived from Eros, the preserver of life? Is it not plausible to suppose that this sadism is in fact a death drive, which under the influence of the narcissistic libido, has been forced away from the ego and has consequently only emerged in relation to the object? [1920, pp. 53ff]

    Freud exemplified his death drive with the help of the sexual drive (part of the life drive) by pointing to its sadistic component. He succeeded in finding the death drive's representative as *derived from the life drive*, which is exactly why it is *not*—as required for any antagonism—*an independent variable from the death drive*. Furthermore, sadism as a component of sexuality or as a sexual perversion does not aim "to injure the object"; rather, it aims at giving and finding sexual pleasure by means of hurting.

And, finally, Freud (1940) did not stay with a unidirectional definition—something like *the death drive wants to die and the life drive wants to live;* instead, he stated that the death drive wants "to lead what is living into an inorganic state" (p. 148).[4] This conveys something like: *the death drive wants the life drive not to live*—thus forming a defense against the life drive, and a defense against a drive requires the involvement of a structure with its regulating measures. This is how Freud came to call his new drive a "drive of death, or destruction," a "destroying drive," or a "destructive drive" (1924, p. 163), and, finally, "a special, independent aggressive drive" (1930, p. 117).

6. It goes without saying that aggression is an important phenomenon in human behavior and mental life, and Freud had long recognized this. Yet its place in his model of the mind shifted over the years from being a component of the sexual drives (1905), to being a capacity of both drives (1909), to originating in the self-preservative drives (1915). It was not until 1920 that Freud—struggling to find a representative for his newly created death drive—shifted aggression or destruction into the position of a primal drive.

    Many contemporary analysts rejected the idea of a death drive, but all embraced the same concept as an *aggressive* or *destructive drive.* Here is the problem that I have with this choice: Freud's original drives of self-preservation and sexuality comprised an antagonism of inward directedness (just as, e.g., the paradigm example, hunger, is characterized by an urge to take in, to swallow, to incorporate—or, more generally, just as the physiological needs of self-preservation are concerned with what goes on inside the body,

---

[4] Experientially, the wish to die (an expression of the death drive) is not necessarily related to destruction. There are numerous stories of old people who, after having lived a long and fulfilled life, and even though in full health, develop a wish to die and then pass away peacefully.

the self) and outward directedness (as the sexual desires focus first on the genitals at the periphery of the subject's body, and only later on the *other*, the sexual object out there). Also, physiologically normal self-preservative activities tend toward calmer states: a slowing down (as in digestive processes or in sleep, during which the immunological system—literally, a system of self-preservation—is most active). On the other hand, normal sexual activities go along with higher alertness, excitement, a speeding up.

Since all life events and mental activities are thought of as driven and infused by both primal drives in varying proportions, Freud's first antagonism allowed for a basically endless variety of nuanced mental states, balanced by a structure that regulates the ratio of plus drive energy (*+energy*) and minus-drive energy (*−energy*), according to a task-related increase and decrease of excitation.

I doubt that this homeostatic regulation is possible with aggression and sexuality as the two primal drives. Aggression, defined as intending to harm, humiliate, or constrain others via violent, destructive motor action (Laplanche and Pontalis 1973, p. 17), is usually thought of as outwardly directed (as is the sexual drive) and as including an increase of excitation (as is the sexual drive). How important this point was for Freud is indicated by his decision to define the death drive or aggressive drive as originally directed inward (as in primary masochism), and only secondarily, with the help of narcissistic libido, can it be turned outward. Thus, he hoped to maintain the idea of a primal antagonism.

Nevertheless, Freud (1940) ended up suggesting two drives that would actually supply *+energy* when he put forth the idea that a "surplus of sexual aggressiveness will turn a lover into a sex-murderer, while a sharp diminution in the aggressive factor will make him bashful or impotent" (p. 149). Simple math shows that here aggression has an increasing, not a decreasing, effect: sexual +energy and aggressive +energy make for a murderer, whereas the lack of aggressive +energy leads to impotency. My point is that, when we stick with aggression as the primal antagonist to Eros, we end up with two drives that provide +energy—which calls into

question the dynamic stability of the system, the homeostatic construction of Freud's model of the mind.

7. Having characterized the death drive as an aggressive, destructive
    drive led Freud (1940) to another hypothesis: that the aim of the life
    drive (Eros) is "to establish ever greater unities and to preserve
    them thus—in short, to bind together; the aim of the second is, on
    the contrary, to undo connections and so to destroy things" (p. 148).
    However, to view *binding* and *unbinding* as properties of the drives
    is again a confusion of the functions of drive and structure.

    In my view, a consistent use of these concepts restricts the drives
    to *driving*, that is, to simply supplying energy to those structures
    that they cathect. It is the function of the structures to *bind* or *un-
    bind*, as well as to *fuse* or *defuse* both drives. It is because of the
    binding function of the structures (and the representations:
    memory traces, ideas, fantasies they carry) that we never experience
    a *single* drive activity, but rather mixtures of them—a momentary or
    enduring balance of the two antagonistic drives.

8. Further, Freud (1940) was unable to designate the death drive's
    sources or its energy term: "We are without a term analogous to 'li-
    bido' for describing the energy of the destructive drive" (p. 149). I
    think the lack of a source and energy term was not accidental; it
    spoke to the consistency crack in Freud's drive theory, which he
    acknowledged in 1924, when he called it "the least complete portion
    of psychoanalytic theory" (see Freud 1905, p. 168). His big change
    of 1920 had installed a new primal drive-antagonism that made
    sexuality and aggression the two basic motivations in the minds of
    generations of analysts to come—and even though we have learned
    a lot in working with these concepts, I believe we can invigorate our
    theoretical and clinical thinking by a reexamination of what was
    once thought to have been set in stone.

I suggest that we stay with the *primal antagonism* of the life drive and
death drive. I do not consider the death drive per se as an aggressive

drive, nor do I think of aggression as a primal drive. As I have elaborated elsewhere (see Schmidt-Hellerau 2002b and 2005b, pp. 1012-1017), I conceptualize aggression as the expression of the intensity of drive energy that is marshaled in order to regulate or overcome the distance to the object of satisfaction.[5]

The Preservative Drive as Part of the Death Drive

In order to rethink the integration of Freud's first into his second drive theory, let us depart from his 1920 notions of *life drive* and *death drive*. Let us not be distracted by what *life* and *death* might mean, but rather focus on their antagonism, their plus and minus directions. This allows us to understand the concept of drive in the sense of a unidirectional force, one that drives virtually endlessly in just one direction. For the newborn, then, everything is a matter of life and death. *Sexuality and self-preservation are introduced only by the intervention of the loving and caring object.*[6]

---

[5] The rationale here is that the psychic apparatus has to muster as much drive energy as is necessary to reach its goal. The goal is always at some distance from the subject—distance in geometrical, but also in psychological, terms: it makes a difference whether the object seems to be psychically absent or present, whether it seems to withdraw or to approach. Thus, the intensity of drive energy corresponds to the anticipated and/or perceived psychogeometrical distance to an object. If the anticipation is correct, aggression will not occur unless necessary (self-defense). However, if there is a distortion in the mental representation of the location of the object in relation to the subject, then it feels to the subject as though, e.g., the sexual or preservative object is too far away and thus unavailable, or too close and thus threatening. It follows that the distance to a drive's object *as it is represented in the mind* will be an important factor in understanding why aggression comes up in general—and (as we will see) why the death drive in particular has been understood as an aggressive drive.

[6] Green (1986, 1999) has suggested a similar idea with regard to the drives in general (even though he held onto the autodestructive function of the death drive and did not discuss a relationship between the death and self-preservative drives). He stated: "Even if drives are considered as basic, first entities, that is to say, primary, we nevertheless must assume that the object reveals the drives. It does not create them—and no doubt it can be said that it is at least partly created by them—but it is the condition for their coming into existence" (1999, pp. 84ff.).

How can we understand this? When the baby is hungry, he/ she might experience a catastrophic feeling, a nameless dread (Bion 1965), a dangerous tension of the whole system, a terrible pain that makes him/her scream and kick. It is only when the nursing mother *interferes* that these powerful strivings, stirred up by hunger, come to a halt in finding their first object—the breast—and the satisfaction of being nurtured. The intervention of the object *stops*, as it were, this general so-called death (or minus) drive and defines what self-preservation is (at this point)—namely, hunger and thirst and being nurtured, but also being dry, clean, warm, comfortable, safe, and so on.

As Freud (1900, 1911, 1950) and others have shown, and as I have elaborated elsewhere (Schmidt-Hellerau 1995, 1997, 2001), the repeated interventions of the caretaking object build up a memory trace, a *structure* that contains the representation of *the hungry self and the nursing object and the whole interactional sequence that produces satisfaction.* From now on, this structure, the first and still undifferentiated represen-tation of self and object, "cuts" the death drive in half; and only then can this particular drive activity—arising from its sources (the stomach, in this case) and ending first at mother's breast and then in the recathexis of the mental representation of the nursing couple—become what we can actually call a *self-preservative drive.* And, consequently, drive activi-ties that reach *beyond that structure* are what we can now conceptualize as the *death drive* (see Figure 1 below).

FIGURE 1

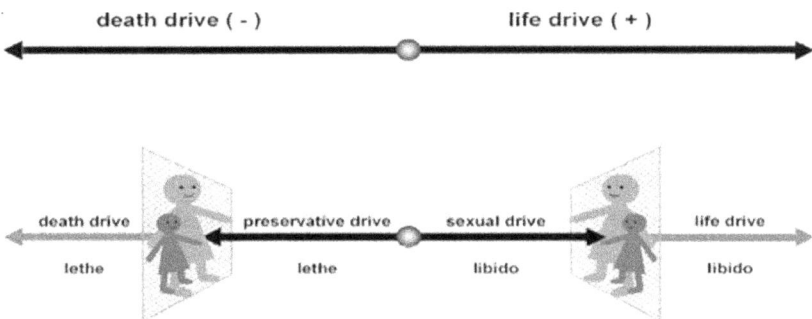

death drive (-)   life drive (+)

death drive   preservative drive   sexual drive   life drive

lethe   lethe   libido   libido

Thus, we can see that Freud's notion of a *self-preservative drive* implied two things that do not make sense:

1. It suggests that this drive more or less "knows," by itself or by some sort of natural endowment, what self-*preservation* is. However, self-preservation is something that needs to be *learned* (even birds teach their offspring how to find and pick up a worm). Although some features of self-preservation and survival are biologically ingrained and thus more basic, reflexive, or spontaneous than others, the way to best preserve ourselves is a capacity that requires quite a bit of mental activity, and needs to be continually considered throughout life (our rich dietary, fitness, and health literature provides ample proof of the complexities of this task).

2. This so-called *self*-preservative drive is not just about our *selves*. Freud (1915) stated that the object "is most variable about a drive and is *not* originally connected with it" (p. 122, italics added). Hence, the self is not the only object; rather, various objects exist for this drive, and that is why we would be better off calling it simply a *preservative drive*. This will help us understand that in the same way that the sexual drive can cathect one's own self (narcissism), as well as one's objects—thus resulting in the experience of self-love and/or object love —the preservative drive can be directed toward the self *or* toward any other object, expressing self and/or object-preservative strivings.[7]

As mentioned above, Freud worked comfortably with the notion of *libido*, designating the energy of the life drive (or Eros), but he never found a suitable energy term for the death and preservative drive—which made it hard to think and speak about the different cathexes and activities of these two drives. This is why I have suggested *lethe* as the

---

[7] That object preservation is something we are literally driven toward is most clearly revealed in the mother's urge to care for her infant, but also in both parents' need to care for and protect their children, and even on occasion to give their lives for them.

energy term of the death and the preservative drive (Schmidt-Hellerau, 1995, 1997, 2001). In Greek mythology, Lethe (*forgetting* in Greek) is the name of the river flowing into the realm of death. The theoretical concept of *lethe* shall indicate some sort of *minus* tendency; it has indispensable health-promoting functions in protecting the system from overexcitation, yet it can also become excessive and then be expressed pathologically (as I will show later). In the list below, I schematically juxtapose some differences between the two.

DEATH-/PRESERVATIVE DRIVE: LETHE	LIFE-/SEXUAL DRIVE: LIBIDO
Biogenic zones (internal organs, e.g., stomach, bladder)	Erotogenic zones (external organs, e.g., mouth, anus, genitals, skin, eyes)
Survival	Intercourse
Hunger	Lust
Digestion, maintenance	Courting, conquering
Excretion of the old, dead	Creation of something new, alive
To console	To charm
Concern	Interest, curiosity
Slowing down	Speeding up
Heavy	Light
To rest	To explore
To sleep	To be awake
Toward the unconscious	Toward consciousness
Introversion-Withdrawal	Extroversion-Reaching out
To be silent	To be talkative
Immobility	Mobility
Care	Love
Sorrow	Joy
Depressive	Manic

It goes without saying that all the above-mentioned tendencies represent complex behavioral patterns and thus composites of both drives—each of them, though, with a predominance of either lethic or libidinal investments, respectively. Now that we have the term *lethe* to describe the energetic force of the preservative and death drive, we might view clinical material somewhat differently. Also, theoretically, it allows us to talk of lethic tendencies, activities, and investments, and of lethic objects—which are primarily nurturing objects or objects to be nurtured—whenever preservative-drive activities are predominant.

The Wooden Reel: Structure

Perhaps the most famous segment of Freud's *Beyond the Pleasure Principle* (1920) is his observation of and reflection on a game that his one-and-a-half-year-old grandson played:

> The child had a wooden reel with a piece of string tied round it. It never occurred to him to pull it along the floor behind him, for instance, and play at its being a carriage. What he did was to hold the reel by the string and very skilfully throw it over the edge of his curtained cot, so that it disappeared into it, at the same time uttering his expressive "o-o-o-o" ["gone"]. He then pulled the reel out of the cot again by the string and hailed its reappearance with a joyful "da" ["there"]. This, then, was the complete game—disappearance and return. As a rule one only witnessed its first act [the throwing away of all sorts of little things] which was repeated untiringly as a game in itself, though there is no doubt that the greater pleasure was attached to the second act. [p. 15]

Freud understood the game as the boy's way of dealing with the (temporary) loss of his mother. He described it not only as a turning-passive-into-active operation, but also as a way of "making what is in itself unpleasurable into a subject to be *recollected* and *worked over* in the mind" (1920, p. 17, italics added).

Even though many have thought and written about the wooden reel game over the years, let us here have another look at this *working over in the mind*. Green (2003) has been particularly interested in how subject and object are related in this game.

What we are dealing with is a double object; in fact, it is doubled twice over. There is the wooden reel and there is the mother. Each of these two objects is duplicated: the wooden reel is both lost and found; and the mother both goes away and returns (fort-da). The object's position in this symbolic organization suggests that it is important, to paraphrase Winnicott on the transitional object, that the wooden reel both is and is not the mother ….

This double and split status of the object may be set alongside a double and split status of the subject. There are two opposing interpretations of the subject here. In the classical interpretation, the subject is the child the child understood as the active pole of the game, as the agent of the game. It is the child who stages the game, throwing the wooden reel away and pulling it back again; it is the child who notices the object's absence or presence; and, finally, it is the child who articulates the different phases of it by uttering the words fort-da …. He plays at making his mother disappear and return, whereas he is played by her, so to speak, in her absence. He only plays to the extent that he is played, however much of a feat he accomplishes in reversing this situation of passivity into activity. [pp. 75ff.]

I think that in this beautiful description, Green captures an important moment of structure building. The question of "who is active and who is passive?" is at this point simultaneously the question of "who is who?" When mother goes and is "lost", the child's (sense of) self goes with her—is pulled away, perhaps as though ripped off by her and lost, too (or else forgotten). Thus, it is essential that the child can come to represent and remember self and object in the absence of their concrete togetherness. The wooden reel, in fact—*by its very shape*—symbolizes both representations, self and object, in their relatedness.

The Wooden Reel: Drive

What Freud and Green did not elaborate in relation to this episode is the specific "outreach" of the drive activity involved. The drive is here symbolized by the piece of string; the length of the string limits the throw, and the reel comes to a halt at the end of the string's maximal stretch. The child must first activate a certain quantity of drive energy (screaming) in order to reach the real object and bring that drive activity to a halt (at the nursing object). In mother's *absence*, the boy's toss of the reel can be understood as an intermediate step, a mental action expressing his need to reach out for the concrete mother-child reunion *and* its mental representation, the capacity to *think it*. The length of the string helps him to get a feeling of *how much energy* he has to put into this throw and how far away the reel will then be—while remaining connected with him. The meaning of this action determines *at what point* (within the mental apparatus) the representation of self and object will be activated and sustained.

It seems to me important to note that our conception of drives applies to the mental apparatus, not to reality. Thus, a drive does not directly cathect any object in the outside world. Drives cathect the *mental object*, the object as it is represented (when it is not there) or as it is represented *and* perceived (when it or its substitute is there). *Thus, it is the anticipated/represented psychogeometrical distance in mental space and time that determines the amount of drive energy to be activated in order to recathect the mental representation—and that will then be applied to the real object out there.*

At this point, both the *concrete present mother* and the *remembered absent* or *"fort"*-mother (her "particular far away" [Green 2003, p. 80], or Bion's [1965] no-breast) become possibilities. And behind this emerging network of representations, still farther away, there is an "indefinite 'far away'" (Green 2003, p. 80), an *absolute nothing* (like a black hole)—and this nothing lies within reach of the death drive.

And what about the second position, *da?* The first toss removed the reel from sight, representing loss of the lethic object (the self-object dyad). Even though throwing the reel is the child's activity, it is, as Green notes, the *gone*-mother who *plays* the child; it is she who elicits his lethic needs. Thus, we can say that the first throw is pulled away by the lethic object (the *gone*-mother) and activates the child's self-preservative strivings (the needy self). The next act is to pull the reel until it can be seen again and is joyfully greeted as *there*. In line with the antagonistic arrangement of the two basic drives, I would suggest that the second movement —pulling the string and making the reel reappear—is initiated by the sexual drives (Eros). The child's excitement and joy at seeing the reel (or the mother) seem to carry a strong libidinal mark. While the *gone*-moment elicits sadness, the *there*-moment elicits happiness. The *there*-reel then symbolizes the reunited libidinal self with the libidinal object in their pleasurable relationship.

To put it differently: As soon as the child has reached the *position of absence*, where the lethic mother-child couple is represented, he is, in his mind, removed from where he actually is (in his bed) to this place of absence (united with mother). It is from there that he (or both mother and child) then—*in his mind*—activates libidinal strivings that reach out for the self that he is (the child in bed) and happily meet him *there* as soon as the reel reappears over the border of his bed. Clearly, the child's happiness mirrors the mother's happy excitement when being reunited with her child. Not only does she play him when she is leaving; she also plays him in coming back. (See Figure 2)

FIGURE 2

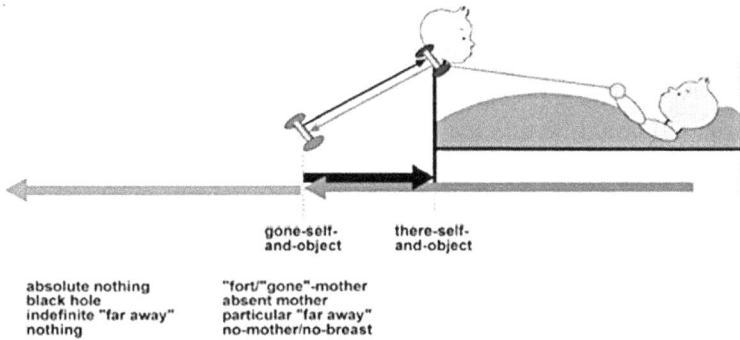

| gone-self-
and-object | there-self-
and-object |

absolute nothing	"fort/"gone"-mother
black hole	absent mother
indefinite "far away"	particular "far away"
nothing	no-mother/no-breast

I have suggested elsewhere (Schmidt-Hellerau 1995, 2001, 2006b) that every structure is formed and held by a libidinal and a lethic cathexis.[8]

---

[8] Green (1988) suggested conceptualizing primal narcissism as a structure that is constituted by the life drives and death drives, thus showing two faces—like Janus—one toward life and the other toward death. I have applied this concept to structure building and structural change in general (Schmidt-Hellerau 2006b).

The *fort/da* game thus demonstrates another relation: the *gone*-self-and-object and the *there*-self-and-object are related in the *specific tension* between lethic and libidinal strivings (stretched between the *position of absence* and the *position of reappearance*). This tension between specific quantities of oppositional energies defines the dynamic stability of the structural unit—as one can see in Figure 2: a unit that forms another, magnified reel by its shape. While the lethic side of this representation stands for the potential of loss, its libidinal counterpart carries the potential of hope—the object's being recalled or recaptured. In this specific example, the predominance of lethic energy (the arrow pointing left in Figure 2) can be held in balance by a rather small portion of libidinal energy (the arrow pointing right).

If we conceptualize two sides for each representation that determine the specific tension between its lethic cathexis and its libidinal one—a tension established as the dynamic stability of this specific structure—and if we think of these representations as placed at different positions along the whole continuum between *death* and *life*, then we assume that each of them will be defined by varying proportions of lethic and libidinal energies. The representation of a *dead self* could then be defined as *balanced* by a predominance of lethic energies—e.g., in a hypothetical proportion of 10:0 or 9:1, while (at the other end of the spectrum) a manic self could be thought of in the reverse proportion, 1:9 or 0:10 (lacking the grounding, calming effects of lethic energies). Thus, what is established as a balance between lethic and libidinal strivings is different in each case.

I suggest that to conceptualize representations in this way is helpful when talking with our patients. It makes us aware of the precarious balances between sexual desires and preservative needs, which is represented in and foundational to every mental event; and if the patient's sense of stability is too threatened by what we address in our interventions (e.g., the lethic need to withdraw versus the libidinal wish to reach out for the analyst), the patient might shut down or react with a *psychic retreat* (Steiner 1993).

We might also come to acknowledge that representations (e.g., of a traumatized self) that are established and stabilized without any contribution from libidinal energies, or with only a tiny one (a hypothetical ratio of 10:0 or 9:1), might be closed and inaccessible via our psychoanalytic efforts. Psychoanalysis cannot awaken what is dead. But of course, we must first determine whether an apparent death is merely a suspended animation.

Preservative Screens

While the many interactions between infant and caretaker result in the buildup of structures of self-representations as a shield, wall, or screen against dread of the *absolute nothing*, the self-preservative strivings become more differentiated, more determined, and develop many specific features. We can assume that lethic strivings concerning intake (prompted by hunger and thirst) create a *nurturing screen;* there are lethic strivings concerning all these palpable and sensitive processes that go on in the belly, building a *digestion screen.* Other lethic strivings, focusing on spitting, burping, urinating, defecating, and passing gas will form an *excretion screen;* and lethic strivings aiming at sleep and rest constitute a *sleep screen* (or blank *dream screen;* see Lewin 1946,[9] 1948). There are lethic strivings to be warm and in positions that feel cozy, represented in a *comfort screen.* These are all examples of the many screens that are gradually built up.

All these possibilities give us a preliminary idea of the multilayered fabric of the emerging structures of self-preservation that increasingly will hold, contain, and specify the need-related lethic strivings. These screens and the representations they are made of form the *mental goals*

---

[9] Lewin (1946) described the dream screen as a "surface onto which a dream appears to be projected. It is the blank background, present in the dream though not necessarily seen, and the visually perceived action in ordinary manifest dream contents takes place on it or before it" (p. 420). Lewin's statement accurately fits the conception of lethic screens, whose function is to hold and limit lethic strivings (since, when these strivings are not limited, no dream occurs), thus providing a "blank background" screen from which the dream (a sexual wish fulfillment, according to Freud [1900]) can emerge. Therefore, the dream is created in accordance with the above statement that every mental event (in the sense of an alpha element [Bion 1965]) is composed of lethic and libidinal cathexes.

(objects) of the different partial self-preservative drives. It is important to realize that these drive activities are not limited to physical needs, but also activate a considerable amount of our daily psychological preoccupations and concerns.

Laplanche (1997) has argued that self-preservation is a biological instinct, not a psychological drive, and explicitly excludes it from psychoanalytic thinking. But I would emphasize that to take something in, to digest something, to let something out, to rest, and to feel comfortable are all *psychological basics* that—while primarily related to bodily needs—become necessary psychological capacities that transform and sublimate the totality of the body's needs for concrete physical satisfaction into the nutritive pleasure of a meaningful thought.

Simultaneously with building up the different self-preservative screens, the primarily undifferentiated self-object unit (from Jacobson 1964 to Milrod 2002) gradually divides into two representational groups, increasingly differentiating self and object. Alongside the growing capacity of the child to care for him-/herself, the representations of lethic objects (dolls, siblings, pets) that need to be taken care of are created. Thus, the protective shield is not only "thickening," as it were, but also "broadening," and increasingly distinguishes what *self/self-preservation* is from what *object/object preservation* is.

It is only at around age four that the concept of death emerges (Weininger 1996), which is another challenge to the child's mind, the buildup of a *death screen* that is supposed to put a definitive mental halt to the death drive. (The many religious and mythological versions of where dead people go—to sit on a cloud as angels, to burn in hell, to be reborn, etc.—merely elaborate this screen, from a psychoanalytic point of view, in order to enhance its holding, protective function.) It is only then that the representations of "what dead means" are emerging. When we lose an object in death and eventually end the mourning process, the representation of this object will have to be moved backward to the death screen. We might still love it (there), yet we have to eventually give up trying to preserve it (with unconscious concern, care, or rescue fantasies)—or else we will be stuck in a pathologically ongoing mourning process.

Trauma

Freud (1920) derives a central argument for a *beyond-the-pleasure principle* from his study of trauma. Trauma is described as the effect of "any excitations from outside which are powerful enough to break through the protective shield" (p. 29). As a result of this "extensive breach" (p. 31). energies from the outside continuously stream into the center of the mental apparatus. The apparatus then defends itself with a libidinal "anticathexis" on a "grand scale ... for whose benefit all the other psychical systems are impoverished, so that the remaining psychical functions are extensively paralysed or reduced" (p. 30).

This is actually quite amazing: Freud reflects on the effects of severe physical and psychic trauma, accidents, war injuries, and so on—and if his idea of a self-preservative drive would ever have been called for, this would have been the moment. When we are hurt and traumatized, we might assume that we will react in strong measure to preserve and restore ourselves.[10] Freud wrote that trauma is paralyzing because all libido is directed to the traumatic breach,[11] and thus all other psychic functions are deprived of energy. I would say, rather, that trauma is paralyzing because *the traumatic hurt activates unusually high quantities of lethic energies in a reparative effort.*

In the foregoing, I have characterized lethic energies as (-)energies, tending toward care and sorrow, and also toward a general slowing down, heaviness, and withdrawal—and at the extreme of this trajectory, we encounter the paralyzing and deadening effect so amply described in the literature of trauma. The difference is that Freud, in keeping his focus on the sexual drive with its libidinal energy, viewed this paralysis as a *lack* of libidinal energy; but with the additional concept of a preservative and death drive, we can understand the traumatic paralysis as

---

[10] Freud (1920) recognized the restorative function of trauma-repeating dreams: "These dreams are endeavouring to master the stimulus retrospectively, by developing the anxiety whose omission was the cause of the traumatic neurosis" (p. 32). Yet he did not attribute this dream-work to the self-preservative drives.

[11] The libidinal investment of the traumatic breach would result in a sexualization of trauma, which might be one—but is certainly not the only—result of it.

the expression of a lethic abundance. This contrast of concepts might lead us to a change in our clinical thinking and in our approach to the same phenomena.

Thus, I suggest that trauma breaks through the protective shield of the preservative screens and *jams the representation of self and/or object into the backyard of death.* (See Figure 3)

FIGURE 3

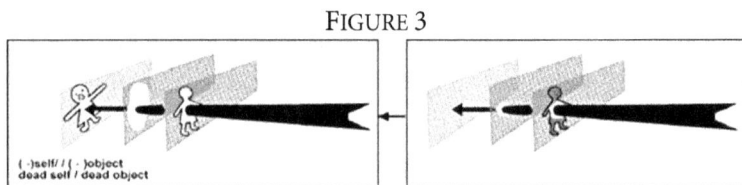

And here my conception of aggression comes into play:

1. Because the traumatized self, or "dead self" or "dead object," is moved much further away than it had been as a result of the trauma, and is thus at a greater distance from the sources of need, much higher quantities of energy must be raised in order to *reach* and *recathect* the dead self's structures.

2. In this model of trauma, since the preservative screens have partly been *destroyed* by the traumatic impact, there will be a lack of structures that could modulate (contain) and thus break down the increasing intensity of these lethic strivings.

3. It is this *intensity* of the intentionally preservative (self or object-resurrecting) strivings that ends up having a destructive effect. And it is this *intensity* of lethic strivings reaching out beyond the self and object-preservative screens that we experience clinically in these cases as the *self-destructive effects of the death drive.*

This now creates a paradox, and often establishes a clinical vicious circle. Within the traumatized psyche, more lethic energies are summoned up in order to *recathect* and recapture self and/or object. Yet, due to the lack of structural modulation, these increased energies become so powerfully intense that they push the traumatized self or object even farther downward, to some sort of *dead screen.* There is no skillful dosage; there is only a wild, intense lethic urge to retrieve what has been lost and may have become a (-)self, or a (-)object (with the minus symbol used to indicate its hypercathexis with lethe), or even a dead self or a dead object, respectively.

This is where we can rejoin Freud, Klein, Bion, Green, and others who have provided so many theoretically and clinically rich contributions to the death drive, conceptualizing it as a *destructive* drive. In the perspective developed here, aggression and destruction arise in the sphere of the death drive, yet I would conceptualize aggression as a *consequence* rather than as a *cause.* Aggression, in my view, comes up *not because a* death drive would be conceptualized as inherently and solely aggressive and destructive, but because—in the case of trauma and severe pathology—a *lack* or a *shutting down* of modulating and interfering preservative structures leads to a *destructive intensification of the lethic strivings,* as is characteristic of many activities in the sphere of the death drive.

In short, what we have learned from experienced clinicians and theoreticians about the pathology and psychic functioning of patients with an *aggressive* or *negative narcissism* (Green 1986; Rosenfeld 1971) who seem addicted to *near-death* (Joseph 1982) remains valuable. Yet I suggest that *what appears to us (and objectively is) self-destructive and object-destructive is actually the patient's intensified striving to PRESERVE him-/herself and to SURVIVE,* as well as to reach out for the—from his/her position—faraway object.

The Sphere of the Death Drive

In order to complete the picture of lethic strivings, I will sketch out a few remarks on some malignant phenomena occurring in the sphere of the death drive.

First, there are the various *eating disorders, addictions,* and types of *physical neglect,* creating very specific representations, all of which seem to express a conflict about self and object preservation, and that struggle with and often tend toward death. There is *hypochondria*, which is linked with the fear of death and a considerably increased self-preservative preoccupation. All of these are, as we know, admixtures that include unconscious sexual fantasies, pleasures, and anxieties; however, I would understand them as dominated by self-preservative issues.

This holds true also for the many variations of masochism, which ties pleasure and lust to physical or mental pain—that is, to the precondition of a strong stimulation of lethic excitations. Libidinal cathexes seem to be less involved in the various *psychosomatic diseases* that have been analytically explored, producing concepts centered around a *lack*, a *minus* of psychic representation and symbolization (as in Sifneos' "alexithymia" or in Marty's "operational thinking" or "essential depression"; see Aisenstein 2006).

Further, there are *depression* and *obsessive-compulsive disorders, mutism, catatonia*, and *stupor*. Also, as Green (1986) pointed out, there are "categories of blankness—negative hallucination, blank psychosis, blank mourning, all connected to what one might call the problem of emptiness, or of the negative, in our clinical practice … traces in the unconscious in the form of 'psychical holes'" (p. 146). That is to say, whether because of a sudden or cumulative trauma, whether by an ongoing subtle neglect or in consequence of a creeping addiction—self and object can be *pushed* or can *slip* beyond the sphere of healthy self and object preservation, ending up with a representation that is tainted as sick, damaged, or depressed, is greedy and insatiable, or is threatened with death.

And beyond these representations of a damaged or sick self and object will lurk those that we could call a *dead self* (or part self) and a *dead object* (or part-object). This is what patients experience as "the presence of death in life" (Green 1999, p. 11)—yet it is still not the end of all drive activity, but rather, as Bion (1965) put it, the border of an ongoing transgression of the never-ceasing power of a "force that continues after • [here the symbol • could stand for *meaning*, I believe] has been annihilated and it destroys existence, time and space" (p. 101).[12] Or, to use

---

[12] Bion (1965) described this force as "violent, greedy and envious, ruthless, murderous and predatory, without respect for the truth, persons or things. It is, as it were, what

228

more Freudian terms, such a state of a *dead self* conveys the virtual endlessness of the death drive's strivings.

The theoretical picture that I am outlining here is basically simple and purposefully schematic, a sort of theoretical scale to be used as an orientation in the background of the analyst's mind: it is the *place* on the axis of drives, and the specifics (the intensity) of energy cathexis, that define *what* is represented and *how* these representations are experienced. In the beginning—until a structure has been built up—all drive activity along the axis of (predominantly) lethic strivings is potentially endless or "deadening." Once the different screens for self and object preservation have been constructed solidly enough, we may find other structures *beyond* these screens, and those are the ones that we would, to varying degrees, define as *a pathological self or object* (or, equally, as *pathological self-object relationships*). It is here, toward this area, that the negative face of Green's (1988) Janus head (his *narcissisme de mort*) is directed; and it is here that Green's (1999) *work of the negative* is dominant and that the *negative hallucination* occurs.

Yet I would not conceptualize these processes—as Green does —in the sense of a *disobjectalizing* function of the death drive. Rather, I would say that the representations of self and object remain *there*, also in the sphere of the death drive. However, they are dominantly (or sometimes solely) cathected with lethic, that is negative or minus, energy. This constitutes them as what we could call *minus-representations*, the *negative self* and the *negative objects*, the *lost* or *absent* or the *dead self-* and *object representations*. They seem to get lost, to disappear into a negative hallucination, or to become totally unconscious as if no longer

---

Pirandello might have called a Character in Search of an Author. Insofar as it has found a 'character,' it appears to be a completely immoral conscience. This force is dominated by an envious determination to possess everything that objects that exist possess, including existence itself" (p. 102). No doubt this is an accurate description of these patients' mental states. However, such an evil characterization makes it hard to see anything other than a destructive and malignant process. It is interesting that Bion also refers to a "search for an author" and for "existence itself." I would hold that even though this search for the dead self is desperate, wild, and uncivilized (greedy, ruthless, murderous), it is not about destruction, but rather about survival.

229

existing; however—as Green's (1986) *dead mother* proves—they can remain powerfully cathected and held onto with the intentionally preservative yet effectively paralyzing energies of the death drive.

How to Build a Fire

Somewhere in the sphere of the death drive was a part of Sam's self as he was with me for a long time: missing, silent, and absent, while being *there* and keeping his place on my couch, in my room—and in my life. Sam was born an unwanted child of the wrong gender. His parents had admitted to him that, after having had his three brothers, who were eight, ten, and eleven years older, they had not planned on more children and certainly not on another boy. He often said to me: "I shouldn't exist at all." He said: "The perfect way of disappearing would be to put myself in a bathtub filled with acid and to completely dissolve—nothing should be left of me." He would disappear, traceless.

However, as far as I can say, Sam was never suicidal. Eventually, we understood that when he did not show up or stayed silent in our sessions, it was as if he fulfilled my/his mother's wish of not having him. His *not being there* was *his way* of staying closest to her (me); it was his way of being the one she wanted: *the absent one.*

It was in this phase of his analysis that I developed a symptom related only to Sam's sessions: in the minutes before he would (and then did or did not) arrive at my office, when I was involved in my usual 10-minute-break activities, again and again, I was startled by thinking that he had already come in and was silently sitting in the waiting room, and that I had not realized it, had completely forgotten about him and about the beginning of our session. I would feel shocked, and even though it was often minutes before our scheduled time, *I had to go see* whether the door to the waiting room was still open (Sam had not yet arrived) or whether it was closed (Sam was in the waiting room). Even though I recognized and analyzed the repetition of this compulsive idea whenever it occurred over many weeks, *I still had to open the door.*[13]

---

[13] The issue of the open or closed door may symbolize the relation between deadened

There are certainly many meanings to my symptom. On the one hand, it indicated a tendency for Sam to *get lost in my mind/ his mother's mind*—the dominance of a lethic cathexis of his self in my concordant or complementary countertransference. On the other hand, it might have represented his secretly being with me and "looking out for me," his having established himself in a temporarily absent part of my mind from which he might be said to *jump* into my awareness, or from which something within me unconsciously tried to pull him out. In a more specific way, my symptom seemed also to repeat his mother's surprise conception of Sam as her fourth child.

This latter aspect was, in fact, enacted one day: Sam (the wrong child) came to his session at the wrong time, and I—momentarily confused and thinking that he might be right—took him in; Sam lay down on the couch, and my office doorbell rang again. I was shocked, realizing that Sam should not be there and that the "right" (scheduled) patient had arrived. However, as Sam was already on the couch, I found that I could not send him away (I managed to schedule a replacement session for the other patient). Sam and I talked a lot about this "error"; however, even though I had obviously decided in favor of Sam at that moment, he insisted that I actually had not wanted to keep him in the session.

I think that an essential task of my being in this analysis with Sam was for me to keep on thinking of him as being *there*, even when he was not physically present. We may sometimes wonder how we can work with patients in absence who are subjected to these powerful lethic strivings (going in the direction opposite to life), which are often experienced as a pull or an urge to remain deadened. More than with our classical neurotics, here the whole enterprise of psychoanalysis, right from the beginning, strains against this pull. Patients with important parts of their selves and objects in the sphere of the death drive usually fight against their analysts' interpretations and fight against progress toward a normal life. Doing so, and desperately making use of all means to ward us off and subvert the analytic process, these patients eventually reveal an envious, arrogant, malicious, and triumphant part self or part-

---

and well-preserved self and objects. See Schmidt-Hellerau 2005c.

object, or the primitive, sadistic superego that we find so amply described in the literature. We have interpreted their destructiveness many, many times, and soon our patients know about it quite well.

Yet I often find that these interpretations do not lead to the insight that changes their mental attitude. Instead, these patients insist that what we call *destructive* is a feature that *protects* them from harm—whereas we (as analysts) threaten and endanger them. They speak about self-preservation, while we speak about self-destruction. Are our patients so wrong? Where is our empathy when we (correctly, from our external perspective) conclude that the patient's "protector" is actually a pervert, a sadist, a Mafia gang member (Rosenfeld 1971) that does *not* rescue, but in fact wants to destroy him or her? The patient conveys his or her inner truth: as malignant as these thought processes might appear to us, they constitute *the patient's struggle to survive in absence.* For him or her, it is the only way to keep an essential part of the dead(ened) self or a dead(ened) object alive.

It seems to me that there are two parts to this struggle to survive, a lethic and a libidinal one. On the lethic side, the *attacks* on the patient's self are actually—and paradoxically enough—meant to be *preservative;* they are intensified lethic investments of this far-removed part of the self or object in the sphere of death. To stop these attacks would mean *for the patient* to *not* reenergize these representations—and thus to have them definitively dissolve and fade away. And that is why he or she withdraws from us when feeling threatened.

The all-too-small portion of libidinal energy, on the other hand, is needed to balance this deadened representation's precarious balance of, e.g., 9:1. Sam said: "I cannot move one step forward because, with each move, I would spend and diminish the tiny bit of energy that I have been left with; thus, I instead stay still in my lukewarm bath of misery." This lukewarm bath of misery provided him at certain times with a "sweet pain"—a masochistic gratification that had compensated him for his loneliness throughout his life, and that he was firmly holding onto over the many years of his analysis.

"You would drop me anyway," Sam went on telling me. For many years, this conviction stood as a rock blocking our analytic path. As we hear in his claims, it was because Sam was afraid to psychically die as soon as he would come to rely on me, to fall into an abyss of death and to lose the rest of his feeling of being *still there* (even though miserable), that he anxiously clung to his self as it was represented in him: depressed, lonely, a failure in a coffin. And with him there was I, the minus or negative object, the disappointing transference mother who would drop him anyway because she did not love him and only wanted to be left alone.

A constellation like this might lead to an analytic dead end. If the analyst mainly focuses on the patient's *destructive* thinking and behavior, the analyst risks interfering not only with the patient's *preservative* efforts (with regard to his or her deadened representations), but also with the cautious libidinal investments of the object (analyst) that are often too subtle to be noticed (Sam more recently came to call it his "secret love story").

On the other hand, the analyst's "gentle" (lethic and libidinal) investment in the patient can feel threatening or even persecutory to him/her—not only as the result of a lethic countermovement aimed at reestablishing the usual balance of misery, but also because, in the sphere of the death drive, the patient's perception of the analyst's "liveliness" can be fundamentally different from what the analyst might think. Sam helped me understand his particular perception of the outside world when he told me many years ago that: "When I'm driving a car, I don't approach things. Rather, things approach me and I have to struggle to avoid a crash. And this is so with everything. Things are just thrown at me, and I must defend and hide myself all the time." His view and experience of himself was that of being at a standstill. Thus, his own as well as any other's libidinal actions—and so the analyst's interventions—merely bombarded or persecuted him (as projective identifications), and drove him even deeper down into his hiding place.

Sam's conviction that I would drop him in fact captured a trauma that we learned about only many years into our analytic work. One day when Sam was about five years old, he was playing alone in front of his parent's house when the news came that his godfather (his mother's brother) had been killed by falling into the wood shredder of his own factory. His mother had told Sam only recently that, despite the fact that it was always called "an accident," she had immediately known it was suicide. Sam's inner life —working on an already rather anxious and shameful oedipal love for his mother—seems to have come to a halt with this event. From then on, it seems, not only was his love met by a depressed and self-absorbed mother, but he had also lost her to a dead object, his godfather/uncle. This dead rival for his mother's attention was invincible.

One way of reacting to a traumatic loss is to identify with the lost object. In Sam's case, there were two lost objects: the lost godfather and the lost oedipal mother. In the coffin of his mind, we found both—first, Sam and me together, and then the dead godfather who was not there (anymore) and the depressed mother who needed to be helped, nurtured, taken care of, and reenlivened by Sam.[14] This single event in Sam's early life certainly did not account for the whole of his mental retreat, yet it did severely traumatize his libidinal development—and even more so in the terrifying threat that he must have felt when his father, shortly after the accident, showed him the shredder machine in which his godfather's body had been cut to pieces. The machinery of death and the fantasies it stirred up had persecuted him ever since.

Sam's fear that I would drop him recaptured in the transference his mother's guilt about having dropped her own brother and failed to rescue him from suicide; it also endlessly replayed Sam's identificatory fantasy of being the one who is dropped into the deadly abyss of a wood shredder. What he held onto in the transference also emerged as an endlessly repeating inner process within his thinking: whenever a new thought, an idea, a fantasy—in particular, a carrier of a libidinal arousal—came up, it was shredded to bits and pieces in his mind, again and again, so that nothing but a deadened feeling remained.

Over the years—and certainly over many failures—I have learned to better understand where Sam is in a particular session, what he is afraid of, what his thoughts and feelings unconsciously express and want to elaborate and what he can and cannot bear to hear from me. In fact, Sam

---

[14] There are many parallels here to the way Green (1986) has conceptualized the dynamics around the dead mother.

taught me how to work with him, and one day he captured it in a beautiful metaphor. He told me that he had recently learned how to build a fire in the open air:

> If you want to build a fire, maybe in order to heat a pot of cold water—for instance, when you're on a mountain hike—you first have to let the fire burn for a while. This allows the wood to heat up and develop the gas inside that burns and maintains the fire. If you put the cold pot on the fire too early, it withdraws the wood's warmth prematurely and the fire can't really develop. Also, there are three mistakes when making the fire: (1) you can let it starve by not feeding it with enough wood; (2) you can put on too much food [wood], and by this you suffocate it; and (3) you can give it the wrong food, e.g., damp logs. However, if the fire is already burning well and you then put a few damp logs on it, that'll be okay; at this point, the fire is strong enough and can first dry and then burn the wood.

The metaphor of *how to build a fire* seems to me particularly helpful in working with patients like Sam. A patient whose *dead self* cowers in the cold and darkness of his inner grave needs a lot of time to warm up. And whenever he is ready—often only for moments at a time—-we have to help him try to keep the flame alive, each time for a little longer. Of course, we will fail many times, and our most patient stance might still communicate and be experienced as urging him to hurry up.

One way to make a fire is to first collect the many thin branches of the patient's lethic concerns and activities, including all that he or she tells us that does *not* work. Thus, we will spend much time exploring the patient's defenses and lethic strivings. This is like gathering wooden materials, all that is at stake (the pyre). However, I came to recognize in Sam's analysis that extensively exploring his defenses eventually became another kind of defense—like an emphasis of his inner "no," like a confirmation of his conviction that it would never work. It was as if the pile of wood were getting higher and higher and thereby suffocating the tiny flames that shot up at times.

This is why I think that, eventually, we need to cautiously emphasize (libidinally cathect) *minor* issues, so-called unimportant and small movements that the patient seems to light by him or herself. It might be as trivial as a sense of warmth or liveliness in the patient's voice that indicates such a shift. Of course, the patient will be watchful and cast suspicion on all that we do; heat is a source of fear. Nevertheless, the patient might eventually accept some of the analyst's interest in addressing a particular topic. For a long time, we might not be able to speak to the patient's deadened state, to painful childhood memories and the like. This would be like putting the cold pot on too early, or a big damp log on a tiny flame: it would kill the flame right away. It is only after a (more or less) steady fire has burned over some time that we might dare to address the bigger issues. Then the fire might momentarily seem to shut down; however, it will have the capacity to revive. Then the hidden longings and the loving feelings slowly come into the process.

In Sam's analysis, I think it was the hot inner tears that had once soaked the log and extinguished the fire. I could feel his pain when he retrieved some of these feelings, saying: "To be so deserted, to not find any access to the loved one, to be so alone with all these feelings, this yearning, this urge—that hurts so much."

What I am suggesting technically is a drive-specific "content" choice: that is, in addition to our careful attention to the dynamic interplay between our patients' wishes and defenses, their progressive and regressive movements—in short, in addition to what we understand about the process—we might think about the proportions of libidinal and lethic issues in the content of the material. According to our sense of the patient's balance (*where* approximately he or she is along the spectrum between life and death), we might choose *what* we address, the lethic or the libidinal side of the material. The task is complicated: on the one hand, we need to appreciate the lethic self and object cathexes in their *preservative intent*, even where they appear to be destructive. That means interpreting the destructive effects of those strivings *not without* linking them to the patient's fears and to his/her intentional struggle to survive—and thereby at least opening an understanding to their essentially preservative intent.

On the other hand, we need to try to slowly emphasize the libidinal cathexis of those representations that are established beyond the screens of secure self and object preservation without challenging the patient's balance too much (thus running the risk of provoking a split or a negative therapeutic reaction). And, last but not least, we need to assign *meaning* to the concreteness of the patient's material, to foster the processes of symbolization—which in itself could turn out to create, essentially, a libidinal link. There is more to think about.

We analysts have to walk a tightrope—and will fall into the abyss ourselves many times. This is a feeling dreaded by the patient, and we dread it, too. However, we might learn to find us in the dark of the abyss and to climb up again. Knowing about our patients' struggles to *survive in absence* might help us to survive in the analysis, and eventually to make life and love first tolerable and then even enjoyable.

References

Aisenstein, M. (2006). The indissociable unity of psyche and soma: a view from the Paris Psychosomatic School. *Int. J. Psycho-Anal.*, 87: 667-680.

Bion, W. (1965). *Transformations*. London: Karnac.

Freud, S. (1900). The Interpretation of Dreams. *S.E.*, 4/5.

Freud, S. (1905). Three Essays on the Theory of Sexuality. *S.E.*, 7.

Freud, S. (1909). Analysis of a phobia in a five-year-old boy. *S.E.*, 10.

Freud, S. (1910). The psychoanalytic view of psychogenic disturbance of vision. *S.E.*, 11.

Freud, S. (1911). Formulations on the two principles of mental functioning. *S.E.*, 12.

Freud, S. (1915). Instincts and their vicissitudes. *S.E.*, 14.

Freud, S. (1920). Beyond the Pleasure Principle. *S.E.*, 18.

Freud, S. (1923). The Ego and the Id. *S.E.*, 19.

Freud, S. (1924). The economic problem of masochism. *S.E.*, 19.

Freud, S. (1930). Civilization and Its Discontents. *S.E.*, 21.

Freud, S. (1940). An Outline of Psycho-Analysis. *S.E.*, 23.

Freud, S. (1950). Project for a scientific psychology. *S.E.*, 1.

Green, A. (1986). *On Private Madness*. Madison, CT: Int. Univ. Press.

Green, A. (1999). *The Work of the Negative*. London/New York: Free Association Books.

Green, A. (1988). *Life Narcissism, Death Narcissism*. London/New York: Free Association Books, 2001.

Green, A. (2003). *Diachrony in Psychoanalysis*. London/New York: Free Association Books.

Jacobson, E. (1964). *The Self and the World of Objects*. New York: Int. Univ. Press.

Joseph, B. (1982). Addiction to near-death. *Int. J. Psycho-Anal.*, 63: 449-456.

Laplanche, J. (1997). Le primat de l'autre en Psychanalyse. *Traveaux 1967-1992. [The Primacy of the Other in Psychoanalysis. Writings 1967-1992.]* Paris: Flammarion.

Laplanche, J. & Pontalis, J.-B. (1973). *The Language of Psycho-Analysis*. London: Hogarth.

Lewin, B. D. (1946). Sleep, the mouth and the dream screen. *Psychoanal. Q.*, 15: 419-434.

Lewin, B. D. (1948). Inferences from the dream screen. *Int. J. Psycho-Anal.*, 29: 224-231.

Milrod, D. (2002). The concept of the self and the self-representation. *Neuro-Psychoanalysis*, 4: 7-23.

Rosenfeld, H. (1971). A clinical approach to the psychoanalytic theory of the life and death instincts: an investigation into the aggressive aspects of narcissism. *Int. J. Psycho-Anal.*, 52: 169-178.

Schmidt-Hellerau, C. (1995). Lebenstrieb und Todestrieb, Libido und Lethe. *Ein formalisiertes konsistentes Modell der psychoanalytischen Trieb und Strukturtheorie*. Stuttgart, Germany: Verlag Internationale Psychoanalyse.

Schmidt-Hellerau, C. (1997). Libido and lethe. Fundamentals of a formalised conception of metapsychology. *Int. J. Psycho-Anal.*, 78: 683-697.

Schmidt-Hellerau, C. (2001). Libido and Lethe. *A Formalized Consistent Model of Psychoanalytic Drive and Structure Theory*. New York: Other Press.

Schmidt-Hellerau, C. (2002a). Where models intersect. *Psychoanal. Q.*, 71: 503-544.

Schmidt-Hellerau, C. (2002b). Why aggression? Metapsychological, clinical and technical considerations. *Int. J. Psycho-Anal.*, 83: 1269-1289.

Schmidt-Hellerau, C. (2003). Die Erhaltung von Selbst und Objekt im Schatten der Freudschen Theorieentwicklung. (The preservation of self and object, a concept in the shadow of Freud's theory.) *Zeitschrift für psychoanalytische Theorie und Praxis*, 18: 316-343.

Schmidt-Hellerau, C. (2005a). The other side of Oedipus. *Psychoanal. Q.*, 74: 187-218.

Schmidt-Hellerau, C. (2005b). We are driven. *Psychoanal. Q.*, 74: 989-1028.

Schmidt-Hellerau, C. (2005c). The door to being preserved and alive. Comment to Ferro, Lisa. The analyst at work. *Int. J. Psycho-Anal.*, 86: 1261-1264.

Schmidt-Hellerau, C. (2006a). Fighting with spoons. On caretaker rivalry between mother and daughter. *Psychoanal. Inq.*, 26: 32-55.

Schmidt-Hellerau, C. (2006b). A shift in the head of Janus. Panel Presentation at a meeting of the European Psychoanalytic Federation, Athens, Greece (April).

Solms, M. (2005). Personal communication.

Steiner, J. (1993). *Psychic Retreats: Pathological Organizations in Psychotic, Neurotic, and Borderline Patients*. Hove, England/New York: Brunner Routledge.

Valenstein, A. F. (1973). On attachment to painful feelings and the negative therapeutic reaction. *Psychoanal. St. Child*, 28: 365-392.

Weininger, O. (1996). *Being and Not Being: Clinical Applications of the Death Instinct*. Madison, CT: Int. Univ. Press.

The Oedipus Complex

CHAPTER 7

The Other Side of Oedipus[*]

The Oedipus complex has been understood as a series of conflicts between feelings of love and hate (sexuality and aggression) in the relationship between the child and his/her parents. In this article I present a different view, defining oedipal struggles as conflicts between love and care, sexual desires and self- and object-preservative needs. The crucial conflict the child has to deal with is: to love the one and nevertheless to preserve the other (the rival). Further, the author distinguishes between monolithic conflicts, which are conflicts between different objects of one drive's strivings, and binary conflicts, which involve the objects of both basic drives. In three illustrative examples, I show that monolithic conflicts can indicate a regressive movement, while binary conflicts tend to foster a progression in the analytic work.

The royal conflict in psychoanalysis is the *Oedipus conflict*. Discovered during his self-analysis in 1897 and formulated in his *Interpretation of Dreams* in 1900, this jewel of Freud's psychic archeology was cherished

[*] (2005). Psychoanalytic Quarterly, 74(1): 187-217
Shorter versions of this paper were presented at the Western New England Psychoanalytic *Society* in New Haven, Connecticut, on November 20, 2004; and at "La Sapienza," Dipartimento di Scienze Neurologiche (the *Child* and Adolescent *Psychotherapy* Program of the University of Rome, Italy), on November 26, 2004.

by him throughout his life, and he did not hesitate to make its recognition "the shibboleth that distinguishes the adherents of psycho-analysis from its opponents" (1905, p. 226n). In fact, Oedipus Rex became the most famous amongst Freud's ancient heroes, and—as frequently portrayed in all sorts of cartoons—Oedipus even advanced in public culture to some sort of representative of psychoanalysis itself. Thus, everybody knows about Oedipus—the man who killed his father and had sex with his mother.

However, this version of oedipal conflict presented only a rough general scheme. In further exploring this important period in human development, Freud eventually realized that the oedipal situation is actually a configuration made up of *several* conflicts—a fact that he acknowledged in 1910 in introducing the more comprehensive notion of the *oedipal complex*. This complex of conflicts was not just about love and hate or sexual fantasies and rivalry; it included the narcissistic injuries of gender and generational differences, castration anxieties and penis envy, the many versions and failures of infantile sexual theories (compromise formations between the eagerness and anxieties to know), and it was complicated by constitutional bisexuality, expressed in the positive and negative Oedipus.

Few concepts have been so extensively elaborated in innumerable papers and books, both in support and in negation of Freud's conception, as has the Oedipus complex. Yet I contend that there is more to it—a whole other side of Oedipus that plays a silent though crucial role in the many conflicts that haunt our patients throughout their lives.

As analysts, we struggle with conscious and preconscious derivatives of emergent neurotic conflicts, while trying to analyze how the dynamic unconscious is involved in them, because

> … the pathogenic conflict in neurotics is not to be confused with a normal struggle between mental impulses, both of which are on the same psychological footing. In the former case the dissension is between two powers, one of which has made its way to the stage of what is preconscious or conscious, while the other has been held back at the stage of the unconscious. For that reason the conflict cannot be brought

to an issue; the disputants can no more come to grips than, in the familiar simile, a polar bear and a whale. A true decision can only be reached when they both meet on the same ground. To make this possible is, I think, the sole task of our therapy. [Freud 1916-1917, p. 433]

What a subtle warning to the clinician: You might lumber with your patient like the polar bear that sometimes catches a fish while the major part of the conflict keeps on moving, like an archaic, mysterious sea-mammal, a whale, in the depths of the unconscious—it takes a while before it shows up for a moment, then disappears again and leaves us back on the ice floe.

Smith (2003), emphasizing the central role of conflict in psychoanalysis, has recently highlighted the essential positions of Freud, as well as those of some prominent American theorists (Brenner, Boesky, Gray, Kris, Bromberg, and Pizer), concluding that conflict is ubiquitous, and can be observed, analyzed, and described with different methods and on different levels of abstraction. The two levels of abstraction on which I choose to explore the basic tenets of the Oedipus conflict are the theoretical and the clinical perspectives of drive theory. I contend that if we resist the trend to marginalize the past (Smith 2001) and to limit ourselves to an "archaic view of drive theory" (Smith 2003, p. 89), we can think in new ways about this most archaic side within ourselves, as it is conceptualized in drive theory, and learn something new about the many conflicts of the Oedipus complex.

Thus, I will not address here either modern developmental theories or infant research. Instead, I will stay with the basic psychoanalytic scheme of the Oedipus complex as presented by Freud and by Klein—because these views still provide our basic, background understanding—and I will add to these perspectives another view, based on the concept of the preservative drive.

The Preservative Drive: A Metapsychological Sketch

It is my understanding (Schmidt-Hellerau 1997, 2001, 2002, 2003a, 2003b) that an important shift in Freud's theoretical thinking with far-reaching consequences, equal to those of the move from the topographic to the structural model, occurred in 1920, when Freud reorganized his drive theory. Up to that year, he had conceptualized the dynamics of mental life on the basis of two primal drives, the *sexual* and the *self-preservative drives*. This idea, borrowed from Darwin, formed part of Freud's lifelong interest in evolutionary biology, and it made sense: *preservation* and *procreation* seemed to be the two success categories in the evolution of each species. Of course, Freud focused his research nearly completely on the sexual drive, leaving the self-preservative or ego drives (as he called them from 1910 on) much on the sidelines. However, he never abandoned the concept of a self-preservative drive, not even in the midst of his struggles with the introduction of narcissism (1914). Yet in his famous essay "Beyond the Pleasure Principle" (1920), he fundamentally rearranged the definition and division of his drives—which had a tremendous impact on the further development of psychoanalysis.

It was not so much the new notion of his pair of primal drives, the *life drive* and *death drive*; rather, it was their conceptualization, and the transition from the first to the second drive theory, that changed things dramatically. In this 1920 turn, the original antagonism of self-preservation and sexuality was *jointly* subsumed under the umbrella of a *life drive* (Eros)—while the new *death drive* was understood as an *aggressive drive*. Thus, *sexuality and aggression* emerged and prevailed as the two basic motivating factors in mental life.

It goes without saying that aggression is an important phenomenon in human behavior and mental life. However, as I have expressed elsewhere (Schmidt-Hellerau 2001, 2002), I doubt that it is wise to conceptualize aggression as a primal drive, or that it is *in itself* a motivating factor. Yet more important here is that, in consequence of Freud's 1920 shift, the concept of a self-preservative drive got lost. Even though sexuality and self-preservation can easily be thought of as contributing to life—at least according to a phenomenological plan fitting the term *life drive*—it seems to me a crucial factor that we are able to distinguish in the material of our patients between what is *sexual* and what is *preservative*, or between what is *love* and what is *care*. And without the concept of a preservative drive, we have a much harder time being aware

246

of these differences and recognizing their specific strivings—if indeed we pay attention to them at all.

It is quite an amazing fact that such a basic and primal need as self-preservation could become marginalized in our thinking, or even excluded from psychoanalysis, as Laplanche (1997, p. 153) suggested.[1] Thus, it has strangely escaped our theoretical and clinical perception that *the struggle to survive*, in its many derivative and often subtle expressions, is something *man is constantly and powerfully driven toward*—something that actually involves and stirs up a considerable amount of our daily mental activity (we cannot help it). Following is a rough outline of what *self-preservation, understood as a comprehensive drive activity*, might be about.

On a physical level, self-preservation concerns our general bodily well-being. This includes, e.g., eating, drinking, digesting, defecating, breathing, resting, sleeping, being warm and clean, and immunologically well defended. Psychologically, anxieties and neurotic, perverse, or pathological derailments around these issues include fantasies of engulfing, stuffing, starving, suffocating, and dying while sleeping, to name a few examples. Further, the different versions of rescue fantasies (both passive and active) revolve around survival; greed and stinginess stem from it; anxieties of becoming infected or poisoned, obsessions with washing oneself and cleaning things are also based in it; and eating disorders, hypochondria, and psychosomatic diseases seem to be parts of this same family. There is no doubt that all these fantasies, anxieties, and pathological formations are complex configurations that need to be analyzed in detail. At the same time, however, I propose that they can be advantageously understood as mainly *driven* by self-preservative and survival needs.

Further, I suggest that we are driven not only to *preserve ourselves*; we are equally driven *to preserve those we care about*. Most prominently, we experience the driven nature of these preservative strivings as mothers

---

[1] In a few *exceptions*, the notion of a self-preservative *drive* has been considered (Loewenstein 1940; Modell 1985; Plaut 1984; Simmel 1924, 1933, 1944; Young-Bruehl and Bethelard 1999).

with babies or parents to our children. To nurture, preserve, and protect one's children is such a powerful drive that we are not surprised to hear of parents' risking or giving their own lives in order to preserve those of their children. Thus, since the object is "what is most variable about a drive and is not originally connected with it" (Freud 1915, p. 122), the notion of a *self*-preservative drive was misleading. We are better off calling it a *preservative drive*, implying that it is viewed as directed toward oneself *as well as* toward another object; its strivings are thus *self-preservative* or *object preservative*.

We are accustomed to talking about what we conceptualize as *sexual drive activities*, making use of the energy term *libido* in speaking simply of libidinal objects, libidinal strivings, or libidinal investments. Freud never came to terms with an energy notion for the self-preservative drive (although he briefly tried using the word *interest*). For reasons elaborated elsewhere (Schmidt-Hellerau 1997, 2001), I have suggested the term *lethe* as an energy term for the preservative drive. Having this notion enables us to talk about a *lethic object* (which can be both an object to nurture, as is the baby, and a nurturing object, as is the parent), or lethic strivings (as in wanting to be taken care of, as well as wanting to take care of someone else), or lethic activities (e.g., eating, cooking, cleaning, and so on, as mentioned above).[2]

On the affective-behavioral side, there is a range of healthy to pathological expressions that I attribute to *lethic strivings*. These include a tendency toward carefulness, introversion, quietude, and silence—on up to mutism—all processes of mental digestion. These represent healthy caution and hesitation, but also rigidity and immobility; the capacity to be alone, but also withdrawal; and, finally, they include hopelessness, coldness, darkness, heaviness, sadness, passivity, absence, falling asleep, depression, lethargy, and suicidal thoughts.

In contrast, we might assume a dominance of *libidinal strivings* when we work with a patient who loves, fights, and talks, but is also chatty or

---

[2] Lethe is a term taken from Greek mythology, meaning forgetting. It therefore captures the quieter tendencies of the preservative drive—including resting, sleeping, and perhaps healthy forgetting (its repressive function).

even logomanic, moves yet also rushes to conclusions. Such a patient may be quick, funny, clear, active, creative, spirited, alert, flexible, cheerful, happy, social, and may show initiative—but is also restless, hyperactive, manic, and so on, just to mention some strong libidinal opposites to the former lethic ones. This indicates a major shift: Freud based his drive antagonism of *sexuality* and *aggression* on feelings of *love* and *hate*. I suggest affective opposites for the antagonism of the sexual and preservative drives, such as *lively* and *deadened, happy* and *sad*—or, as Freud (1930) put it, *noisy* and *silent* (p. 119), or, in Damasio's (2003) terms, *joy* and *sorrow*.

Binary and Monolithic Conflicts

Amongst the different ways of thinking about conflict, I want to show how drive theory can illuminate our understanding of psychic conflict. In 1910, Freud stated:

> Our attention has been drawn to the importance of the drives in ideational life. We have discovered that every drive tries to make itself effective by activating ideas that are in keeping with its aims. These drives are not always compatible with one another; their interests often come into conflict. Opposition between ideas is only an expression of struggles between the various drives. From the point of view of our attempted explanation, a quite specially important part is played by the undeniable opposition between the drives which subserve sexuality, the attainment of sexual pleasure, and those other drives, which have as their aim the self-preservation of the individual—the ego-drives. As the poet has said, all the organic drives that operate in our mind may be classified as "hunger" or "love." [pp. 213-214]

Here as well as on many other occasions, Freud not only links *ideas* directly with *drives*—thus, whatever comes to mind can be viewed as representative of an ongoing drive activity—but he also conceptualizes conflict as a struggle between the two basic drives, namely, sexual and self-preservative. Whichever drive is stronger (i.e., supplies more energy) will prevail and suppress the other and its related ideas. It follows that in this conception, the energetic side of repression (the force required to suppress any drive activity) is provided by the opposite of each of the two drives (Schmidt-Hellerau 1997, 2001).

Conflicts that involve *both* basic antagonistic drives can be called *binary conflicts*. According to Freud's statement, they would manifest in a struggle or shift of the guiding *ideas*, which include the aimed-for *objects* and/or the kind of *satisfaction*. For example, thoughts about the libidinal object might be repressed and become permanently replaced by an increase in self-preservative thinking (such as obsession about nutrition or other concerns with health issues); or, if self-preservative needs seem unacceptable (shameful), they can be defended against by a surge in a promiscuous sex life.

In these examples, both drives involve different objects—the libidinal (love) or the lethic (care) object—with the repressed one fading out of sight or being replaced by the self as an object of this very drive activity. In a mature version of binary conflict, both drive objects stay cathected, e.g., "Shall I clean my apartment, or shall I go for a weekend trip with my lover?"—and the answer would be: first the one, and then the other (whichever comes first). Yet both drives can also aim for the *same* object and cause conflicts expressed by the question of, e.g., "Do I want to have sex with my partner, or do I want to take care of him/her?" While a healthy decision might momentarily opt for the one *or* the other, a rigid either-or choice indicates a neurotic defense.

In his two "Contributions to the Psychology of Love" (1910, 1912), Freud talks about people who fail to resolve these kinds of conflicts: "Where they love they do not desire and where they desire they cannot love. They seek objects which they do not need to love, in order to keep their sensuality away from the objects they love" (Freud 1912, p. 183). Freud describes patients who suffer from total or psychical impotence or frigidity, or who show passion only for unavailable partners or for prostitutes. The interesting point here is Freud's explanation based on the strivings or currents of his two basic drives:

> Two currents whose union is necessary to ensure a completely normal attitude in love have, in the cases we are considering, failed to combine.

250

These two may be distinguished as the *affectionate* and the *sensual* current.

    The affectionate current is the older of the two. It springs from the earliest years of childhood; it is formed on the basis of the interests of the self-preservative drive and is directed to the members of the family and those who look after the child.… It corresponds to *the child's primary object-choice.* [1912, p. 180, italics in original]

It is worthwhile to note that in these failed love relations, Freud sees the conflict as not between *love* and *hate* (sexuality and aggression), but between *love* and *care*, the sensual (sexual/libidinal) and the affectionate (preservative/lethic) currents. In his understanding, mature love necessitates the union of both drives' currents. To put it differently, mature love requires a structural integration of the love and the care object, a convergence of both drives onto one object. Love relations fail when the self-preservative drive's *affectionate* strivings for the *primary object* remain *divided* from the sexual drive's *sensual* strivings. Thus, we must not mistake the *affectionate* for the *libidinal*. The distinction might become more apparent if we stay with the above wording and differentiate between the *caring* current of the preservative drive and the *sensual* strivings of the sexual drive. If there is a split of objects between the sexual and preservative drives, the sexual object cannot be preserved in a maturing relationship (i.e., the lover does not care for the love object), leading either to promiscuity, or—as we will see later in this paper in the example of Eveline—to a caretaker without a love life.

    All the examples above involve the activity of both drives, and thus they are binary conflicts. However, other conflicts may also play out between different objects without involving both drives, but instead only one of them—and I call these *monolithic conflicts*. Monolithic conflicts struggle with the choice of the aimed-for objects. In a developmentally early state, we might find on the side of the preservative drive an expression such as, for example, "Shall *I* eat all the cookies or give some to *my sister*?" Later in life, this same conflict may read: "Shall I take advantage of my insider knowledge and sell my stocks, or shall I care for all the other stockholders and notify the authorities of the state of accounts?"

The failure of a mature resolution of this conflict—correctly called a greed crime—might indicate an unconscious exaggeration or perversion of self-preservative needs, and even more so when there is no awareness of any wrongdoing. An example of monolithic conflict on the side of the sexual drive is the unconscious struggle in narcissistic states of: "Shall I love *myself* or shall I love (give some of my love to) the *object*?" Or, in the oedipal phase, a monolithic conflict may be expressed in the choice of parental objects: "Do I love *mother* or do I love *father*?" Or later: "Do I love *mother/my analyst* or do I love *my spouse*?"

In wondering "what is a conflict about?", I suggest a basically simple answer: Conflicts are about drives and their objects. *Binary conflicts* play out between the preservative and the sexual drives (both of which might aim for different as well as the same objects). Since each of these drives involves its own cathexis of object representations, binary conflicts are more complexly structured, thus indicating a progressive line of psychic processes. By contrast, monolithic conflicts involve just one of the two primal drives and the struggle between its different objects—with the self's usually being one of them. I suggest that monolithic conflicts presuppose a powerful repression of the opposite drive's strivings, and/or a deep split between the two drives' objects, followed by a regressive state or movement. All fantasies, objects, or actions are then either sexualized or relate to being taken care of. When this is the case, we have to first deal with this division or split in order to equally balance the spheres where the whale and the polar bear move—that is, to help the whale surface again.[3]

A Case in Point: Eveline

In order to illustrate lethic drive activities, as well as the above outlined types of conflicts, let us look at "Eveline," one of James Joyce's *Dubliners*

---

[3] My suggestions resonate with Kris's (1985) notion of divergent and convergent conflict—except that here, convergence and divergence are specified as applying to the drives and/or their objects. Thus, monolithic conflicts are always divergent, while binary conflicts may be divergent or convergent.

(1914). (In the section below, the original text is printed in italics.)

> Eveline is nineteen years old, and she is about to leave home in order to marry Frank. On the day of her departure, she sits at the window, *the evening invades* her thoughts and she is *tired*. She looks around at her home, *all its familiar objects which she had dusted once a week for many years.* She thinks *she would never see again those familiar objects from which she had never dreamed of being divided.* She wonders, *was that wise? ... In her home anyway she has shelter and food; she had those whom she had known all her life about her.* As she promised her mother when she died, Eveline has always worked *hard ... to keep the house together and to see that the two young children who had been left to her charge went to school regularly and got their meals regularly.* Her father is hard on her—he is stingy, and Eveline *sometimes felt herself in danger of her father's violence.... he had begun to threaten her.... she had nobody to protect her.*

This has been Eveline's life, a mostly lethic life: the hard work of cooking, cleaning, and caring for younger siblings, thus replacing the dead mother. This heightened demand and promise to be object preservative toward the family seem to have recently come into a (monolithic) conflict with Eveline's basic needs for self-preservation: she is *threatened* by the *violence* of her father and *has nobody to protect her.* Yet now she is about to embark on a new life.

She was about to *run away with a fellow, she would be married.... People would treat her with respect.... She was about to explore another life with Frank. Frank was very kind, manly, open-hearted. She was to go away with him by the night-boat to be his wife and to live with him in Buenos Ayres....* He took her to the theater, and *she felt elated.... He was awfully fond of music and sang. People knew that they were courting and, when he sang about the lass that loves a sailor, she always felt pleasantly confused.... First of all it had been an excitement for her to have a fellow and then she had begun to like him.* When her father found out that she was having an *affair,* he demanded that it stop, and *she had to meet her lover secretly....* She felt *she had a right to happiness.*

Here comes the love object, arousing pleasantly confusing feelings in Eveline when he sings of love and takes her to the theater and has *fun* with her. It seems as if sexual wishes have been stirred up, and Frank has become a libidinally cathected object: this fellow, this kind, *manly*, open-hearted sailor. Yet the *invading evening* has already cast a dark shadow on her mind:

> Eveline is thinking about her *home*, her *shelter*, that *her father was becoming old lately.... He would miss her.... She remembers the last night of her mother's illness; she was again in the close dark room.... The pitiful vision of her mother's life laid its spell on the very quick of her being.... She trembled.... Escape! She must escape! Frank would save her. He would give her life, perhaps love, too. But she wanted to live....* She was standing with Frank *in the station. He held her hand and she knew he was speaking to her.... She felt her cheek pale and cold and out of a maze of distress, she prayed to God to direct her, to show her what was her duty.... Their passage had been booked. Could she still draw back after all he had done for her? Her distress awoke a nausea in her body.... All the seas of the world tumbled about her heart. He was drawing her into them: he would drown her.* Having let go of him, *she gripped with both hands at the iron railing.* He called her again: "*Come!*" But *No! No! No! It was impossible.... Amid the seas she sent a cry of anguish!* He, already on the boat, called her to follow because the barrier was closing. "*Eveline, Evvy!*".... *She set her white face to him, passive, like a helpless animal. Her eyes gave him no sign of love or farewell or recognition.*

This is the end of the story. How can we understand it psychoanalytically, in terms of Eveline's inner conflict? If we deal with this literary figure as though it portrayed the essentials of human conditions, and if we follow Freud's statement that "every drive tries to make itself effective by activating ideas that are in keeping with its aims" (1910, p. 213), then we can be deliberately simple and say: Eveline's conflict plays out between her preservative and her sexual drives and the objects and ideas/fantasies about them.

For a brief moment, she struggled with a *binary conflict* between love and care: *She had a right to happiness—yet was it wise* to go away from *food* and *shelter*? Praying that *God* would *direct her*, she seemed to give up resolving this conflict between her duties (of caretaking) and her rights (for love). Instead, her preservative strivings prevailed: *she wanted to live*—and yes, to *love*, too, but love took a back seat when she felt she had to rescue herself. Self-preservation (the familiarity of her home) and object preservation (caring for father and siblings) succeeded in completely repressing her sexual longings for the man who wanted to marry her and sing with her. Her *lethic thoughts* started to grow profusely, and the whale of her sexual strivings—having recently shown up and filled her with hope—disappeared again in the ocean of her unconscious.

At this point, we are no longer witnessing a conflict between going with the libidinal object or staying with the lethic objects, a binary conflict between *love* and *care*. Instead, it all turns *lethic*, ending up with simply the wish to be *saved*. At first, Eveline thought *Frank would save her*—but Frank did not carry the same familiar lethic cathexes as did her old objects. Thus, she let go of Frank's hand (and, with it, of his libidinal investment), completely falling prey to an excessive self-preservative panic. Who would rescue this *pale and cold, nauseated and helpless animal* that she then felt herself to be—and her conviction was: *Frank would drown her*. Was it her libidinal self that was drowning with the lost love object? In the vortex of her struggle to survive, Eveline could think only of rescuing herself by turning back to the poor and dusty, yet familiar, safety of her father's home. Her eyes had lost all signs of *love* or *recognition* for her lover.

What was for a little while a binary conflict between the two drives and their objects—*love* and *care*—has regressed to a monolithic preservative conflict between different objects: Would Frank take care of Eveline? Or should she take care of her aging father and younger siblings—in order to be taken care of herself by her family, in the end?

But couldn't staying with her violent father also represent a masochistic surrender to an unconsciously loved oedipal object? No doubt, there is masochism present, if only in its moral version. However, if we call Eveline's father an oedipal object, it might still be helpful to scrutinize whether her (a patient's) attachment to him is libidinal at all (tinged with infantile sexual longings), or whether it is predominantly object- and self-preservative (limited to issues of taking care of the object that is supposed to save oneself). This latter notion, at least, is where Eveline ends up in this story: all she can think of is the need to rescue her very survival.

Klein's Early Stages of the Oedipus Complex

While for Freud, the Oedipus phase takes place between the ages of about three and five, Klein places the early stages of the Oedipus complex within the first year of life. The difference between the formulation of these two concepts was not rooted in factors related to the sexual drive—of which, as is well known, Freud acknowledged the existence from the time of an individual's birth onward. However, his understanding of structural development made it difficult for him to reconcile his views with Klein's. Freud postulated the mental representation of *one object* in the oral phase (a "me" who incorporates the mother and everything relevant to the infant's needs), *two objects* in the anal phase ("me" and "you"—with father and mother and everybody else being "you"), and *three objects* only in the genital phase, when gender differences start to divide objects into *male* and *female*. Since the mental representation of an object is a crucial determinant of a drive's purposeful strivings, and since triangulation is basic to Freud's Oedipus complex, he called those phases preceding the mental acknowledgment of three different objects *preoedipal*.

Klein (1928), by contrast, proceeded from different assumptions about (inner) objects and object relations. Since she conceptualized objects as an active part of the infant's mental life from birth on, the existence of phantasies of triangular relationships—and, consequently, of the early stages of the Oedipus complex—were consistent with her thinking.[4] She suggested that, for both sexes, the Oedipus complex

---

[4] The Kleinian spelling of the word phantasies, used specifically to refer to unconscious fantasies, is respected in this paper.

usually starts with weaning, and then takes on specific oral- and anal-sadistic features, mostly revolving around the mother's breast and phantasies about the good and bad contents of her body, urine, and feces, mingled with phantasies about the father's penis and the babies. Sadistic expressions of these early phantasies and actions were attributed to a primary *aggressive drive* that conflicted with the sexual drive. Thus, a failure to resolve early oedipal conflicts would weigh heavily (most often in an inhibitory way) on later sexual life.

I will use one of Klein's famous case examples, that of 10-year old Richard, as a model to rethink, from my point of view, not the object concepts of Freud and Klein and how they differ, but instead, a different view of the *drives activating these early objects or their representations*. It is my view that conflict in these early years does not arise between aggression and sexuality, but rather between self-preservation and sexuality.

Klein (1945) portrays Richard as a boy who was "excessively preoc-cupied with his health and was frequently subject to depressed moods" (p. 340). His "suckling period had been short and unsatisfactory." His mother was depressive and was "very worried about any illness in Rich-ard, and there was no doubt that her attitude had contributed to his hypochondriacal fears"; she "lavished much care on him and in some ways pampered him." Richard "was over-anxious and over-affectionate towards his mother and clung to her in a persistent and exhausting way" (p. 340). In analysis with Klein, Richard drew a starfish, explaining that it was "a hungry baby which wanted to eat" (p. 342), and then an octo-pus, representing "his father and his father's genital" and unconsciously a "monster." He identified himself with a "destroyer" named "Vampire" and had it "bump into the battleship 'Rodney' which always represented his mother" (p. 344). Klein understands the bumping of the two ships as symbolizing sexual intercourse, and Richard's then pulling away from this as a "repression of his genital desires towards his mother" because of his fear of the "destructiveness of sexual intercourse" (p. 344), in conse-quence of the oral-sadistic character he attributed to it.

Richard, who suffered from an "unsatisfactory feeding period" (p. 362), and shared with his mother a heightened concern about both his and her health and well-being (depressed moods), seemed not to have been able to establish a solid sense of good self and object preservation. However, a child's feeling of safety for the self and the nurturing object is a precondition for the capacity to phantasize about sexual penetration not as an act of destruction (endangerment), but as a pleasurable and procreative drive activity. Richard was afraid of his own penis because it seemed to him a "dangerous organ that would injure and damage his loved mother" (p. 365). *Thus, his sexual strivings were in conflict with his object-preservative needs.*

> Because of his unconscious fear and guilt about his own oral-sadistic impulses, however, infants predominantly represented to him oral-sadistic beings. This was one of the reasons why he could not in phantasy fulfil his longing to give children to his mother. More fundamental still, oral anxiety had in his early development increased the fear connected with the aggressive aspects of the genital function and of his own penis. Richard's fear that his oral-sadistic impulses would dominate his genital desires and that his penis was a destructive organ was one of the main causes of his repression of his genital desires. [Klein 1945, pp. 363-364]

It seems to me that Richard could not maintain a binary-conflict level in which his preservative and sexual strivings for his mother were sufficiently balanced. Instead, he seemed caught in a vicious cycle: oral, self-preservative frustration with his depressive mother might have (aggressively) intensified his lethic drive activity—making him a "vampire" who would attack and endanger his mother. Thus, he needed to withdraw, which increased his frustration and greed—and, consequently, his concern about his potential to attack his nurturing object ("He often asked, even after quite harmless remarks to his mother or to myself: 'Have I hurt your feelings?'" [p. 346]). His developing sexual urges further complicated these difficulties. The increased push of the sexual drive aroused phantasies of penetration and of intruding on the mother's body, which appeared as a catastrophic danger—thus necessitating a defensive regression to a lethic preoccupation with self and object-preservative concerns.

Klein (1945, pp. 365-ff.) confirms Freud's above-mentioned contribution to the psychology of love as she formulated it in Richard—namely, the presence of a split between the affectionate (preservative) and the sensual (sexual) strivings (Freud 1912, p. 180), or, as Klein (1945) also puts it, a split between the "good breast-mother" and the "bad genital mother" (p. 346). Presupposing destructive damage, Klein then emphasizes a "drive for reparation" (p. 380) that counters aggression and supports feelings of love. This drive for reparation is *part* of what I would conceptualize as (object-)preservative drive activity. Klein describes Richard's conflicts, as well as early oedipal conflicts in general, as binary: struggles between sexuality and aggression. I would agree with her analysis and general conclusions while understanding these struggles as a conflict between the sexual and the preservative drives, with a hyperactivity of the latter.

The Libidinal Side of Oedipus

Freud (1900) describes conflicts within the oedipal complex as what I would call *monolithic* conflicts (affecting the different objects of just the sexual drive), even though they seem to exist as conflicts between sexuality and aggression: "It is the fate of all of us, perhaps, to direct our first sexual impulse towards our mother and our first hatred and our first murderous wish against our father" (p. 262). It is worth noting that *this is not a conflict between love and hate*; rather, these murderous wishes are fully in accord with sexual strivings for the mother; they occur in order to eliminate the paternal obstacle on the way to the libidinal object, and can be understood as a reinforcement or *intensification*—or simply as an expression of the sexual drive (Schmidt-Hellerau 2002). In fact, this conflict is not with mother, but instead arises because there are positive feelings (identification) for father as well (Freud 1923, p. 32). Yet are these feelings primarily "affectionate" (lethic), or are they "sensual" (libidinal)?

Freud bypassed this question by introducing his notion of *bisexuality* and the *negative Oedipus complex* (p. 33). Thus, he focused on conflicts between homo- and heterosexual fantasies about a *male* or a *female self* who is in a sexual relationship with a *male* or *female* object—stating that the boy also behaves as mother does and wants to be loved by father, just as mother does. This might bring up another conflict, one occurring around a confusion between *passive* as in "wanting to be loved" (receptive), and *passive* as female or homosexual. Thus, the child struggles between wanting to love mother, wanting to love father, wanting to be loved by the one, and by the other—and all of this at different times and without any annoying interference by the respective other.

With all these facets, Freud described a whole range of conflicts on the *libidinal side of Oedipus*. They all concern the sexual drive and its objects and work on the structural development of what I have called the *erotogenic self* and the *erotogenic objects* (Schmidt-Hellerau 2001, pp. 219-ff.). In the end, complete resolution of the Oedipus complex will require not so much the *repression* of the negative Oedipus as the *integration* of male and female identifications and strivings, in order to foster the formation of an erotogenic self that strives for and is empathic with the desires of the erotogenic object.

The Lethic Side of Oedipus

Earlier, I suggested that monolithic conflicts tend to be more regressive than binary conflicts. Calling the conflicts Freud outlines for the Oedipus *monolithic* thus seems to contradict our common understanding of the progressive nature of this developmental period. Therefore, we might wonder whether lethic strivings and structural formations are occurring simultaneously with libidinal ones that so far have not been part of our general Oedipus concept, since their presence would elevate these struggles to the more advanced, binary-conflict level.

Freud (1923) suggests the arousal of considerable aggression not only within the jealous oedipal child, but also within his/her parents, which eventually—at the height of the Oedipus complex—leads to the threat of castration and the "demolition of the Oedipus complex" (p. 32).

> If the satisfaction of love in the field of the Oedipus complex is to cost the child his penis, a conflict is bound to arise between his narcissistic

interest in that part of his body and the libidinal cathexis of his parental objects. In this conflict the first of these forces normally triumphs: the child's ego turns away from the Oedipus complex. [Freud 1924, p. 176]

Freud (1923), in focusing on the sexual drive, again presents this centerpiece of his Oedipus as a conflict between object-love (mother) and narcissistic self-love (penis); this conflict leads to the "transformation of object-libido into narcissistic libido," which is understood as a "desexualization—a kind of sublimation" (p. 30). However, if we are serious about Freud's concept of a self-preservative drive, then we understand castration anxiety as creating a binary conflict: on the one side, there is the libidinal desire to love mother; on the other side, there is the lethic need to preserve the penis/oneself—and, interestingly enough, self-preservation "normally triumphs," as noted in Freud's remarks above. I suggest that, in the shadow of the glamorous libidinal side of the oedipal conflicts, there are important processes going on to deal with the child's self and object-preservative urges and their conflicting, as well as balancing, potential; they constitute the other side of Oedipus, and advance these processes to an altogether more integrated binary conflict level.

It should not come as a surprise that self-preservative strivings conflict with sexual ones when the latter begin to gain strength. Without reference to self-preservative issues, Freud (1932) speaks to the heart of these new difficulties by quoting Heine: "*Was dem Menschen dient zum Seichen/Damit schafft er Seinesgleichen*"[5] (p. 192). He elaborates:

> The sexual organ of the male has two functions; and there are those to whom this association is an annoyance. It serves for the evacuation of the bladder, and it carries out the act of love which sets the craving of the genital libido at rest. The child still believes that he can unite the two functions. According to a theory of his, babies are made by the man urinating into the woman's body. [1932, p. 192]

---

[5] Strachey translates in a footnote: "With what serves a man for pissing he creates his like."

While these and other infantile sexual theories (Freud 1908) are well known—and we are certainly familiar with some children's and patients' worries about the genitals being dirty, sexuality being disgusting, and/or masturbation making people sick—we have not conceptualized these conflicts as *driven* by the *need for self-preservation* (e.g., being clean, healthy, not harmful, and also decent) and the *desire for sexual pleasure*. To conceptualize the "antithesis between the two functions" (Freud 1932, p. 192) of one organ (and later one object) is a mental challenge that affords the resolution of conflicts between lethic and libidinal drive activities.

Thus, a complicated task in the genital phase is to differentiate between what I have called the *biogenic* (preservative) and the *erotogenic* (sexual) functions and zones, and, further, between a *biogenic* and an *erotogenic self and object* (Schmidt-Hellerau 2001). The *biogenic self* demands to be taken care of and is preoccupied with taking care of him-/herself in order to be healthy and to feel safe and well. The *biogenic object* is the object who has to take care of, nurture, and protect the child and has self-preservative needs of his/her own that might require being taken care of by others. By contrast, the *erotogenic self* is pleasure seeking, as is the *erotogenic object*, which is also required as a pleasure-providing partner for sexual encounters in both direct and sublimated ways. *It follows that the complicated task of the oedipal phase is not only to differentiate between a male and female self and object; it is also to differentiate between biogenic and erotogenic self and object representations.*

The subsequent step will afford this re-*union* of "the affectionate and the sensual current" (Freud 1912, p. 180). That is to say, the preceding *differentiation* (elimination of confusion) is the necessary precondition for a subsequent mature *integration* of both functions. Then the self will be represented as capable of taking care of him-/herself and others, while also having sexual pleasures, and, in addition, the object will be represented as self and object preservative, while also being sexually exciting and enjoying him-/herself.

The active and passive strivings of sexual and preservative drives aiming for parental objects create a full range of conflicts within the triangular situation of the Oedipus. For the positive Oedipus, the formula says that the child's aim is to establish a two-person relationship that would eliminate the third—*the boy wants to love mother and fights against father*. Yet the child also expects to be taken care of by this third. This situation constitutes a conflict between *the wish to get the love object*— which requires fighting the rival —*and the wish to be taken care of by this very rival*. One way to resolve this conflict is to distribute the sexual and preservative strivings to both parental objects, keeping father and mother simultaneously cathected with different drive energies. We could thus visualize two sides to the oedipal structure: a libidinal front side that is balanced by a lethic reverse side.[6]

If we look at it this way, the *active libidinal side of the positive Oedipus* would read: "The boy wants to love mother (as father does) and fights against the paternal rival." On the reverse side, however, another silent wish might occur: "The boy wants to take care of father (as mother does), and fights against the maternal rival." That is to say, the identification with both parents, father and mother, is constantly at work (the boy internally enacts the relationship with the parental couple). Further, we realize that feelings of rivalry are not limited to libidinal (erotic) strivings; they also come into play with lethic (caretaking) needs and urges (who does and gets the "better" caretaking?).

On the *passive libidinal side of the positive Oedipus*, we then find: "The boy wants to be loved by mother (as father is) and fears the father"—with its reverse side: "The boy wants to be preserved/protected by father (as mother is) and fears mother." The boy's wish to be also taken care of by father (as mother is) might feel competitive with mother's being cared for by father, thus creating the (later unconscious) fear of an envious, retaliatory action by her. Therefore, if we wonder why preservative wishes need to be repressed and become unconscious, we might remember that it is the gratification of these wishes within a meaningful relationship with parental objects, together with fantasies of envy and rivalry (arising from the infantile idea that *all love* or *care* goes to only *one* object, with nothing left for a second or third), that appear

---

[6] A more detailed scheme of these conflicts was published in Schmidt-Hellerau 2001, p. 225.

to be too dangerous to know about. The same active and passive configuration as described with the opposite objects would then apply to the
scheme of the negative Oedipus as well.

In thinking about different combinations of libidinal-lethic conflicts,
a much more complex picture emerges. We realize, for example, that
there is a subtle but crucial difference between a negative homosexual
wish (*the boy wants to be loved [penetrated] by father [his penis]*) and a
lethic wish (*the boy wants to be protected by father*)—in short, there is a
difference between *love* and *care*. I think that the creation of structures
to organize issues of care (for both male and female objects) is essential
for psychic development and growth—and that these structures must
exist *separately* from issues of sexual love. Analysts must know about
these differences (which do not presuppose aggression, I might add).
This conception also ensures that the libidinal wish *to love mother* is
counterbalanced by the antagonistic drive's wish *to preserve father*,
which modulates the impulse *to fight against the father*—and thus, the
sexual strivings for the maternal love object are eventually relinquished.
Therefore, it seems to me that *the classical Oedipus conflict is not between love and hate, sexuality and aggression; it is between love and care:
to love one parent and to preserve the other (rival), nevertheless* (see also
Schmidt-Hellerau 2001).

In this manner, the basis for a triangular representation of object relations can be established—even though there is still one more step for
the child to master: that is, to keep on loving and caring for his/her
parental objects, even while realizing that they have loving and caring
relationships with each other without the child's being part of the parental couple.

The outcome of these developmental achievements at the end of the
oedipal phase is understood to be crucial for the development of the
superego. As I have elaborated elsewhere (Schmidt-Hellerau 2001), the
preservative drive's structures will form the foundation of the superego's
protective functions (which could not be explained by aggression as a
primal drive), while the libidinal precipitate (ego ideal) creates its orienting function; and both interact favorably in a balanced way.

Lora

In order to illustrate the complexity of conflicts of differentiation between sexual and preservative strivings, I will briefly sketch representative vignettes from the third and fourth years of a five times-per-week analysis with Lora, a 35-year-old, married mother of three. She came to me because she often felt depressed and suffered from migraines, backaches, and frequent incontinence; she also had great difficulties in her marriage.

Lora grew up as the only girl among five brothers. She always felt devalued, incapable, and sad, and she remembered that she cried a lot when she was little. She thought that people behaved "as if I weren't there." She might enter a room and nobody would look at her. Nowadays, she might cook an elaborate meal, but people would thank her husband when leaving. For a long time, she did not want to apply for a job because she was afraid people would find out that she could not do it. All her efforts seemed never to yield the appreciation she wanted so badly. She said: "I'll never be good enough; I'll never have it all. There is something missing." Our work often centered around understanding the links she made between being a girl/woman (not male) and the many disappointments and frustrations she had experienced in her life.

One day in the third year of her analysis, she told me of her recent birthday party. The band had played for her and she had danced all night. Eventually, the bandleader asked her on stage and she had sung a song. She felt great. "I walked around having the sense that my inside was out. I felt so powerful—it was really exciting!" That night, she dreamed the following: "I had to use the bathroom. I was standing over the toilet—it was a men's toilet—the water started bubbling up, and I was torn between having to go to the bathroom and the feeling that I could have an orgasm. I was so excited, yet I had to go to the bathroom."

Later in the same session, Lora wondered: "What do men do when they get excited and have an orgasm?" I said, "Your dream seems to say that there is a conflict with urinating." Lora answered, "Yes, I only learned at age nineteen that I had a vagina, and it was extremely uncomfortable to use tampons." She told me that she could not wear pantyhose;

the stockings always wound around her legs oddly. "It drives me nuts being a woman!" she exclaimed. Many sessions followed that wrapped around penis issues, highlighting her fantasies, worries, and curiosities.

Lora lived with the unconscious wish to have an inner penis—which, as it turned out, was one of the reasons that she was unaware of having a vagina until she was nineteen. As a part of her sexual fantasies, this was an important source of hope: one day, she would make it; and it was also a constant source of renewed disappointment: she would never have it all. In this brief vignette, she demonstrated that she finally felt recognized and accepted by the men in the band at her birthday party, joining them as alike (male). She had the sense that *her inside was out*, and this made her feel *powerful*. Proudly, she presented this feeling to me. But how to deal with this new achievement? The dream spelled out that it aroused a binary conflict: "I was torn between having to go to the bathroom and the feeling that I could have an orgasm." Her question to me was: "What do men do when they get excited and have an orgasm?" The sexual excitement (having an orgasm) conflicted with the preservative urges (having to urinate).

In the fourth year of her analysis, Lora told me another dream: "I was in a clothing store, trying on a white dress. I had taken up my other clothes and my necklace with a golden-heart pendant and put them somewhere. The new dress looked very round on me, as if I were pregnant. After I had changed back into my clothes, I couldn't find the necklace with the heart pendant. I searched on the couch. A security man said, 'It isn't there.' I put my fingers in the slit of the couch, pulling out a fold, and behind this fold I found it."

Lora found this dream interesting. She said that when the fold came out, it looked like a woman's genitals. She thought that she often had dreams about searching and finding her jewelry. She concluded that in this dream, she found her womanliness in the slit of my couch—because it looked like my couch. What she was searching for she found here, she said, in my office—it was her *self*, her womanliness. The heart of the matter, reflected in her pendant, was to be found here in analysis. She said it was hard to bring her love here and to put it on the couch, but now she *found* love in my couch—she had found *my* love. And she talked of the dress, white like a wedding dress, in which she also looked pregnant.

The next day, Lora came in angry with Pete, her husband. Eventually, she wondered: "What has my anger to do with having found your love here? I can only love one at a time. How is it different—Pete's love and your love and my love for you and my love for Pete? It is so confusing. I don't feel comfortable in myself, my legs hurt, it's so unfair, why can't I be comfortable with myself?"

The next day, she came in angry with me and did not feel like talking. We gradually understood that she had thought I would push her to be with Pete. She felt offended, thinking that I did not love her. She had thought that her life was going so well, and yet deep down, there was still a tiny spot where she felt she would kill herself. She knew she would not really do it, but there was this feeling, and she thought she would not tell me about it because she was mad at me. "I thought, I could do it alone, without you. But this isn't really the case until I have understood how I can love people—separately and differently."

I understand this dream as part of Lora's negative Oedipus, her wish to find my love (heart) by using her finger-penis to penetrate the slit in my couch, representing my vagina. By doing so in her dream, she created a concept of a woman's genitals. This helped her to find her womanliness and to fantasize herself as pregnant. Unconsciously, it was *I* impregnating *her* while she was doing the same with me; we were the wedding couple. This made her angry with her husband, who interfered with our relationship.

I think the patient had correctly picked up some subtle countermovements on my part in the second of these three sessions, which had offended her and made her express her anger with me in the third session. However, she came to an important insight: even though she had been disappointed with me, she would not withdraw; she would stay with me until she had understood how she could love people *separately* and *differently*—which meant how to *love* and how to *care for* both her *husband* and her *analyst*, or for both her *father* and her *mother*.

All these conflicts provoked aggression. Lora was angry with herself, angry at her husband, and angry at her female analyst. Most of this anger focused on impatience and annoyance for not *getting it*, or for feeling prevented from *getting it.* Yet this anger and the aggressive out-bursts it triggered did not represent a conflict, but rather emphasized sexual strivings and their aim: wanting to get *it* and get *through* to the sexual object—and, in the end, to do so without losing the care and protection of the preservative objects.

These few analytic moments—from the patient's *never having it all* (the missing penis/the parental love objects), to this *powerful* and *exciting* feeling of *having it out*, to the question of *what it does*, to *using it* (putting her fingers in the slit of my couch) in order to *find the heart of the matter, her womanliness = her jewel, in the vagina*—illustrate how our patients need time and space to sort out their different and conflicting fantasies and feelings about love and care, and about being male and/or female with a male and/or female transferential object, the analyst. It is not just about finding out what one *really* is (gender identity); rather, it is about trying all this out in order to integrate it into a gendered sense of one's *erotogenic self* as coexisting with an *erotogenic object* in a sexual *and* caring relationship.

Conclusion

The other side of Oedipus is the lethic side of structure formation, the side that is at work during all these difficult developmental processes in childhood. In the pregenital phase, the lethic demands of self- (and object) preservation dominate the expression of early libidinal strivings, but in the genital phase, it seems crucial that the sexual drives prevail, simultaneously retaining the preservative currents in a stabilizing function. Both drives must and will at times be pursued aggressively, whenever they seem to be thwarted. However, I suggest that, instead of an aggressive drive, we might conceptualize the *preservative drive* as the primal antagonist to the sexual drive. Thus, we might better comprehend the *two directions* of man's motivational strivings that shape the oedipal complex, two basic demands of the body to the mind: the need for safety (preservation) and the desire for love (sexuality).

The concept of a preservative drive existing alongside sexuality helps us grasp the difference between monolithic and binary conflicts. Further, appreciating the direction of lethic strivings prevents us from interfering with their expressions (e.g., in not interpreting concern and care as veiled hostility or guilt and reparation for preceding aggression) when they are about (progressively) building up the structures of self and object-preservative functions. Such an appreciation also helps us understand when a patient's clinging to safety needs eventually becomes a defense against sexual strivings, and—if not analyzed as such—might even lead to malignant regression.

Thus, knowing about the importance of the lethic side of Oedipus by no means implies *favoritism* of preservative issues. Green (1995) is concerned that our interest in early disturbances leads to a *predilection* of the preoedipal issues, with a corresponding neglect of oedipal ones, a trend he describes as a shift from the penis to the breast. Yet "the role of a sexual relationship is not to feed and nurture but to reach ecstasy in mutual enjoyment" (p. 877). Green emphasizes the importance of sexual drives for achieving and working through the oedipal phase and reaching a certain stability of psychic functions.

> We should ask: what is important? What has the greatest value? The price of life is attached to what all human beings share and are longing for: the need to love, to enjoy life, to be part of a relationship in its fullest expression, etc. Again, here we are confronted with our ideology of what psychoanalysis is for. What is its aim? Overcoming our primitive anxieties, to repair our objects damaged by our sinful evil? To ensure the need for security? To pursue the norms of adaptation? Or to be able to feel alive and to cathect the many possibilities offered by the diversity of life, in spite of its inevitable disappointments, sources of unhappiness and loads of pains? [p. 874]

Can this be an either-or choice? Isn't it always about both? While in both psychoanalysis and in life, we might hope to develop sexual pleasure within a loving relationship, as long as we are haunted by primitive anxieties and basic threats to our security, there will be no room for erotic enjoyment. And even after we have overcome these primitive fears in a healthily neurotic life, the basic threats to our survival travel with us as an ever-lurking potential to regress that flings open as soon as we feel endangered. That is why I think psychoanalysts need to know about the power of both the preservative and the sexual drives, because this knowledge will help them analyze, and thus to structure, their patients' capacities to love and to care for themselves as well as their objects.

Finally, the other side of Oedipus is also the other side of the ancient myth—the parental failure and its consequences, which were left out of Freud's conception. Laïos, reacting to the oracle that his son will kill him, pierces (that is, penetrates and hurts) Oedipus's feet and abandons him in the wild, thus hoping to kill or get rid of the child and *to preserve his own life*. If this is meant to imply a conflict at all, it is a monolithic one—self-preservation versus the preservation of a newborn son—that is decided regressively in favor of Laïos's own survival needs. The father's decision amounts to a murderous plan shared by Jocaste, the baby's mother. Thus, the story says that both parents want to enjoy sexuality, but are not willing to care for their offspring.

Whether we take this to encapsulate the horrendous fantasy of the oedipal child who is excluded from the parental couple (Britton 1998, p. 36), or whether we take it as a failure in parenting, the myth tells us that Oedipus—even though he was accidentally saved and well reared by his foster parents—unconsciously carries on what has informed his early mind. He lacks the very object-preservative concerns toward his real parents that they failed to provide for him. The wisdom of Greek mythology implies what psychoanalysts know: that a defense against an imagined threat (oracle) brings about the very danger that attempts are made to avoid. Thus, the tragedy makes sense to us when Oedipus ends up killing Laïos—not only as a failure of the incest taboo, but also, and most important, as a failure of object preservation.

References

Britton, R. (1998). *Belief and Imagination. Explorations in Psychoanalysis.* London/New York: Routledge.

Damasio, A. (2003). *Looking for Spinoza: Joy, Sorrow, and the Feeling Brain.* Orlando, FL/New York: Harcourt.

Freud, S. (1900). The interpretation of dreams. *Standard Edition*, 4/5.

Freud, S. (1905). Three essays on the theory of sexuality. *Standard Edition*, 7.

Freud, S. (1908). On the sexual theories of children. *Standard Edition*, 9.

Freud, S. (1910). A special type of choice of object made by men. *Standard Edition*, 11.

Freud, S. (1912) On the universal tendency to debasement in the sphere of love. *Standard Edition*, 11.

Freud, S. (1914). On narcissism: an introduction. *Standard Edition*, 14.

Freud, S. (1915). Instincts and their vicissitudes. *Standard Edition*, 14.

Freud, S. (1916-1917). Introductory lectures on psycho-analysis. *Standard Edition*, 16.

Freud, S. (1920). Beyond the pleasure principle. *Standard Edition*, 18.

Freud, S. (1923). The ego and the id. *Standard Edition*, 19.

Freud, S. (1924). The dissolution of the Oedipus complex. *Standard Edition* 19.

Freud, S. (1930). Civilization and its discontents. *Standard Edition*, 21.

Freud, S. (1932). The acquisition and control of fire. *Standard Edition*, 22.

Green, A. (1995). Has sexuality anything to do with psychoanalysis? *Int. J. Psycho-Anal.*, 76: 871-883.

Joyce, J. (1914). *Dubliners*. New York: Penguin Books, 1993.

Klein, M. (1928). Early stages of the Oedipus conflict. In *Contributions to Psycho-Analysis, 1921-1945*. London: Hogarth, 1945.

Klein, M. (1945). The Oedipus complex in the light of early anxieties. In *Contributions to Psycho-Analysis, 1921-1945*. London: Hogarth.

Kris, A. O. (1985). Resistance in convergent and in divergent conflicts. *Psychoanal. Q.*, 54: 537-568.

Laplanche, J. (1997). *Le primat de l'autre en psychanalyse. Travaux 1967-1992*. Paris: Flammarion.

Loewenstein, R. (1940). The vital or somatic instincts. *Int. J. Psycho-Anal.*, 21: 377-400.

Modell, A. (1985). Self preservation and the preservation of the self. *Annu. Psychoanal.*, 12/13: 69-86.

Plaut, E. A. (1984). Ego instincts: a concept whose time has come. *Psychoanal. St. Child*, 39: 235-258.

Schmidt-Hellerau, C. (1997). Libido and lethe. Fundamentals of a formalised conception of metapsychology. *Int. J. Psycho-Anal.*, 78: 683-697.

Schmidt-Hellerau, C. (2001). *Libido and Lethe. A Formalized Consistent Model of Psychoanalytic Drive and Structure Theory.* New York: Other Press.

Schmidt-Hellerau, C. (2002). Why aggression? Metapsychological, clinical and technical considerations. *Int. J. Psycho-Anal.*, 83: 1269-1289.

Schmidt-Hellerau, C. (2003a). Die Erhaltung von Selbst und Objekt im Schatten der Freudschen Theorieentwicklung. *J. Psychoanal. Theory & Practise*, 18: 316-343.

Schmidt-Hellerau, C. (2003b). Driven to survive: rediscovering the clinical value of a forgotten Freudian concept. Paper presented at the American Psychoanalytic Association Meetings, Boston, MA, June.

Schmidt-Hellerau, C. (2005). We are driven. *Psychoanal. Q.* 74:989-1028.

Simmel, E. (1924). Die psycho-physische Bedeutsamkeit des Intestinalorgans für die Urverdrängung. *Int. Z. Psychoanalyse*, 10: 218-221.

Simmel, E. (1933). Prägenitalprimat und intestinale Stufe der Libidoorganisation. *Int. Z. Psychoanalyse*, 19: 245-246.

Simmel, E. (1944). Self-preservation and death instinct. *Psychoanal. Q.*, 13: 160-195.

Smith, H. F. (2001). Obstacles to integration: another look at why we talk past each other. *Psychoanal. Psychol.*, 18: 485-514.

Smith, H. F. (2003). Conceptions of conflict in psychoanalytic theory and practice. *Psychoanal. Q.*, 72: 49-96.

Young-Bruehl, E. & Bethelard, F. (1999). The hidden history of the ego instincts. *Psychoanal. Rev.*, 86(6): 823-851.

CHAPTER 8

The Lethic Phallus

Rethinking the Misery of Oedipus*

Here I rethink Sophocles' dramas Oedipus the King *and* Oedipus at
Colonus *with a special focus on how self-and object-preservative drives
are expressed in the protagonist's thoughts, feelings, and actions. What
endangered Oedipus' survival at the beginning of his life—the planned
infanticide—becomes the disease that later befalls his kingdom and finally
culminates in his self-mutilation, which entitles the blinded Oedipus to be
cared for by Antigone until he dies. The concept of the* lethic phallus
*demonstrates how trauma and the resultant failure in structuring the
lethic energies of the preservative and death drives can result in a specific
pathology in which disease is used as a trophy and a means to bind the
object in an ongoing caretaker relationship.*

I will never forget my first class reunion. Twenty-five years after we had
vanished with the winds, we all came together again in the little town

* (2008). Psychoanalytic Quarterly, 77(3): 719-753
This paper is dedicated to my colleague and friend, Dr. Martha Eicke-Spengler of
Zürich, on the occasion of her 80. birthday, November 26, 2005 (†2011).
An Italian translation of this paper, "Il Fallo Letico," was published in the Rivista di
Psicoanalisi's 2008 monograph entitled Parricidio e figlicidio: croce-via d'Edipo (Patri-
cide and filicide: The Crossroads of Oedipus), edited by Patrizio Campanile (Edizioni
Borla, Rome, Italy; pp. 101-121). A shorter version of the paper was presented in
Venice, Italy, on June 11, 2005.

where we had graduated. One classmate after another stood up to up-date everyone on what he or she had achieved.

Alex was first: he had studied economy and politics, he was married with three children, and had recently been appointed assistant to the chairman of a big international insurance company. Betty had studied art; she was a photographer and had shows in Paris, London, Tokyo, Boston, and an upcoming one in Sydney. Charlie was a lawyer and a happy bachelor. Dora was a professor of German literature, divorced, had one child, and was soon to become a grandmother. Eddie, happily married with five children, was a plastic surgeon and ran the community hospital in a state capital. Frank was a high school teacher, now in his second marriage, with three-year-old twins. The list went on alphabeti-cally, revealing the typical life and career stories that usually emerge from an academic background of this type. Even my being a psychoana-lyst was greeted with pleasure and applause.

Finally, Zeno got up. I hardly remembered him from my school days. He was one of those silent guys who are there and are not there at the same time. Zeno had his head shaved. He looked pale and stoical when he started to speak:

I first studied psychology for three years in B [he named a city]. I had a girlfriend. Then I found out that psychology wasn't what I wanted. I quit university. My relationship broke up. I moved to M [another city] and went to social work school. I found a new girlfriend—then that re-lationship failed, and I didn't pass the final exam. I got into a crisis and was hospitalized for three months. Then I went to Calcutta and worked as a nurse in a charities hospital. I learned to meditate. Then I got sick and couldn't work for a long time. I spent five years in a Zen Buddhist cloister in the north of India before coming back here. Now I live in a group home and work in a protected carpenter shop. My life has been an ongoing failure, and I believe I have to sink all the way down to the bottom before I'll ever be able to climb up again—if at all.

Zeno sat down. There was a moment of total silence—amazement and awe in the atmosphere. Then Alex, the insurance executive, got up and interjected: "You say *you've* failed? What do *I* do, other than moving papers from the left side of my desk to the right side, day after day? I tell you, I'm slowly but surely becoming an idiot while doing this! *You* at least meditate, that's something!"

Frank, the high school teacher, joined in: "Right—you say *you've* failed? Do you think it's fun to teach all these kids year after year, always the same stuff? And don't think that even my second marriage is an ongoing honeymoon. Maybe some people are better off if they're on their own!"

Eddie, the surgeon, raised his voice: "Exactly. Your life—a failure? Can you imagine how stupid *I* feel, walking from bed to bed every day, listening to the same kind of people complaining about the same sort of problems, and explaining to them the same procedures over and over again? *You* got around in the world, you think about things—life and death and so on—-and I don't even know how to write the word *Buddhism* correctly"

Zeno, with an unmoved face, silently listened as one after another of his former classmates bowed to him and praised his feat of having accomplished nothing. After all who wanted to had spoken up in his favor, he softly but firmly said: *"Yet—I—suffer!"*

In fact, Zeno taught me something important. At first, *pride* had filled the room; everyone was happy to present their *success stories* of twenty-five years of life and work. Then Zeno presented his *total failure*, a *nothingness* that stood there nakedly, monumental and unrivaled. At this point, the group process took a striking turn. Zeno's failure seemed to become the biggest of all accomplishments, and everyone felt like subordinating their own bursting lifelines to this extraordinarily depressing non-achievement.

I think Zeno presented us with a deeply anti-oedipal stance, the celebration of a powerful *no* to all the frightening challenges of competition, castration, and narcissistic defeat. One might think the group showed a regressive move in identification with Zeno, the non-achiever. However, Zeno did not say that to achieve nothing was better than to achieve something. It seemed to me that my classmates were struggling to lift him up, to make him feel better about what he had done (or not done) with his life. Yet Zeno insisted: He did *not enjoy* having lived an alternative life or being the biggest non-achiever. *He was suffering!* He was in pain—maybe he was the biggest in pain. What Zeno presented was something categorically different; and this is what I will call the *lethic phallus*, a concept that will be further elaborated in this paper.

Oedipus and Drive Theory

What does Zeno have in common with Oedipus? For us, Oedipus is Freud's Oedipus, presenting the drama of man's early sexual awakening, filled with fantasies about the murder of father and the incest with mother (the classical duality of sexuality and aggression), leading to guilt and punishment. That's what Sophocles concentrates on—or seems to concentrate on—when he artfully reveals the sins of this ancient hero. However, we know about another story at the bottom of this tragedy: the planned *infanticide.* Only a few psychoanalytic authors (e.g., Faimberg 2005; Forrest 1968; Ross 1982) have focused on this aspect of our most famous house myth. Freud's (1900) compelling interpretation of Sophocles' drama and his subsequent elaborations are so central to psychoanalysis that there seems to be no room left even to wonder whether this tragedy might also teach us something about other aspects of mental life.

I find it interesting to rethink Sophocles' (5th century B.C.) two Oedipus dramas while keeping in mind the concept of self- and object preservation as primal drive activities and as part of the death drive (see Schmidt-Hellerau 2001, 2002, 2005a, 2005b, 2006). While a review of these plays from the perspective of object relations would probably be readily accepted, an analysis of them from a drive perspective nowadays seems to require some explanation. Just how is drive theory helpful in understanding a clinical hour, the analytic process, or the development of a drama?

Most of all, I think that drive theory helps us capture the *unconscious current*, the *directedness*, the *trajectory* of the material: Where are all the associations of the patient aimed during an hour, and where are they aimed during a particular phase of the analysis? What is the patient unconsciously *driven to achieve?* Is his major, basic, or predominant concern safety, the activation of preservative drive activities, so that everything he does or says has the goal of enhancing his (neurotic) need to be safe? Or is he driven to find sexual excitement, pleasure, satisfaction?

The question I often encounter, "Why drive theory?", indicates that we have lost sight of the importance of what *propels*, what *forces*, what *motivates* us to do anything at all. Drive theory helps us think about what activates particular representations, and hence images, fantasies, wishes, and thoughts. Is it predominantly the lethic energies of the preservative drives, or is it the libidinal energies of the sexual drives? In examining these questions and their possible answers, we might better understand what particular need or desire makes us relate to an object in a specific way (Schmidt-Hellerau 2005b, p. 1023). It is the psychoanalytic concept of drives that brings into focus these basic and ongoing urges, the wishes and needs that inform *all* mental processes.

As an example, imagine that person X shows up at a party, and person A greets X by saying: "Hi, you look great, I want to introduce you to my friend"—while B greets X by saying: "Hi, is everything okay? You look a little distressed and pale. Can I help with anything?" While X looks as X looks, A *sees* X from the perspective of locating a possible sexual partner for a friend (a libidinal cathexis of X), whereas B *sees* X as a distressed or near-to-sick person who needs help (a lethic cathexis of X). This example does not tell us how X really (predominantly) looks. It only shows that A saw X and was struck by a sexual idea, while B saw X and was motivated to be a caretaker. These ideas can be related to a momentary predisposition or to character traits of A and B. They can be totally reality oriented, rather defensive, or mostly neurotic; in all cases, though, they express the individual's predominant (unconscious or conscious) urge to do or to communicate something sexual or preservative.

As the example is intended to show, my premise is that preservative and sexual strivings can be observed in the analytic material, as well as in a poetic text, because "every drive tries to make itself effective by activating ideas that are in keeping with its aims" (Freud 1910b, p. 213). These drive-activated ideas can be more or less obvious, they may be expressed directly or merely implied, they travel on different levels of disguise and repression, and, on top of all that, the ideas of *both* drives always travel together, combined into compromise formations or creating conflicts, and it is not easy to separate out what each is all about. However, more often than not, it is possible to hear a dominant theme.

Whenever a person—the patient or the hero in a play—is preoccupied with preservative or death issues, concerning, e.g., nutrition, cleanliness, and health, but also disease, misery, suffering, pain, sadness, death, and survival, then we see the preservative and death drives and their lethic cathexes at work. In this sense, my former classmate Zeno presented his life as an endless chain of failure, misery, disease, and loss—and he succeeded in stirring up our urges to be momentarily helpful, to take care of him and be supportive: a lethic life-account called for a lethic response in his objects' countertransferences.

Thus, rereading the two dramas about Oedipus, I wondered: Does the traumatic assault on the hero's early life—as portrayed in the myth—reverberate in the adult character as put onto the stage by Sophocles? Do we see the play's protagonist driven by self- and/or object-preservative urges and needs? Is there a lethic trajectory in these dramas that might sensitize us to similar currents in our patients' material?

As I reflected on these questions, to my surprise, I discovered a very different Oedipus from the one I had known since I first read Freud. And even more surprising was the fact that what I was discovering was openly there—it was as explicit and present in the text as it was absent from our psychoanalytic awareness. Could we not realize and reflect about the lethic needs of Oedipus (had we even dismissed their importance) because we watched the drama through our conceptual binoculars—one eye for libido, one for aggression —that did not allow us to see that this man was driven by issues around self- and object preservation and the lurking death behind them? This, then, would seem reason enough to reconsider these two ancient dramas from the perspective of the lethic drives.

What I am suggesting here is *not an alternative* to all that we have learned from Freud and throughout more than a hundred years of psychoanalysis, but an *addition*, a complement, *an other side* to this complex drama of *Oedipus the King* and *Oedipus at Colonus*.

The Unknown Known: A Story to be Revealed

The tragedy of Oedipus is rooted in a disturbance in his father Laius' mind. In consequence of Laius' homosexual assault on Chrysippos, he entertains the oracular belief—his "Laius Complex" (Ross 1982)—that, had he a son, this son would murder him and have sex with his wife: a horrifying projection, it seems, that prevented him from having sex with his wife and impregnating her in the first place. Thus, the prehistory of Oedipus is already characterized by a threat to Laius' *survival*—or what I would call a *binary conflict* (Schmidt-Hellerau 2005a) between sexuality (having sex with his wife) and self-preservation (his fear of being murdered).

Here versions of the myth vary[1]: one version tells us that, despite these fears, Laius had sex with Jocasta. Another says that Jocasta made Laius drunk and seduced him. Either way, with Oedipus' birth, Laius and Jocasta's oracular anxieties that they will be killed by their son (1299[2]) become concretized, and they regress to a *monolithic conflict* (Schmidt-Hellerau 2005a) between *self-preservation and object preservation:* that is, *their lives* versus *the life of their son.* Driven to survive, they decide in favor of their own self-preservation and order that the baby be abandoned in the woods or drowned in a box. We see that their aggression arises in the service of self-preservation.[3]

This is the family background for Oedipus-baby (or Oedipus' unconscious belief): he is not cathected as a lethic and libidinal object (an object to be preserved and loved); instead, he is *represented in the minds*

---

[1] My sources for the myth are Rose (1982) and Graves (1955).

[2] All quotations are referenced with the verse number as annotated in the 1984 Fagles translation of Oedipus the King and Oedipus at Colonus (Sophocles, 5th century B.C.).

[3] Forrest (1968) is one of the few authors who have focused on parental failure in the Oedipus myth, which he notes "reveals the effects of parental deprivation on the individual, and of familial and social deterioration that ensues from marital dysfunction. When the father's anxiety interferes with his function of stabilizing the mother, or worse, unbalances her, it results in maternal deprivation. The mother infected by the father's anxiety may ward off her fears by rejecting either infant or husband, seeking thenceforth the satisfaction of her needs for both from one, thus robbing the child of appropriate mothering" (p. 158).

of his parents as dead before he is even born. Thus, Jocasta does not carry life in her womb, but death. Moreover, since Oedipus represents a threat to his parents' life, he becomes a survival tool for them: *he is supposed to die in order to preserve their lives.* Thus, Oedipus-baby is delivered to physical assault and psychic pain in an abusive and murderous parental plot. His feet are pierced and pinned together so that he can be carried like an animal, and *this wound*—we must not forget its specifics—this "dreadful mark" (1134) gives him his name: Oedipus, *swollen foot* (thus, not *swollen penis* in actuality, even though we are used to thinking of his name as a displacement). He got his "name from that misfortune" (1135), and this name, the Swollen Foot, screams into the world forever: *he has been hurt, he is the injured hero*—and we might very well expect that in consequence of this hurt, his self-preservative needs are "swollen," increased, perhaps aggressively intensified.

Next, we meet Oedipus as a young adult. To be called a bastard stirs up a deeply unconscious question about his parents—his primary caretakers. In Delphi, his father's oracular belief is transmitted to Oedipus (Faimberg 2005), or, as we might think of it: he becomes obsessed with the *projective identification* of Laius—that he would kill his father (which also entails the idea that his father is too fragile to survive his son's aggression)—and wed his mother. Oedipus reacts in an *object-preservative* way: he decides never to return to his adoptive parents, Polybus and Merope, in order to *protect* them from any murderous and sexual assault.

Quinodoz (1999) suggests that the play's two sets of parental couples, the *abandoning* one and the *adopting* one, represent a dichotomization of Oedipus' parental imago, which allows him to avoid his ambivalent conflicts and, in terms of "the drive forces involved in an unresolved conflict," to temporarily repress his "destructive aggression" (1999, p. 17). Might we conclude also that it is the dichotomization between the *preservative* and the *sexual parental* imagoes that led Oedipus to be all object preservative with Polybus and Merope, and all rivalrous and sexual with Laius and Jocasta?[4]

---

[4] See also Schmidt-Hellerau (2005a) and Freud (1910a, 1912).

When Oedipus meets Laius at the crossroads, his father—*again!* — wants to get him out of the way.[5] Yet Oedipus, now grown up, *preserves* himself and fights for his right to be there. As he later tells Jocasta:

> And the one in the lead and the old man himself
> were about to thrust me off the road—brute force—
> and the one shouldering me aside, the driver,
> I strike him in anger!—and the old man, watching me
> coming up along his wheels—he brings down
> his prod, two prongs straight at my head!
> I paid him back with interest!
> Short work, by God—with one blow of the staff
> in this right hand I knock him out of his high seat,
> roll him out of the wagon, sprawling headlong—
> I killed them all—every mother's son!
> [888-898]

We cannot miss the ring of pride in this account: this time Oedipus has successfully defended himself. Was this an act of his aggressive drives—did he *want* to kill these people? Or was it an act of his self-preservative drives? Think for a moment of a patient who tells his analyst that he was attacked in an alley by thugs, and that he *did*—or *did not*—defend himself. Would the analyst think it psychically healthy if the patient did not fight for his life?[6]

---

[5] Some versions of the myth tell us that Laius wanted to consult the oracle about the riddle of the Sphinx. Other versions say Laius went to Delphi because he was afraid that his son might still be alive, thus constituting an ongoing threat to his life. It makes sense that Laius could not rid himself of threats to his survival by ridding himself of his son.

[6] The right to defend and preserve himself is exactly what Oedipus confronts Creon with twenty years later in Oedipus at Colonus:

> One thing, answer me just one thing. If,
> here and now, a man strode up to kill you,
> you, you self-righteous—what would you do?
> Investigate whether the murderer were your father
> or deal with him straight off? Well I know,
> as you love your life, You'd pay the killer back,

However, as healthy as his own actions seem to the adult Oedipus, we might also wonder: was there no way for his father and he to get past each other without one of them killing the other? Think of those narrow Italian roads where only one car seems to fit, but whenever two cars come from opposite directions and meet up, they always find a way to get past each other. The simultaneous wish to preserve one *and* the other makes these solutions possible. Thus, the crossroads encounter shows that both Laius and Oedipus do not have a stable representation for good object preservation. The tragic consequences of this lack are revealed in Oedipus' last line: killing the old man, *his father*, is like killing "every mother's son!"— and thus killing himself.

After having resolved the riddle of the life-threatening Sphinx[7]— thereby becoming Thebes' rescuer (a grandiose lethic idea)—Oedipus comes to live in an incestuous relationship with his mother. Or should we say, instead, as Stimmel (2004) emphasized, that Jocasta, not having overcome her separation from and yearning for her son, lives in an incestuous relationship with Oedipus? As in any case of incest, we might suspect that this relationship speaks of profound confusion in the minds of both parties in the relationship, a confusion of what is sex and what is care, a lack of differentiation leading to the sexualization of preservative needs.

---

not hunt around for justification. Well that,
that was the murderous pass I came to,
and the gods led me on,
and my father would only bear me out, I know,
if he came back to life and met me face-to-face!
[1132-1142]

[7] The Sphinx rips off (in one version) or strangulates and swallows (in another version) everybody who cannot solve her riddle. Can we say that those who cannot solve it are the children who are killed by her, one after the other? Isn't it striking that Jocasta and Laius do not know the answer to the Sphinx's questions—do not know that what crawls on four legs is a baby, and what walks with a cane is an old man, both asking to be taken care of? Oedipus, however, does know, and spelling it out saves his life. The Sphinx suicides, as will Jocasta many years later, when she is confronted with a human condition that requires not only sexual intercourse, but first and last the caretaking of a helpless human creature.

It is striking that in this drama, we do not hear anything about love or sexual excitement; it does not seem to be about sex at all. Instead, the scenery is soaked by an outpouring of lethic concerns, feelings, and imagery: they are all about *sorrow* and *threatening death*—which elicits in Oedipus the pervasive need to *take care of the spreading disease*. For despite being the king of Thebes, Oedipus is not happy; he is a "lone man unknown" (281), dragging out "his life in agony" (283); and, furthermore, "a raging plague in all its vengeance" (36) is devastating his kingdom.

Danger is all that Oedipus can see, all around him, and eventually it dawns on him that *he* "is the plague" (276) that has epidemically befallen the world of his objects. *His conviction that everyone around him is sick* speaks of a surge of his object-preservative needs and strivings. This is the opening scenario of the drama and the *reason* for its unfolding. Oedipus finds himself surrounded, overwhelmed, "with cries for the Healer" (5), and he *is driven to preserve his objects*. To his citizens (he calls them children), he says:

> You can trust me. I am ready to help,
> I'll do anything.
> [13-14]
> I pity you. I see—how could I fail to see …
> you are sick to death, all of you,
> but sick as you are, not one is sick as I.
> Your pain strikes each of you alone …
> But my spirit
> grieves for the city, for myself and all of you.
> [69-76]

It is interesting that here, in the drama's first minutes, we hear that *no one is as sick as Oedipus is—he is the biggest in pain and grief*. Accordingly, when he spells out the curse of the illness, he actually curses himself: "I curse myself as well" (284), and even seeks to be struck down by his own curse: "With my full knowledge, may the curse I just called down … strike me!" (287).

We all know how things unfold as the drama progresses and how the truth is unearthed "step by painful step" (283). Warnings that the findings of this investigation might be painful and devastating cannot stop Oedipus. He makes up his mind: "The time has come to reveal this once and for all" (1152). It is fascinating to note that the drama's focus shifts here from searching for the murderer of Laius to Oedipus' relentless inquiry of *who his parents were and what they did to him* (1161). The revelation of this mystery, forced out of the shepherd by Oedipus, is the climax of this drama:

SHEPHERD:

All right! His [Laius'] son, they said it was—his son!
But the one inside, your wife,
She'd tell it best.

OEDIPUS:

My wife—
she gave it [the baby] to you?

SHEPHERD:

Yes, yes, my king.

OEDIPUS:

Why, what for?

SHEPHERD:

To kill it.

OEDIPUS:

Her own child, how could she?

SHEPHERD:

She was afraid— frightening prophecies.

OEDIPUS:

What?

SHEPHERD:

They said— he'd kill his parents.

OEDIPUS:

But you gave him to this old man—why?

SHEPHERD:

I pitied the little baby, master, hoped he'd take him off to his own country, far away, but he saved him for this, this fate. If you are the man he says you are, believe me, you were born for pain.

OEDIPUS:
O God— all come true, all burst to light!
O light—now let me look my last on you!
I stand revealed at last— cursed in my birth, cursed in my marriage, cursed
in the lives I cut down with these hands!
[1286-1310, italics in original]

No doubt the account is shocking—its consequences overwhelming, devastating. Who would dispute that this is the worst of the worst that could happen to anyone? Now it is most striking that, when Oedipus gets the full picture, only once and briefly does he express his amazement: how could a mother—his wife, his mother—do this to her child, to him? Yet there is no outcry of rage, no blaming, no effort to excuse himself by pointing out how hard he has tried to avoid all the oracle's sinister prophecies. Instead, it seems as though Oedipus immediately absorbs the primal crime, infanticide, into the range of his own misdeeds; he did it all. He, who was "born for pain," now has his full share of it to live with.

Oh, ohh
the agony! I am agony—
Where am I going? Where on earth?
Where does all this agony hurl me?
Where's my voice?
Winging, swept away on a dark tide—
My destiny, my dark power, what leap you made!
[1443-1448]
Dark, horror of darkness
my darkness, drowning, swirling around me
crashing wave on wave—unspeakable, irresistible
headwind, fatal harbor! Oh again,
the misery, all at once, over and over
the stabbing daggers, stab of memory
ranking me insane.
[1450-1456]

I am misery!
[1510]
The blackest things
a man can do, I have done them all!
[1541-1542]
Kill me, hurl me into the sea
where you can never look on me again. Closer
it's all right. Touch the man of grief.
Do. Don't be afraid. My troubles are mine
And I am the only man alive who can sustain them.
[1545-1549, italics in original]

As much as we empathize with Oedipus' pain, more and more, we come to hear a tone of hubris in his ongoing laments. His self-proclaimed "I am misery" carries no defeat or shame; it is his "dark power" that provides him with "stabbing daggers," concretized in the gold pins of Jocasta's brooches that he uses to irreversibly enter the darkness of the blind. And, as if to concretely portray how much Oedipus is locked in the grip of death drive forces, Sophocles has Oedipus say, "*my* darkness, drowning, swirling around me/crashing wave on wave—unspeakable, irresistible/ headwind, fatal harbor!" Unspeakable, this irresistible head wind— a storm in his head—is pulling Oedipus away from life, forcing him into a fatal harbor of misery. This puts him, nonetheless, into the highest lethic rank of insanity, we might surmise: Oedipus is now "the only man alive who can sustain" such agony.

Creon, who wants to protect Oedipus, demands: "Get him into the halls …. Piety demands no less" (1564-1565). Creon seems increasingly repelled by this screaming exhibition of shame and guilt: "This is obscene" (1566). Oedipus, however, insisting that he is "the worst of men" (1568), doesn't want to be hidden in secrecy:

Let me live in the mountains, on Cithaeron,
my favorite haunt, I have made it famous.
Mother and father marked out that rock
to be my everlasting tomb—buried alive.

Let me die there, where they tried to kill me.
Oh but this I know: no sickness can destroy me,
nothing can. I would never have been saved
from death—I have been saved
for something great and terrible, something strange.
[1589-1597]

The Lethic Phallus

We see no gesture of humility in this last quotation; we find none of the modesty of someone who is sorry for what he did, no apology. Instead, Oedipus wants to live at the place that he made famous, where the parental assaultive intent was *to bury him alive*. His having been victimized, traumatized in his self, pierced in his feet, becomes a strange and terrible but great *something*, an indestructible, powerful, dark trophy: *his lethic phallus*.

This lethic phallus is not something to be hidden; on the contrary, it can be used to exercise power over others. Although he has asked to be driven "out of the land at once, far from sight, where I can never hear a human voice" (1571-1572), Oedipus claims his favorite daughter, Antigone, to accompany him. Blinded by self-mutilation, he now needs a guide, and, finally, *he can claim the right to be taken care of till the end of his life*. We need to be clear about what he suggests and carries out: Oedipus forces Antigone into a hidden incest, a lethic incest, an incest in caretaking. His lethic phallus powerfully intrudes into the beautiful life of this young woman and ties her forever to her father's misery. He denies her the joys of love, banquets, and marital delights, and casts bitterness, tears, and disgrace on her. "What more misery could you want?" (1638), he asks—as if she, too, would not know any other delight than tending to his lethic phallus, reflecting his entitlement to be cared for.

With stunning ease, Oedipus strips his daughter of any future sexual pleasure: "You'll wither away to nothing, single, without a child" (1644-1645). There shall be no room for her sexual drives; she is supposed to be all object preservative, a lifelong caretaker of her father. In a complete reversal or denial of generational roles, he forces her to live with him to fulfill the role of the "nursing couple" whose care he did not enjoy as an infant. The sexual boundary violation with his mother turns into a boundary violation in caretaking with his daughter/sister.

Creon, sensing this abuse, tries to stop Oedipus: "Enough. You've wept enough" (1662-1663). "Come along, let go of the children" (1673). He senses that Oedipus is far from being a penitent who offers apologies, but instead presents himself as "still the king, the master of all things" (1675)—and Oedipus is now the king of pain, guilt, and misery. He will later get his way and take Antigone with him into his exile.

Traumatic Reversal and Depression

Let us now return to the brief moment of amazement when Oedipus learns that his wife—his mother—actually handed him over to have him killed: "Her own child, how could she?" He learns that Jocasta was afraid—still how could she? Oedipus does not ponder this point; he concludes that it is his fault—*he* is "the worst of men," the one who did it all. In this moment, Sophocles calls upon us to witness a trauma (in the classical Freudian sense) and the way in which Oedipus struggles with its disorganizing effects. When he was a baby and his parents punched his feet and gave him away, he had no means to know what was happening. This early assault remained deeply buried, an *unthought known* (Bollas 1987), which was partially unearthed by another assault, his being called a bastard.

Now, as the shepherd tells Oedipus the whole truth, it hits him with the full power of *Nachträglichkeit*. What the shepherd says is: "No, you did *not* have a mother who cared for you [in the way your adoptive mother, Merope, did]; on the contrary, your mother [Jocasta] was after your blood—your parents tried to kill you, endangered your life!" The force of this blow to Oedipus' inner world is so overwhelming that he has to defend himself against the unbearable loss of his primal objects; he has to seal the hole it punched in his psyche—his pierced mind swells and reverses the deepest and most terrifying abyss into a huge and powerful monument: his incomparably big, erected lethic phallus.

In her famous contribution to the negative therapeutic reaction, Riviere (1936) describes the patient's fear of an inner world without escape, where "one is utterly alone, there is no one to share or help …, there would be no one to feed one, and no one whom one could feed, and no food" (p. 313). Thus, a patient in this situation is completely absorbed by warding off danger:

> To save his own life and avert the depth of despair that confronts him, such energy as he has is all bent on averting the last fatalities within, and on restoring and reviving where and what he can, of any life and life-giving objects that remain. It is these efforts, the frantic or feeble struggles to revive the others within him and *so* to survive, that are manifested. [Riviere 1936, p. 313, italics in original]

Riviere's early clinical observations focused on narcissistic patients with an unconscious depressive condition that is shielded by a manic defense. From a Kleinian perspective, she beautifully described the patient's struggle with his inner objects, in which he "feels undeserving of help from the analyst until he has helped restore and cure his internal objects" (Spillius 2007, p. 67). We can add here that the particular unconscious inner object relation of the patient, as Riviere described it, is predominantly spurred on by his self- and object-preservative drives: it is the *loss of the representation of a preservative object* that is experienced as life threatening to the subject, and it is this imagined threat to his survival that propels his "frantic and feeble struggles" *to feed and to be fed, and to find food.* To rescue and maintain "any life and life-giving objects" is object preservative, as Riviere points out, for the sake of one's own self-preservation.

Interestingly enough, we might then consider that the negative therapeutic reaction to the analyst's food (interpretations) might not only indicate a rejection—e.g., a depressive reaction to an unconscious sense of guilt (being undeserving), or an envious attack on the analyst's capacity to nurture; it might also express what goes on in the mind of the patient: that he is handing over all that he receives from the analyst to an insatiable maw. Or, to put it another way, the patient's voracious inner objects swallow up all they can get without giving anything in return, leaving the patient with nothing. This keeps the patient in a permanent, melancholic identification with his objects, equally hungry (sick) and voracious, and never to be satiated by his analyst—unless the analyst, rather than fighting these objects, joins the patient and helps him understand what his efforts are all about; and joining the patient means acknowledging and mourning his objects' unbearable, frightening, and enraging feebleness and carelessness.

Object Loss and Fetishism

Here, from a French psychoanalytic perspective, Denis (1992) offers an important addition. He conceptualizes the "depressive object" as an "internal fetish" that is "intended to preserve a broken link," a powerful "refusal to contemplate any detachment" (p. 90) from the lost object, suggesting that:

> Something else has taken the place of the lost object and has been appointed its substitute; it has inherited the *interest* formerly directed to its predecessor and *this interest has suffered an extraordinary increase because the horror of object loss has set up a memorial to itself in the creation of this substitute*, which will be found in the core of depression. It is "the shadow of the object" which constitutes this substitute or memorial; it is its fetishistic cathexis which sets it up as an object of depression, or "depressive object." [p. 89, italics added]

The link between object loss and fetishism goes back to Freud's writing. The fetishistic object is an unconscious substitute for the phallus, the symbol of the penis. Indicative of narcissistic pathology, as well as of a massive regression, the fetishistic object functions not only as a defense against castration and separation anxiety, but also as a protection against trauma, depression, and psychosis (Lussier 2002, pp. 604-606). Denis' *depressive object*, when used defensively as a fetish, leads us to recognize its phallic status. This phallus, however, is not erotically exciting and does not have a lust-promising potential, not even in the sense of masochism. It is a *lethic phallus*. It is devoted to the preservation of the lost object, the "lost object-me" (Abraham and Torok 1984, p. 229), the preservation of its shadow and death. Its perverse quality expresses itself in the hypercathexis of the affective state of suffering.

This fetishistic defense has grave consequences for the ego. As Denis (1992) points out, "the ego may be said to develop in mourning" (p. 90). Yet the fetishistic use of suffering exhausts the ego, and it "becomes spent; all cathectic capacity is devoted to upholding the structure threatened by the absence of the object" (p. 90).

Object Loss as Trauma

If these frantic lethic strivings are all aimed at *preserving* representations of a lost object, how can there be such a strongly perceived danger of their getting lost in the subject's mind—which is part of what the anxiety is about? As I can sketch only briefly here (see Schmidt-Hellerau 2006), I suggest that trauma affects, transgresses, and even destroys the very structures that define, hold, and modulate the preservative drives, and that, as a consequence of this structural rupture, the representations of a well-preserved self and/or object are pushed back into the realm of the death drives, where they will, in the end, energetically figure as a *dead self* or *dead object* (see Figure 1, taken from Schmidt-Hellerau 2006, p. 1082).

FIGURE 1

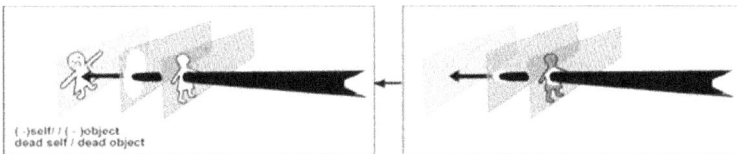

(-)self/ / (-)object
dead self / dead object

In a simplified way, this graphic depicts how the traumatic blow (the black dart) might push a self- or object representation from a preservative screen (on the right) to the structural screen of death (on the left). Once represented as a dead self-object, the blow itself becomes hypercathected. The traumatic intrusion is, as it were, turned inside out and becomes a black phallus, a lethic phallus (often symbolized in the material of our analysands by a "black snake" or a "poisonous snake").

Much has been written about this pathology, mostly focusing on narcissism, masochism, primitive rage, and aggression, as well as on primitive mechanisms of defense, such as splitting and disavowal. All these contributions have helped increase our insight into the specific mental functioning of these patients. What I wish to add from a drive perspective is that *it is the hypertrophy of a self- and object-preservative phantasm*, created by and continuously recathected with lethic energies, that feels deadening in the minds of these patients. It is the boundlessness, the *excessive intensification of the preservative drive*, that we see in certain patients as the destructiveness of the death drive—just as we see this in Oedipus (Schmidt-Hellerau 2006).

Freud ended up conceptualizing self-preservation as part of Eros. However, *to love* and *to care for* are two basically different drive activities, two very different functions, two different movements toward the object—which must first be represented separately before any mature integration can take place (Schmidt-Hellerau 2005a). To love and be loved gives *pleasure;* to care for and be cared for provides *satisfaction* (from Latin *satiare*, akin to English *to satiate*). To hold onto the love object is different from holding onto the care object; the latter results in melancholia, while the former is accessible to mourning.

The Search for a Caretaker

Laius and Jocasta failed as care objects in both Sophocles' account of the myth and in the mind of Oedipus. From babyhood, a gnawing question has long plagued his unconscious: who will ever care for him? Oedipus, (re)traumatized by the shepherd's revelation, is *driven* to blind himself. By piercing his eyes, he repeats his parents' piercing of his feet, thus revealing his fusion with the parental objects: he does to himself what they did to him—he did it all.

This act of self-mutilation also enacts what happened in the moment of trauma: a breakthrough of his preservative structures. Oedipus cannot protect his body and mind from insanity; he cannot take care of himself any longer. Therefore, the piercing of his eyes symbolizes the traumatic rupture of his preservative structures, the piercing of his self- and object representations (as sketched in Figure 1). The act of self-blinding underscores Oedipus' wish to pull away from the libidinal pleasures of any erotic relationship, and instead to embark on a lethic journey through the darkness of his lifelong misery.

By blinding himself irreversibly, Oedipus turns into a *beggar for care*, dependent on his daughter for the rest of his life. Here the very specific object relatedness of personalities with the structure of the lethic phallus becomes apparent. Such personalities do not self-sufficiently suffer; they are extremely dependent on others, and those others are reduced to and abused as full-time caretakers. This differentiates them from masochistic and narcissistic personalities. As Green (2001) points out, *masochistic* patients relate to their objects by seeking punishment and pain in order to enjoy unpleasure, while *narcissistic patients*—particularly in cases of what Green calls "moral narcissism" (pp. 131-157)—renounce the whole world, its pleasures *and* unpleasures. These narcissistic patients want to be pure and alone; they do not seek to avoid pain and misery, but strive for a state beyond pleasure and unpleasure (p. 135), and all they ask of their analysts is the recognition of their sacrifice (p. 137).

However, patients with the structure of a *lethic phallus* do not seek and enjoy punishment and pain (as does the masochist), nor do they renounce their objects and what they might receive from them (as does the narcissist). They have greatly suffered in the past, not so much in their love lives as in their need for self-preservation. They do not strive for further sufferings; rather, *they claim reparation*. What they demand is not erotic love (even in the broadest sense) or some sort of sexual pleasure; they simply want preservative care (in every way they can get it).

I call such a psychic structure—one that is excessively or predominantly energized by the preservative drives—a *lethic phallus:* it is *phallic* in its monumental urge and power, and it is *lethic* in preserving a failed primary caretaker union. This structure is thus the carrier of a lethic hyperexcitation, the potency of which penetrates its objects and fills them with sorrow, pain, depression, and concern. It is the opposite of, and even inimical to, any erotic pleasure. Instead, subjects with this psychic structure constantly try to draw in the object to cater to their misery in an exhausting and never successful effort to cheer themselves up, to lift their burden, and to make themselves feel better. The *lethic phallus* is a black phallus, but as a phallus, it irresistibly attracts the object (as we saw happening with Zeno's classmates), eliciting others' object-preservative drives, the urge to provide care and nurturing. I have found that the notion of the *lethic phallus* has a simple, symbolic, imaginary power that makes it clinically useful.

Ingres and Bacon: Oedipus and the Sphinx

Two famous paintings visually portray the distinctions I am talking about and thus are representative icons of my argument. I will briefly muse on these paintings as a psychoanalyst, not as an art historian.

Jean-Auguste-Dominique Ingres' idealizing version of "Oedipus and the Sphinx" (see Figure 2), painted in 1826, shows Oedipus as a young man. The beauty of his naked body conveys the *aesthetic idea* of Eros as incorporated in a mature male figure. Here Oedipus appears as a man who overcame and resolved the Oedipus complex—indicated by his forefinger that charmingly points to the Sphinx, a reminder of the penis that was not lost through castration. Observe, also, how Oedipus and the Sphinx look at each other in an object-related way. Death has been overcome, as indicated by the skull and bones next to the rock at Oedipus' feet.

In 1983, Francis Bacon responded to Ingres' Oedipus of 1826 as if he wanted to reveal "the other side of Oedipus" (Schmidt-Hellerau 2005a). In his version (Figure 3), Oedipus is all pain and blame. "See what you have done to me!" he seems to yell at Mother Sphinx. Or maybe he doesn't yell—maybe this is just what Gaddini calls a "fantasy in the body" (1982, p. 379), a mute presentation of our hero's wounded soul/foot on a pedestal. No bandage can contain the blood that bursts through the white tissue. This pierced foot is his lethic phallus, the trophy of his trauma that he exhibits on a plinth, higher than the socle of the Sphinx.

While the rock on which Ingres' Oedipus comfortably rests his foot is small compared to the size of the adult man, Bacon's Oedipus seems himself small, like a youngster, compared to the pedestal that he has stretched his leg toward in order to rest his foot. Also, Bacon's Oedipus, even though he is dressed in some sort of body-wear, is much more *body* than Ingres' naked Oedipus; Bacon's Oedipus is actually *all* body, all

FIGURE 2[8] AND 3[9]

Oedipus and the Sphinx
Jean-Auguste-Dominique Ingres 1826

Oedipus and the Sphinx (after Ingres)
Francis Bacon 1983

tortured body, all blame and demand for help. Whether on purpose or by accident, there is something wrong in this picture: Oedipus lifts his right leg but exposes his left foot, perhaps indicating the conversion of weakness into strength—psychoanalytically, a perverse misuse of neediness as a power-providing tool.

Also, interesting in comparison to Ingres (and typical for Bacon) are what we might call the faceless faces of both Oedipus and the Sphinx— the lack of individual representation. And, last but not least, in the background, there seems to be another bloody body part or part-object, emphasized by a dart pointing to what this whole picture is about: a celebration of pain and suffering—or, as Cappock (2004, p. 248) would have it, a hint to the Furies, the goddesses of revenge. Bacon's art consistently focuses on the tortured body, thus making him a master of Lethe in twentieth-century art.

---

[8] Oedipus and the Sphinx, by Jean-Auguste-Dominique Ingres, 1826. This image is © The National Gallery, London, 2008. Used by permission.

[9] Oedipus and the Sphinx (After Ingres), by Francis Bacon, 1983. This image is © 2008, Estate of Francis Bacon/Artists Rights Society (ARS), New York/DACS, London. Used by permission.

Oedipus at Colonus

About twenty years after writing *Oedipus the King*, only a couple of years before he died, Sophocles picked up the thread of his famous hero's fate in order to end his life. So we meet the aged Oedipus again on the stage, finally arriving at Colonus. Through all these years, Antigone has been with him, has endured grief, misery, and hunger, so that her "father had some care and comfort" (383-384). Now her sister Ismene arrives, concerned about her father because of the latest oracle:

> Soon, soon the men of Thebes will want you greatly, once you are dead, and even while you're alive—they need you for their welfare, their survival.
> [425-427]

The men of Thebes are Creon, his brother-in-law, and Polynices, his son. They need Oedipus as a means to preserve themselves. He struggles with the news: "So, when I am nothing—then I am a man?" (430-431) Ismene confirms this: they want him, dead or alive, because *their safety* depends on their control over his tomb near Thebes. Oedipus still seems ready to assume the best: "But surely they will shroud my corpse with Theban dust?" (450) The answer is no, not even this is granted to the old man. And this is the tipping point. Oedipus decides: "Then they will never get me in their clutches—never!" (454). When Creon shows up, Oedipus angrily refuses his request to return to Thebes:

> What brazen gall! You'd stop at nothing!
> From any appeal at all You'd wring
> some twisted, ingenious justice of your own!
> Why must you attack me so, twice over,
> catching me in the traps where I would suffer most?
> First in the old days, when I was sick to death
> with the horror of my life,
> when I lusted to be driven into exile,
> you refused that favor—for all my prayers.

But then, when I'd had my fill of rage at last
and living on in the old ancestral house seemed sweet …
then you were all for cutting, casting me away—
these ties of blood you maunder on about
meant nothing to you then. And now,
again, when you see me welcomed well,
embraced by this great city and all her sons,
again you'd attack me, drag me off and away,
your oily language smoothing your brutality.
[865-882]

And with even greater fury, with desperate bitterness and irreconcilable rage, Oedipus curses Polynices to "die and be dammed" (1568). Clearly, Oedipus cannot forgive his sons for driving him into exile and not caring for him. Moreover, it sounds as though Oedipus simultaneously curses his father when he shouts at his son:

You destroyed my life! You made me brother
to this, this misery—you rooted me out—thanks to you
I wander, a vagabond, abandoned,
begging my daily bread from strangers through the world.
And if these two girls had not been born to nurse me,
I'd be good as dead—for all you cared! But now,
look, they safe my life, they feed me, tend me,
why, they're men, not women, look when it comes
to shouldering my burdens. But you, my brace of boys,
you're born of a stranger, you're no sons of mine!
[1541-1550]

Steiner, who has written three thoughtful interpretations of the two dramas (1985, 1990, 1996), sees Oedipus at Colonus as predominantly in his "manic triumph which frightens us by its power and ruthlessness, and which impresses us through its grandeur" (1990, p. 230). He suggests that:

We no longer see a man who could acknowledge his guilt and who was subsequently shattered by the discovery of the true nature of the oedipal crime, but instead, we meet a haughty, arrogant man who makes repeated and devious self excuses, who adopts a superior grandeur and relates to others, including his sons, with coldness and cruelty, and who in taking on divine characteristics sheds the very humanity he fought so hard to achieve. [Steiner 1990, p. 231]

What a condemning conclusion! Psychoanalytic empathy (Bolognini 2004) is difficult to maintain in the face of an enraged patient who seems ready to take revenge and cut all bonds. However, should psychoanalysis fail to acknowledge any right and reason for a person to feel disappointed, hurt, and furious? In our theory of mental functioning and mature personality organization, is there no place for self-preservation, the right to protect oneself from exploitation and abuse? If we maintain the concept of self-preservation as a basic, primal drive activity (as well as a human right), we might find a different way of understanding the wrath of the older Oedipus. He has come a long way. Earlier, we left him traumatized by the revelation of truth, omnipotent in his guilt and misery, all lethic phallus. We also linked his grandiose attitude of saying "it was all my fault" to his need to deny the loss of his inner care-objects, a preservative need to secretly keep this bad-and-sad union of self and object alive, and to justify the abusive claim on his daughters' helping hands (and he continues to state that they were "born to nurse" him).

Yet something decisive happens here: Oedipus says: "*No, it was not all me. This is what I did and these were my reasons—and this is what my parents did.*" I suggest that what we are seeing here is the *dissolution of a traumatic fusion of self and object*, a redifferentiation that was worked out over a long period of time through a very difficult process. Wouldn't it have been easier for Oedipus to stay with the feeling that it was all his fault, to stay with this monumental guilt until his death, than it was for him to say: "This is who my parents were; what they did to me informed my whole life"?

Oedipus describes the long process of working through that he has undergone as follows:

… as time wore on
and the smoldering fever broke and died at last,
and I began to feel my rage had far outrun my wrongs,
I'd lashed myself too much for what I'd done,
once, long ago—
[486-490]

This sounds as if Oedipus has gained the insight (Michels 1986) that allows him to shed the former grandiosity of his lethic phallus and to become a normal human being with feelings of disappointment, anger, and revenge, but also with gratefulness and the capacity to realize that he, like everyone else, has the right to preserve himself and the right to act in self-defense without guilt. He responds to the necessities of life and human nature because he is driven to survive. To the Leader of the Chorus, he says:

How could you call me guilty, how by nature?
I was attacked—I struck in self-defense.
Why even if I had known what I was doing,
How could that make me guilty? But in fact,
Knowing nothing, no, I went … the way I went—
but the ones who made me suffer, they knew full well,
they wanted to destroy me.
[288-294]

Of course, the claim of the older Oedipus of "knowing nothing," were it to be made by a patient, might cause an analyst to suspect the continuing denial of unconscious guilt; and it is interesting that Sophocles has his hero stop himself right afterward when he says: "no, I went … the way I went." Could Oedipus have stopped himself from saying: "no, I went *too far?*" Might there emerge the thought: *I didn't need to kill— however, I did want to take revenge.*

Something he said in the first drama, "I paid him back with interest!" (894), now reveals its deep roots: his revenge does not address only the attack at the crossroads, but is also in response to the original infanticidal assault ("they wanted to destroy me"). So, yes, the frightening thought might have peeked out briefly: had Oedipus preserved the object (Laius) who wanted to kill him—twice—his life would have taken a different turn. To put it another way, he might have best preserved himself by sparing the one who had set out to kill him. This is where Greek tragedy pushes our limits and plunges us into conflicts beyond clear judgments of right and wrong. Yet Oedipus is not Jesus; he is the common man with whom all of us can (and have to) identify.

Oedipus not only had to painfully acknowledge that his parents did not protect him and wanted to murder him; he also had to recognize that even his own sons did not care for him:

> When I, their own father,
> was drummed off native ground, disgraced,
> they didn't lift a finger, didn't defend me, no,
> they just looked on, they watched me driven from home.
> [476-479]

However, Sophocles also shows us that Oedipus is not just a victim, tossed about and threatened by selfish people. There was the shepherd who pitied the little baby; there were Polybus and Merope, who carefully raised him; and, after the disastrous revelation, Oedipus experienced the care of his daughter Antigone for many years—making up for his lack of maternal care. Finally, he also finds a *preservative father*, Theseus, who reassures him of his unconditional protection, saying to Oedipus:

> Whatever you decide,
> I will stand behind you all the way.
> [729-730]
> Trust to this:
> your life is safe, so long as a god saves mine.
> [1376-1377]

These are the words that we all hope to hear from our fathers. In this respect, a conciliatory light seems to be cast on the closing phase of

Oedipus' life. He has experienced object preservation, and now he has one more chance to be object-preservative. Oedipus has something to offer, and this is his "own shattered body … no feast for the eyes, but the gains it holds are greater than great beauty" (650-651). Its final resting place will *protect* those who care for it.

Oedipus chooses not to turn over his body to Creon and Polynices because they do not care for him; they only want to drag him home, either with words or by force, in order to preserve themselves. But Oedipus does not allow another abuse of himself or his body, not even by his own sons. He ends, once and for all, his exploitation as a survival tool for others. Thus, he decides to stay, to die, and to have his grave located at the place of his host, Theseus, in Athens. Oedipus chooses to preserve Theseus because Theseus is the one who preserves him:

> For all his kindness, all he did for me,
> now I would give that gift I promised him. [1686-1687]
> There, in that last kindness, I harvest all the rest. [659]

Oedipus' last speech, and his understanding of the preservative value of his death, is all about safety and defense: Theseus shall keep his daughters "safe forever" (1733), and will never reveal the spot where Oedipus will die.

> Then it will always form a defense for you. [1724]
> Then you will keep your city safe from Thebes. [1738]

In the end, there will be no monumental gravestone, not for the lethic phallus of Oedipus' previous misery, nor for his last gift of safety to Athens. However, this could be taken to mean that Oedipus will remain a memory "without legal burial place" (Abraham and Torok 1984, p. 223), either in Antigone's mind or in the drama's reality. Thus, we might assume that, in the end, the daughter, too, will be left in an "endocryptic identification" (1984, p. 223) with her lost object and all the lethic consequences this entails. When the Chorus has spoken the final words, "All rests in the hands of a mighty power" (2000-2001), and Antigone leaves the stage, she is freed from taking care of her father; yet she rests in the hands of her family's history (Faimberg 2005), with this mighty, dark power weighing heavily on her mind.

The Threat of Castration

Finally, let us return to my former classmate Zeno. I do not know anything about his life, not before nor after his remarkable presentation at our class reunion. I can only muse on the event I have described. It seemed to me that he was not ashamed of his failures; on the contrary, his report was delivered with calm pride. His narcissism seemed to exist beyond question, safely established—different from those states of grandiosity that are easily shaken by the suspicious detection of any possible devaluation. Perhaps he felt some triumph or sadistic pleasure when he heard my brave colleagues degrading themselves in order to provide helpful reactions to boost him up.

However, I'm not sure about this. I felt that Zeno inhabited a different planet, in a sense, and he had a project. He did not aim at getting better by our standards, but on the contrary, he aimed at getting worse: "I believe I have to first sink all the way down to the bottom before I'll ever be able to climb up again—if at all," he said. He held onto his life as a failure to take good enough care of himself or of others (and he did not even talk about loving others or being in a sexual relationship). Instead, he had established himself in a totally lethic environment, living in a group home and working in a protected carpenter shop, surrounding himself with caretakers around the clock. Zeno related to others solely with his lethic phallus, and it was fascinating to experience its effectiveness: we all immediately felt sorry for him, and there was an *urge to be object-preservative; we literally felt driven to help him*, and to cater to (or rival with) his misery that had become his greatest asset.

If we call this attitude *phallic* in the lethic sense, then we immediately understand that for him to get off this track would equal *castration*—castration in the sense of being cut to normal size, and starting to struggle to get better like everyone else. However, there seems to be a crucial difference: the flight from castration of the libidinal phallus—say, for the oedipal child—is supported by the self-preservative wish to protect the penis (Schmidt-Hellerau 2005a), which means that, in addition to the external force (the parental prohibition), there is an internal force (the self-preservative drive) that cooperates with the former and promotes the necessary renunciation of the oedipal object.

Yet in the case of the lethic phallus, we cannot count on an internal motive to accept a form of castration. Since the lethic phallus is all about self-preservation, the threat of castration will *erect* rather than *deflate* the lethic phallus. Libidinal sparks here do not seem to have the power to elicit sexual desire; they are instead used to enjoy a mild masochistic pleasure in suffering, reassuring the subject of the usefulness of the lethic phallus. These are—from the perspective of the preservative and death drives—the reasons why such cases are so long in treatment and often lack the success we hope for, and why the negative therapeutic reaction is so hard to overcome. However, once we understand that, for these patients, *getting better* unconsciously means, first of all, a threat to their own and their objects' survival, and that, consequently, they are endlessly driven to enact a futile, malignant rescue mission—to interpret one way or the other what they dread to lose, which is the *dread of castration*, the *loss of the lethic phallus*—we might eventually find that this understanding makes the difference, clinically, that we hope for. Oedipus needed twenty years to work it all out on his own.

References

Abraham, N. & Torok, M. (1984). "The lost object-me": notes on identification within the crypt. *Psychoanal. Inq.*, 4:221-242.

Bollas, C. (1987). *The Shadow of the Object: Psychoanalysis of the Unthought Known*. London: Free Association Books.

Bolognini, S. (2004). *Psychoanalytic Empathy*. London: Free Association Books.

Cappock, M. (2004). Bacon und Ingres. In *Francis Bacon und die Bildtradition*, ed. W. Seipel, B. Steffen & C. Vitali. Zürich, Switzerland: Pro Litteris, pp. 247-251.

Denis, P. (1992). Depression and fixation. *Int. J. Psycho-Anal.*, 73:87-94.

Faimberg, H. (2005). *The Telescoping of Generations: Listening to the Narcissistic Links Between Generations.* London/New York: Routledge.

Forrest, T. (1968). The family dynamics of the Oedipus drama. *Contemp. Psychoanal.*, 4:138-160.

Freud, S. (1900). The Interpretation of Dreams. *Standard Edition*, 4/5.

Freud, S. (1910a). A special type of choice of object made by men. *Standard Edition*, 11.

Freud, S. (1910b). The psycho-analytic view of psychogenic disturbance of vision. *Standard Edition*, 11.

Freud, S. (1912). On the universal tendency to debasement in the sphere of love. *Standard Edition*, 11.

Gaddini, E. (1982). Early defensive fantasies and the psychoanalytical process. *Int. J. Psycho-Anal.*, 63:379-388.

Graves, R. V. R. (1955). *The Greek Myths.* London/Baltimore, MD: Penguin.

Green, A. (2001). *Life Narcissism, Death Narcissism.* London: Free Association Books.

Lussier, A. (2002). Fétichisme. In *Dictionaire International de la Psychanalyse*, ed. A. De Mijolla. Paris: Calmann-Lévy.

Michels, R. (1986). Oedipus and insight. *Psychoanal. Q.*, 55:599-617.

Quinodoz, D. (1999). The Oedipus complex revisited: Oedipus abandoned, Oedipus adopted. *Int. J. Psycho-Anal.*, 80:15-30.

Riviere, J. (1936). A contribution to the analysis of the negative therapeutic reaction. *Int. J. Psycho-Anal.*, 17:304-320.

Rose, H. J. (1982). *Griechische Mythologie. Ein Handbuch.* Munich, Germany: C. H. Beck.

Ross, J. M. (1982). Oedipus revisited—Laius and the "Laius Complex." *Psychoanal. St. Child*, 37:169-200.

Schmidt-Hellerau, C. (2001). *Libido and Lethe: A Formalized Consistent Model of Psychoanalytic Drive and Structure Theory.* New York: Other Press.

Schmidt-Hellerau, C. (2002). Why aggression? Metapsychological, clinical and technical considerations. *Int. J. Psycho-Anal.*, 83:1269-1289.

Schmidt-Hellerau, C. (2005a). The other side of Oedipus. *Psychoanal. Q.*, 74:187-217.

Schmidt-Hellerau, C. (2005b). We are driven. *Psychoanal. Q.*, 74:989-1028.

Schmidt-Hellerau, C. (2006). Surviving in absence: on the preservative and death drives and their clinical utility. *Psychoanal. Q.*, 75:1057-1095.

Sophocles (5th century B.C.). *The Three Theban Plays: Antigone, Oedipus the King, Oedipus at Colonus,* trans. R. Fagles. New York: Penguin Classics, 1984.

Spillius, E. (2007). On the influence of Horney's "The Problem of the Negative Therapeutic Reaction." *Psychoanal. Q.*, 76:59-74.

Steiner, J. (1985). Turning a blind eye: the cover-up for Oedipus. *Int. Rev. Psycho-Anal.*, 12:161-172.

Steiner, J. (1990). The retreat from truth to omnipotence in Sophocles' *Oedipus at Colonus*. *Int. Rev. Psycho-Anal.*, 17:227-237.

Steiner, J. (1996). Revenge and resentment in the "Oedipus situation." *Int. J. Psycho-Anal.*, 77:433-443.

Stimmel, B. (2004). The cause is worse: remeeting Jocasta. *Int. J. Psycho-Anal.*, 85:1175-1189.

CHAPTER 9

The Kore Complex

On a Woman's Inheritance of Her Mother's Failed Oedipus Complex[*]

The Greek myth of Kore/Persephone captures a particular psychopathology of women who are torn between a deadened and often asexual husband (Hades) and an ongoing close relationship with a caretaking mother (Demeter). Psychoanalytic work often reveals that these women live in the shadow of their mothers' failed oedipal complex. Their identificatory preoccupation with maternal object preservation disrupted or distorted their oedipal development, and ever since continues to serve as a defense against sexual strivings. Thus, these women are trapped in a Kore complex: as maiden caretakers, they remain attached to and torn between a "grain mother" and a grandfather transference object.

Two Brief Clinical Outlines

Cindy

Cindy, a single nurse who is thirty-seven years old, has been in a four-times-per-week analysis with me for two years. She came to treatment because she desperately wanted to get married, but never seems to get past the first weeks of a new love relationship. She feels like a failure, she says,

[*] (2010). Psychoanalytic Quarterly, 79(4): 911-933

A shorter version of this paper was presented on March 14, 2008, at the 21st Annual Conference of the European Psychoanalytic Federation in Vienna.

for not being able to have someone who loves her in the way she wants to be loved. However, she continually finds fault with her various lovers—in particular with how they treat her, how they communicate with her, and in what they demand sexually from her. Her biological clock is running out, she tells me, and she blames me for not being more successful in my analytic work with her. Her biological clock is a reality, I understand, and I do find myself sometimes wishing she would find a good mate—even though I notice that this wish is part of a complicated countertransference.

Cindy subscribes to an Internet dating service and tells me at length about the different candidates she chooses from their list, as well as about those who choose her. Here is how her encounters with these men usually go:

First, Cindy is interested. The profile of a man whom she gets in contact with—let us call him John—sounds promising. John is divorced and has an adult daughter; he is interested in jazz, literature, gardening, and hiking—things Cindy enjoys a lot. Also, he is a gourmet, which is a particular area of Cindy's expertise. The two meet, and Cindy comes into her next session raving about John. They really hit it off right away. He is so smitten with her that he said he would terminate his dating service subscription the next day. The conversation went very well, and he seems to have good manners, something Cindy cares about.

"John is too good to be true," Cindy says to me. "Where are the flaws?" She will soon find them—so soon that there is not even time for us to watch the early signs of mismatch sneak in. As if out of the blue, the just-blossoming romance is abruptly crushed under a sudden load of ice. What happened?

Having turned delight into indignation, Cindy now finds John's sexual behavior odd, to say the least. She complains that he urged her to allow him into her bedroom, which she was not ready for, but finally agreed to anyway. Then his performance seemed to prove that he was impotent. On top of all that, it turns out that he is a smoker! The whole love story unravels in a few hours (or days, or a couple of weeks at best, depending on the individual man involved).

Then part two of the drama unfolds. Cindy now accuses me of having pushed her to pursue this relationship despite the fact that she had uttered some early doubts. Did I do that, I silently wonder? She would never have gone so far as to go to bed with John, she claims, had I not indicated that she could do so. Why would I think that she did not deserve someone better than this elderly, conservative man, divorced for murky reasons, who still has a strange relationship with his ex-wife, has neglected his daughter for years, is currently unemployed, lives on his dwindling assets without health insurance, and has looming kidney failure?

Well, this now sounds horrible to me, too. Cindy is furious with me. Why do I think her unworthy of someone better? Even worse, she claims that, time and again, I have let her rush headlong into these disastrous sexual encounters. She stops short of saying that I delivered her to these rotten, dependent, sickly, passive, demeaning, and depressing guys; but she does say that she feels I would be happy if she settled down with any one of them. Then I would feel I had reached my goal. I silently wonder, *is* this my goal—to see Cindy settled with *a sickly, depressed* man?

Jane

Then there is Jane, who is very different from Cindy. Five years ago, she came to analysis depressed and rather desperate because she had discovered that her husband, Frank, had a secret collection of pornographic videos that he would watch at night. She tells me of the many problems they have had almost from the beginning of their six years of marriage: difficulties in talking with each other, a lack of sexual intimacy, and an inability to forget the many hurts that each felt had been inflicted by the other.

At age twenty-eight, engaged in a teaching position that she seems to do very well in, Jane is always tired. She speaks to me dutifully in analysis, but with little interest in what she is saying—or in what I might say to her. Jane always talks about how much work she has to do, how much she has already done, and how hard it is for her to accomplish all this. And when she comes home from work, Frank sits in front of the television, and she has to first shovel the snow, then bring in the groceries, go through the mail, cook dinner, and finally clean up the kitchen, all by herself.

Does she address this with Frank, I wonder? Frank does not seem to hear her, she replies, because he does not react to what she is saying—

that is, to what she needs, which is some help. He says that he has his own stress and that he needs to rest. And Jane continues to restlessly perform all the work.

Soon something very similar seems to be established in her analysis. She "works" all by herself, I feel—or rather, she launches into some sort of analytic routine that starts to bore me not long into her sessions. I wonder aloud about that with her, too. She reacts as though I had not heard what she was saying and continues in the same vein.

One of Jane's complaints is that she is all alone in her marriage, but she feels helpless to change this, and—as it turns out—she also feels alone in her analysis; she thinks this is how it has to be, and that something will change over time to make her analysis better. But she actually has no idea how I could possibly help her. And regarding the redundancy with which she fills her sessions, and her resistance to considering that there might be something to notice or to think about, I sometimes *do* feel helpless, as if overwhelmed by this ongoing repetitiveness that seems to cancel out any possibility that something I say could make a difference.

Discussion

Now, there is something very similar in the histories of these two seemingly very different patients that eventually began to intrigue me. As remarkably little as they told me about their childhoods, both Cindy and Jane seemed to have grown up in an atmosphere that I would characterize as *oppressive* in a particular way.

Jane's parents had a hard time making ends meet. Her mother was a cook in a government-run drop-in facility for homeless people, and worked eight hours a day for very little money. Her father, a freelance salesman, was on the road most days of the week, and was wiped out when he came home on Saturday afternoons. Jane and her younger brother were latch-key children. After school, Jane prepared the meals for her brother and helped him with his homework. She also did most of the cleaning in their apartment so that her mother could rest when she came home. There was little praise for all the hard work she did.

Cindy's family, on the other hand, was financially comfortable. Yet she, too, had a somber childhood. She was the only child of a mother who worked part-time in a museum, restoring ancient pottery, while her considerably older father, once a successful lawyer, became a diabetic invalid when she was just nine years old. He eventually lost his sight as well as one foot, and from then on rarely left the parental bedroom; instead, he spent most of his time listening to a radio through headphones.

Cindy's widowed maternal grandfather, a wealthy former real estate broker, maintained an apartment nearby, but could most often be found in Cindy's home, ensconced in a corner of the kitchen from which he ordered her mother around. Cindy says that she hated to see how submissively her mother behaved toward him, in an exhausting and fruitless struggle to please him.

The Object Of the Preservative Drives

In discussing the repetition compulsion, Freud (1920) mentions the case of a woman who "married three successive husbands each of whom fell ill soon afterwards and had to be nursed by her on their death-beds" (p. 22). In contrast to other well-known cases, in which love relationships or other relationships repeatedly fail according to a certain pattern that can be analyzed as related to the early infantile neurosis of the patient, cases like this one, where the subject apparently suffers from "a passive experience" (p. 22) beyond her influence, seemed to Freud to confirm a *compulsion to repeat*, a dark force behind his pleasure principle.

However, was the woman who was widowed three times merely the victim of some uncanny fate? She was the one who chose her spousal objects, after all. So we might wonder: did she unconsciously pick *sickly* objects? And if so, what might have driven her to do so? Did she perhaps feel the need, the urge, to take care of others and to ultimately nurse them to death?

Freud—who fiercely held on to, but never elaborated on, his concept of a self-preservative drive—did not consider that the urge to preserve others could be as primal as the self-preservative urge or the sexual one.

Thus, it did not occur to him that this woman's object choice could have been an expression—an unconscious striving—of her *preservative drives.* And this will be the particular focus of my discussion here, in relation to a particular kind of failed oedipal conflict.

As I have shown elsewhere in my revision of drive theory (Schmidt-Hellerau 1997, 2000, 2005b, 2006b), we can reintegrate Freud's neglected concept of the preservative drives as part of the death drives, if we take into account that it is the structuring intervention of the nurturing object that tames, limits, and modulates the power, reach, and intensity of the death drives—and brings self- and object preservation into being. To conceptualize the preservative drives as a necessary, healthy part of the death drives is to recognize the fact that, in the end, self-preservation is about walling up the dangers of death; it is a matter of survival. *We are all driven to survive.*

Regarding the relation between drives and structures: representations are built up and elaborated following experiences with various objects; they are the structures of our mind. However, the complex *representation of father*, for example, can be activated predominantly by preservative or by sexual strivings, leading to two very different (momentary) experiences or needs/desires of father, in the former case as a protective, nurturing object, and in the latter case as an exciting erotic object. It is the energetic investment with libido (the energy of sexual drive) or lethe (the energy of the preservative drive) that determines the function and meaning of the activation of the representation of the object *father* in a particular moment.

The need for self- and object preservation is so basic and powerful that it can temporarily or permanently cancel out the major portion of an individual's sexual strivings. In this case, a *powerful preoccupation with survival* ensues, with severe consequences for the individual's fantasy life and state of mind. Whereas sexual strivings elicit *desire*, and aim at joy, pleasure, romance, success, happiness, and related representations—thus structuring an imaginary world that colors our experience and guides our daily life—preservative strivings are expressed in the *need* for maintenance, repair, and safety; they go with sadness, sorrow, aches, and pains, and they stir up anxieties about starvation, suffocation, and dying, leading to rescue and escape fantasies. See Figure 1, in which the preservative and death drives, with their energy, lethe, and related feelings and fantasy formations, are depicted.

FIGURE 1

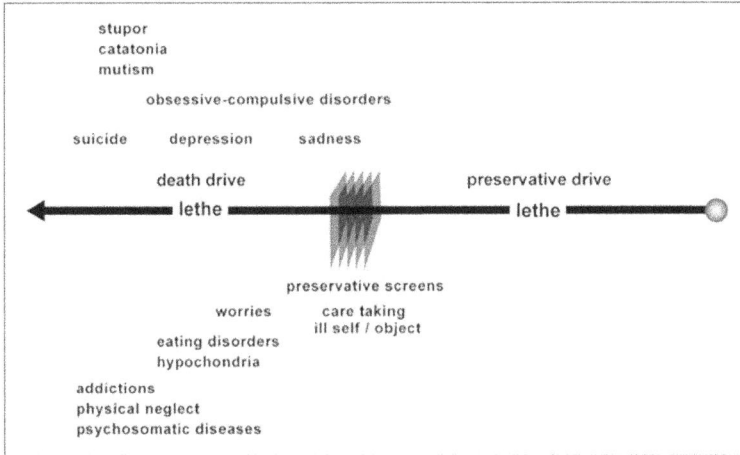

The Oedipal Phase in Women

In two previous papers (Schmidt-Hellerau 2005a, 2008), I have shown how the preoccupation with self- and object preservation impacts an individual's Oedipus complex. Here I want to explore the effects of the parent's preoccupation with self- and object preservation on the daughter's oedipal phase.

The importance of the aforementioned opposition between the preservative and death drives on the one side, and the sexual and life drives on the other, has become apparent to me in my clinical work with certain young women who are married or in stable relationships, but who do not have a sexual life. Instead, they have been mostly and often exclusively devoted to taking care of children, husband's or boyfriend's more mundane needs, and the needs of other family members, as well as household duties and/or the tasks of their professional lives. These women tend to be dutiful, on the obsessional side, rather depressed, easily worried, and frequently consult doctors for physical concerns.

Also, amazingly enough, they do not miss having a sexual relationship, nor do they complain about a lack of fun and amusement.

Some of these women have declared to me: "After my children were born, I didn't feel like sleeping with my husband anymore; I just didn't care about it." Others have said: "With menopause, or with my depression, my libido is gone—actually, I don't need it. Maybe I never did." Or: "Men always want sex—it makes me furious!"

Instead, they have established themselves, or so it seems to me, in a land far away from amor's lust and passion. They have been preoccupied with self- and object-preservative activities. And when the patient and I, often after years of analysis, unearth traces of an oedipal conflict, it unfolds in a strangely dull way. It seems as though, in their minds, there is no *sufficiently attractive father* who could spark excitement, longing, and dreaming. Yes—there had been rivalry and fury, yet it was in the area of caretaking; for example, one patient said: "Whenever I set the table, my mother came and finished it up so that she could say she had done it." Or: "I remember once in winter, when my father wanted to go out, I hurried to bring him his woolen scarf, as my mother used to do, saying, 'Daddy, you should keep warm when you go outside'—and he brushed me off, saying, 'I know what to wear!' and left. It hurt me so much!" Or: "My mother and I, we always have this fight about how to load the dishwasher. I've done it for many years and it always works fine. But when she visits, she takes out what I have just put in and starts to rearrange things, saying it works better her way—it drives me nuts!"

Notice how different these struggles sound from clearly erotically charged complaints, such as: "Mother did all the exciting things with Daddy, like staying up late, dancing rumba, going for fun trips on weekends, dressing up for the opera with her long gowns and high-heeled shoes, and on top of it all, they slept together in one bed and would chat and laugh together in the bathroom."

Kore between Demeter and Hades

As so often, Greek mythology provides us with a story that can help capture a major problem in failed female oedipal development as I have outlined it here. It is the story of *Kore*—and Kore is not an individual name, it simply means *girl* or *maiden* (which is interesting in itself: if she has no name of her own, is she really just a narcissistic extension of her mother?). Kore's mother is *Demeter*, the barley mother or goddess of grain. Demeter has important powers in the preservative sphere: mythology has it that she can condemn a person to eternal hunger, for example, or free someone from stomach pains forever. She presides over fields and harvests and can threaten the world with starvation and death.

Demeter has no husband, which is also interesting. It is Demeter's brother Zeus who fathered Kore. And Hades, who will wed Kore, is another brother of Demeter and Zeus. Thus, there is no other, *new object* outside the family circle in this story, as is essential for a mature love relationship. (Incest is such a pervasive feature in Greek mythology that I will not discuss it here.)

One day, Kore is out with friends collecting flowers, and just as she starts to pick a narcissus, her uncle Hades, god of the dead, emerges. He abducts and rapes her, and makes her his wife and the queen of the underworld. From then on, Kore is called Persephone. Demeter, desperately searching for Kore for nine days, is furious when she eventually learns that Zeus cowardly gave in to Hades's desire for Kore. (Thus, we learn that Kore's father does not *protect* his daughter—or, as I would express it, he shows a lack of object preservation that increases Kore's dependency on her mother for her protection, and thus severely impairs a healthily balanced structuring of Kore's own self-preservative drives.) In her pain, Demeter withdraws into year-long mourning, thus causing a famine that threatens everyone with starvation.

Finally, Zeus negotiates a compromise with Hades that allows Persephone to return to her mother. However, since Hades has fed her the seeds of a pomegranate, she has to return to Hades in the underworld for four months each year. Thus, Persephone is trapped between her mother, the goddess of nutrition, and her husband, the god of the dead. Eros is not in the picture, and in at least some versions of this myth, Persephone has no children, which makes sense: how could the king of death father a child? Persephone, who by marriage became the queen of the underworld, is wedded to death, destined to wander endlessly between the living and the dead (which is in some way the realm of the transference). She must shuttle back and forth between tending to her deadened husband and following her mother's preoccupation with nourishment.

In recent years, the Persephone/Demeter myth has been used to emphasize aspects of female development and oedipal conflict that were not captured in Freud's classical analogy drawing on Sophocles. Fairfield (1994) presents a thorough analysis of a whole cluster of myths related to Persephone, Demeter, and Hades in order to illustrate unconscious anxieties of both male and female preoedipal children who struggle with separation-individuation conflicts—causing anxieties of which separation (from mother Demeter) is experienced as equal to death (being drawn into the underworld).

Better known is the extensive work of Kulish and Holtzman (1998) on the female oedipal complex. They argue that the Persephone/Demeter myth captures the oedipal dilemma of a little girl who finds herself in a conflict of loyalty between father and mother, struggles with the fear of losing her virginity, and defends against a sense of agency over her sexuality before eventually coming to a peaceful resolution of her adult sexuality.

Closer to my own understanding is Krausz's (1994) view of the Demeter/Persephone myth. Emphasizing the transgenerational transmission of *pathological mothering*, Krausz shows that it is Demeter's refusal to separate from her daughter, her pathological mourning, that prevents Persephone from safely expressing her desire to her husband, or from wishing for a husband worthy of her feminine desire. It is this transgenerational, unconscious legacy that keeps Persephone trapped between a mother dedicated to excessive mothering and a husband who is merely a shadow of death. Krausz goes on to explore the fantasy of invisibility in women.

My interest centers around the psychic drives. Staying close to the narrative of the myth, I explore Persephone's entrapment between Demeter and Hades, and I focus on self- and object-preservative issues in relation to the threat of death—which, when unresolved, severely inhibits, taints, or even prevents female sexual development to a degree that requires our psychoanalytic attention.

Further Oedipal Challenges

As I have previously emphasized (Schmidt-Hellerau 2005a), the oedipal phase is a challenge to the child's mind that extends beyond the well-known, classical issues of positive and negative erotic desires, murderous rivalry, castration anxiety, narcissistic defeat, and acceptance of the law of the father and the generational difference. All of these important and more prominent features are infused by Eros, the libidinal instigator of this crucial developmental phase.

But in the shadow of these dramatic processes, another challenge must be met simultaneously: the child has to differentiate between preservative and sexual aims and functions (e.g., in recognizing that the genitals are the organs of excretion as well as procreation), between needs and desires, care and love, protective and erotic objects and interactions. If there is a serious "confusion of tongues" (Ferenczi 1949) in which the child's tenderness and attachment to her parents and her need to be taken care of is interpreted as a seductive gesture that requires a sexual response from the parent, or if the child's oedipal seductive behavior, rather than being understood and contained by her parents, is misconstrued as a heightened worry and need for caretaking, this process of differentiation will be impeded and will ultimately fail. The result is the child's permanent sense of threat, as well as a severe inhibition of sexual pleasure.

However, if the work of differentiation (which is basically a working through of conflicts between preservative needs and sexual desires) has taken place, then the two types of strivings do not need to be anxiously kept apart, but can instead be integrated on a new level (where it is possible for a single object to be an object of care as well as an object of desire), leading to a well-structured, balanced mental life in which both preservative and sexual strivings can be pursued and fulfilled.

In order for these processes to take place in a good enough way, the child's parental objects must be both good enough caretakers and good enough lovers. They need to communicate that care is about safety and the preservation of health and well-being; it is calming and comforting. Erotic desire, on the other hand, is about joy, pleasure, and making babies; it is exciting and enlivening.

As I have suggested elsewhere (Schmidt-Hellerau 2006c), structure building is the consequence of a dynamic process between subject and object. It differs depending on the libidinal and lethic components that infuse the dynamic process between subject and object, demand and response, action and reaction. The mind's structures represent not only one's own drives, with their related objects and all the memories, fantasies, and feelings associated with them, but also one's *object's* needs and desires—the "enigmatic messages," as Laplanche (1997) would call them, that are continuously perceived, even if subliminally and unconsciously. Both these sets of psychic elements together weave the dynamic tapestry of mental structures.

One of the key points in the resolution of the Oedipus complex is that a child experiences her parents as being in love with each other, when she observes them exchanging a tender hug, a kiss, a stroke, when they have a good time with each other. As jealous as an oedipal child may become, in the end it is the safe nature of her parents' happiness that proves to her that her jealous and rivalrous fantasies, her angry outbursts and secret murderous wishes, could not do any real harm to her parents' relationship. This assures her of the stability of her own romantic future. I have heard more patients in my office complain about and mourn the *absence* of their parents' loving gestures and romantic vibes (which can also represent denial, of course) than I have heard of the classical oedipal jealousy that Freud focused on. (Were marriages at the beginning of the twentieth century happier than in recent years?)

If we listen to our patients who talk about a lack of erotic affection between their parents, and also between their parents and themselves, we will frequently discover an accompanying overemphasis on what I would call *preservative* measures: order and routine, a search for harmony at all costs—often embedded in strictness or hyper-cleanliness, for example, at times combined with anxiousness. We may uncover a smoldering disease or distrust in the family, a persistent financial crisis, a sudden professional defeat, or the like. Subtle or more open signs of disaster have clouded the family atmosphere; causes for worry are everywhere, and self- and object preservation are the highest priority.

How will such a situation influence a child's development during the oedipal phase?

Types of Object Choices

Freud (1914, p. 90) describes the individual's object choices, characterizing the *narcissistic type* as a man who loves:

(a) what he himself is (i.e., himself),
(b) what he himself was,
(c) what he himself would like to be, and/or
(d) someone who was once part of himself.

Freud's counterexample of a non-narcissistic or "real" object choice is the *anaclitic* or *attachment* type, according to which a man seeks:

(a) the woman who feeds him, or
(b) the man who protects him.

Clearly, the two latter types function as the lethic or preservative object. Even though Freud intended to show how the "real" object choice develops out of the nurturing one, it is intriguing that he stayed with the preservative choices (at the time, an expression of his self-preservative drive, it would seem), and despite his predilection for sexuality, missed spelling out a *third type* of object choice, which I think is important to include here for the sake of differentiation: the *erotic type*, of which examples would be:

(a) the sensual, exciting, physically attractive man or woman, or
(b) the funny, intellectual, artistic, high-spirited woman or man. (The latter type indicates a focus on the more sublimated forms of sexual strivings.)

To *distinguish between the attachment and the erotic type of object choices* seems important when we work with patients who split the preservative object from the sexual object—for example, the man who wants a care-taking wife at home but seeks sexual relations elsewhere; in effect, this expresses the classic Madonna/whore dichotomy. "Where they love they do not desire, and where they desire they cannot love. They seek objects which they do not need to love, in order to keep their sensuality away from the objects they love" (Freud 1912, p. 183). Here we see that differentiation between preservative and sexual strivings and functions has not been accomplished, and thus needs to be—most often forcefully and obsessionally—maintained and enacted. Integration cannot take place when fusion looms.

From a drive perspective, we can wonder what object choices might result as a consequence of different parent-child constellations in the female oedipal phase. First, let us consider the *ideal or mature type of constellation:* A good enough parental couple that is *loving* and *caring* toward each other and toward the child can help her resolve her Oedipus complex, which would then lead to a *mature object choice*, in which the woman will choose:

(a) a man whom she loves (the sexual element) and whom she wants to take care of (the preservative one), and
(b) a man who loves her (sexual) and wants to take care of her (preservative).

In the above, (a) presents active strivings, and (b) passive ones. The same is true for a man's mature heterosexual object choice (with a woman as the object, of course).

However, the child's experience of an imbalance between love and care within the parental couple—whatever the cause of this (e.g., one parent's or both parents' physical or mental health problems, or the child's unresolved infantile conflicts involving frightening fantasies and related distortions of sexual and/or preservative functions)—will gravely impact the child's development. Such an experience can result in a distortion of oedipal conflict, leading in turn to various consequences; for instance, a woman might choose her husband based on the model (or anti-model) of either parent.

Thus, in the *imbalanced (neurotic) object choice*, a woman may choose her transferential father-husband as either:

(a) predominantly an erotic lover (the "sex-machine"),
(b) predominantly her caretaker (the "sugar-daddy"),
(c) an object of mutual caretaking (in which both partners will be preoccupied with taking care of each other), or
(d) predominantly an object to take care of (as was the case in Freud's example of a woman who nursed three husbands to their deaths).

These types of object choices express important differences: In the first two cases of the imbalanced type, (a) and (b), there is either a lack of differentiation between what is care and what is sex—with the consequence that every action is aimed primarily at satisfying just one of the two drives—or (a) and (b) are used in a counterphobic way, so that the choice of a "sex machine" can defend against feelings of shame around wishes to be dependent and cared for, and the choice of the "sugardaddy" can turn out to be a defense against an infantile hypersexuality, expressed as a compromise in the attitude of a "sex-vamp" (who sucks blood money from her provider) while maintaining a childlike dependency.

The second, third, and fourth imbalanced types (b, c, and d) express the predominance of self and object preservative strivings (primary or defensive ones): either the wish to be taken care of by an omnipotent provider (the permanent breast), or, in the case of a caretaker couple, the common worry that is jointly defended against by being careful, neat, concerned, and so on. This couple might get into a sort of caretaking rivalry that threatens their safety and survival, which might then be responded to by a heightened need to preserve the couple, defending against competition and hence increasing the anxiety level in an endless vicious circle (Schmidt-Hellerau 2006a).

In the fourth imbalanced type, a woman chooses a man whom she can take care of, either because he is sickly (as in Freud's example) and will need to be nursed, or because he demands caretaking (e.g., men who prefer to marry the stereotypical housewife), or because he is totally absorbed by his career (the "absent-minded professor" type) and leaves all caretaking responsibilities to his wife. Whatever the complaints of our women patients about their husbands or partners, we are mindful that the patients have chosen to be with them, and hence these men are fulfilling some unconscious wish or need of the patients (even if this becomes ego-dystonic to them).

We can fairly say that a woman who makes a predominantly preservative object choice (imbalanced types b, c, and d) at the expense of her sexuality (in the broadest sense of this notion) suffers from a heightened feeling of insecurity. Her own as well as her object's survival unconsciously feels to her as if it is always in jeopardy; thus, she must first ensure that she establishes herself close to the larder, so to speak (type b). She might also behave defensively against her own needs by projecting them onto her objects, and calming herself down by taking care of them (types c and d).

If a girl's father was experienced, portrayed, or fantasized as weak, if he was in fact sick, invalid, or actually died from a disease or addiction, or if he was or seemed to be an object in need of being cared for, this might become the focus of a woman's way of relating to a man—not in the sense of a simple replication of her childhood situation, but in terms of the subtext of all her object communications, namely: "There is a threat that father is going to die." The little girl, instead of developing sexual fantasies toward her father, will then feel *driven to rescue, protect, and preserve him*, because she is in a constant state of anxiety about losing him. (Of course, an overemphasis on preservative urges can also be a defense against the girl's forbidden sexual longings, or a compromise formation that allows her to be close to the desired object without having to feel guilty, competitive, or bad.) In these situations, oedipal development is thwarted by object-preservative needs. The girl's father, instead of being a model for her erotic strivings, comes to be represented as an object to care for; the lack of resolution of this attachment and the resultant conflicts will later stir up *an urge to preserve the man.*

This exaggerated urge to preserve should not be confused with a strong superego. On the contrary, it is my impression that in these cases, the superego is often only rudimentarily structured. Having missed out on a clear shift from predominantly preservative needs in early infancy to predominantly sexual strivings in the oedipal phase, these women have not had much to renounce and repress. Consequently, there does not seem to be a clearly designated, separate mental unit within the patient's psychic apparatus that can exert the potentially mitigating influence of a superego, which would create a conflict with urges from the id, to be resolved by the ego. Rather, there is an overriding, essentially unconscious threat to survival that expresses itself in fundamentally anxious, overprotective fantasies and activities, and makes these women prioritize always being "nice" and "good."

Furthermore, it is because of the lack of a solid superego structure that occasional breakthroughs of anger (aggression toward the object that thwarts preservative needs, as well as aggression toward the self) cannot sufficiently be contained and internally worked through—with the consequence of an even greater need to repair, heal, and protect. And where we do find a set of superego ideas at work, they tend to be rigid, limited, and predominantly preservative—while the libidinal (narcissistic) investment in the ego ideal that could promote progress and renewal, and that could spur development, can do little to counterbalance the anxiousness of the woman's conscience.

These cases follow the classical transference model in that they relate the patient's choice of husband or boyfriend to an unfulfilled childhood wish in relation to the father. This wish by no means needs to be, or to genuinely include, a sexual wish, but can in fact be a predominantly preservative one. The fact that these relationships might initially embrace sexuality—sometimes just until a woman's wish for children (who will need to be cared for) is sufficiently fulfilled—does not prove that sexuality is a major motive. The unconscious wish to be preserved by the object can still be the decisive one, if sexuality is understood to be the price for staying safely in a relationship.

I suggest that *women who choose and create their marital relationships in a way that excludes or marginalizes sexuality, who instead focus predominantly on self- and object preservation* (in order to fight off the idea of looming death), suffer from what I would call the *Kore complex*[1] Like

---

[1] Fairfield's (1994) notion of the Kore complex has a different meaning (see earlier description).

Kore, they must remain trapped between a nurturing "grain mother" and a deadened spouse who is to be rescued from dying or to be nursed to his death. Actually, they remain girls in a deeper sense, and have yet to discover and represent their sexuality—an implicit goal of their analyses—in order to become mature women.

Looking at genealogy allows us to trace the situation even further back. Careful analysis more often than not reveals that the patient's deadened husband is her mother's own transferential oedipal father, cast onto and picked up by the little girl in order to perpetuate her mother's failed Oedipus complex. Failed in the very sense that I outlined before: be it for reasons of conflict, deep anxieties, or a predominance of their preservative drives' strivings, the mothers of these patients had chosen to relate to their fathers at the oedipal stage not as potential sexual objects, but as objects of care taking. Thus, they avoided their sexuality and remained attached to their fathers in an object-preservative stance. Later, these women married considerably older, sick, or alcoholic men for whom they functioned as caretakers—remaining depressed themselves (and often abused), while yearning for a better life. Since these mothers could not or could only barely represent their own sexuality, they often lacked the necessary desire and determination to leave these malignant relationships. Instead, they continued to aim at providing better and better care, and to draw their daughters into this vortex of misery and exhaustion as their allies.

The daughters of these mothers—our patients—present themselves to us as overshadowed by their mothers' failed Oedipus complex. Identified with a caretaker mother and confronted in their early oedipal love with a sick and/or weak father, they have aborted their own oedipal development and are trapped in a Kore complex. As maiden caretakers, they are bound by the need to help their grain mothers with the burden of caretaking and to heal their mothers' paternal transference objects. Yet the inherited dead father is too heavy to be carried, too sick to let go of, and too sad to be an enjoyable object. Such an impossible task pulls these women into a vicious cycle of guilt and/or rage, which defensively increases their preoccupation with caretaking, nurturing, and repair.

"So Many Men Who Struggle"

Jane recently told me that, when she was eighteen years old, she and her brother accompanied their father on a trip to Paris. For most of the trip, they were on their own and arranged their own sightseeing. One day, however, their father took them to the red-light district, Pigalle, and it was revealed that he had been going there every day. She started to wonder what he had actually been doing during all the years when he was on the road for his work.

"He never was at home much," Jane says to me, "and he became an alcoholic, like my grandfather. Why couldn't he have a job in town— why couldn't he be happy with my mother? But when he got her roses on Valentine's Day, my mother would complain that he had spent too much for flowers, and anyway they would die in a few days. There were so many problems, and we were always short of money."

I say: "There were so many problems to worry about, and the lust sneaked out to a secret and unexpected place."

Jane then tells me that she had lunch with her brother Barry the previous day. "He reminded me of this trip to Paris," she says, "and then he told me that his girlfriend has broken up with him. He always has problems in his relationships, and he also loses his jobs—or at least he never stays at one place for long. And he has this allergy—he itches all the time, it drives him nuts. If he would deal with these problems on a deeper level, they would go away. [She cries.] I have the fantasy of being a therapist. I would talk with him, and I could help him, because I wouldn't charge him. He can't afford therapy. He would get better. [She sobs.] I think there are so many men like Barry! I found help here, and I will get better. But there are still so many men out there who struggle— and Frank [her husband] is one of them, too."

What makes these constellations so inescapable? Sorrow, concern, and care always trump lust, pleasure, and fun. If there is something to worry about, going for the fun things seems careless and inconsiderate. Jane deeply cared for her brother, and it pained her to see how lost he was in his life. She felt she could not let go of him until she had saved him. Just as Jane had always felt driven to protect her brother, she had

325

wished to save her father from becoming an alcoholic like her grandfather. Moreover, she felt the need to help her mother with the burden of making ends meet, a burden that thwarted the pleasure of roses and killed the potential for happiness.

And that was how Jane continued on in her marriage to Frank. In a lethic atmosphere full of misery, sorrow, and oppression, libido—the very energy that could turn things around for the better—is often split off; it "sneaks out" and finds a perverse release (as in Frank's use of pornography).

Something I learned over time from Cindy was that her mother had worshipped her own father, Cindy's grandfather. She had submitted to him so completely that she did not hesitate to dutifully sacrifice everything—her marriage, her daughter's well-being, and even her own life—to this complaining old man. Mother limited her professional career in order to stay home and take care of her father; she catered to her father's food predilections (his favorite was pasta) at the expense of her diabetic husband's health. And she would send her daughter Cindy to sit on his lap and cheer him up. Cindy had hated to sit on his hard knees, uncomfortable with his unrelatedness and disgusted by the two warts on his chin and the slightly rotten scent that exuded from his worn-out sweaters. But she felt she had no right to protest. "Be quiet!" her mother would say, "Grandpa had a bad day. He is old and sick."

And Cindy would tiptoe away—disappointed, sad, furious, and guilty for being enraged. Yet she continued to do her household jobs, to fold the laundry and clean everybody's shoes. Thus, Cindy found herself in a dilemma: she wanted a man and wanted a child, but she could not go out to play and find a fun man; instead, she felt guilty about abandoning *me*, her analyst, and was angry at my wanting her to "come in every day." And when she met a man and felt for a moment smitten by him, the uncanny fear crept in that she would lose her freedom and end up as a provider for a needy old grandfather. On top of all this, it felt as if it were not *her* choice, but her mother's (her analyst's).

So we seem to have ended up with quite a classical constellation in which sexuality is repressed and filled with conflict. However, this is not because it is shameful or forbidden; it is because of an *overbearing sense of misery* that continuously stirs up the need for self- and object preservation.

What I would like to emphasize here is that self- and object preservation are not part of a life drive (Eros)—in line with sexuality, an expression of libidinal strivings. On the contrary, they are its *antagonists.* If exaggerated (as is the case when one is overprotective), they oppose and sometimes completely suffocate lust and pleasure. Analyzing the overwhelming urge to help, and working through the pain and defeat of not being able to preserve, protect, and rescue, means to alleviate survivor guilt (in the most general sense of the term). It eventually frees the patient's libido and enables her to balance love and care in more fulfilling relationships.

Concluding Remarks

It goes without saying that typologies are rough abstractions put forward in order to highlight a particular aspect or phenomenon. Real life, psychic pathology, and neurotic conflict are always more complex than a bare scheme. Furthermore, we recognize that differences in constitution allow one person to flourish despite miserable circumstances, while another becomes discouraged and gives up all hope, and still another endeavors to fix all the problems in the world. And there are always more objects around a little girl as she grows up than her primal family offers; hence she might find pleasure and a good, suitable man for her awakening sexual strivings outside her own home, and she might then transfer what she experiences with others to her sickly father, thus investing him with all he needs to be the frog-turned-into-a-prince whom she can build her fantasies around.

And finally, too much misery can also lead to a compensatory erotic fantasy life that might at first glance look rather normal and oedipal (even though it is most often split off)—until the heavy weight that is attached to it finally reveals its defensive function, and sometimes even an overwhelming preservative undercurrent in need of being analyzed. Yet despite the fact that these and other possibilities necessarily complicate the simple picture sketched in this paper, the differentiation between sexual and preservative strivings seems to me to be crucial for an awareness of this particular dynamic in our psychoanalytic work with patients.

References

Fairfield, S. (1994). The Kore complex: the myths and some unconscious fantasies. *Int. J. Psycho-Anal.*, 75:243-263.

Ferenczi, S. (1949). Confusion of tongues between the adults and the child (the language of tenderness and of passion). *Int. J. Psycho-Anal.*, 30:225-230.

Freud, S. (1912). On the universal tendency to debasement in the sphere of love. *Standard Edition*, 11.

Freud, S. (1914). On narcissism: an introduction. *Standard Edition*, 14.

Freud, S. (1920). Beyond the Pleasure Principle. *Standard Edition*, 18.

Krausz, R. (1994). The invisible woman. *Int. J. Psycho-Anal.*, 75:59-72.

Kulish, N. & Holtzman, D. (1998). Persephone, the loss of virginity and the female oedipal complex. *Int. J. Psycho-Anal.*, 79:57-71.

Laplanche, J. (1997). The theory of seduction and the problem of the other. *Int. J. Psycho-Anal.*, 78:653-666.

Schmidt-Hellerau, C. (1997). Libido and lethe: fundamentals of a formalised conception of metapsychology. *Int. J. Psycho-Anal.*, 78:683-697.

Schmidt-Hellerau, C. (2001). *Life Drive and Death Drive, Libido and Lethe. A Formalized Consistent Model of Psychoanalytic Drive and Structure Theory*. New York: Other Press.

Schmidt-Hellerau, C. (2002). Why aggression? Metapsychological, clinical and technical considerations. *Int. J. Psycho-Anal.*, 83:1269-1289.

Schmidt-Hellerau, C. (2005a). The other side of Oedipus. *Psychoanal. Q.*, 74:187-217.

Schmidt-Hellerau, C. (2005b). We are driven. *Psychoanal. Q.*, 74:989-1028.

Schmidt-Hellerau, C. (2006a). Fighting with spoons: on caretaking rivalry between mothers and daughters. *Psychoanal. Inq.*, 26:32-55.

Schmidt-Hellerau, C. (2006b). Surviving in absence: on the preservative and death drives and their clinical utility. *Psychoanal. Q.*, 75:1057-1095.

Schmidt-Hellerau, C. (2006c). A shift in the head of Janus: metapsychological reflections on the analyst's contribution to psychic transformation. *Bull. European Psychoanalytic Federation*, 60:135-143.

Schmidt-Hellerau, C. (2008). The lethic phallus: rethinking the misery of Oedipus. *Psychoanal. Q.*, 77:719-753.

CHAPTER 10

The BAD Superego

Reflections on a Subversive Myth[*]

Between 2000 and 2010, three prominent analysts in Boston resigned. Whatever the legal or official statements about their sudden disappearances from their institutes, their resignations occurred in the context of alleged boundary violations. In the aftermath of these shocking events, the Boston Psychoanalytic Society and Institute (BPSI) formed a task force to look at and reflect on boundaries in all aspects of the institute's life. The aim was to better understand the determining factors of an institutional culture that could contribute to or fail to prevent boundary crossings and violations. This paper, continuing these reflections, was presented and discussed at BPSI in October 2010 and followed up with a panel on "Love and Hate" in March 2011, all of which contributed to a serious process of working through. A boundary violation could happen in any psychoanalytic institute. That's why I decided to include this paper in this volume. The appendixes will raise related issues, one of which explicitly addresses boundary violations in the context of self- and object-preservative questions.

---

[*] This paper is dedicated to Dr. Ellen Pinsky who, as the then-Program Chair of the Boston Psychoanalytic Society and Institute, had the audacity to invite these reflections for a presentation and controversial discussion with the whole membership in October 2010. In this, as in many other instances, she was the trusted reader of early drafts of my writings. Her sensitive and astute comments on the basis of our shared love for Freud and writing were an invaluable help and support throughout the years, for which I feel deeply grateful.

No analyst is allowed to have sex with a patient because, due to the transferential nature of the patient-analyst relationship, sexual relations between the two are incestuous. Whatever the individual ramifications, incest between parent and child always relates—directly or via deferred action—to the Oedipus complex: by breaking the law that "you shall not sleep with your parent," the boundary violator unconsciously kills the father (Laius)—if not the mother (Jocaste's suicide)—leading to misery (disease) for the community (Thebes's plague), and finally the expulsion of the perpetrator (Oedipus). Hence boundary transgressions in psychoanalysis relate to unresolved oedipal conflicts, revealing the erosion, subversion, or resexualization of the superego.

In this sense, I want to apply psychoanalytic thinking to psychoanalysts ourselves as we are organized in institutes, societies, and associations, in the hope of increasing our insight into processes of which we are all a part.[1] In doing so, I am not primarily interested in individuals or their psychology (Gabbard and Lester 1995). Rather, I'm concerned with *how we think about the issues under consideration*, and specifically, how our thinking can be understood when examined through the narrow lens of the superego.

Noticing

In 2000, I moved from Switzerland, where I did my psychoanalytic training, to the United States, where I became a member of the American Psychoanalytic Association and a Training and Supervising Analyst of the Boston Psychoanalytic Society and Institute. Such a move is as exciting as it is daunting. At the new place, most everything is unfamiliar: colleagues, procedures, locations—so much is different, surprising, challenging, and at times alienating. One doesn't immediately understand or get everything right. Nothing goes without saying; everything needs to be studied and verified. But this may offer the newcomer the

---

[1] Much has been written about the dynamics within psychoanalytic institutes, organizations, and education. My contribution is limited to a discussion of the relevant processes in relation to the applied concept of the superego.

chance to take a fresh look at habits that to insiders seem too much a matter of course to be even tentatively questioned.

In this context, I made the following observation: Whenever there was a clinical presentation, I noticed a phrase that came up in many iterations, namely: "The patient cannot allow himself to acknowledge his success." Or the analyst would interpret to the patient, "You cannot allow yourself to have a good analysis," or would state, "Now you can allow yourself to relax." The general meaning seemed to be that if the patient were healthy, he would allow himself to enjoy all the good things he was capable of. Thus the analyst was working to help the patient to allow himself more gratification and to lead a less restricted, happier life—and there is nothing wrong with that.[2]

But what was striking to me in this habitual way of speaking was the "allow" part. I thought to myself: internally "allowing" and "not allowing" are functions of the superego. The *id* needs and desires; the *superego* demands, allows, and forbids; and the *ego* perceives, struggles, compromises, and decides. Thus the implication of these "allow" statements seemed to be that the patient suffered from a bad superego that would not allow him to enjoy all the good things available to him.

There are many possible reasons for a state of mind that prevents a patient from enjoying a good feeling or thought about himself or his surroundings. For instance, there is narcissistic grandiosity that feels abased when a seemingly small accomplishment sparks happiness; or there is a projected paranoid fear of being enviously attacked when feeling pleased about having something good; or there is a weak ego that cannot deal with intense joyous excitement—and these are just a few possibilities that are not primarily related to the superego. But the phrasing of the comments I was hearing was not "the patient is ashamed or afraid"; rather, it was that he would not *allow* himself something. Whether explicitly spelled out or not, the focus seemed to be on a *bad superego* looming large somewhere in the patient's—or in the analyst's—mind.

---

[2] Freud, more modest than we might sometimes feel today, cautiously aimed for less— that is: to turn neurotic suffering into ordinary misery—which in most cases is already a lot and certainly good enough.

A while ago at a meeting of the American Psychoanalytic Association, I heard a case presentation in which a patient was said to be complaining and swearing that this was shit and that was shit, thus shitting throughout and all over the hour, which his analyst correctly interpreted, but the patient couldn't hear him and make use of what his analyst said; instead, he went on to crush all interventions with his verbal diarrhea. Regressive states like these are difficult for all of us to cope with; they require our analytic thinking in order to figure out how best to help such a patient to gain or regain a more workable level of psychic functioning.

However, I was struck when one of the discussants of this case said: "This patient is great fun! He is like an adolescent. The analyst allows him to do what the patient's father never allowed him to do, to swear and fully express his anger. This is fun!" Here again, we hear that something is *allowed:* the analyst allows the patient to shit all over the hour, and somehow this is fun. But I didn't think that the analyst actually allowed the patient to enjoy his shit monologues; rather, the analyst couldn't stem the fecal flood.

However, if what this adult patient exhibited was adolescent behavior, wouldn't we have to analyze what was keeping him in deep shit—rather than simply having fun listening to its evacuation? Further, if this is understood as adolescent behavior, then it might as well be called rebellious—and then this discussant's implication could have been that the analyst was siding with his patient's rebellion against a strict, paternal, criticizing superego that would not allow him to shit all over the hour. To put it differently, the discussant enjoyed the idea of an analyst who sided with and allowed rebellion against a critical or *bad* superego.

This is not the only such example. These case descriptions are part of our scientific literature. In "Defining the Goals of a Clinical Psychoanalysis," Renik (2002) tells us of his first session with Sheila, whose

thoughts turn to the film director Luis Bunuel and his depiction of the Last Supper in *The Discreet Charm of the Bourgeoisie,* in which people eat in the bathroom and defecate in the dining room. She chuckles, thinking about it. I suggest that perhaps the appeal of the scene in the

Bunuel movie is that it shows the absurdity of received morality by turning it on its head. Sheila agrees, and adds that she likes Bunuel because of his refusal to accept orthodoxy. (p. 120)

Note that Sheila has fun—she chuckles—when talking about these people who, as she remembers it,[3] "defecate in the dining room." Her analyst sides with her, saying that the movie shows—he doesn't say *seems to sh*ow or that *Sheila thinks it shows*, but that it *does* show "the absurdity of received morality"—thus he is joining the patient in a subversive attack on an absurd superego that does not allow people to defecate in the dining room.

Now one could argue that I am making too much of this little *allow* word, and in the end, it may not even have much to do with the superego at all. However, I was again struck in hearing colleagues say of senior analysts in their community: "He is the superego of our institute!" Or: "He is so superego-ish!" These remarks weren't really meant as compliments. So, I wondered, what is so wrong with the superego?

The next thing I noticed was an emphasis on *safety*. "The patient needs to feel safe," I heard. Was this statement meant simply to emphasize the general safety of the analytic environment? I don't think so. Having read a number of case reports, it seems to me that phrases such as "the patient didn't feel safe enough to express himself" speak instead to the patient's fear of being criticized or shamed by the analyst, and to the analyst's effort to reassure the patient that his analyst isn't so critical, or that the patient isn't as bad as his own bad superego would suggest.

However, as Gray (1991) has shown, if the patient's "infantile needs for safety" (p. 3) meet in a defensive collusion with "the analyst's wish to be regarded as non-critical" (p. 4), then a "false sense of safety" (ibid.) is created that merely bypasses the patient's terrifying and debilitating

---

[3] Interestingly enough, (the original version of) this movie (that I watched again in this context) does *not* include a scene where people "eat in the bathroom and defecate in the dining room." So it is possible that Sheila communicated a *fantasy*, her *inner* spectacle, which was taken by Renik as the film's *reality* rather than as an issue Sheila was struggling with. Anyway, the very fact that she talks about this scene to her analyst makes it an analytic event rather than a cinematic one.

superego conflicts. Good old Freud might still have gotten it right when he taught us that the persistence of the patient's bad conscience tells us that his unconscious ego knows more about his secret hostile strivings than his consciousness might want to acknowledge.

But the emphasis on safety is not limited to our patients. When we discuss matters of training, I frequently hear the statement that our candidates need to feel safe. What is it that would make them *not* feel safe, I wondered? Criticism, I learned, was the issue; the candidate should not feel anxious about being criticized or ashamed of not knowing something. Nor should the candidate be embarrassed about having engaged in an enactment, something one "shouldn't" do—and this *shouldn't* is always gestured with both arms flying up into the air to indicate quotation marks around *should,* thus questioning or even mocking a critical, bad superego that tells us what we should and should not do (rather than remaining open to discussion, e.g., of what the enactment might have meant in the moment).

Certainly, being anxious and ashamed are unpleasant feelings. But they are part of everyone's development and actually give the necessary impetus for change and growth. Our work is difficult; a candidate is a candidate and a supervisor is a supervisor, and the candidate comes to us so that we can teach him analytic thinking and the meaning and variety of technical skills. If we turn an open and critical mind toward the work of our candidates and reflect together with them, they will build a sense of safety of their own. It helps them if we are critical—yet being "critical" is something that I often hear equated with being really bad. So it seems we are dealing here with a bad superego, a ghost that haunts our culture.

Yet there is something puzzling, something that might at first seem like a paradox—but isn't, as I will show. The puzzle is: the more we counteract a supposedly bad, critical superego by being willing to *allow,* the more we need to emphasize *safety.* To say it differently: There seems to be a connection between *allowing more* and *feeling less safe.*

The Superego as Heir of the Oedipus Complex

As we all know, the superego is the heir of the Oedipus complex with all the personal traces, scars, and ruptures that determine its more or less successful resolution in the individual's early history. But here already we must pause. As the title of Greenberg's bestselling book *Oedipus and Beyond* (1991) insinuates, we are nowadays more *beyond* than *with* Oedipus, it seems. Several years ago, after having taken my elective course on "The Many Faces of Oedipus," a candidate told me that he had only signed up for it out of curiosity. Like many of his cohort, he thought that the Oedipus concept was outdated, of no use any more. Now he was surprised to find that it helped him understand his patients' material in ways he hadn't before.

Have we really marginalized the Oedipus complex—this, as Freud (1905) famously called it, "nuclear complex of the neuroses" (p. 226), with all its many challenges that recur in mental life and in every analysis—for everyone, with no exception? "Times have changed," a colleague recently stated, and he is right. But our unconscious hasn't changed, not a bit. Despite the intellectual and scientific progress that provides our Google-connected minds with seemingly unlimited knowledge from early on, the minds of our children are still preoccupied with the questions and mysteries of their parents' intercourse and procreation. They still fight the unavoidable oedipal battles, and that's why our unconscious remains a wild forest populated with heroes and haters, snakes and sinners, the monsters and murderers of our ancient infantile prehistory. In this sense, we will never get beyond Oedipus.

Maybe, then, the idea of being beyond Oedipus speaks, rather, of a movement within our psychoanalytic community: a movement away from what Freud called the shibboleth that distinguishes analysts from non-analysts, and thus away from psychoanalysis—or is it a regression to narcissism, a movement against Oedipus, an *anti-Oedipus*?

As we know, oedipal challenges are manifold and complex: gender and generational differences, triangulation, exclusion and primal scene fantasies, jealousy, rivalry, castration anxiety and penis envy, the differentiation between needs and desires, fear and fury, love and hate, the positive and negative Oedipus and all the challenges that a five-year-old's still fragile narcissism must face. Only when all these confusing tasks and conflicts of passion and exploration have been sorted out can there be a dissolution of the Oedipus complex that will establish the superego.

As Freud discovered, the superego is the result of a complex integration of many elements, including the earliest identifications with and object choices of both parental objects, as well as the reaction formations against these choices (Freud 1923, p. 34). The superego not only demands that "you ought to be like this" (like your father); it also comprises the prohibition that "you may *not* be like this" (like your father)--that is, "you may not do all that he does; some things are his prerogative' Against this parental *NO* the child mobilizes a considerable amount of anger, "but he is obliged to renounce the satisfaction of this revengeful aggressiveness." (Freud 1923, p. 34). And in order to accomplish this difficult task, the infantile ego borrows strength from the father by taking "the un-attackable authority into himself" as his superego (p. 34), which is invested with all the aggression that had originally been mobilized against it (Freud 1930, p. 129). Hence the strictness of the superego is not merely a testimony to the experience of parental rigidity; it also operates—and maybe even more so—in the service of the child's own aggressive reaction to parental prohibition.[4]

This is the genesis of a harsh, critical superego, leading to fearfulness, inhibition, and guilt exuding from a never-silent bad conscience, the critical voice within.[5] Is this, then, what we want to protect or free our

---

[4] The superego structure merges representations of parent and child; it looks and acts like the parent but has a passion that betrays the child's own murderous wishes. This, as Freud recognizes, can become a terrible vicious cycle, "for the child's vengeful aggressiveness will be in part determined by the amount of punitive aggression which he expects from his father" (1930, p. 130). So the more furious the child is over the parental *no*, the more horrible he imagines his father's punishment will be, which makes him even more anxious and more furious, thus more threatened by a potentially still-more-devastating paternal response, and so on. The original parental prohibition can be minor but can nevertheless spiral within the child's mind into a dangerous and aggressive inner monster that will become a building block of his bad superego.

[5] The most extreme case of a murderous superego was first described by Rosenfeld in his paper "Destructive Narcissism and the Death Drive" (1971), in which he depicts the

patients from by *allowing* instead of prohibiting, and by making them feel safe? The equation wouldn't add up were we to offer ourselves as a gentler countermodel. Freud's theoretical analysis points out that the harsh and overcritical superego is a subject-object unit (a co-creation, if you will) characterized and infused by parental as well as infantile aggression. Try to obliterate the object's role and you will throw out the subject's with the bathwater. That's why our patients resist doing away with it. We want to hold on to our father's borrowed strength—or else we would feel weak and endangered; and we keep blaming our vengeful aggression on his iron fist because it provides justification for our hot-headed revenge. However, if we don't own our aggression, we will always feel persecuted, afraid of this inner monster that we once created, submissive even though intending revolt. And this is the trap: In order to finally escape the fear of punishment, we must admit to the very bad thing—our own aggression and wish to defeat authority—that we fear will subject us to terrible punishment.

Defensive Strategies, or the Battles of Oedipus

What to do? There seem to be different strategies. One is to abolish the concept of the superego altogether. No less of a psychoanalytic giant than Charles Brenner (2002, 2003) suggested trashing it when he, late in life, discarded Freud's structural theory, replacing it with his own notion that every mental event is a compromise formation.[6] But discredited or not, this bad superego didn't go away—or it's hard to let go of for the reasons just pointed out.

The next strategy is the reexternalization of the superego and, in an effort to limit its influence, it may be projected onto a few people in a

---

superego as a ruthless Mafia gang relentlessly persecuting a small intimidated self that cannot move and cannot love for fear of total destruction. However, these extreme expressions of a destructive superego apply only to a relatively small group of severely narcissistic patients.

[6] This is not exactly a contradiction. Since every psychic structure can be conceptualized as a drive-defense unit (including compromise formations), the structural model merely offers the same principle on a higher level of organization.

sort of pin-the-tail-on-the-donkey. If this worked—if there were only a few colleagues, sort of impersonating superegos—we could just avoid these guys, and all would be fine. But fine it isn't. Occasionally these people make a critical comment, and that is scary, annoying. So next we question their right to say something in the first place, or at least to say something critical. However, since their criticism comes from a position of authority anchored in the structures of our national organizations (we might say our mega-superegos), we now have to dispute the right of these organizations to mix in our local affairs—to judge, regulate, mandate, and evaluate what we are doing. That's a tricky task. In order to get these larger organizations to give up the power, authority, and oversight that we once invested them with and that is now inscribed in our laws and bylaws (our depersonalized superego), we claim that these laws are destructive and crippling (thus betraying our threat of castration).

As a case in point: it has been said that the requirement of Certification and Training Analyst (TA) appointment for those who shall be *allowed* to analyze candidates can be a destructive interference with an applicant's ongoing productive analysis; and this can be seen as crippling an institute because it could exclude some people from applying for training. However, let's keep in mind that the TA requirement doesn't ask anyone to interrupt his analysis; it simply defines one of the conditions for training, and of course an application can be delayed if an individual doesn't yet meet a particular criterion. All training institutions define their conditions and are in this sense exclusive to those who don't meet them.

Now, in case the reader already sees me as squarely in the orthodox corner and as an ultraconservative who is against any change, I want to make my stance explicit: I am not against amendments that provide more flexibility; in fact, I have voted for and supported many of them. However, I take issue with the rationale for this change. Our thinking matters. If we modify our standards because we declare them to be destructive, then we discredit everyone who has ever adhered to these standards, viewing each of them as either an aggressor or a victim of our organization's bad superego laws. And in that way, we lose sight of what made these standards appear reasonable and necessary when they were first put in place (I'll get back to this later). It is this kind of argument that may persist in our meeting rooms and corridors and infuse our institutional climate.

Further, it has been argued that evaluation for a TA appointment is basically impossible because there are no clearly defined criteria for deciding whether someone has the capacity to be a TA or not. However, to deny our overseeing bodies the right to judge competency and establish criteria for evaluation essentially means decapitating (or castrating) our analytic fathers, tantamount to saying that "they don't have the brains to conduct such an evaluation. Meanwhile, those of us who have served on evaluative committees, whether for candidates or for TA appointments, know that there is usually a broad consensus about the qualification of an applicant, even across differing theoretical schools. We all know that. We also know that sometimes evaluators err, possibly even in derogatory or sadistic ways, which is hurtful to the one being evaluated. However, if the process fails, consistency prevails.

My comments are not about excusing evaluation failure; they are about upholding the principle of evaluation because it meaningfully relates to oedipal essentials such as paternity, seniority, and maturity—in short, the acceptance of a generational difference. And there is another wrinkle to this debate: evaluation always elicits anxiety. Thus, to remain firm and to continue thinking analytically while going through an evaluation process proves that the applicant is sufficiently grounded and competent in what he is doing to be able to persevere even if he is challenged—be it by the stress of the evaluation itself, by a provocative candidate in training, or by the defiance of a patient in the midst of a negative transference. So I wonder about the wisdom of the suggestion that new, ad hoc TAs should not be evaluated, for if we believe that their work is good enough, this can easily be confirmed by a brief evaluation, and if we doubt this, it would be irresponsible for us to let that work continue.

But I think that opposition to the evaluation of ad hoc TAs is actually about something else, namely, the idea of a bad superego, impersonated in some mean-spirited evaluators who would not allow what is desirable. The serious problem with this idea is its basis in a smoldering suspicion about our senior colleagues, a distrust that can undermine our community. And finally, if we stick to this belief, we end up in a paradox: we want to teach candidates to become good analysts of their patients while at the same time suggesting that we cannot tell if their analysts are good enough for them.

It is remarkable: all organizations are hierarchical—the political system in our national democracy is hierarchical; the organization of our schools and universities is hierarchical; even our organism, the interaction between body and brain, functions hierarchically. So if every organization requires hierarchy—bottom-up and top-down regulation included—why, then, are these all-engulfing and split-producing battles periodically stirred up in psychoanalytic institutes over the decades and throughout the world?

There is substantial literature addressing this question, which can't be summarized here. Let me mention only Kernberg (1998), for one, who suggests that exploration of the unconscious (as in candidates' analyses) liberates "radioactive fallout" that increases regressive group processes in social organizations, particularly in psychoanalytic institutes (1998, p. 214f.). Also, it is well known that displacement, splitting, and projection of current and lingering transferences infuse many processes in psychoanalytic institutions (ibid.). In the context of my subject here, I think, we analysts are more prone to oedipal fights than other professionals may be because—whether we see it as such or not—we are continuously exposed to the unconscious of our patients; their unconscious Oedipus complexes stir and rub against our own and never give it a rest. So perhaps our organizational struggles are an expression, at least in part, of the smoldering heat that arises from our own never-ceasing desire to topple what impedes our path to the forbidden object—a leakage, as it were, from our own oedipal wounds.

As long as we don't know about it, the ghost that haunts us won't leave; it will keep circulating, sometimes more openly and at other times rather covertly. Where does it come from? I have heard that in earlier decades, senior colleagues tended to be harsh and shaming toward candidates, prohibiting their progression as well as the appointment of new Training Analysts. This earlier generation held onto its power and stood in the way of the younger generation. This phenomenon happens everywhere, repeatedly! It is the reverse of the Oedipus complex, the *Laius complex*. Remember that Laius, the father, wanted to kill Oedipus, the son, because he was afraid of one day being replaced (killed) by him. Hence the *Laius complex* is simply the mirror of the Oedipus complex (in the same way that a dreamer may present his father as a child and himself as a parent); it's the same principle—namely, the elimination of the rival within a generational conflict. We could say that senior analysts who act not to promote but rather to kill their candidates' progress are exhibiting either a revival of their own oedipal battles or that they never succeeded in resolving them in their own analyses.

I can appreciate the achievement of establishing a better intergenerational dialogue, having overcome the various hurts and animosities, having finally reconnected in a respectful and civilized way. There is good reason for a society to be proud of building a warm, collegial atmosphere, of providing a thorough training program, and of organizing the processes of decision-making in democratic and transparent ways on all levels of hierarchy. Still, our capacity to share responsibility and transparency within our organization and our institute does not translate as such into our unconscious life, where we simultaneously experience the world with radical, primitive, and passionate feelings. Outer and inner lives differ, and our reality perception is always an amalgam of both. That's why we cannot disregard Oedipus. And that's why I am concerned that a lack of awareness of and reflection about ongoing oedipal dynamics will end up undermining our achievements and strength in far-reaching ways.

Some of the problems I'm seeing in this context are these:

1) Our friendly collegiality may at times be mistaken as compliance with a silent requirement to consistently be "nice" and accepting. It seems as if being nice (i.e., making people feel safe) has secretly become a guiding principle—a *being-nice principle*, perhaps a variation of the pleasure principle—turned into a group ideology to replace the principle of the strongest, the wisest: the paternal principle. Does this replacement casually suggest that there is no need for a particular leader, that all can be leaders simply by being nice?

2) A *being-nice principle* would constrict our scientific debates. If we cannot criticize or contradict anyone, we cannot freely reflect, openly question, probe, or discuss our assumptions and opinions, nor can we strive for better ideas, answers, and solutions.[7] This is so because a better argument by definition claims superiority, and hence a hierarchy is established—so that, if we fight against hierarchy, we cannot support or maintain a strong and healthy competition among arguments.

3) It follows that all aggression, even when it is necessary in the sense of benign assertiveness, has to go underground. Where does it go from there? One of its outlets, I think, infuses the demand for equality—equality that by definition decries what is superior. I think it is here that anxiety and vulnerability shine through, and here that we risk being stuck in the weakness of a narcissistic, preoedipal safety position, for if we cannot confront inferiority in the face of superiority, we cannot improve. Then we will always fear that our weaknesses will be found out.

4) The fight against hierarchy and the prerogatives of the parental generation deprives us of protection and challenge. Psychoanalytically speaking, there is no longer a father to lean on and learn from. Consequently, we cannot profit much from those in our community who have proven, usually elsewhere and often internationally, that they have something special to offer. The question is: can the excellence and intellect of our best colleagues be a source of pride within our societies and of attraction to them, or do they merely exist as hidden truths because equality wouldn't allow for such differences to become apparent?

5) This is important because subduing difference for the sake of equality would lead to mediocrity, which would make us less

---

[7] In our discussions, we rarely if ever hear a contributor say: "I disagree with x." Instead, the typical speech-act goes like this: "I find x very interesting. I might only add y."

interesting and hence less attractive in the greater world of competition. For instance, on the occasion of our institute's 75th anniversary, a focus on "the areas of commonality that bridge every modality from supportive psychotherapy to psychoanalysis" meant emphasizing that others also do what we do. Thus, our institute inadvertently communicated that the essentials don't matter much, and that the differences in what we offer lie in marginal conveniences. In fact, I am concerned that it may be considered "politically incorrect" to emphasize that there is a difference between psychoanalysis and psychotherapy, and that psychoanalysis is first and foremost what we offer, that this is special, unlike anything else, and if you want to become a psychoanalyst, you have to come to our institute. This might sound a bit too bold or too restrictive for some, but yes, that's what I believe in. Not everybody may want to become an analyst; we also offer courses in psychoanalytic psychotherapy, which are valuable and teach analytic thinking and skills, useful for therapists and helpful for their patients. Still, there is and remains a difference between psychoanalysis and psychoanalytic psychotherapy with regard to where it can reach and what it can accomplish.

Throughout this exploration of the bad superego, many of the classical oedipal issues have been touched upon: exclusion, castration, genital and generational difference, competition, triangulation, fights against the parental no, and fights against feeling small and taking the necessary time to grow and become an analyst. All these struggles reverberate in tales of Greek mythology, where the gods feared and castrated their sons and the sons feared and castrated their fathers—the theme of Sophocles's *Oedipus Rex*. It's simply part of our nature! If we listen carefully, we can always hear Oedipus cry. To recognize and acknowledge his scream reaching across centuries and echoed in our contemporary hallways does not mean to pathologize our political or institutional discussions; it means simply to be aware of the oedipal issues that these institutions stir up in all of us. Nor does it mean to infantilize our candidates—rather, it means to respect and honor their willingness to regress during the time of their training analysis in order to recapture and reassess a vital though repressed piece of early personal history as an essential tool for their future work as analysts.

In his paper "The Oedipal Conflicts of the Analyst," Grunberger (1980) emphasizes the particular necessity to thoroughly work through the many aspects of a candidate's Oedipus complex so that he will be able to resist the siren song of narcissistic regression. To be idealized by our patients without falling prey to the temptation of "merger narcissism," and to meet the challenge of oedipal rivalry without shying away from the murderous fantasies that spur it, requires structural stability as well as flexibility. We can learn from Grunberger that an insistence on equality and sameness in the fight against authority and hierarchy is actually a narcissistic attack on difference and otherness. Narcissism, he says, cannot tolerate failure witnessed by authority; in order to erase the ensuing unbearable shame, the narcissist will try "to abolish the principle of paternity itself and the whole frame of reference of which it was the organizer" (ibid., p. 621). By contrast, the mature, stable oedipal structure is capable of tolerating defeat without giving up and of persisting in order to eventually prevail—something we would wish for everyone at the end of their analyses, and in particular for our candidates[8] and analysts.

---

[8] "In general it is the Oedipus which opens the analytic treatment in emerging constantly during the session in all modes of psychosexual relations; it functions like a structuring element of the ego and as a source of energy nourishing the process of individuation; as the oedipal strivings must be taken up repetitively during the evolution of the subject in order to flesh itself out, it must be worked through continuously during the treatment. In the absence of this repeated analysis and appropriate timing, the subject may not be able to maintain his Oedipal position to the point at which it could really be considered definitively acquired. He will be particularly exposed to a regression to the level of identification with the primal mother. This is particularly valid for the so-called training analysis, a deep didactic treatment, the only guarantee actually at our disposal while we suffer the pressure of the reigning narcissistic, antioedipal and therefore anti-analytic, collective super-ego and collective ego ideal" (Grunberger 1980, p. 615f.).

The Good Superego

Maybe it's easy for me to think that way; it might be part of the female oedipal fabric to want a strong father figure rather than a weakened one. And maybe the lifelong competition between sons and fathers will always carry a murderous undercurrent ready to trigger the enaction of some version of Freud's *Totem and Taboo* (1912-1913). There Freud described the slaughter of the powerful father by his sons, the ensuing depression of the primal horde of equal brothers, and the erection of the totem—represented today perhaps by the analytic couch that stands in offices where no analysis takes place any more. In such instances, the couch becomes a memento of the Ur-father Freud, a sad trophy from costly years of training—or a prestigious fetish with which some pretend that they still care about this never-ending endeavor of exploring the depths of the unconscious mind, rather than just about making patients feel better.

We don't need to murder Freud, nor do we need to worship him or uncritically preach his theories. On the contrary: studying them will inspire us to creatively work with them. So let us finally cast another glance at his superego conception. Freud based its emergence on the acceptance of the incest prohibition. However, there are many other parental prohibitions. Think, for instance, of a child who is not allowed to play soccer on the street. The parental *no* wants to *protect* the child from being killed by a car. These kinds of prohibitions and parental demands are much more frequent and important than those thwarting the child's erotic advances. Most of them aim at *preserving* the child from harm, and that's what the child has to learn and internalize into his superego in order to preserve himself and his objects and to be safe in his inner and outer world.

Freud appreciated the importance of not murdering our fathers: "We understand," he writes, "it is the preservation of the object that guarantees the safety of the ego" (my translation from the original German text[9]). Clearly, when the child is in a situation of danger, the parental *NO*

---

[9] Strachey's translation reads: "We can see that what guarantees the safety of the ego is the fact that the object has been retained" (Freud 1923, p. 53).

will come back to his mind and he will safely charter his course. This is true even in the context of oedipal love, of incestuous love—and hence the forbidden love between analyst and patient. It is the preservative function of the superego that helps the analyst not to go overboard when his desires push him into dangerous territory.

So, again, it turns out that we cannot do without the preservative drives; they are simply indispensable in our lives as well as in psychoanalysis. With this conception in mind, we don't need to focus so much on the aggressiveness of the superego—albeit while not denying it—but will better recognize its preservative functions or the lack thereof. More precisely, the superego spreads two wings: (1) the *challenges* represented in the *ego ideal* that is invested with narcissistic *libido* and activated by the sexual drives; and (2) the *precautions* represented in the protective voice of our *conscience* that is activated by the *lethic* energies of the preservative drives (Schmidt-Hellerau 2001).[10]

It is particularly this latter side, the preservative function of the superego, the conscience, that is contained within the idea of the *bad superego*. To say that "he is superego-ish" suggests: "He is too critical, too restrictive; let's do away with this exaggerated conscience that won't allow us to have some fun." However, the fun of today can be the misery of tomorrow.

So even if we don't quite call it, with Schafer, "the loving and beloved superego" (1960), we might still hold onto it as the caring and protective superego, because the refusal to internalize and integrate the laws of our analytic fathers / parents doesn't liberate us. On the contrary, it keeps us anxious about and furious at criticism. As long as we cannot accept the critical voice of our conscience that will sometimes not allow but prohibit for the sake of our own and our object's preservation, we won't feel safe in what we are doing—be it training for our profession, teaching and evaluating young colleagues, or analyzing our patients!

---

[10] Chasseguet-Smirgel (1975) distinguishes between the ego ideal, the heir of primary narcissism, and the superego, the heir of the Oedipus complex; the former creates the positive demand ("you should strive for A") while the latter ensures prohibition ("you are not allowed to do B").

Also, if we fully comprehend the superego's protective function, we will gain not only a sense of safety; we will also gain the freedom to accomplish creative and secure change. If we grasp what our laws want to accomplish, then we can think of substitutes that retain their essence and preserve what is useful, while also making them accessible for transformations that better suit a changed environment.

Having thought about all of this, I have come to this conclusion: holding onto the values of our personal as well as institutional and organizational superegos does not mean being stuck in orthodoxy. It means being free to responsibly answer to the demands of a changing culture. It means to understand and uphold the good reasons behind our laws and morale, the rationale for our *can-do* and *can't-do* rules, in order to preserve our objects and ourselves. Or, to put it differently, it means to first think through and understand the essence of the rules in place that we intend to change. Freud's dictum "Where id was, there ego shall be" (1933, p. 80) can then be supplemented by: "Where superego was, there ego shall be."

Annex 1: On Metapsychology and Freud

Metapsychology is another area to which the above-described reflections can be usefully applied because it represents the general laws of how the mind works. Thus, metapsychology actually operates in the service of the ego. But since it guides us and exerts the demands of an extra-individual reference frame (Busch and Schmidt-Hellerau 2004), it can easily be felt as "superego-ish." If we relate to a theory of the mind—whichever one we adopt—we are restricted in arbitrarily responding to our patients; we can no longer say or do what we feel like saying without explaining to ourselves and our colleagues—at least in hindsight—how our intervention relates to our general psychoanalytic understanding of the patient's mental functioning.

In this sense, psychoanalytic theories about the mind represent a third, a paternal structure, that holds and protects the analyst from losing himself in the regressive pulls of fusion and symbiosis with the patient. To put it another way: reflecting on our analytic work in relation to our preferred theory of the mind cracks the narcissistic dyad with the patient and makes room for the introduction of the object, the separate object, and eventually for the oedipal object that we cannot "fuck around" with.

Elsewhere (Schmidt-Hellerau 2001, 2005), I have elaborated on my view of the deteriorating effects of the great metapsychology debate that spanned the period from the 1960s to the '80s, as a consequence of which many of our basic concepts were called into question and finally abolished. Gill famously stated: "Metapsychology is not psychology" (1976); Klein reassured us that one theory, clinical theory, is enough (1973); and Holt finally declared "the actual death of metapsychology" (1985). Was it the seemingly "superego-ish" function that made metapsychology so despicable?

Be that as it may, relief was short and merely ushered in the next wave of rebellion—this time against our technical guidelines: abstinence, anonymity, and neutrality, as well as interpretation, were decried as stifling, authoritarian, or simply impossible. We heard statements such as: one cannot not enact—everything is an enactment; self-revelation is unavoidable and actually beneficial; and interpretation is authoritarian—how would an analyst know better than his patient what he feels? Aren't we all equal?

Now we frame our interpretations as questions: "Could it be that you felt left out by me over the weekend?" we ask the patient, who then answers with "I don't know; I haven't thought about this." Are we afraid to say simply: "You felt left out over the weekend" because the patient might respond with "no," and we have come to dislike *no* for an answer—in particular, when the patient's *no* seems to include a narcissistic retort: "Who do you [the analyst] think you are that I would care what you're doing on your fucking weekend?" Exactly! Do we hear in this statement the oedipal rage over being *excluded* and proceed to analyze it? Or do we hear it as *despair* over feeling *abandoned,* as a threat to the patient's safety, and intervene in order to repair the narcissistic hurt and reestablish us in an analytic dyad of protection? Both can apply at different points in the analysis. Whatever we decide needs to be explained with arguments about how we think the patient's mind works.

However, unfortunately, there is a deep reluctance to engage with our theories of the mind—and there's even a warning not to delve into *too much theory*, as if theory were bad. In our discussions, I often get the sense that theoretical thinking itself isn't honored and enjoyed as an exciting accomplishment that furthers our understanding, but on the contrary, it is depreciated as "not clinical."

Maybe all these ideas are linked together: no theory, no superego, no authority, no hierarchy—and no boundaries? Isn't the fight against theory, in the end, a rebellion against our primal father, Freud? I wonder about this because Freud has been devalued and banished when his theories have been discredited in favor of our personal styles, of our individual playfulness, and of all that makes us feel more comfortable as analysts and analysands.

Such struggles are ongoing in many institutes, which can help shed more light on these processes. As Auchincloss and Michels note, there was a Freud controversy at Columbia in which "senior faculty advocated the shortening of the Freud course," while the younger faculty "flocked to join study groups for the purpose of reading the complete psychological works of Freud" (2003, p. 393). The authors' analysis remains interesting: "Ultimately, we understood the phenomenon of our 'generational gap' to reflect the fact that our senior faculty were educated in an era of extreme Freudian orthodoxy during which Freud's metapsychology was presented as dogma. Many of them worked hard to demystify the work of Freud and to challenge the religious approach to teaching Freudian theory" (p. 393). Thus, when younger faculty turned their interest back to Freud, senior faculty saw this as "evidence of disturbing neo-orthodoxy or alarming atavism." They wanted younger analysts to carry on "what it is we think now and what it is we really do" (Cooper quoted in Auchincloss and Michels 2003, p. 393). But even though the younger generation was mindful of the previous battles of their analytic parents, they didn't want to merely swallow "the leftovers of someone else's totem dinner" (Auchincloss 2000, p. 71); they wanted to develop their own take on Freud. This shows that perhaps all fathers want their sons to carry their banners, while all sons fight to pick up and display a banner of their own. Intergenerational relations are complex and ambivalent, incorporating power and rebellion. And so is our relationship to our superego.

Annex 2: On Loewald's
"The Waning of the Oedipus Complex"

As one of the great fathers of American psychoanalysis, Hans Loewald has certainly had a formative influence on its current culture. In his seminal paper "The Waning of the Oedipus Complex" (1978), Loewald makes two important points: (1) we are never done with the Oedipus complex; again and again, it rears its head and requires ongoing mastery throughout life. Consequently, it is not limited to our childhood or our associations on the couch—it also drives our institutional dynamics and group processes. (2) Already in 1978, Loewald noticed a decline of our interest in the Oedipus complex in favor of preoedipal and postoedipal developments—and he held that an "increased understanding of pre-oedipal issues, far from devaluating oedipal ones, may in the end help to gain deeper insights into them" (p. 386f.). I fully agree with both these assessments.

Where I do not agree with Loewald and where I think he erred is in this formulation: Loewald asserts that "the assumption of responsibility for one's own life and its conduct is in psychic reality tantamount to the murder of the parents, to the crime of parricide" (1978, p. 389). "By evolving our own autonomy, our own super-ego,…we are killing our parents. We are usurping their power, their competence, their responsibility for us" (p. 390). "Not only is parental authority destroyed by wresting authority from the parents and taking it over, but the parents… are…destroyed as libidinal objects as well" (p. 389)—all of which leads to guilt and the need for "atonement for that crime" (ibid.).

Ogden (2006) warned us not to water down Loewald's blunt language by taking it as *just metaphorical*. And Loewald repeatedly emphasizes that "parricide" as a "developmental necessity" is "more than a symbolic action" (1978, p. 395); for him, it is a "psychic reality." He even claims: "Without the guilty deed of parricide there is no autonomous self" (p. 393).

While Loewald's description aims at characterizing the generational struggle inherent "in the process of becoming and being an adult" (1978, p. 388), I would argue that he is instead portraying the infantile, oedipal fantasy of a four-year-old *before* any resolution (let alone analysis) of the Oedipus complex has taken place. It is the child's *illusion* that it is merely the person of the powerful father who blocks his way to the desired maternal object: were the rival killed off, the child could usurp his power, competence, and privileges. But in reality this isn't so. Competence—be it marital, parental, professional, or other—can never be *usurped;* true authority can never be wrested from a senior, and competence and authority are achieved only by growing, learning, and maturing, and by proving that one can hold firm in experiencing the challenges and tests of life. Only then may we enjoy privileges—yet even these entail responsibilities, the fulfillment of which require mature competence.

This is what the acceptance of generational difference means. Conflicts do not arise because the father is a selfish guy who wants to control his son; no, it is a matter of the oedipal son's smallness and sexual immaturity. The son lacks the capacity to anticipate the consequences of his decisions, doesn't know how the world works, and needs the guidance and protection of his parents; he is not autonomous and cannot do what his father does. To understand the fact of his own nonreadiness, unfitness, and imperfection is an unavoidable blow to the child's narcissism, a symbolic castration, that needs to be understood and worked through in the child's mind in order to resolve the Oedipus complex and transform it into the secondary identifications of a solidly structured, benign superego.

What happens in the process of superego development is not only the restriction and repression of the child's early erotic strivings; this process is simultaneously and to no lesser degree a build-up of structures on the side of his self- and object-preservative drives. First, the child cannot murder her baby brother because mother intervenes and says *no;* then she cannot do so because the internalized voice of her mother demands that she not hurt him but be gentle with him. Finally, it becomes a general superego value to respect others and to protect them from harm. In this process, mature superego values will be established that are increasingly detached or independent from the individuals who taught them. Thus, it is a process of abstraction in that it requires us to

351

differentiate between the significant persons in our lives (our parents, teachers, or analysts) and the values they taught us.

In the end, these values stand for themselves; they structure the libidinal and lethic ideas of the superego, and can be upheld, discussed, criticized, developed, expanded, and rejected with arguments and without killing or destroying the fathers and mothers who taught us. *This, I think, is true, mature autonomy and emancipation: to preserve another person even when disagreeing with his or her ideas*; or, to put it differently: to hold on to the affectionate bond with and the respect for parental objects while criticizing their ideas and striving for better accomplishments.

Also, Loewald's idea that in this process we are destroying our parents as libidinal objects misrepresents the complexity of this task. Yes, we do have to reject them as libidinal objects for ourselves, but simultaneously we have to hold onto them and accept them as libidinal objects for each other. The decisive step from the anal to the oedipal phase is the discovery of sexual relations between the two parental objects, relations that exclude the filial subject. To mentally destroy the former as libidinal objects would be a regression to a narcissistic position. This is what we may find in the adolescent's conviction that his parents are, at any rate, too old to have sex; the adolescent is thinking: "If I can't do it now, neither can they" (which is another narcissistic refute of the generational difference that claims, "We are alike, and neither of us can do what I can't do").

I wonder if Loewald's call for "emancipatory murder" ushered in a culture that simultaneously fears and destroys *the law of the father*. If some sort of *generative parricide and matricide* were required in order to transit from adolescence to paternity and maternity, the adolescent would feel emboldened to "kill" his parents for the sake of his own autonomy—yet then he would fear becoming a parent who is therefore next in line to be destroyed. The adolescent would grow up to be like Laius or Jocaste, who tried to kill their offspring in order to save themselves.

Are we then stuck in an adolescent culture, never really growing up but playfully cultivating or enjoying adolescent destruction as a "necessity" in the process of maturation, rather than seriously analyzing

352

infantile oedipal murder fantasies and the catastrophic anxieties beneath them? As Winnicott showed, in infancy, the survival of the object is solely the object's task. I would add that the parents' survival is foundational to the child's survival and is indispensable to the structuring of his/her preservative drives. For this very reason, the parents should never allow to be destroyed, nor self-destroy, their authority. As Ogden reminded us, the "absence of genuine parental authority leaves the child with little to appropriate" (2006, p. 656).

Throughout the long history of the object's development, his or her survival increasingly becomes the growing child's task, the task of the preservative drives, eventually represented as *conscience* and demanded by the superego. To love and preserve the parental objects rather than killing them to usurp their authority and autonomy means sharing with them the responsibilities for the survival of all; it means jointly carrying burdens, as well as enjoying the pleasures of a civilized life.

Annex 3: On Boundary Violations in Psychoanalysis with Regard to Self- and Object Preservation

My reflections in this paper have started off from the topic of boundary violations, and that's where they will be concluded. Here, too, the literature is rich and cannot be comprehensively summarized. Instead, I will limit my comments in this respect to Gabbard and Lester's groundbreaking study, *Boundaries and Boundary Violations in Psychoanalysis* (1995). In looking at a great number of psychoanalysts who committed boundary transgressions, they were concerned with questions of character pathology, unresolved neurotic conflicts, and transference-countertransference enactments in cases of sexual and nonsexual boundary violations. Nonsexual boundary transgressions can be harder to research because victims may feel less justified in filing complaints, compared to sexual boundary violations where the abuse is blatant, and once it becomes apparent (which may take a long time), the psychoanalytic community usually reacts strongly. As required by the International Psychoanalytical Association, member institutes implemented a set of procedures to deal with ethical violations, usually resulting in the exclusion of the violator—unless the latter forestalls any prosecution by terminating his membership affiliations first. In any case, the psychoanalytic community is left wondering what happened—and *how* could this happen?

Strikingly, analysts may often justify or explain their boundary violations by claiming a "benign intent"—namely, an extraordinary affection for the patient, be it based on love or concern. However, what does it mean, and what does it require, to love or worry about an object in a mature and professional way? We could say that mature, erotic *love* sails along the desires of sexuality (in the all-inclusive sense), combined with the wish to take care of and protect the loved object: it integrates libidinal and lethic strivings. Mature *concern* is felt with regard to objects we care about (libido) and care for (lethic) when they are helpless or endangered. While we may enact our erotic desire, as well as our wish to help with the objects we are close to (our partners, family members, and friends), it is the analyst's task—his or her only task!—to analyze these urges, especially as they are part of the patient's transference or the analyst's countertransference. Boundary violations break this essential contract between patient and analyst, which stipulates that the analyst will analyze and will not enact.[11]

Gabbard and Lester developed three categories[12] of psychic disturbances typically found in sexual boundary violators, for which they offered thorough analyses and relevant insights. The three categories of disturbances are: (1) psychopathy and severe narcissistic personality disorders, (2) lovesickness, and (3) masochistic surrender. I want to briefly sketch out the characteristics of these three groups and comment on them from the point of view of drive theory.

Analysts with a *psychopathic or severely narcissistic personality disorder* were found by Gabbard and Lester to behave "dishonest[ly] or

---

[11] We know that mini-enactments take place in all analyses; I am not denying this. The decisive point is that such enactments must be analyzed, interpreted, and hopefully understood, a process that replaces action with reflection.

[12] A small number of analysts commit boundary transgressions as a consequence of an outbreak of psychosis or brain disease; they form an extraneous category that will not be addressed here.

unethical[ly] in a variety of ways" (1995, p. 94); they are "masters at manipulating" and treat their patients in sadistic and demeaning ways as sexual objects, feeling that these patients should even feel "lucky to have had sexual favors" from them. Such analysts may have sex with a number of patients, one after the other, or with several during the same time period. "Because they lack empathy or concern for the victim, they are largely incapable of feeling remorse or guilt about any harm that might have been done to the patient," note Gabbard and Lester (p. 95). This lack of conscience shows a "massive failure of superego development."

Does the sadism and recklessness in these cases prove the usefulness of an aggressive drive? I doubt that sexual predators want to destroy their sexual objects; they are simply ruthless in the pursuit of their sexual satisfaction. In my view, this ruthlessness displays a lack of object-preservative structures and hence any mitigating influence through lethic defenses. Analysts with this character pathology don't care about their patients or about what their actions do to them. The object is not represented as in need of being preserved and protected. Hence, rather than investing patients with a benign mixture of libidinal and lethic energies, the narcissistically aggrandized analyst-self uses its objects only to satisfy its own sexual urges (we can call these urges *primitive* because they are not mitigated by preservative concerns).

The second category of disturbances, that of *lovesickness*, accounts for analysts who fall madly in love with one patient while continuing to work more or less professionally with others. As Gabbard and Lester point out, here, too, narcissistic needs and situational stress—such as "divorce, separation, illness of a child or spouse, death of a family member, or disillusionment" (p. 96) with life or career, as well as the challenges of aging—may trigger a breakdown of ethical and professional barriers. Lovesickness often creates a complex situation in which both participants, analyst and analysand, feel love for each other. However, since the analytic relationship always stirs infantile transferences in which the analyst figures as a parental object, sexual boundary violations are incestuous, without exception. As subsequent analyses of these cases show, the patient's erotic feelings are either part of a revived oedipal complex or a counterphobic defense against preoedipal lethic wishes (such as to be protected and taken care of).

The realization of this love affair between analyst and patient means that either the analyst disregards the generational gap and mistakes the patient's infantile longing for adult sexual desire, or he misconstrues an erotic *defense* against lethic needs as a sexual *wish*, showing the very confusion of tongues that Ferenczi (1949) described. Here again we can see that this is not a confusion of sexuality with aggression; it is a confusion of the language of *tenderness* with the language of *passion*—or, as Freud put it (1912, p. 180) of the *affectionate* with the *sensual* current. In the terminology of the drive theory presented here, this confusion is between *lethic needs* and *libidinal desires*.

The third group of analysts committing sexual boundary violations displays a dangerous tendency toward *masochistic surrender*. In a "heroic" commitment, they accept the most difficult cases: extremely aggressive borderline patients (often incest victims or patients with PTSD) who have thwarted or disrupted previous therapeutic efforts and have been rejected by a number of analytic colleagues. These patients may soon challenge the therapeutic boundaries with demands for special treatment or extra-hour contacts as proof that the analyst really cares about them. "Probably the most common scenario involves the male analyst who allows himself to be intimidated and controlled by a demanding patient who badgers him into increasingly escalating boundary violations as a way to prevent suicide" (Gabbard and Lester 1995, p. 113).

The more that such a patient tries to seduce and blackmail the analyst, the more resentment the analyst might build up, followed by guilt feelings about his negative reaction to the patient, causing him to then overcompensate. In a desperate effort to rescue the patient and prevent her suicide, the analyst may surrender to her demands for "healing love" and a sexual relationship. When this occurs, the patient may file an ethical complaint against the analyst, which often ends up destroying his career, his family, and his finances.

As Gabbard and Lester note:

> The analyst-patient relationship begins as a rescuer-victim paradigm until the analyst has "run the extra mile" by descending down the slippery slope to the point that he feels relentlessly tormented by the

patient. At this point the roles change and the patient becomes the abuser while the analyst becomes the victim. Finally, in an effort to rescue the patient, the analyst colludes with a reenactment of early abuse in which he becomes the abuser and the patient is once again the victim. (p. 116)

As we can see, here the victim-patient has the power to destroy the analyst. This brilliant description of masochistic surrender clearly shows a dangerous dynamic: the analyst has overextended himself on behalf of his patient's survival, to no avail, and finally ends up making a final, frantic effort to prevent her imminent suicide; in doing so, he suffers the consequences of the neglect of his own self-preservative needs. His enacted rescue operation turns out to be his own professional suicide.

Referring again to Gabbard and Lester's three categories of disturbances of analysts who commit boundary violations, we can see that the first group, that of psychopaths and malignant narcissists, lacks object preservation. The second group of analysts—the lovesick ones—demonstrate confusion between sexual desires and preservative needs (they are literally *love-sick*). The third group of analysts, those with the masochistic surrender syndrome, show a blatant lack of self-preservation. The aggression in these cases merely enhances the ensuing tendencies and deficits.

Finally, there is a broad range of nonsexual boundary violations, which relate to *active and passive lethic needs of either one or both partners* in a therapeutic relationship. Such needs may touch on financial temptation (Rothstein 1986, 2004)—any financial deal that involves the patient—or on exploitation of the patient for the financial, professional, or narcissistic gain of the analyst. It seems to me important to know that the lethic need to take care of or be taken care of by the analyst may come up in the transference and should be addressed, or else these needs can grow into one-sided or mutual enactments.

Seemingly endless analyses that are the result of iatrogenic, malignant regressions may be prolonged by the patient's unconscious transference assumption that the analyst doesn't want her to get better, to be independent and to leave him, because the analyst needs the patient to perform the analytic function, to feel good about himself, or simply to safeguard his income. This urge may reveal an unconscious vicious cycle: the child needs to feed the parent so that the parent can feed the child, which keeps both entangled in an eternal, two-way feeding loop, any escape from which seems to threaten starvation. In particular, when the analyst is frail, sick, or in the beginning stages of dementia, the patient may feel concerned and have the urge to protect him from any loss or blow to his fragile narcissism. Even if this situation is never fully realized by either of the two participants (the patient may be more aware of it than the analyst, but may not know how to break the bond), it constitutes a lethic boundary violation if the patient's object-preservative urges and conflicts are not analyzed but instead are enacted.

References

Auchincloss, E. L. & Michels, R. (2003). A reassessment of psychoanalytic education: controversies and changes. *Int. J. Psychoanal.*, 84:387-403.

Brenner, C. (2002). Conflict, compromise formation, and structural theory. *Psychoanal Q.*, 71:397-417.

Brenner, C. (2003). Is the structural model still useful? *Int. J. Psychoanal.*, 84:1093-1096.

Busch, F. (2010). Distinguishing psychoanalysis from psychotherapy. *Int. J. Psychoanal.*, 91:23-34.

Busch, F. & Schmidt-Hellerau, C. (2004). How can we know what we need to know? Reflections on clinical judgement formation. *J. Amer. Psychoanal. Assn.*, 52:689-707.

Chasseguet-Smirgel, J. (1975). *L'Idéal du moi. Essai psychanalytique sur la "maladie d'idéalité."* Paris: Tchou.

Ferenczi, S. (1949). Confusion of the tongues between the adults and the child—(the language of tenderness and of passion). *Int. J. Psychoanal.*, 30:225-230.

Freud, S. (1912-1913). *Totem and Taboo: Some Points of Agreement between the Mental Lives of Savages and Neurotics. S. E.*, 13.

Freud, S. (1923). *The Ego and the Id. S. E.*, 19.

Freud, S. (1930). *Civilization and its Discontents. S. E.*, 21.

Freud, S. (1933). *New Introductory Lectures on Psycho-Analysis. S. E.*, 22.

Gabbard, G. O. & Lester, E. P. (1995). *Boundaries and Boundary Violations in Psychoanalysis.* Washington, DC/London: American Psychiatric Publishing, Inc.

Gill, M. M. (1976). Metapsychology is not psychology. In *Psychology Versus Metapsychology: Psychoanalytic Essays in Memory of George S. Klein,* ed. M. Gill & P. S. Holzman. New York: Int. Univ. Press, pp. 71-105.

Gray, P. (1991). On transferred permissive or approving super-ego functions: the analysis of the ego's super-ego activities, part II. *Psychoanal. Q.,* 60:1-21.

Greenberg, J. (1991). *Oedipus and Beyond: A Clinical Theory.* Cambridge, MA: Harvard Univ. Press.

Grunberger, B. (1980). The oedipal conflicts of the analyst. *Psychoanal. Q.,* 49:606-630.

Holt, R. (1985). The current status of psychoanalytic theory. *Psychoanal. Psychol.,* 2:289-315.

Kernberg, O. F. (1998). *Ideology, Conflict, and Leadership in Groups and Organizations.* New Haven, CT: Yale Univ. Press.

Klein, G. S. (1973). Two theories or one? *Bull. Menninger Clin.,* 37:102-132.

Loewald, H. W. (1979). The waning of the Oedipus complex. In *Papers on Psychoanalysis.* New Haven, CT: Yale Univ. Press, 1980, pp. 384-404.

Ogden, T. H. (2006). Reading Loewald: Oedipus reconceived. *Int. J. Psychoanal.,* 87:651-666.

Renik, O. (1993). Analytic interaction: conceptualizing technique in light of the analyst's irreducible subjectivity. *Psychoanal. Q.,* 62:553-571.

Renik, O. (2002). Defining the goals of a clinical psychoanalysis. *Psychoanal. Q.,* 71:117-123.

Rosenfeld, H. (1971). A clinical approach to the psychoanalytic theory of the life and death instincts: an investigation into the aggressive aspects of narcissism. *Int. J. Psychoanal.,* 52:169-178.

Rothstein, A. (1986). The seduction of money: a brief note on the expression of transference love. *Psychoanal. Q.,* 50:296-330.

Rothstein, A. (2004). The seduction of money: an addendum. *Psychoanal. Q.,* 73:525-527.

Schafer, R. (1960). The loving and beloved super-ego in Freud's structural theory. *Psychoanal. Study Child,* 15:163-188.

Schmidt-Hellerau, C. (2001). *Life Drive and Death Drive, Libido and Lethe. A Formalized Consistent Model of Psychoanalytic Drive and Structure Theory*. New York: Other Press.

Schmidt-Hellerau, C. (2005a). The other side of Oedipus. *Psychoanal. Q.*, 74:187-218.

Schmidt-Hellerau, C. (2005b). We are driven. *Psychoanal. Q.*, 74:989-1028.

Clinical Applications

CHAPTER 11

Fighting with Spoons

*On Caretaking Rivalry Between Mothers and Daughters**

I present an aspect of my version of modern drive theory with a preservative and a sexual drive as basic motivating factors in mental life. To consider self-preservation and object preservation as primal drive activities allows me to focus on the many issues of caretaking as they play a major role between mother and daughter. I discuss three different ways that mothers deal with object-preservative concerns in the interaction with the child with regard to competition and rivalry. An extended psychoanalytic example demonstrates how I use these concepts in my clinical work. The article ends with some reflections on specific countertransference difficulties in the context of self-preservative and object-preservative urges and needs.

What if Freud had been a Woman—S. Freud: Not Sigmund But Sigrid Freud? What would psychoanalysis look like? Would we understand and conceptualize man's mind differently if it had originally been analyzed by a woman? Did Freud miss something essential from his male vantage point that needs to be added to our psychoanalytic universe? Or is it politically incorrect to ask these questions, assuming any difference in the first place?

   Balsam, interested in female psychology in general (1991, 1999, 2001) and in motherhood in particular (1996, 2000, 2003), has shown how

* (2006). Psychoanalytic Inquiry, 26(1): 32-55

difficult it was for the first woman in the Vienna Society, Margarete Hilferding, to make herself heard. The minutes of her presentation on January 11, 1911, "On the Basis of Motherlove" (Nunberg and Federn, 1974) not only tell us how disappointed Hilferding felt about the discussion of her article by her all male colleagues but also indicate that she was missing a psychoanalytic language to address certain aspects of motherhood. She struggled to think about how the body speaks in the mind of a woman. Trying to capture some of what she called "physiological motherlove," she wondered whether it was inborn or not, linked it to the issues of breast feeding and caretaking, lingered on failed motherlove, the refusal to nurse the baby, and even included cases of child abuse and murder. Freud (1905) responded with focusing on the mother's repressed infantile sexuality, very much in line with his take on the different stages of libidinal development in the *Three Essays*. However, it is striking that in one of his earliest publications, Freud (1892-1893) struggled with the same problem posed by a mother who couldn't feed her baby.

> The patient intended to feed the infant herself. … Nevertheless, though her bodily build seemed favorable, she did not succeed. … There was a poor flow of milk, pains were brought on when the baby was put to the breast, the mother lost appetite and showed an alarming unwillingness to take nourishment, her nights were agitated and sleepless. At last, after a fortnight, in order to avoid any further risk to the mother and infant, the attempt was abandoned as a failure and the child was transferred to a wet-nurse. Thereupon all the mother's troubles immediately cleared up [p. 117].

Freud (1892-1893), interested at that time in "antithetic ideas" and the "counterwill" treated this mother with hypnotic suggestion. At that time, even though intrigued, he was not yet capable of analyzing what was going on in his patient's mind, nor was he curious about the fact that on the occasion of this woman's second child, when the same symptoms reoccurred, his hypnosis was met with undisguised hostility. Freud noted: "Far from being welcomed as a savior in the hour of need, I was obviously being received with a bad grace and I could not count on the patient's having much confidence in me" (p. 119). Freud's hypnosis—some sort of therapeutic counterwill to the patient's anxieties—not only bypassed her defenses (which eventually led him to drop this technique in favor of psychoanalysis) but also bypassed the question that Hilferding raised nearly 20 years later and that we keep on wondering today[1]: what about motherhood is so disturbing to these women? How can we understand the specifics of neurotic derailments in motherhood and, within the particular focus of this volume, in mother-daughter relationships?

Driven to Preserve Self and Object

In my contribution to this inquiry, I want to suggest that caretaking, with all its related thoughts, fantasies, feelings, and actions, can advantageously be conceptualized as a drive activity, namely of the preservative drive (Schmidt-Hellerau, 2001, 2005). This means to reach back and to finally elaborate and explore an early conceptualization of Freud that he never made much use of. Despite the fact that he held on to the idea of self-preservation as one of the two primal drives in his theory of mental functioning,[2] it didn't appear to have ever really occurred on his male radar screen as something to think about. How could that be? It is well

---

[1] Of course, the history of psychoanalysis acknowledges the important contributions of women analysts since these early days. Yet it is as if only more recently the growing number of women in our profession has led to focus an on the specifics of female attachment, development, and separation anxieties; on women's sexuality, aggression, and super ego structures; on the many shapes, functions, and languages of the female body; on maternal transferences and countertransferences; and on the bonds and conflicts between mothers and daughters (e.g., Chodorow, 1978; Silverman, 1987; Schmidt-Hellerau, 1988; Kulish 1991; Lax, 1994, 1995; Holtzman & Kulish, 1996, 1997; Kulish & Holtzman, 1998; Lax, 1999; Holtzman & Kulish, 2000; Kulish 2000, 2002; Hoffman, L., 2003; Holtzman & Kulish, 2003; Kulish & Holtzman, 2003; Balsam and Fischer, 2004; overview in Bernstein, 2004).

[2] Freud's first theory of self-preservative and sexual drives related to Darwin's theorem that self-preservation and the preservation of the species are the two success categories in the evolution of all species. Darwin's preservation of the species embraces two functions: procreation and object-preservation. Although Freud adopted the one of Darwin's categories telquel as the "self-preservative drive," he focused for the other entirely on procreation and postulated a "sexual drive." This represented a remarkable shift for the foundations of his psychology of drives from a phenomenological-behavioral to a biological-functional perspective.

known that Freud thought of himself as a very masculine man, and he acknowledged difficulties with understanding female psychology. Masculinity for him appears to have been linked with the sexual—he even suggested tentatively "that libido is invariably and necessarily of a masculine nature" (1905, p. 219). Thus, Freud might have considered a preservative drive—that would, by its his very notion, embrace all the many issues of caretaking—as necessarily of a feminine nature, a trait hardly compatible with his view of himself. At any rate, even though he did continuously quote both of his primal drives, often as *hunger and love*, Freud only explored the sexual drive[3] and widely ignored his self-preservative drive.

As I have elaborated in greater detail elsewhere (Schmidt-Hellerau, 2001; 2002; 2003; 2005), it is quite an amazing fact that self-preservation has been kept offshore in psychoanalysis for more than a hundred years[4], because we all are literally driven to survive. In the first months

---

[3] Freud focused on the "Sexuality in the Aetiology of the Neurosis" (1898); he declared the sexual infantile wish to be the main producer of our dreams (1900); he wrote the "Three Essays on Sexuality" (1905)—and never planned to write "Three Essays on Self-Preservation" (which, I think, is sorely missing today); he explored the sexual cathexis of the self in his introduction "On Narcissism" (1914); and he addressed the vicissitudes, the repression, and the unconscious of sexual wishes in his metapsychological writings of 1915.

[4] Only a few analysts have addressed this issue. Most interesting here is Ernst Simmel (1924, 1933, 1944), who elaborated on an "instinct to devour" with the goal of reassuring self-preservation and self-development; however, Simmel stayed with Freud's final decision to conceptualize the self-preservative drive together with the sexual drive as libidinal. Loewenstein (1940) focused on the self-preservative instincts, suggesting rather to call them the vital or somatic instincts. Laplanche (1997) then excludes the self-preservative drive explicitly from psychoanalytic thinking, arguing that self-preservation is a biological instinct, not a psychological drive. Khantzian and Mack (1983) elaborated extensively and most carefully on the function of self-preservation and self-care as an ego capacity. Plaut (1984) proposed to work with the concept of the "ego-instinctual drives" as a third basic drive category besides and in addition to sexuality and aggression. Modell (1985) defined narcissism as a "system for self-preservation" and proposed to view it as one causative factor of neurosis while the other remains the Oedipus complex. Silverman (1991) suggested reviving Freud's "self-preservative instincts" as an essential part of attachment behavior; she differentiated between "drives and attachment activation" (1991, p. 180), yet proposed for the latter "the same status as drives" (1991, p. 183).

of life, we might think of the infant's self-preservative strivings as simply related to all the issues of physical well-being. Yet from the beginning, these basic needs to be taken care of (to be nursed, warm, dry and clean; to be able to breathe, digest and defecate; to feel free of pain and protected against any assault) necessarily include an object that does the caretaking. Thus the strivings of a self-preservative drive lead to building up structures in the infant's mind, representations of the caretaking dyad, within which physical and relational pleasures and meanings are combined (the pleasure of need-relief with the pleasure of the accompanying playful interactions between mother and child).

Despite his own conception that distinguished hunger from love, Freud (1905) viewed the infant's early needs and pleasures predominantly through his libidinal glasses. For instance, musing on the child's thumb sucking he writes:

> It was the child's first and most vital activity, his sucking at his mother's breast, or at substitutes for it, that must have familiarized him with this pleasure. The child's lips, in our view, behave like an erotogenic zone, and no doubt stimulation by the warm flow of milk is the cause of the pleasurable sensation. The satisfaction of the erotogenic zone is associated, in the first instance, with the satisfaction of the need for nourishment. To begin with, sexual activity attaches itself to functions serving the purpose of self-preservation and does not become independent of them until later. No one who has seen a baby sinking back

---

Quoting Freud's description of the self-preservative drives as eliciting everything that has to do "with the preservation, assertion, and magnification of the individual" (1933, p. 96) Silverman's notion of attachment as including "a need for proximity, care, and security" (1991, p. 183) emphasizes similarity. Her distinction from Freud's drives is made with regard to the object-relational aspect: attachment, as she sees it, occurs in relation to an object that "can be experienced as separate from the self," including self-objects, excluding however, "merged or non-differentiated relationship(s)." (1991, p. 183) This latter distinction dissolves if one, as I would hold, considers the object as an integral part of Freud's drive conception. More recently, Young-Bruehl and Bethelard (1999) viewed the ego instincts as "primarily object related" (p. 838) with regard to "safety, security, caretaking, and affection" (p. 839) and suggested a "growth principle" related to the ego instincts (p. 840), analogous to the pleasure principle of the sexual instincts.

satiated from the breast and falling asleep with flushed cheeks and a blissful smile can escape the reflection that this picture persists as a prototype of the expression of sexual satisfaction in later life [p. 181f.].

Freud recognized that this satisfaction is about "the need for nourishment." However, the child's pleasure appears to him as sexual and is limited to the erotogenic zone of the mouth. We might not want to dismiss his idea that sexual pleasures are "attached" to the activities of the self-preservative drive. However, are there no specific pleasures of a self-preservative drive different from the sexual ones? Are the tastes of the food, the feelings of being well nourished, full and round in the stomach not pleasurable? What about the pleasures of having slept well? What about the pleasures of being well taken care of or of taking care of someone else well? What about this slight but distinctive feeling of pleasure when we finally have cleaned up our apartment, have fixed our clothes, or slip into a bed with fresh clean sheets? What about the feeling of satisfaction when we effectively warded off a serious attack?

I would state that preservative needs, and in the extreme case survival issues, are basically separate and at times even opposite to sexual strivings. As soon as we feel our life endangered—be it by an assault from the outside, by a disease, or by a deprivation of essentials to our physical health and well-being—everything else, and even the most attractive lover, is instantly pushed aside, and all we aim for is to preserve ourselves. The inheritance of Freud's focus on sexuality barred our view for a more differentiated conception, which would have enabled us to explore and conceptually grasp the many tasks, perils, confusions, and conflicts related to the strivings of a preservative drive that preoccupy us daily with making sure that we preserve ourselves and those we care about.

The fact that we are driven to care about others is an important part of the concept of a preservative drive, as I suggest it, that hasn't been recognized. Freud's rare remarks and those contributions who picked up on this concept, are all focused on and aimed at the subject, casting preservative strivings as self-centered; thus, self-preservation often appeared to be covered by the umbrella concept of narcissism. Yet as much as narcissism can (but doesn't need to) be involved in self-preservative strivings, we are not only driven to preserve ourselves (as Freud's notion self-preservative drive suggests) but also equally and powerfully driven to preserve others. Parents are driven to preserve, nurture, and protect their children[5] (not so different from any mammal's care of the brood). If something or someone appears to do harm to them, they furiously interfere and fight the assault. In the same way we are all driven to help, to protect, and to take care of those who need it: our family, our friends, our colleagues, and, with varying degrees of passion, our neighbors, our citizens and our nation.

It appears to be important that we explore and reintegrate into our theory and clinical thinking this urge not only to preserve ourselves but also to preserve others. This will help us to be better aware of this important part of human strivings—and its failures—that shape our inner landscape and are an essential part of our unconscious and conscious motivations. The dual theory of preservative and sexual drives also allows us to better distinguish the libidinal strivings and cathexes of self-love and object love from the lethic strivings and cathexes of self-care and object care (I suggested the term *lethe* as an energy term of the preservative drive [Schmidt-Hellerau, 1997, 2001]). To put it differently: it is not the object directedness that distinguishes the drives but the specific satisfaction (their function) they are striving for that tells us what moves us in a specific fantasy, dream, anxiety, association, or action.

---

[5] A moving example for this urge to preserve the other rather than oneself can be found in Bodenstab's (2004) analysis of Rosalie's (mother) and Jolly's (daughter) interaction, when they, both near death from starvation in the concentration camp Bergen-Belsen, negotiate the sharing of a bowl of soup. Their capacity to not regress to pure self-preservation (greed) but to instead keep the object cathected—they mutually feed each other the soup—speaks of the strength of their structures (object representations) that contained and tamed their hunger and thus might have been an essential part of their psychic survival.

Gender-Specific Differences in
Preservative Drive Activities

If we conceptualize self-preservation and object-preservation as primal drive activities, then we consider them to be basic for men and women alike. However, I suggest that there are important differences between the expressions of female and male preservative needs and strivings. Here our experience and intercultural observations will lead the way to what appears to be a common place: some of the basic caretaking activities—for example, nursing, cooking, feeding, cleaning, comforting, and attending to the sick, all activities inside the house—usually are performed by women, whereas building the house, hunting for food (be it in the forest or on Wall Street), and protecting the home against all kinds of dangers from the outside world are most often performed by men. This is not (or even less) specific to our modern Western culture but can be found worldwide in primitive as well as developed societies. Whether we like it or blame it on religious, social, and cultural influences, I think Freud was right when he stated that social education will not trespass beyond the lines that are laid down organically, just "impressing them somewhat more clearly and deeply" (Freud, 1905, p. 178). Compliance with gender-specific roles could not prevail in the long run if we were not—at least to a certain degree—driven to do and enjoy what we are supposed to do, if there were not these predilections that we all are so familiar with and have over the years been confirmed by scientific research.

Silverman's (1987) analysis of a great number of studies of female infants shows there is an earlier and greater need and capacity in girls for attachment to their mothers and female caregivers compared with male neonates. In addition, mothers showed a greater involvement in their interactions with infants than fathers or male caregivers even if these men were the primary caregivers. Further, female neonates show greater calm, experience earlier and longer nighttime sleep, and use feeding or diaper changing more for social bonding, whereas male infants are more easily cranky, distressed, and restless. Somewhat exaggerating we could say that the less stable and less attached state of the male infant already displays the little hunter ready to go into the world, whereas the more stable and attached female behavior indicates her predilection to develop and explore things while staying at home—and possibly clinging to mother.

From a different angle, O'Connell (2005) presents a beautiful example highlighting gender-specific differences:

> One summer my daughter, Chloe, then three years old, stepped on a bees' nest and was stung many, many times. I didn't know exactly what these stings meant to her, but she was very hurt, very frightened, and generally very stirred up. Her mother and I went about helping her in fundamentally different ways, not by design, but as you will hear, by our essential differing natures. For several nights, while the pain and distress kept her awake, my wife stayed up with Chloe, talking with her about her experience of bees, pain, surprise, fear, itching, and every other experience imaginably related to bee stings.
>
> I, on the other hand, was not content with soothing and understanding. I needed to do something. While her mother sat with her by night, I plotted with her by day. We scouted out the bees' nest and made careful, elaborate arrangements to kill the bees. Importantly, the complexity of our military operation paled in comparison to what was going on emotionally. Chloe was certainly angry at the bees, and the prospect of taking out the hive was an exciting one, but she worried about all this killing. As she once put it, "I feel angry, I feel sad, I feel scared, and I feel all of them A LOT!" Eventually, however, she resolved her concerns with the realization that, if we didn't get the bees, someone else was likely to get stung. Thus decided, we carried out our mission and had a great time. Many months later Chloe still talked about bees and bee stings with a bit of fear. But she also talked about killing bees with a fair bit of excitement, and a great deal of pride [p. 64f].

O'Connell characterizes the maternal response to Chloe's hurt as "nonhierarchical"; mother focused almost exclusively on the girl's needs, "instinctively matching her own agenda, rate, and rhythm to that of our child" (p. 66). By contrast, father basically set the agenda on his own and then asked his daughter to join him. Thus the maternal and paternal reactions differ in terms of their being "homeostatically attuned" or "disruptive" (Herzog, 2002).

With regard to self-preservative and object-preservative drive activities, O'Connell's example can also teach us a lot about gender-specific expressions of lethic urges. The mother, stirred up by her daughter's hurt, reacted with an increase of caretaking: her preservative actions unfolded "indoors," focused on soothing, healing, tending, and talking. While being all object preservative toward her daughter, mother was completely unaware of her own exhaustion from staying up with the little girl for three nights in a row (O'Connell, 2005, p. 66). Her object-preservative needs clearly exceeded her self-preservative concerns. Father's preservative actions instead were directed to fight back the "outdoor" enemy and thus prevent it from future assaults; by inviting Chloe to join him, his object-preservative strivings also aimed at teaching his daughter "about agency, self-protectiveness, aggression, planning, and much more." (O'Connell, 2005, p. 70) Clearly both, the female and the male way of preservative actions are indispensable for the child in the aftermath of the assault and are an important learning experience (structuring) that will help her to preserve herself and others well on her own later in life. Also very interesting is Chloe's reluctance to kill the bees; I would suggest that here she struggled with a monolithic conflict (see footnote 6) between taking revenge (self-preservation) and protecting the bees (object preservation). It was only the thought that someone else could get as badly stung by these bees as she was that helped her decide to take out the hive (any potential human victim was closer to her object-preservative needs than the insects).

All of these findings are meaningful for the issues of caretaking rivalry, because competition is always fiercest where we are driven to enjoy the same activities, as in the case of females, for example to nurture, pamper, and keep things tidy and less fierce where our urges rather complement each other, as between males and females, that is to fight and to soothe. This competition creates the specific conflicts in the area of the preservative drives between mother and daughter that is the focus of my article.

Rivalry in the Caretaker Dyad

The nursing couple is a paradigm example for a broad variety of activities that we could understand as driven by self-preservative needs (the baby) and object-preservative strivings (the mother). Although these needs and strivings are at best attuned to the baby's needs and mutually satisfying disturbances, derailments, and conflicts with self-preservation and object-preservation occur in the interaction between mother and daughter on a broad spectrum between too little and too much that spans, for the infant, between deprivation and intrusion and, for the mother, between neglect and overprotection. I want to look at the interactions in the female-female caretaker dyad with a particular focus on their driven nature, and I will highlight in a very schematic way and limited to the issues at stake three different types of these interactions, which certainly does not do justice to the complexity of issues we encounter in any individual case. With a clinical example, I will then focus on rivalry between mother and daughter as it played a crucial role in my analysis with Jane.

The Good-Enough Mother A
Mother A has enough confidence in her own bodily functions. Consequently, her self-preservative strivings are healthily modulated (well structured) and feel safe. Health concerns are not a big issue on her mind. Thus, the changes of her body during pregnancy and her fantasies about giving birth are not experienced as a major threat. Also, she has already developed a mature care for the other, a sound capacity for object-preservation, is not lacking support where necessary, is not imposing help where not necessary—in short: she takes good care of herself and she cares for others. Even though mother A has the usual worries about the health of her fetus, she balances these concerns with her growing love for the fetus and delightful fantasies about a happy future of her child. When the child is born, she will enjoy taking good care of her. She doesn't do everything right and problems might occur; however, these are resolvable within her family or, if necessary, with outside help. Mother A will also gradually and appropriately hand over

the tasks and challenges of self-preservation to her child, teaching her how to care for herself and eventually how to care for others. She respects and enjoys the developmental steps of her child. She is what Winnicott (1971) called the "good-enough mother."

The Threatened Mother B

Mother B feels consciously or unconsciously unsafe and threatened in her self-preservation or even her survival. (This could be a mother who was as a child overprotected or neglected and couldn't learn (structure) the tasks of self-preservation; she experiences the world as a dangerous place.) This mother might feel unconsciously threatened by all the changes in her body, with the challenges of giving birth, with pain and blood and milk. The fetus becomes a menace to her survival, the enemy within who wants to damage and kill her. (Her distress might increase when there are narcissistic issues playing into it, a resentment of becoming gross, threatening in her fantasy her capacity to attract a man, and thus ensure his support and protection and the like.) When her baby is born, she might bite her breasts, disturb her sleep, pull her nerves (see Freud's early patient). Even though she might struggle to love and nurse her baby, mother B is at least unconsciously totally preoccupied with her self-preservation in defense against her "attacker child." She tends to neglect, control (limit), or suspiciously watch and ward off the child's needs. Consequently, this child will internalize that she and her needs are a threat to her mother and that her mother is fragile and endangered. Thus her hunger will create a monolithic conflict[6] between "I want to engulf all that I need" and "I need to feed everything to my mother because if she would starve I would starve as well." Sensing this dilemma, the child might prematurely develop object-preservative urges

---

[6] I distinguish monolithic from binary conflicts (2005). Monolithic conflicts are usually more regressive; they involve different objects of one primal drive; for example, shall I eat all the cookies or shall I give some to my sister (preservative drive), or do I love mother or father (sexual drive)? Binary conflicts involve both primal drives and the same or different objects; for example, shall I clean my apartment or meet with my lover (different objects); shall I take care of my partner or have sex with him; shall I present myself needy or sexy (same object/self)?

(concerns for the breast) without having established yet stable representations of a well-preserved self.

The Competitive Mother C

Consciously, mother C appears not very much concerned with her self-preservation; instead she pours all energy into object preservation. (Mother C could be a defensive version of mother B or could be the daughter of a mother B.) She is driven to care for others, anticipates all their possible needs, and finds a million ways of forestalling the efforts of others to do something on their own. Unconsciously she might be scared of wanting to be taken care of herself (self-preservative needs) and defends herself against her neediness and dependence with increased object-preservative activities that lead her to the borders of exhaustion.[7] Yet her ongoing message is this: "you don't need to do that, I can do it!" In her tireless "altruism," she competes with others in being the better caretaker. In the beginnings, her newborn is a wonderful prey to her urge to be helpful. Mother C finds total satisfaction in nursing, caring, and understanding. Her fantasy of "the perfect mother" is imperceptibly and successfully enacted as she senses with nearly uncanny empathy all her baby's needs—even before the child can feel them. She is the "overprotective mother," and soon her urge to take care of the baby will interfere and disrupt the growing infant's capacity to take over and enjoy her own self-preservative and object preservative strivings. As soon as the small child wants to do things on her own— does not want to be fed anymore but wants the spoon in her own fist to feed herself and to feed mother—this mother will say something like, "I know you want to do this now, and this is wonderful, however, you're still too little, I'll do it for you." The daughter of this mother will always be "too little," she will always be deprived of the pleasures and satisfactions of successfully performing her self-preservative and object-preservative strivings—and her relentlessly "helpful" mother will unconsciously become her greatest threat and her worst enemy.

---

[7] This is a special form of a monolithic conflict in that it is negotiated between giving (active) and receiving (passive) with the self as the central object.

There are two major outcomes: The child ends up in a state of malignant regression showing permanent helplessness, dependence, and entitlement, now demanding that mother (and all later mother substitutes) take care of her until the end of her life. Or the child doesn't give up but fights for her self-preservative and object-preservative pleasures, thus getting enmeshed in an endless circle of lethic competition. This competition goes as follows: mother C wants to feed her child with all sorts of food; however, the child pinches her lips and responds with a "vast array of no-entry defenses" (Williams, et al., 2004), or the child takes what mother gives and then throws up and spits it out. Both responses indicate mother's care is bad, doesn't nurture, but poisons the child.[8] Mother C, realizing that her food wasn't good, will increase her efforts in giving good stuff, desperately wanting to make it right, achieving the goal of being the perfect caretaker—and the daughter rejects or evacuates everything right away again and again and all over again. At the same time, the daughter too wants to care for mother, partly in an effort to repair the damage she did to her in rejecting her metaphorical milk, partly to demonstrate to mother how the good caretaking works. So the daughter too furiously tries to force something into her mother, that her mother can't take, because she wants to be the caretaker, and the child is supposed to be the one taken care of. Mother and daughter mutually want to exercise and satisfy their object-preservative drives and feel continuously interfered with and frustrated in it by the other. The situation becomes desperate when to preserve the object unconsciously means to secure ones' own self-preservation (the preservative object). From here terrible anxieties erupt and lead—often in an escalating vicious circle—to furious attacks on the one who refuses to be nurtured in order to nurture oneself.

---

[8] Williams, et al. (2004) relate a particular reason for feeding difficulties to a reversal of Bion's "container-contained" model (1962): "The infant or child is not only not contained (by the mother, addition by CSH), but is at the receiving end of parental projections. ... For some, the introjection of projecting objects can become unbearable, and there is an imperative need to disgorge, emit, or block off these 'missiles'" (2004, p. xiv).

Fighting With Spoons

Jane, a slim woman in her late thirties came to me for analysis because she continuously got into difficulties in her relationships with the women at her workplace and in particular with her mother. She had never married, lived on her own, and, even though doubtful, she was hoping to still find someone with whom to build a family. I remember that my first impression of Jane was mixed: on the one side, she appeared to me lively and willing to relate and change; on the other, I felt her to be highly guarded and suspicious when I said something. These first impressions would fit to what I experienced later on. Jane has a lively, colorful, creative, and funny side; she loves to surprise her friends with a nice present or to organize a birthday party with music and dance, and she is able to become excited when she does research on a complicated issue and finds a smart solution. However, Jane also has a rigid, stubborn, oppositional side to her, and at times, she was constantly preoccupied with control and power issues, which we came to struggle with a lot in the transference-countertransference occurrences.

Jane grew up in a rural area in the Midwest. She was the only child of her parents. Her mother divorced her father a few months after Jane was born, and Jane hadn't seen much of him. On the few occasions during her early childhood when her father came to visit, Jane remembered that she felt very uncomfortable. Her mother worked first as a part-time secretary and then later in a full-time position in a big company. Jane described her as often melancholic and exhausted. She worried a lot about everything, in particular about her daughter's health and whether Jane would eat enough. Jane slept with her mother in the parental bed until age 15, when she started to rebel against her mother and finally refused to sleep one more night together with her in the same room. Her adolescent years had been filled with fierce fights with her mother because Jane felt she was controlling and intruded her private space. Jane left home to go to college with some anxieties but also with much relief. After college, she had settled down on the East Coast where she found a good job and felt herself to be at a reasonable distance from her mother. However, she also loved her mother who appeared to be the only person who ever really cared for her. A year before Jane first came to see me, her aging mother had decided to move into an assisted living home only three blocks from her daughter. Jane was sympathetic with her mother's wish to be closer to her. She now wanted to show her mother more affection and provide more entertainment than she could while living far away from her. However, mother and daughter soon got into the familiar old fights that often ended in furious outbursts on Jane's side, which left both women in tears and exasperation.

During the first years of her analysis, these fights between Jane and her mother were a major issue. Jane often went over to see her mother in the evenings or on the weekends. Wanting to spoil her mother, she dragged bags of food to cook for her and spent much energy cleaning up her mother's apartment or organizing medical checkups. Yet no matter how good Jane's spirits were when doing these things, mother was always defensive, struggling with concerns that it was too much for her daughter to do all these things for her. She worried that Jane would be exhausted from the burden she put on her, and when Jane cooked for her mother, she usually ate little and urged her daughter to take the food home to use it for herself. Mother, on the other hand, also used to buy all sorts of food and wanted her daughter to drag it home. Jane felt her mother only pretended that she had meant to buy these things for herself and only later discovered that she couldn't digest them and had to give them to Jane. When Jane explicitly refused to accept, mother tried to smuggle it anyway into Jane's bags, which often led to an outburst of rage on Jane's side that made her mother cry and apologize. Also, both women competed in who would do more "good" for whom, for example, washing and creaming the other's feet, massaging the back, paying the bills in restaurants and so on, which usually ended with blaming and complaining that the other wasn't able to accept anything and wasn't appreciative of what was offered. In addition, Jane's mother would go into Jane's place and clean her kitchen or iron her blouses while Jane was working. Even though Jane had given her a key to her apartment, she hated it when her mother came in and suspected that she was going into her closets and drawers to look at what she had. All of these interactions between Jane and her mother were extremely painful—and even to listen to them was sometimes hard for me as her analyst, because all of this was presented as pure realities, and when I tried to reflect with her about what was going on, she accused me of siding with her mother—and shut down completely.

Soon our work in analysis recreated this dynamic. Our sessions revolved around the complex issues of who is giving and who is taking or who is in need of whom? Jane had different ways of talking to me: sometimes she spoke to me as if she were my boss and gave me orders in a friendly though cool manner, or she talked as if she were a mother who has everything and would gorge me with it; at other times she presented herself as dense or like a regressed child, needy and near to starving. Both sides changed rapidly. If she was in the mother position, she talked to me like to a child who doesn't know anything (e.g., describing to me in simple language and great detail certain processes at her workplace), and I would feel more stuffed than nurtured.

The material itself wouldn't stimulate my analytic thinking—but, realizing this, the process did. I wondered whether Jane was feeding me with a specific (indigestible) idea of what a child needs. When I would bring this up by saying, "It is as if you need to give me so much, as if I needed a lot" Jane would agree, she did feel I wanted to hear all of this, and she did need to explain it in all detail so that I could follow her. When I would link this to her feeling of exhaustion, she would sometimes become somewhat anxious and defensive. In these moments, she was troubled by realizing that I might think differently than she did, which made her feel like a child who fears an unbearable withdrawal and separation from her mother that basically threatens her survival. Sometimes she got very anxious and agitated, as if a huge unconscious hunger had come up; then Jane would bombard me with questions and get desperate or furious if I wouldn't immediately answer to all of them.

With the following vignette I want to show how early competing self-preservative and object-preservative strivings together with changing activations of "self-as-mother" and "self-as-child" representations came up in the transference and how we tried to work on them.

Jane starts her Monday session telling me that she is very tired—first linking this to the summer's heat and then suggesting she doesn't feel like working. It's exhausting to be with people. She goes on telling me that she went to a professional meeting on Saturday, and one of her colleagues talked and talked and talked—Jane just felt like telling her to shut up. She felt insignificant in this group and didn't find much to say. Later in the evening, she had suggested to have the next meeting with a dinner at her place. One woman responded by saying, she can't eat so much in the evening. This made her mad—as if what she would serve wouldn't be good enough. She goes on telling me that she thought she'd rather make a trip to Cape Cod that day than sitting in this stupid meeting. She elaborates on that and then says, "Actually first I had thought you might have gone to the Cape, you might have a place there for the weekends—and this felt to me as if I was getting somehow into your suction—as if you were pulling me behind you."

I say: "It is my suction that pulls these thoughts out of you." Jane says: "Well, these are my thoughts, but it is your attraction which makes these thoughts come up."

I say musing: "Suction comes from sucking." Jane goes on: "This speaks to the vacuum that I felt on the weekend, an empty room, which I can't escape (esCape); that's why I have to follow you, but I do it reluctantly, because this suction has something devouring, it scares me. If I approached you—you would swallow me up …"

I say: "… because I'm so greedy." Jane is silent for a moment, then: "You are not greedy, but I am. Then it's not you who wants to suck me in, it's me. This has to do with the weekend. You didn't see me for three days. This makes me feel that I'm not attractive enough to suck you in. I would need to have something to give that you couldn't get elsewhere, that you would need—then you would want to see me even on the weekends." She goes on, musing that I might have filled my weekend with paperwork, not with pleasure on the Cape. Then she says: "I wouldn't be as patient as you are with someone like me—I'm glad you are." Then she talks about her work and how often she feels like dumping everything. "I was exhausted on the weekend—I would have been anyway too tired to go to the Cape. I felt as if I wore lead shoes." She sighs, pauses.

I say: "It's tiresome to wear these lead shoes." Jane says: "In fact—and now I'm thinking I'm talking like my mother, she was always exhausted. I recently saw myself in a photo, and was shocked: I made the same face that my mother showed so often, tired and a little cranky. I thought I'm like my mother. There is something unresolved, something that I didn't understand so far …"

I say: "Maybe you are so exhausted because you feel like a little girl walking in mother's shoes which are sooo heavy, much too heavy to go where you want to go—instead you then feel just sucked in."

Jane says: "Hmm, an interesting thought … to be active—like yesterday when I had this exciting thought to go to the Cape—why would I be reluctant to have these thoughts. Reluctance affords a lot of energy."

I say: "Maybe one part of you feels like little Jane who wants to go to the Cape thinking you might find me there. Yet another part feels exhausted like mother, who has to do the cooking for everybody and then is too tired to go anywhere. That puts these big lead shoes on your feet."

Jane agrees: "That's a good way to put it. I just thought of something else: I'm invited to a garden party in two weeks. I just wondered: how will I dress myself. There was a totally new thought: I would like to buy a hat—I have a nice dress, but no hat." Then she goes on to tell me in a lively way about the party, how she would dance, that many of her old classmates would come—and that she even could meet an interesting man there.

Microanalysis of the Session

In this session, we had struggled with Jane's huge hunger, her need to suck me in. Her wish that I be totally attracted to her and her depressive idea that I instead didn't want to see her, appeared to reflect her feeling that she couldn't suck her mother in. It also reflects (what had been more in the center of other sessions) her narcissistic defense against acknowledging difference (the other), dependence (her need), and, at the end, the generational gap between parent and child. Thus the scary question for her always is "who sucks in whom?"

Jane had started out with a defense: she is too tired to "talk and talk and talk" (to work) with me in this session, which simultaneously states she can't give me anything and she doesn't want anything from me. On the weekend she had felt little (insignificant) at her Saturday meeting (a reversal of our no meeting) and had warded off this feeling with introducing herself as the food-providing host (mother) of the next meeting. She got mad when one colleague (child) did not appear to want to eat much. This touched on this empty room (her empty stomach, an emptiness in her mind because of my being away), which brings up her fantasy of going to the Cape—her wish to be with me. Yet this longing for me appears to stir up a dangerous devouring hunger (self-preservative); thus it is projected onto me (my suction) to better defend against: she is anyway too tired to go to the Cape (object-preservative: she doesn't want to swallow and loose the nurturing mother). However, after it has become my hunger, she feels afraid: "you would swallow me up"—I suck these thoughts out of her. When I then say "because I am so greedy" I accept "the spoon" that she wants to feed me (her concern) as "my greed," I show her that this is eatable, this is digestible, and this isn't poisoned food: it is possible to acknowledge need and greed. This being said, Jane can now reject my spoon, my last "I am so greedy" interpretation (food), and interpret (feed) herself better: she can own her greed-wish to suck me in—which however, makes her feel dependent. This is worrisome, because she feels she has nothing that would guarantee that I stay with her—that she could keep me close to her. So again, she wants to be the mother rather than the baby. In this conflict between wanting to eat me up and wanting to feed me, she is stuck like in her mother's lead shoes—it is in this exhaustion that she recognizes her mother in herself. I don't interpret at that moment that she had sucked in her mother's heavy depression, thus her mother's food was in fact sickening.

I stay more with her defense (wanting to be mother), her guilt (she felt her huge hunger caused this exhaustion in her mother), and her anxiety (it threatened her that her mother would withdraw/esCape). The moment when we understood in the transference that her feet express her wish to go to see me as well as her defense against it—an interpretation which appears to have been heard by Jane in a permissive sense that she could come to see me—puts a cap/hat (a limiting, containing structure) on her unlimited (greedy) self-preservative strivings, which turns the psychic movement toward libidinal fantasies: Jane gets out of her lead shoes and shifts to an enthusiastic chain of thoughts about wanting this hat for the garden party where she would dance (!) and meet a man. Even though these thoughts are clearly and affectively more libidinal—I think at this point Jane's unconscious wish to "marry" (me) is still mostly self-preservative and a wish to build with me the perfect unit of a mutually nurturing caretaking-couple.

Jane and I have mused on the question why she needs so much, why she is so deeply threatened in her survival and still has to give all the time. She tells me she was always indulged by her mother and never got the chance to learn how to do things on her own. That's why she is so afraid to lose her mother; she thinks she wouldn't be able to make it alone. She knows this isn't true, but that's how it feels. She also felt guilty for wanting so much, because her mother was tired and had to carry the burden of making a living for the two of them all by herself. Jane remembered having fantasized as a little girl that her mother would break down and she would take care of her and the little house. However, Jane also tells me how much she hated to be stuffed by her mother and how incapable her mother made her feel when Jane offered to help with cooking or cleaning, and her mother just waved her out of the room. On the one side, there is her feeling of needing to be fed; on the other side there is her wish to be the one who does the feeding without knowing how to do this. As a compromise, she has to reject what is fed, ending up with not taking in what she needs and gets (e.g., in the transference: my interpretations) and staying in this state of constantly being threatened to starve out.

Self-Preservation and Object Preservation
in the Countertransference

To work with patients like Jane is a challenge to the analyst's countertransference. The patient's open or more subtle demands to be fed and provided for by her mother-analyst (more interventions, more time, and the like) create strong self-preservative and object-preservative pulls and pushes that strive to suck the analyst into an unconscious caretaking rivalry with the patient. This can become a trap or a dead end to the analysis. The difficulty is that the analyst principally wants to help. However, prolonged "feeding" help—instead of the analysis of the patient's feeling of needing to be fed— might turn into the "too-much spoon" that in the end prevents the patient from growing and even can lead to potentially malignant regressions. Further, if the analyst gives in to the demand for "feeding" help, she responds to one side of the patient's conflict, the hungry-child part (and this part—as much as the analyst might feel it—is, for a long time, unconscious), thus challenging the other side, the providing-mother part, that is an important constituent of the patient's identity ("I'm always doing everything for everybody, I'm all exhausted"). To put it differently: the patient defends herself against the child within (her frightening neediness and her overwhelming greed) with fantasizing herself in the position of a mother who controls the spoon[9]; to directly point out that she is the one who actually needs to be nurtured would bypass her defense (Busch, 1993, 2000) and most often initiate a new round of "no-entry" defenses—a patient with pinched lips.

I think to understand our wish (sometimes our impulse) to help and to provide as part of our self-preservative and object preservative strivings, as

---

[9] I am not talking about the mother's breast and the infant's/patient's omnipotent fantasy to possess it and thus to be independed from the object. I think that these early stages that have been very well elaborated by Melanie Klein and her followers lie before, sometimes also at the bottom of what I am describing, when I'm talking about the difference between self-preservative and object-preservative strivings. This differentiation, as preliminary and incomplete as it might be, starts as it were with the baby's grabbing the spoon (see also the conflicts of seven-month-old Margaret seizing the spatula [Winnicott, 1941]).

an urge that might be called up by the patient in our countertransference response, will help us to decide whether the patient needs our caretaking in a certain moment (e.g., when the patient needs to be hospitalized[10] or more metaphorically in the beginning of an analysis), or whether providing rather follows our own needs. For instance, the analyst might unconsciously be afraid of her patient's greed and then might provide to the patient (words, lowered fees, and the like) to protect herself against any possible attack (self-preservation), or the analyst follows an unconscious urge to be a "good caretaker" (object preservative) instead of tolerating the transference of a bad and neglectful parent.

Most difficult, yet unavoidable, appears to me to bear and deal with the patient's "infant transference" to the analyst. I think there is a natural tendency in analysts to see themselves in mother-transference or father-transference, sometimes also in sibling-transference positions. Much more complicated are transferences that want to force the analyst into the regressive position of an infant that is to be fed and taken care of by the patient. To unconsciously defend against this demand for regression (instead of realizing and reflecting it) can limit our capacity to listen to and capture what the patient might need to tell us about how her mother-self is represented in her and what it is driven to do. For instance, the patient might act as an unempathic and at times desperate or even furious mother who wants to force into her child (the analyst) what she thinks the child needs. If the analyst clings to her own need to see herself rather in a mother-transference than in a daughter-transference, she not only misses the patient but might react with the very same "no-entry defenses" (to what she is supposed to swallow) as her patient—and both might end up in a vicious circle of caretaking rivalry (who feeds whom) that is often hard to capture right away and difficult to slowly untangle.

Whether it is about confused self-representations and object representations or about more differentiated identifications with the mother as the primary caretaker—in both cases we can ask ourselves, what is the patient driven to do and to communicate, whom is she driven to preserve in a

---

[10] Patients who openly or in a smoldering way threaten their analysts with suicide— under this perspective—scream for a concrete object-preservative action.

certain moment? It is not that psychoanalysis has missed to see the neediness of the regressed or early-deprived patient. However, to capture this need as a compelling drive activity, as an urge to preserve oneself and one's objects, reveals a compelling dynamic beneath depression and aggression, an unconsciously motivated trajectory that will help us to understand the patient's ongoing open or more hidden fights with the analyst. To sort out the meaning of these urges within us, within the patient and within our interactions is a first and important step to make our interventions more acceptable and digestible for the patient. It won't always be easy to find the right words, because they all will touch on the basic threats to our survival. Yet in the end the analyst might learn from the patient like a mother learns from her child what and when and how much is needed to build up the representations of a well-preserved self and object. Spoons then cease to be weapons and turn into being simply the right tools for the pleasures of a nurturing relationship.

References

Balsam, R. H. (1991), Thinking fragments: Psychoanalysis, feminism, and postmodernism in the contemporary west, *Int. Rev. Psycho-Anal.*, 18: 128-130.

Balsam, R. H. (1996), The pregnant mother and the body image of the daughter, *J. Amer. Psychoanal. Assn.*, 44 (Suppl.): 401-427.

Balsam, R. H. (1999), Becoming and being a woman, *J. Amer. Psychoanal. Assn.*, 47: 266-269.

Balsam, R. H. (2000), The mother within the mother, *Psychoanal. Q.*, 59: 465-492.

Balsam, R. H. (2001), Integrating male and female elements in a woman's gender identity, *J. Amer. Psychoanal. Assn.*, 49: 1335-1360.

Balsam, R. H. (2003), The vanished pregnant body in psychoanalytic female developmental theory, *J. Amer. Psychoanal. Assn.*, 51: 1153-1179.

Balsam, R. H. & Fischer, R. S. (2004), Mothers and daughters, *Psychoanal. Inq.*, 24: 595-600.

Bernstein, P. (2004), Mothers and daughters from today's Psychoanalytic Perspective, *Psychoanal. Inq.*, 24: 601-628.

Bodenstab, J. (2004), Under siege: A mother-daughter relationship survives the Holocaust, *Psychoanal. Inq.*, 24: 731-751.

Busch, F. (1993), In the neighborhood: Aspects of a good interpretation and a developmental lag in ego-psychology, *J. Amer. Psychoanal. Assn.*, 41: 151-177.

Busch, F. (2000), What is a deep interpretation?, *J. Amer. Psychoanal. Assn.*, 48: 237-254.

Bion, W. R. (1962), *Learning from Experience*. London: Heinemann.

Chodorow, N. (1978), *The Reproduction of Mothering*. Berkley: University of California Press.

Freud, S. (1892-93), A case of successful treatment by hypnotism. *Standard Edition*, 1. London: Hogarth Press, 1955.

Freud, S. (1898), Sexuality in the aetiology of the neurosis. *Standard Edition*, 3: 263-285, London: Hogarth Press, 1962.

Freud, S. (1900), The interpretation of dreams. *Standard Edition*, 4 & 5, 1-621, London: Hogarth Press, 1953.

Freud, S. (1905), Three essays on the theory of sexuality. *Standard Edition*, 7: 130-243, London: Hogarth Press, 1953.

Freud, S. (1914), On narcissism: An introduction. *Standard Edition*, 14: 73-102, London: Hogarth Press, 1957.

Freud, S. (1920), Beyond the pleasure principle. *Standard Edition*, 18: 7-64, London: Hogarth Press, 1955.

Freud, S. (1933). New introductory lectures on psycho-analysis. *Standard Edition*, 22: 5-182, London: Hogarth Press, 1964.

Herzog, J. M. (2002), *Father Hunger*. Hillsdale, NJ: Analytic Press.

Hoffman, L. (2003), Mothers with babies and toddlers: Mastering conflicts with aggression, *J. Amer. Psychoanal. Assn.*, 51: 219-1240.

Holtzman, D. & Kulish, N. (1996), The hymen and the loss of virginity, *J. Amer. Psychoanal. Assn.*, 44 (Suppl.): 303-332.

Holtzman, D. & Kulish, N. (1997), *The hymen and the loss of virginity*. Northvale, NJ: Aronson.

Holtzman, D. & Kulish, N. (2000), The feminization of the female oedipal complex. Part I: A reconsideration of the significance of separation issues, *J. Amer. Psychoanal. Assn.*, 48: 1413-1437.

Holtzman, D. & Kulish, N. (2003), The feminization of the female oedipal complex. Part II: Aggression reconsidered, *J. Amer. Psychoanal. Assn.*, 51: 1127-1151.

Khantzian, E. J. & Mack, J. E. (1983), Self-preservation and the care of the self—ego instincts reconsidered, *The Psychoanalytical Study of the Child*, 38: 209-232. New Haven, CT: Yale University Press.

Kulish, N. (1991), The mental representation of the clitoris: The fear of female sexuality, *Psychoanal. Inq.*, 11: 511-536.

Kulish, N. (2000), Primary femininity: Clinical advances and theoretical ambiguities, *J. Amer. Psychoanal. Assn.*, 48: 1355-1379.

Kulish, N. (2002), Female sexuality: The pleasure of secrets and the secret of pleasure, *The Psychoanalytical Study of the Child*, 57: 151-176. New Haven, CT: Yale University Press.

Kulish, N. & Holtzman, D. (1998), Persephone, the loss of virginity and the female Oedipus complex, *Int. J. Psycho-Anal.*, 79: 57-71.

Kulish, N. & Holtzman, D. (2003), Countertransference and the female triangular situation, *Int. J. Psycho-Anal.*, 84: 563-577.

Laplanche, J. (1997), Le Primat de l'Autre en Psychanalyse. [The primary of the other in psychoanalysis] *Travaux 1967-1992*. Paris: Flammarion.

Lax, R. F. (1994), Aspects of primary and secondary genital feelings and anxieties in girls during the preoedipal and early oedipal phases, *Psychoanal. Q.* 63: 271-296.

Lax, R. F. (1995), Freud's views and the changing perspective on femaleness and femininity, *Psychoanal. Psychol.*, 12: 393-406.

Lax, R. F. (1999), Nevermore: The hymen and the loss of virginity, *J. Amer. Psychoanal. Assn.*, 47: 1461-1464.

Loewenstein, R. (1940), The vital or somatic instincts, *Int. J. Psycho-Anal.*, 21: 377-400.

Modell, A. (1985). Self preservation and the preservation of the self, *Annu. Psychoanal.*, 12/13: 69-86.

Nunberg, E. & Federn, P., eds. (1974), *Minutes of the Vienna Psychoanalytic Society, Vol. 3, 1910-1911*. New York: International Universities Press.

O'Connell, M., (2005), *The Good Father. On Men, Masculinity, and Life in the Family*. New York: Scribner.

Plaut, E. A. (1984), Ego instincts: A concept whose time has come, *Psychoanal. St. Child*, 39: 235-258. New Haven, CT: Yale University Press.

Schmidt-Hellerau, C. (1988), Über das Rätsel der Weiblichkeit. Neue Thesen zur weiblichen Entwicklung, herausgearbeitet aus dem Werk Sigmund Freuds, [The enigma of femininity. Suggestions on female development deducted from the works of Sigmund Freud.] *Psychiatry*, 42: 289-306.

Schmidt-Hellerau, C. (1997), Libido and lethe. Fundamentals of a formalised conception of metapsychology, *Int. J. Psycho-Anal.*, 78: 683-697.

Schmidt-Hellerau, C. (2001), *Life Drive and Death Drive, Libido and Lethe. A Formalized Consistent Model of Psychoanalytic Drive and Structure Theory*. New York: Other Press.

Schmidt-Hellerau, C. (2002), Why aggression? Metapsychological, clinical and technical considerations, *Int. J. Psycho-Anal.*, 83: 1269-1289.

Schmidt-Hellerau, C. (2003). Die Erhaltung von Selbst und Objekt im Schatten der Freudschen Theorieentwicklung, [The presentation of self and object in the shadow of the development of Freud's theory] *J. Psychoanal. Theory & Practise*, 18: 316-343.

Schmidt-Hellerau, C. (2005), The other side of Oedipus. *Psychoanal. Q.*, LXXIV, 187-217.

Silverman, D. K. (1987), What are little girls made of? *Psychoanal. Psychol.*, 4: 315-334.

Silverman, D. K. (1991), Attachment patterns and Freudian theory. *Psychoanal. Psychol.*, 8: 169-193.

Simmel, E. (1924), Die psycho-physische Bedeutsamkeit des Intestinalorgans fuer die Urverdraengung, [The psychophysiological meaning of the intestinal organ for primal repression] *Internat. Zschft. Psychoanalyse*, 10: 218-221.

Simmel, E. (1933). Praegenitalprimat und intestinale Stufe der Libidoorganisation, [The pregenital primacy and the intestinal stage of libido organization] *Internat. Zschft. Psychoanalyse*, 19: 245-246.

Simmel, E. (1944), Self-preservation and the death instinct, *Psychoanal. Q.*, 13: 160-185.

Winnicott, D. W. (1941) The observation of infants in a set situation. *Int. J. Psycho-Anal.*, 22: 229-249.

Winnicott, D. W. (1971), *Playing and Reality*. London: Tavistock Publications Ltd.

Williams, G., Williams P., Desmarais, J. & Ravenscroft, K. (2004), Exploring Feeding Difficulties in Children. *The Generosity of Acceptance*. Vol. 1. New York: Karnac.

Young-Bruehl, E. & Bethlard, F. (1999), The Hidden History of the Ego-Instincts, *Psychoanal. Rev.*, 86 (6): 823-851.

CHAPTER 12

"You've Hurt me!"

Clinical Reflections on Moral Sadism[*]

I was boarding a shuttle from New York to Boston. Three rows in front of me, a mother seemed to be in some sort of struggle with her four-or five-year-old son. "You've hurt me!" the boy exclaimed. The mother responded with a comment. "You've hurt me!" the boy insisted. More talking followed. "You've hurt me," the boy kept complaining. Eventually, the mother grew silent. "You've hurt me" the boy reiterated throughout the flight in what seemed to become an increasingly demanding tone—pausing at times, but continuing to repeat the words until we arrived in Boston an hour later. "You've hurt me!"

This interaction reminded me of patients who do just what the little boy did: they blame us and cannot stop blaming us for having hurt them. In order to outline the general dynamics I am referring to, let me sketch a typical situation with my patient Peter, who in his mid-thirties is married, has five-year-old twins, and is a hardworking lawyer in a successful practice. Peter came to treatment depressed and angry because, despite all his efforts and care for everybody, he continuously feels treated unfairly and unappreciatively by his wife, his clients, and even his two little sons. The very fact that he was recommended for analysis made him feel hurt.

[*] (2009). Psychoanalytic Quarterly, 78(1):233-241
A shorter version of this paper was presented at the International Psychoanalytical Association Congress in Berlin on July 26, 2007.

Soon the two of us have a similar situation between us. I make some small intervention, even something that seems of minor importance, and Peter feels hurt. "You've hurt me," he says, seemingly disgusted (more than wounded) by my misdeed. I acknowledge that he feels hurt. "That's what I said!" he rebukes. "And … ?"

"'And … ?'" I echo. Peter stares at me. I wonder aloud to him what it was that felt so hurtful. "Isn't that obvious?" he says. "You've hurt me! I wonder how you could say that." All efforts to explore and clarify fail. Peter insists that I have hurt him, throughout this and the following sessions.

In the meantime, the event itself has become blurred. I am under the barrage of my patient's attacks. His eyes pierce me, and he clearly enjoys my struggle with this complication. I feel I am supposed to apologize, to confess that I *did* hurt him, to explain how I could do this—and I do not want to do so. As much as I understand the importance of this enactment (more than I do the complexity of the enactment itself), I feel unjustly accused. His claim to having been brutalized by me is brutalizing me. Whatever I say, he continues trying to corner me, hoping to force me to my knees in front of him while he tells me that I am using bad technique and he is paying all this money for nothing. "You've hurt me!" As I try to awaken his sense of what is going on, interpreting aspects of the particular interaction we are engaged in, he counters with something like: "Am I supposed to feel sorry for you? You didn't answer my question! How could you do this!?"

After some time, Peter seems to be finished, and the blame fades from his attention—readily available, though, to be picked up again whenever it fits the purpose. Real insight has not been achieved, I feel. And a little while later, after another intervention of mine, sure enough, we will get into another cycle of this kind in which his feeling hurt by me justifies his persecuting me with his accusations.

We have all seen patients who, for quite a while, engage in this kind of repetitions with us before they open up to the idea that such enactments have meaning. Of course, we can understand and conceptualize their occurrence from various angles. Narcissistic issues are always involved, as are primitive sadomasochistic fantasies played out in the transference with the analyst. Triumphantly observing how the object is humiliated serves as a manic defense against feeling small, helpless, and not in control of what is going on.

These functions have been widely discussed in the literature. Here I want to limit myself to a particular aspect while leaving aside all the other secondary gains that form a part of these clashes. Drawing on my counter-transference feelings whenever I am in this kind of struggle with a patient, I am most impressed by what I would call the patient's *moral sadism*. For example, it is with strong sadistic satisfaction that Peter crashes on my psychoanalytic conscience and makes me feel bad—how could I possibly be so insensitive, thoughtless, and technically clumsy as to say something that hurt him so much, that he was not ready to hear and not able to bear?[1]

My patient is not simply trying to humiliate me. Rather, it feels as if he wants to force a sense of guilt into my analytic conscience. If the moral masochist says, "I did it all wrong, I shouldn't have done it, I'm a bad person," the moral sadist says: "*you* did it all wrong, *you* shouldn't have done this, *you* are a bad person!"

In thinking about these clinical moments, I became intrigued with the fact that Freud conceptualized *moral masochism* but not *moral sadism*, even though he certainly saw masochism and sadism as an inseparable couple. Until 1915, he understood sadism as primary, and masochism as a result of turning sadism around "upon the subject's own self" (1915, p. 127). In 1919, sadism was still viewed as primary, and—in light of repression—the unconscious masochistic masturbation fantasy of "my father is beating me" was taken to be a compromise between morality and lust, combining a "sense of guilt and sexual love" (1919, p. 189). As Freud explains: "*It is not only the punishment for the forbidden genital relation, but also the regressive substitute for that relation*" (p. 189, italics in original).

In revising his whole drive theory (1920, 1924), Freud finally stated his formulation of a primary masochism, in which the death drive fused

---

[1] Of course, when a patient feels hurt, we always have to wonder in what way our intervention might have been hurtful; e.g., it might have been stirred by an unconscious sadistic or retaliatory impulse in the analyst. Here, however, I am referring to interventions that seem to have been arbitrarily picked out and designated as hurtful.

with libido is directed toward the self; sadism occurs when a part of this mixture is directed toward the external object. As much as the erotogenic masochism seeks sexual pleasure via physical pain, moral masochism seeks the satisfaction of a sadistic superego (or its more primitive precursors) because of an unconscious sense of guilt. As always with his predilection for sexuality, Freud understands moral masochism as a dissolution of oedipal achievements, a resexualization of morality.

This latter idea certainly can hold for moral sadism as well. Moral sadism then represents the sadistic side of resexualizing morality. Here the refusal to feel oedipal guilt leads to the externalization of a bad conscience (its projection onto the analyst), which allows the patient to feel morally superior, even flawless, while enacting the unconscious erotic fantasy of intercourse as a sadistic subjugation and penetration of the object. As in Freud's concept of moral masochism, this aspect of moral sadism can be viewed as an expression of aggressive sexuality.[2]

It is worth noting that Freud's and these latter approaches represent two different—if not opposite—perspectives on sadism, both of which are clinically valid. The first is focused on sexual perversion guided by the sexual drives; the second on the threat to survival and thus, as I see it (Schmidt-Hellerau 2001, 2005a, 2005b, 2006, 2008), is guided by the preservative drives. This is the perspective I want to develop here: *moral sadism in the service of self-preservation.*

It is my countertransference feeling when entangled with a patient in one of these "you've-hurt-me" episodes that has led me to think of moral sadism in this particular function. When I am blamed for having harmed or wronged someone, I can react in one of two ways: (1) I can acknowledge the

---

[2] Leonoff (1997) explores the use of sadism with regard to annihilation anxieties, when the fear of losing an object deemed essential for the subject's survival becomes overwhelming: "Faced with unarticulated primitive dread ... the sadist triumphs over death by becoming its agent. Clinically, such dread can be expressed through a malignant fear of passivity, helplessness, or ego collapse, as well as in the wordless panic of nonexistence. These may be defended against through moments of sadistic triumph, which, through omnipotent control of the object, symbolically guarantee the survival of the sadist. Sadism, therefore, garners grandiosity and through aggression sidesteps psychic death by becoming the harbinger of it." [p. 100]

correctness of the blame, consequently wanting to apologize and repair the damage (showing an urge to be object-preservative), or (2) I can dispute or deny my wrongdoing (thus being essentially self-preservative). And both feelings are usually stirred up in my countertransference and present the two sides of a monolithic conflict (Schmidt-Hellerau 2005a, 2005b). I feel urged to, and sometimes tempted to, apologize and repair—yet I also feel that I did not mean to do it, and that in fact I did not do anything wrong.

First, I want to address my patient Peter's feelings: he is hurt. Consequently, in his view, my duty is to apologize and remedy the injury. If this is what my patient wants to coerce me into doing, then I contend that his *moral sadism* is his effort to provoke an object-preservative response in me—an increase of care in the form of soothing his pain, healing his wound, reassuring him of his intactness, and helping him with something that seems unmanageable. "You've hurt me—now repair the damage!" would be his claim to be taken care of.

To be sure, understanding my countertransference in this way is not the means simply to enact the required reparation, but to work toward analyzing the patient's need to bring me into this corner. "It is true," the moral sadist says, *"you are a bad person"*; however, this accusation does not mean *"Go away"*—it rather expresses the idea that the object owes something to the subject. The expectation is that the object will then make up for it, will do the restoration. This view strips this particular form of moral sadism from its erotic core, seeing it not as primarily about gaining anal-sadistic pleasure, but instead about a heightened need to be cared for.

I think we should make a clear distinction between the *pleasure* of our sexual strivings and the *satisfaction* of our preservative needs. Pleasure and satisfaction do feel quite differently. And it is satisfaction, not pleasure, that I sense when Peter seems to notice that he has brought me close to an admission of my guilt and an apology for my supposedly hurtful intervention. He is then briefly satisfied, while also feeling the previous extension of his narcissistic boundaries reestablished. Now he can let go for a little while.

But the issue is not resolved and reemerges—even jumps up without warning, it seems, soon after. Again, Peter claims that I have done some-

thing hurtful to him and pursues my assumption of guilt with all the cruelty and sadism of which he is capable. I notice it is not that he merely wishes
I would take good or better care of him—as do those patients who emphasize their neediness, thus evoking in us a countertransferential urge to be
helpful. His issues are more pressing, more intense; his transference message to me is: "Not only did you not take good enough care of me—you
even hurt me by doing something bad!"

My patient wants to force guilt into me (using projective identification), and I feel like refusing to accept it. He does not stick something
into me like a symbolic knife (penis) that would cut or hurt me; the
unmanageable something that he wants to force into me is *guilt*—and
that is what makes this form of sadism a *moral sadism*. It is a guilt that
he wants to get off his chest, that he himself refuses to accept, and that
he wants me to take over. I have to apologize for it —which, if I do, gives
him relief for a short time, until the whole cycle starts again, because as
long as we have not understood what this unconscious guilt is all about,
he will continue to feel guilty.

Guilt that is so unbearable to a child's mind that it potentially leads to
moral sadism usually goes beyond normal oedipal fantasies. It can be the
consequence of a traumatic event in the family (e.g., the death of a sibling
or parent or mother's miscarriage, possibly during the oedipal phase) for
which the child takes omnipotent responsibility. It may also be evident in
patients whose parental objects have used them as containers for their own
excessive projective identification with guilt (Williams et al. 2004). In these
latter cases, the patient's use of a moral sadistic attack on the analyst represents an attempt to get rid of the indigestible parental guilt while
simultaneously reenacting the moment of guilt intrusion (a turning of
passive into active). Having once been the victim of such a guilt intrusion,
the patient feels quite justified in blaming the transferential object—the
analyst—of hurting or wronging him or her.

The idea of justice is central to moral sadism: it not only defends the
patient against the perception of his or her own sadism; it also expresses
a deep-seated sense of the right to be oneself, authentic and separate, the
need to purge oneself from one's bad objects in order to restore, preserve, and develop one's own pure self. When the guilt is less particular

and more pervasive, when there is confusion about what the object and what the subject might have contributed to the crime, the patient often insists on "misunderstanding."

In severe cases, the claim of "misunderstanding" does not aim at clarification, but rather at bolstering the "reality" of the patient's having been hurt by the analyst, if only by accident. Nevertheless, despite the difficulties in working with these aspects of "malignant misunderstandings" (Britton 2003), it may be helpful to keep in mind that these patients' attachment to moral sadism includes a reparative offer extended to subject and object alike: it is as though the patient is suggesting, "Neither of us is truly bad; we just misunderstood each other." However, this offering to the analyst can be a trap if both parties agree that this is what took place. In fact, moral sadism is never based on misunderstanding, but on an intrusion of guilt that requires analysis.

With these few strokes, my goal has been to elaborate on a clinical concept that, to my knowledge, has not previously been made explicit as such in the literature. "You've hurt me" seems to be the central formula that promotes the secret strivings of the moral sadist to force guilt into the object, with the expectation of repair and compensation. The apology of the object never helps because whatever was originally the object's guilt has since become the *patient's* guilt. Analyzing and helping the patient to own his or her guilt by differentiating between which aspects belong to the object and which to the subject will provide the relief the patient yearns for. Owning one's guilt means to transform some of the moral sadism into healthy moral masochism (Rosenberg 1991)—including the acknowledgment of one's sadism and one's need to repair.

We can leave open Freud's question of whether masochism or sadism is primary. Rather, I would say that the primal need to be taken care of becomes sadistic, as in moral sadism, when a part of the self that was in need of being cared for by the object feels unbearable, even dangerous to the subject—the child, the patient—since the maternal/parental object has closed off that part and refused to take it over, leaving the child with the feeling of being bad.

Moral sadism is then an intensification of the subject's claim for help, piercing the object's wall of refusal and loading it with all the indigestible badness that was once stirred up within the child. Thus, in an ines-capable vicious cycle, the object becomes the bad object, avoided by the subject as a source of direct help, but used for further evacuation of all that feels bad inside. Signs of "moral masochism"—or rather of true feelings of guilt and sorrow—eventually indicate to the analyst that the patient has become capable of containing some of his or her guilt and working it through.

References

Britton, R. (2003). Narcissistic problems in sharing space. In *Sex, Death and the Superego: Experiences in Psychoanalysis*. London: Karnac, pp. 165-178.

Freud, S. (1915). Instincts and their vicissitudes. *Standard Edition*, 14.

Freud, S. (1919). A child is being beaten (a contribution to the study of the origin of sexual perversions). *Standard Edition*, 17.

Freud, S. (1920). Beyond the Pleasure Principle. *Standard Edition*, 18.

Freud, S. (1924). The economic problem of masochism. *Standard Edition*, 19.

Leonoff, A. (1997). Destrudo ergo sum: towards a psychoanalytic under-standing of sadism. *Can. J. Psychoanal.*, 5:95-112.

Rosenberg, B. (1991). *Masochisme mortifère et masochisme gardien de la vie*. Paris: Presses Universitaires de France.

Schmidt-Hellerau, C. (2001). *Life Drive and Death Drive, Libido and Lethe: A Formalized Consistent Model of Psychoanalytic Drive and Structure Theory*. New York: Other Press.

Schmidt-Hellerau, C. (2005a). We are driven. *Psychoanal. Q.*, 74:989-1028.

Schmidt-Hellerau, C. (2005b). The other side of Oedipus. *Psychoanal. Q.*, 74:187-217.

Schmidt-Hellerau, C. (2006). Surviving in absence: on the preservative and death drive and their clinical utility. *Psychoanal. Q.*, 75:1057-1095.

Schmidt-Hellerau, C. (2008). The lethic phallus: rethinking the misery of Oedipus. *Psychoanal. Q.*, 77:719-753.

Williams, G., Williams, P., Desmarais, J. & Ravenscroft, K. (2004). *The Generosity of Acceptance*, Vol. 1. London: Karnac.

CHAPTER 13

Anxiety in the Negative Therapeutic Reaction*

Freud introduced the negative therapeutic reaction as a clinical concept. But, as always, he also reflected on it on a metapsychological
level. At the end of his 32nd lecture, in which he considers the relation
between "Anxiety and Instinctual Life" (1933), he reveals how he came to
develop his second drive theory: It was the negative therapeutic reaction
that gave him pause. Hence, Freud's conception of the negative therapeutic
reaction is the clinical root of his second drive theory and his introduction
of the death drive. In order to fully appreciate and explore the meaning and
value of these concepts in contemporary psychoanalysis, it seems sensible
to consider this particular connection from the perspective of my revised
drive theory (Schmidt-Hellerau 2002, 2005, 2006). This will provide us
with new, clinically relevant insights into the particular anxiety that feeds
the negative therapeutic reaction.

Self-Preservation, Anxiety, and the Fear of Being Ill

As I have stipulated throughout this book, from the beginning of life
memory traces of interactions with the caregiving object will structure the

---

* An earlier version of this paper was published in *Nothing Good Is Allowed to Stand: An
Integrative View of the Negative Therapeutic Reaction,* edited by L. Wurmser and H.
Jarass. New York: Routledge, 2013, pp 149-159.

death drive and introduce the goals and functions of self- and object preservation. Throughout the child's development, these preservative structures will form increasingly stable screens that *represent* the tasks of how to be safe and healthy. From here we can take a further step (Figure 1).

FIGURE 1

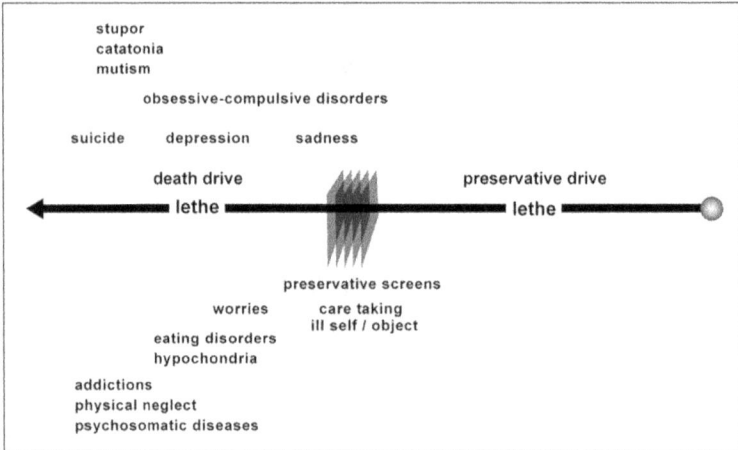

If we agree that it is the structures that halt, organize, or bind the unbound, unruly urges of bare drive activity, thereby giving them meaning, we can see that we will also need next to the structures of healthy self- and object preservation others that represent malady and sorrow, the memory traces of physical and psychic pain. Intensified strivings of the preservative drives will reach beyond the representations of sound self- and object preservation and activate the representations of self and object in the state of disease, suffering, and the fear of approaching death. It is necessary that we are able to represent ourselves and our objects as sick or sad because this will lead us to initiate what fosters healing, helps recapture sanity, and provides solace. However, these representations can also be neurotically emphasized or distorted, producing self- (and object) representations such as those seen in hypochondria, germaphobia, or obsessive-compulsive disorders with a heightened concern and fear of being sick or infected or not clean, resulting in an anxious or overprotective attitude with regard to self and/or object.

Thus we come to roughly distinguish three layers of structural screens on the lethic side of drive activities (Figure 2).

FIGURE 2

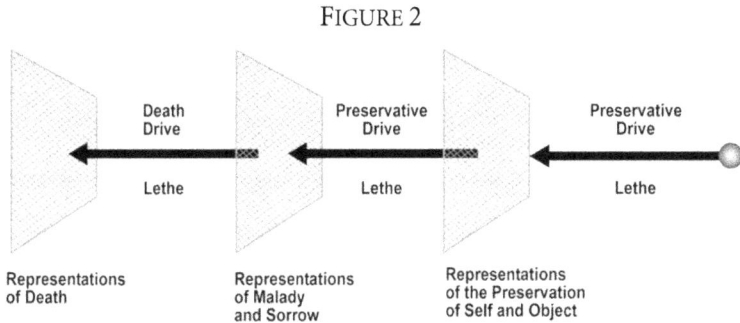

1) The most densely structured area of the death drive (on the right side of Figure 2) is the layer containing the basic representations of self- and object preservation. It is permanently invested with lethic energies, continuously at work, and triggers all the specific actions necessary to ensure safety and health. Many of its functions may not be noticeable as long as all requirements are fulfilled, but even slight deviation from average comfort levels will immediately arouse further lethic investments in the affected section, promoting remedial action.

2) The next layer of representations is activated by increased amounts of lethic energies in states of malady and sorrow. It is an equally important structural area organizing the ideas about disease and survival threats with related anxieties and concerns, with fear of helplessness and the ensuing rescue fantasies. If the threats to safety and survival are real, the intensified activities of the preservative drives will be aimed at protection and healing. But even if the perceived threats are based on neurotic imagination, the subject's inner reality is one of being endangered in his/her survival, stirring the same measures of precaution and protection. Or, viewed from the perspective of the first layer: if there is a lack of solidly established preservative structures, the excitations of the self-preservative drive

(e.g., hunger urges) will not be sufficiently contained and limited, thus ushering in a lethic surge into the area of disease (e.g., insatiable greed, as in addictions) and potentially death.

3) The final layer of lethic representations is crucial in coming to terms with death, something that goes beyond words, images, knowledge, and meaning. This *nameless dread* (Bion) is countered by the subject's *ideas* of physiological and psychological death, represented in this third layer; it may also contain a collection of infantile beliefs, religious faith, the residues of forgotten fantasies—which were once vital—and further memories of dead and lost objects, as well as the shadows of a dead or deadened, traumatized self or object—all of these being organized or loosely connected in what we could call a *death screen*. The function of the conscious and unconscious representations of this third and final layer is to halt and contain what otherwise might be experienced as the terrifying and virtually endless striving (the ruthless force) of the death drive.

Anxiety Turns the Page

How do these reflections relate to anxiety? Freud consistently conceptualized anxiety in quantitative terms. What elicits anxiety is a certain amount of drive energy (in response to an external stimulus or an inner need/desire) that exceeds the apparatus's capacities for containment (binding), and thus not only interferes with its working properly and effectively, but also threatens to damage or even destroy psychic structures. This idea postulates that a surge of drive energy, an overwhelming excitation, causes trauma from within (possibly by the effects of *Nachträglichkeit*).

The second theory of anxiety also relates to the quantitative—now refined to a signal, a tiny portion of drive energy that allows the ego to probe *en miniature* (by investing a fantasy in the unconscious) the possible consequences of a full-fledged enactment of the unconsciously aroused need or desire. The possible use of only a small amount of drive energy to arouse *signal anxiety* that then activates protective defenses is a sophisticated, ingenious, and economical way for the psychic apparatus to preempt damage—initially not available but eventually achieved in the course of the structural development of the ego.

In his 32nd lecture, Freud emphasizes that, starting from birth, anxiety is a response to danger. The danger can be real (toxic, external), leading to *realistic anxiety*. If there is no real danger but anxiety comes up all the same, we call it *neurotic*. In struggling to find a theoretical explanation for the latter type of anxiety, Freud suggests: "What he [the neurotic] is afraid of is evidently his own libido. The difference between this situation and that of realistic anxiety lies in two points: that the danger is an internal instead of an external one and that it is not consciously recognized" (Freud 1933, p. 84). Using libido as a synonym for drive energy (excitation), Freud here captures that neurotic anxiety is stirred by an unconscious (but also at times preconscious or even conscious) fantasy of danger (e.g., separation from the caregiving object, castration). This fantasy is entirely psychic; it is the expression of a specific drive activity, because "every drive tries to make itself effective by activating ideas that are in keeping with its aims" (1910, p. 213). And since Freud acknowledges that "anxiety serves the purposes of self-preservation" (1933, p. 84), we might very well conclude that *anxiety is the expression of the self-preservative drives in response to a realistic or imagined danger to the subject's (or the object's) well-being and survival,* hence the release of quantitatively increased lethic energies reaching into the area of disease or even death, because "what is feared, what is the object of the anxiety, is invariably the emergence of a traumatic moment, which cannot be dealt with by the normal rules of the pleasure principle" (1933, p. 94).

Freud describes his concepts of *anxiety* and *drives* in order to summarize for his imaginative audience the most important of his theoretical developments since his first lecture series in the winter of 1916-17. He ends his reflections by declaring that the starting point for his introduction of the *death drive* was the *negative therapeutic reaction,* the patient's resistance to getting better because of an unconscious sense of guilt, a powerful masochistic "need for punishment" that is "satisfied by the suffering which is linked to the neurosis, and for that reason holds fast to being ill" (Freud 1933, p. 108). Freud presents the example of a woman whom he had freed from the symptoms of a long-tormented existence; however, as she eagerly plunged into the activities of her life, she started to experience a series of accidents (hurting her ankle, knee, and hand) and then illnesses (catarrhs, sore throats, influenza, and rheumatic swellings), "which put her out of action for a time and caused her suffering" (p. 109). Freud explains this chain of new physical suffer- ings as caused by an "unconscious sense of guilt," a superego aggression turned against the ego and hence a need for punishment—in short, a negative therapeutic reaction.

Let us remember Freud's finding: "What is feared, what is the object of the anxiety, is invariably the emergence of a traumatic moment." We can picture the effect of trauma (Figure 3) as I have developed it previ- ously: "Trauma breaks through the protective shields of the preservative screens and jams the representation of self and/or object into the back- yard of death" (Schmidt-Hellerau 2007, p. 1066).

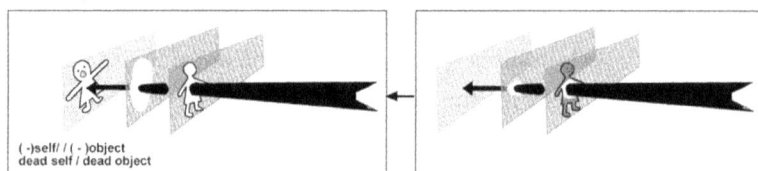

(-)self/ / (-)object
dead self / dead object

Figure 3: A traumatic assault on the representation of a healthy self or object (on the right side) will lead to a break or rupture of the preservative structures, as a result of which self and object will be represented as dead/deadened (on the left side).

As we know, anxiety seeks to protect against the damages of trauma. Not all threats would end up causing trauma. Not all anxiety patients show the negative therapeutic reaction, but those who do can be considered as traumatized. They require long-lasting analytic work and only slowly show signs of progress. And when these traumatized patients step only briefly out of the backyard of death and for a moment reenliven those parts of their self-representations that have been deadened by trauma, they often develop physical symptoms or depression, withdraw fearing breakdown and disease, or don't show up for a while in order to get back to where they had been before. At a later state, when their capacity for verbalization in this area has considerably increased, they might say: "If

I'd get better, I'd surely be diagnosed with cancer!" Or they may be convinced that any bit of further progress will end in disaster. All these occurrences seem to be the signs that Freud emphasized, signs of the patient's "wish" not to get better: the negative therapeutic reaction.

However, looking at the organization of representations on the continuum of lethic drive activities in Figure 3, we can come to a different interpretation.

A traumatized patient with (parts of) his self represented in the area of death (third layer) doesn't show much, if any, concern for his survival. He is numb or indifferent as to whether he lives or dies. It is only when he gets better in his analysis, when he has built up structures beyond the quiet area of his deadened self, that all of a sudden he becomes capable of fearing for his life. It is only then that he cathects self-representations in the anxiety-laden area of disease and suffering (second layer). *This actually makes him feel worse.* It is precisely through these newly developed (often physical) symptoms that he can express his heightened concerns for his self-preservation. These anxieties signal a surge of lethic cathexis, comparable to that summoned in a normal person during illness. I suggest that anxiety about falling ill, as well as intermediate illnesses, are an unavoidable and necessary transitional phase on the reconstructive way from a traumatized, deadened self-state to the safely established representation of a well-preserved self and object (first layer).

What Freud called the negative therapeutic reaction is therefore not a *resistance against* getting better, but *evidence of* getting better, and should be interpreted as such. Borrowing from Quinodoz (1999), I would hold that these worries and affections are symptoms that "turn over a page" and should be interpreted progressively as a newly achieved capacity to elicit the analyst's object-preservative concerns, as well as the patient's own self-preservative ones. That is to say: instead of interpreting a resistance against getting better, a regressive move, or an expression of aggression turned inward, we interpret to our patients that they now (finally) worry about themselves, that these symptoms can be understood in the context of their progression, because it is necessary to be concerned about one's health, well-being, and survival. And when there is no real cause, we can work them through like any other neurotic symptom.

This does not mean that Freud was wrong in identifying an unconscious sense of guilt (often borrowed from an early love object) underneath the negative therapeutic reaction. However, in the light of what I have just described, this unconscious guilt reveals its defensive function; it can be understood as a grandiose denial of the helplessness experienced in the traumatic assault. "I am guilty" says "it was *my* doing; *I was in charge*"—while the trauma had overwhelmed the individual's capacity to manage and protect him-/herself from the devastating blow of the onslaught (be it from within or from outside). The same accounts for "borrowed guilt," which entails a grandiose denial of *not* being able to lift up or repair the object's failure. Thus, at the bottom of the negative therapeutic reaction is helplessness, the most terrifying feeling of all—helplessless so dramatically increased in the moment of trauma that from then on, survival will forever require and refuse the object's preservative assistance.

The negative therapeutic reaction of the patient holds on to the numbness of a deadened state; it not only shies back from the frightening acknowledgment of being vulnerable (in not cathecting the anxiety-ladden representations of malady and sorrow), it simultaneously, by not allowing the patient to get better, tries to make sure that he/she remains in the analyst's care—thus clinging to the analyst while foreclosing his or her helpfulness.

The difficulty of working through this unconscious guilt as a denial of helplessness has to do with the patient's unconscious anxiety over an overwhelming rage in response to the trauma that would come up—a rage that always looms large and threatens to destroy not only the caregiving object (analyst) outside, but also the fragile self-preservative structures inside the traumatized psyche. This anxiety about losing or fighting off the object on whom one totally depends envisions a repetition of the old trauma, leading the patient to continue a suffering that he is used to and can manage on his own, rather than risking any step forward that might first lead him to feel worse in order to eventually get better.

Thus the anxiety in the negative therapeutic reaction is that of an overwhelming helplessness and rage. It is the patient's aggressively intensified self-preservative response to his or her trauma that needs to be analyzed as such in order to structure and limit the patient's lethic energies according to the requirements of normal healthy self- and object preservation.

References

Freud, S. (1905). *Three Essays on the Theory of Sexuality. S. E.*, 7:123–242.

Freud, S. (1910). The psycho-analytic view of psychogenic disturbance of vision. *S. E.*, 11:209–218.

Freud, S. (1915). Instincts and their vicissitudes. *S. E.*, 14:109–140.

Freud, S. (1933). *New Introductory Lectures on Psycho-Analysis. S. E.*, 22:1–182.

Green, A. (1993). *Le travail du negatif* [The work of the negative]. Paris: Editions DeMinuit.

Laplanche, J. (1997). Une metapsychologie a l'epreuve de l'angoisse [Metapsychology as a test of anxiety]. In *Le primat de l'aure* [The predominance of the aura]. Paris: Champs/Flammarion, pp. 143-158.

Quinodoz, J.-M. (1999). "Dreams that turn over a page": integration dreams with paradoxical regressive content. *Int. J. Psychoanal.*, 80:225–238.

Schmidt-Hellerau, C. (1997). Libido and lethe: fundamentals of a formalized conception of metapsychology. *Int. J. Psychoanal.*, 78:683–697.

Schmidt-Hellerau, C. (2001). *Lifl Drive and Death Drive, Libido and Lethe: A Formalized Consistent Model of Psychoanalytic Drive and Structure Theory*. New York: Other Press.

Schmidt-Hellerau, C. (2002). Why aggression? Metapsychological, clinical and technical considerations. *Int. J. Psychoanal.*, 83:1269–1289.

Schmidt-Hellerau, C. (2005). We are driven. *Psychoanal. Q.*, 74:989–1028.

Schmidt-Hellerau, C. (2006). Surviving in absence: on the preservative and death drive and their clinical utility. *Psychoanal. Q.*, 75:1057–1095.

CHAPTER 14

A Shift in the Head of Janus

Metapsychological Reflections on the Analyst's Contribution to Psychic Transformation[*]

W hat do we do—what do we hope to achieve—when we do psychoanalysis? The general answer is: make the unconscious conscious or strengthen and enlarge the ego. This is curative, said Freud, because it ensures better control over the drives (1937, p. 229f). If what we are driven to is elaborated, hence structured, it can become conscious and be part of the more reality-oriented choices in our life. Thus psychic transformation in the psychoanalytic process is seen as an expression of the change or building of psychic structure, which leads to a change in the regulation of drive activity. This is the point I want to address here, first on a metapsychological level and then with two clinical vignettes: how can we think about the analyst's contribution to the modification of psychic structure and the ensuing modulation of drive activity?

Freud's paradigmatic formulations on structure formation (1895, 1900, 1911) are based on the activation of the infant's self-preservative drive: the baby is hungry, screams and kicks, mother comes, feeding takes place, and the hunger subsides. Countless repetitions of this same sequence eventually are retained and result in a memory trace, a first structure, in which the excitation of this particular self-preservative drive—hunger—is associated

---

[*] Paper presented at the EPF Congress in Athens in 2006.

with the sensory representations of the satisfying object—mother—and all the affect and motor representations—screaming, kicking, sucking—that will be formed as part of the nursing interaction. From now on, whenever hunger arises, this structure is recathected, and its reactivation is perceived as what Freud calls a *hallucination*: the infant knows that he/she is hungry and wants to be fed.

How can we think in more detail about the structure, the activation of which produces this hallucination? It is clear: whatever might be hallucinated speaks only to the part of this structure that is available to conscious perception (as fleeting or momentary as it might be), while there may be other parts equally important for its stability and constitution that remain unperceived and unconscious (Schmidt-Hellerau 1997, 2001). Knowing about all elements of psychic structure gives the clinician the chance to intervene more precisely according to the patient's needs.

Departing from Freud's 1910 statement that "every drive tries to make itself effective by activating ideas that are in keeping with its aims" and that "all the organic drives that operate in our mind may be classified as 'hunger' or 'love'" (Freud, p. 213f), we can trace or "reimagine" how structure formation involves both primal drives, the preservative and sexual drives: they are the two antagonistic forces that will be balanced in various proportions in every structure that is built and thenceforth exists.

Structure Formation

Stipulating two primary drives—namely, the preservative and sexual drives, which oppose each other and express themselves through the ideas that indicate their aims—lays the foundation of structure formation within the psychic apparatus. For its minute (albeit hypothetical) description, we can relate to Freud's paradigm example, *the hungry baby*.

1) Hunger, at first not recognized as such but probably sensed as pain in the *pit of the stomach* combined with the threat of general physiological derailment, is one of the body's first demands on the nascent mind. It may be something like a *nameless dread* (Bion), a huge gap,

a black hole, a devouring abyss, maybe a sense of pain and terror. These are all words when in fact there are no words yet. However, hunger registers as a rush toward death, a *death drive*; it may not yet be represented as a veritable "idea," but for the sake of theoretical elaboration, we can call this basic threat the original (permanently unconscious, primary repressed) *lethic idea of the death drive.*

2) Mother's object-preservative response (feeding, articulating the need) associates the infant's first "idea" of death (starvation) with the lethic idea of the object's aid to survival (breast/nursing), thereby *transforming a previously nameless dread into a self-preservative need*: hunger. Thus the idea of *hunger* is composed of *two lethic layers* linking the infant's quest/need with mother's response/satisfaction.

3) Interacting with the nursling, mother is also delighted and erotically stimulated; she cathects or envelops her infant libidinally (smiling, stroking, having reveries, etc.). Her baby is an object to be preserved *and* to be loved. This erotic/narcissistic investment—energized by the ideas of mother's *sexual drives* and the whole potential of her desire (her enigmatic messages, to use Laplanche's term)—adds a libidinal layer to the emerging representation, establishing the foundation of the infant's narcissism.

4) The experience of mother's love and sensory stimulation in turn reveals the infant's sexual drives (Green 1993, p. 117), an erotic response felt as pleasure within the undifferentiated mother-child matrix, which adds a second libidinal layer to the buildup of the memory trace of the feeding experience.

The two layers of libidinal representations attach themselves to the two layers of lethic representations. This is what Freud called *anaclisis*. Hence these *four layers of ideas, two lethic and two libidinal*, associated and combined within the experience of the nursing interaction, will create a memory trace or representation of the whole feeding experience, which (1) connects self and object, (2) "fuses" or "binds" preservative and sexual drives (the former tending toward the unconscious, the latter allowing for its conscious memorable part), and (3) shapes the pleasure principle for this particular structure in the very ratio that corresponds to the body's predominant demand on the mind at this point in time. In this ratio, the preservative drives might also provide a structure-preserving, maintaining, and stabilizing function while the sexual drives might promote its ability to change.

This detailed conceptualization of the first hypothetical structure can apply to structure formation in general: any complete structure can be viewed as a complex configuration composed of lethic and libidinal representations. To put it differently: it is the two antagonistic drives, balanced in whichever ratio in each case, that activate a structure and its particular functions. Hence we can say: each structure is composed as a Janus head.[1] Freud used this metaphor, and Green (2001) elaborated it for his conception of narcissism as a structure, one side of which is organized by the life drives and the other by the death drives. I take this conception as a model for every structure and would only slightly modify

---

[1] Janus fits so well for this conception of structure because, in Roman mythology, he is the god of gates and doors, beginnings and endings, and he represents the transition between primitive life and civilization—as structure certainly does. He is usually depicted with two faces looking in opposite directions, corresponding to the general idea of the two antagonistic drives and their representations; however, sometimes Janus is also presented as four-faced, and this version corresponds to the differentiation between self- and object-preservation as well as self- and object-love. Finally, the Romans had a particular custom: the gates of the Janus temple were open in times of war, reminiscent of a situation when Rome was attacked, and Janus made a hot spring erupt that put the attackers to flight. The opening of the gates in times of war was meant to allow the hot water to pour out of the temple and fight off the enemies. In times of peace, the gates were closed. Let's transfer this idea to our concept of structure: in times of peace, the gates are closed—the structure is balanced and can hold, contain, and modulate drive activity; it is a buffer, a limit that prevents the flooding of the mental apparatus with excessive drive excitation. However, in times of war, the gates are opened, and the structures do not modulate or "tame" the drive energy but instead allow an enforced expression: aggression, as I have elaborated elsewhere (2002), is the intensification of the primal drives' energies, made possible by a reduction of the structures' inhibitory effects; and this is necessary when the drives' goals of satisfaction seem to be interfered with and endangered.

it, inasmuch as the libidinal side is representative of the sexual and life drives, while the lethic side represents the preservative and/or death drives.

Clinical Application

Returning to our initial question about the analyst's contribution to the transformation of structure, I suggest that transformation requires a shift in the head of Janus. The patient's neurosis, even his most disturbing symptom, stands for a relatively balanced state of his mind that he or she fights to maintain. Hence the analyst's contributions—his or her chosen interventions—aim at shifting this neurotic balance. Two short vignettes illustrate the application of the above-described ideas to the clinical moment.

Intervention on the lethic side:
First, a clinical example from Marilia Aisenstein (2000). A patient, Pierra, tells her:

"I dream that I fall asleep, I try to fight against an invasive and dangerous sleep, I drown and a black veil will cover my head, I am scared, I feel my brain captured as if in a net, it will grow numb forever. Is this my accident? Is this death? In the dream I fight to wake up; I wake up in reality.

I'm sweaty, my heart is racing, I turn on the light, I go to the toilet, then I drink some water—strangely enough this calms me down."

Here the analyst says: "Because you made sure that you are alive, physically and psychically."

Now Pierra says: "Ah, I have forgotten a piece of this dream: I succeeded in waking up, perhaps because an unknown man came into the room and gave me his hand, which was reassuring" (Aisenstein 2000, p. 1066).

When an interpretation is good, it will free and further the patient's associations (Green 2005). This is exactly what happens: the patient can remember a forgotten piece of her dream. Here is the way I understand this clinical vignette: the patient dreams her real, traumatic experience of a vascular accident that had previously ripped her out of sleep with a pain "beyond imagination" (Aisenstein 2000, p. 1066). Now in her dream she can imagine or *represent* her traumatic experience, being threatened by death. She fights for her life, fights to wake up. Since her self-preservation at this point is not represented as sufficiently secure, Pierra has to wake up in reality and drink water, and by doing so she feels strangely calmed.

Now the analyst says: "Because you made sure that you are alive, physically and psychically." The analyst hears the patient's survival threat, and with her intervention, she backs the fragile representation of her self-preservation by saying, "You are alive." That is one part: the representation of the patient's self as preserved and alive, as well as the confirmation of her perception of this.

Yet why does the analyst say something here and not simply keep quiet? I think the emergency of her dreaming patient, struggling to survive, elicited a necessary object-preservative response in the analyst's countertransference. In saying, "Because you made sure that you are alive," she is also saying: "I know and reassure you, too, that you are alive." It is the adult's presence when her child wakes up out of a night-mare that secures the child's (patient's) survival.

Now Pierra can associate to another part of her dream, an unknown man who gave her his hand; this was reassuring and helped her wake up. "An unknown man," Aisenstein muses—"the contrary of a known wom-an"—as is the analyst (ibid.). So one possibility is that the unknown man represents the object-preservative analyst—or, we might say, the other side of the Janus structure, the preservative parental couple that was completed between patient and analyst: the man-father in the patient's dream and the analyst-mother behind the couch.

However, Aisenstein also wonders about her patient's failure to feel erotically excited by men and asks herself whether she, the analyst, might feel jealous of Pierra because of the presence of this man in her dream. Thus the man in the dream might also represent the libidinal, erotic part of this emerging structure, the patient's implicit—still faint—wish for a man, her unconscious idea that the lethic rescuer could turn into a libidinal prince (another Janus). Ultimately, it seems to be the libidinal part that helps her become conscious of her dream: Pierra succeeds in waking up because this man offers her his hand (a proposal). The analyst's manifest intervention on the preservative side ignites a subtle libidinal part—here allowing for the emergent scheme of an erotic couple—thus establishing a more balanced structure in which the lethic strivings are attached to and balanced by libidinal ones.

Intervention on the libidinal side:

The following vignette from my analysis with a severely traumatized patient addresses the effects of an intervention on the libidinal side of the representations actualized in the moment. Sam, who for years has been withdrawn and often silent in his analysis, says:

"Before our session, I fell asleep. I had a dream. I dreamt I was diving in a swimming pool and someone was with me, I don't know who. Swimming was so interesting. I felt something was wrong, I felt as if I was getting sleepy—and I had to defend myself against getting sleepy, I woke up in time. This kind of getting sleepy is dangerous. When scuba diving, one can get into a certain state, a depth intoxication, and then you don't want to go up any more—it's a loss of reality. It's very similar to my depressive spirals downward....I became so sleepy—as if I wanted to disappear out of reality and just dive...."

I say: "There was something interesting..."

Sam says: "Yes. We were the two of us, and we were looking at something in this swimming pool. Before that, I actually wasn't underwater. I was with a group of people, those I train with for running—they got transformed into divers. I'm thinking right now: what I was interested in....I was interested in a woman—it's an interesting memory....There was some kind of flirting....[with emphasis] She was someone from this group!"

I say: "You want to make sure that I don't think it was me."

Sam (laughs a bit): "I wanted to make sure that it was nobody in particular...."

I chose this vignette because of its similarity to and difference from the previous one. Both patients are traumatized; both struggle to wake up from a dream that threatens to drown them, to pull them down toward death. At this point of his analysis, Sam is in a less immediately threatening situation; however, he, too, feels a dangerous pull toward depth intoxication (a familiar topic to both of us). He, too, struggles to preserve himself, and he finally wakes up. In telling me his dream, Sam again seems tempted to dive down and disappear from our session, despite knowing about these dangers.

At this point, I say: "There was something interesting"—picking up on this short libidinal spark in his dream report. With this intervention, I back the libidinal part of what is represented in this dream, indicating that I, too, am interested in what was so interesting. And in consequence of this intervention, there is a shift; he now can look at something together with me, which turns out to be the first part of this dream that had then been drowned or kept out of sight. Now he gets his feet on the ground; it is no longer about merely sleeping, but about the interesting something that becomes a woman, a memory, a flirtation—with his analyst. With this short intervention, "there was something interesting," I interpret his sexual interest. I am saying: "You are interested in something and I am interested in it, too"—meaning that I can deal with and represent the patient's sexual interest in me. I am saying, "Let's look at that," and, implicitly, I am also saying: "This is not something danger-ous, not an emergency, nothing to shy away from." Since we had worked through Sam's many anxieties and survival threats over a very long period of time (he knew the situation very well, even in his dream), my interpretation at this point is focused on his libidinal representations in order to promote a shift in the head of Janus toward sexuality and life.

Concluding Remarks

Both clinical examples show something of the complexity of our interven-tions and how they are received in the patient's mind. They might also help us understand how transformation occurs in the psychoanalytic process. Within this frame, we have (theoretically) four choices at any particular moment: we can focus more on the preservative or the sexual side of the patient's representations, each time with a greater emphasis on the patient's self or his objects. In most cases—or I should say, in all cas-es—we will make a combined intervention that is processed and organized within the patient's mind according to his needs and capacities, gradually elaborating and building up representations that will contribute to a more healthy balance within the structures of his or her mind.

References

Aisenstein, M. (2000). Élaboration, perlaboration, cicatrisation. *Revue Française de Psychanalyse,* 64(4):1065-1076.

Freud, S. (1895). A project for a scientific psychology. *Standard Edition,* 1.

Freud, S. (1900). *The Interpretation of Dreams. Standard Edition,* 4-5.

Freud, S. (1910). The psycho-analytic view of a psychogenic disturbance of vision. *Standard Edition,* 11.

Freud, S. (1911). Formulations on the two principles of mental functioning. *Standard Edition,* 12.

Freud, S. (1920). Beyond the pleasure principle. *Standard Edition,* 18.

Freud, S. (1937). Analysis terminable and interminable. *Standard Edition,* 23.

Green, A. (1993). *Le travail du négatif.* Paris: Éd. De Minuit.

Green, A. (2001). *Life Narcissism, Death Narcissism,* trans. A. Weller. London/New York: Free Association Books.

Green, A. (2005). Issues of interpretation; conjectures on construction. *EPF Bulletin,* 59:81-100.

Schmidt-Hellerau, C. (1997). Libido and lethe. Fundamentals of a formalised conception of metapsychology. *Int. J. Psychoanal.,* 78:683-697.

Schmidt-Hellerau, C. (2001). *Life Drive and Death Drive, Libido and Lethe: A Formalized Consistent Model of Psychoanalytic Drive and Structure Theory.* New York: Other Press.

Schmidt-Hellerau, C. (2002). Why aggression? *Int. J. Psychoanal.,* 83:1269-1289.

Schmidt-Hellerau, C. (2005). We are driven. *Psychoanal. Q.,* 74:989-1028.

Musings

CHAPTER 15

Professional ethos and personal integrity

The history of German psychoanalysis in the Third Reich[*]

In 1977, for the first time since the war, the German Psychoanalytic
Association (GPA) invited the International Psychoanalytic Association (IPA) to hold its congress in Berlin. The IPA's rejection of the
GPA's offer (many Jewish colleagues threatened to boycott a congress in
Berlin) made German psychoanalysts painfully aware that they had not
yet thoroughly worked through their history. Since then, they have made
great strides in coming to terms with the behavior of their predecessors
in the Third Reich. They have shed light on portions of their institutional unconscious that had previously been closed off. The subject of this
essay is the professional ethos and personal integrity of analysts during
the Third Reich, and it will pose and respond to three fundamental
questions. First, how could the analysts in Germany so misjudge the
political situation in Germany that they were unable to subject the
National Socialist movement to psychoanalytic reflection? Second, how
did it happen that the German analysts as a group became so corrupted
by fascist ideology that they placed their work at the service of the

---

[*] Über Berufsethos und persönliche Integrität—Zur Geschichte der deutschen Psychoanalyse
im Dritten Reich. (1990) Zeitschrift für psychoanalytische Theorie und Praxis, 5(3):262-272.
Translated into English by Kenneth Kronenberg.
Revised version of a presentation at an exhibit on the history of psychoanalysis in
Germany, given at the University of Zürich on April 19, 1989. This paper is dedicated to
Prof. Dr. Fritz Meerwein († 1989).

Göring Institute, which was founded by Heinrich Göring, a cousin of Hermann Göring? And finally, why did no one from the Göring Institute at the end of the war question his suitability as a founder of the new GPS and later the GPA?

Let us begin with a brief history of organized psychoanalysis in Germany. In 1908 Karl Abraham founded a psychoanalytic working group in Berlin, which in 1910 was officially accepted by the International Psychoanalytic Association (IPA) as the Berlin Psychoanalytic Association (BPA). In 1926 the BPA became the German Psychoanalytic Society (GPS). From 1933 until 1938 the GPS participated as Working Group A in the Göring Institute before dissolving. In 1945 Carl Müller-Braunschweig refounded the former GPS as the Berlin Psychoanalytic Society, which in 1950 received permission from the Allies to reuse the old name, the German Psychoanalytic Society. Clashes within the new GPS between Harald Schultz-Henke's neo-analysis and Carl Müller-Braunschweig's Freudian analysis led to a split; in 1950, under the guidance of Müller-Braunschweig, a group of analysts formed the German Psychoanalytic Association (GPA), which one year later, in 1951, was accepted as the German member society of the IPA.

During the immediate postwar period in Germany, the behavior of German analysts did not differ from that of other Germans, regardless of profession. The country was caught up in the hustle and bustle of reconstruction, and people needed to make a living. Even before Germany's official capitulation, representatives from the Göring Institute had been in touch with government officials for permission to form a successor institute. And after the reestablishment of the GPS in 1950 and the founding of the GPA in 1951, the analysts in the two rival organizations threw themselves into the effort to regain their standing in relation to institutes abroad and particularly in their competition with each other. Not a moment to spare for looking back, for reflection. No work of mourning.

In *The Inability to Mourn: Principles of Collective Behavior*, first published in 1967 (English translation 1975), Alexander and Margarete Mitscherlich produced what is perhaps the most careful analysis of this postwar tendency. The Mitscherlichs proceeded from the observation that despite the rapid reconstruction, despite West Germany's "Economic Miracle," the political and social culture of the country was marked by what they viewed as an astonishing lack of creativity and blocked by rigidity and provincialism. The Mitscherlichs concluded that this intellectual and affective blockage indicated a resistance to dealing with the events that had taken place during the Third Reich. It was, they held, a defense against overwhelming feelings of guilt, shame, grief, and fear. According to the authors, the Germans had collectively retreated from their historical responsibility, denied the reality of their own past (a complete withdrawal of emotional cathexis), because everything that had given their lives value and guided their actions had depended either directly or indirectly on the Führer, their personified new ego ideal. The unmasking of this Führer as a fanatic madman guilty of crimes against humanity, in other words, the loss of this collectively internalized narcissistic ideal object, led to a profound sense of devaluation, a narcissistic depletion that ought to have plunged Germany into a general state of depression. Instead, the Mitscherlichs observed a manic undoing manifested in this counterphobic restless effort to rebuild. And while the compulsive busyness served as a defense against collective melancholy, Germans were unable to fend off the ensuing ego-impoverishment, resulting in their inability to find progressive and creative solutions to social problems.

Just how this could have come to pass, the Mitscherlichs explored in a social-psychoanalytical study of the economic and political situation in Germany before 1933. In their analysis, the economic depression that took hold after World War I brought about real frustrations and long-term disappointments about the social order. These, in turn, led to feelings of powerlessness and worthlessness that made the Germans especially susceptible to a charismatic leader whose grandiose claims promised to give them back their sense of self-esteem.[1]

---

[1] Addition in 2017 from my perspective of self-preservation as a primitive drive activity: The Nazis murdered more than 6 million Jews. Afterwards, people asked how this could have happened. What had become of the Christian ideal of brotherly love? Were previously apparently well-intentioned citizens simply given permission to act on their long-

This did not apply to German psychoanalysis, or at least not to the same extent. After all, it had been well institutionalized before the rise of the Nazis, and spirits were high: two teaching facilities had been established, one in Berlin and the other in Frankfurt. Pioneering work was being done; the institutes were developing well, and although their financial situation was not especially rosy, they were fully engaged and successfully run. In other words, the frustration overrunning Germany and blunting people's critical faculties was not felt within the psychoanalytic movement. So why were German psychoanalysts unable to respond to National Socialism with a psychosocial analysis that might have helped them better diagnose its danger and perhaps kept them from making a pact with the fascists?

This seems especially mysterious because as early as 1921 in his essay "Mass Psychology and Ego Analysis," Freud had provided a model for psychoanalyzing mass movements. In it he had shown that a key feature

---

suppressed aggressive urges? That argument was never convincing, and we now know better: a propaganda mix of nationalism, racism, and anti-Semitism stoked paranoid survival fears, anxieties about whether Germans would even be able to feed themselves. "The foreigners are cheating us and hollowing out our economy," "The world Jewish conspiracy is bent on enriching Jews and driving us to the wall," "The Jews steal our money, and that is why the Jewish race is a threat to our survival. They not only threaten us economically; their bacteria-like infiltration of German society subverts our values, imperils the health of the German *Volk* (the People), and as a result of miscegenation defiles our racial purity with their alien blood." According to this thinking, friendly Jewish neighbors were in fact treacherous exploiters and parasites fit only to be exterminated like rats and insects. All of this is well-known. My point here is that the murderous persecution carried out by the Nazis on a grand scale may be understood as the violent expression of incited paranoid fears about the survival of the *Volk* in which delusional threats to self-preservation eventuated in an insane frenzy of murder. To preserve oneself (in this instance, the oneself includes one's own family, race, and nation in the sense of object preservation), the Other, defined as threatening and harmful, must be eliminated. In the United States we are currently getting just such rhetoric from Donald Trump, whose claims come to this: foreign countries are taking advantage of our generosity and cheating us economically. "Illegal aliens" take our jobs; Mexicans rape our women and smuggle drugs; hundreds of thousands of immigrants invade our country, where they live like maggots on bacon; Islam is un-American and sends terrorists out to murder us.... These slogans are effective and will remain so because they hook into primary fears for survival that can be manipulated and radicalized.

of the libidinal constitution of a mass is that its members have all substituted one and the same leader for their own personal ego ideal; as a consequence they identify with each other through this commonality. It is as if they are saying, "We are all the same before Him." In such a situation, the individual's boundaries dissolve, and the de-differentiated self merges into the mass with an attendant loss of self-awareness, independence, and sense of identity. This process increases a person's dependency on the personality of the leader. For his part, the charismatic leader, secure in his function as ego ideal of the masses—and by extension of each individual—responds, "You are the Chosen Ones."

But what exactly is the ego ideal as Freud conceptualized it, and how does it develop? Over the regular course of psychic development, a child goes through a normal narcissistic phase, during which her/his original sense of perfection includes first the mother and then the father. When the child finally realizes that s/he is not perfect, s/he continues to idealize her/his father for a time. As the child develops s/he builds stable relationships with her/his parents, which makes it possible to view the father more critically. Over time, the idealized father will slowly be transformed into a normal person with strengths and weaknesses that the child has come to understand from her- or his own imperfections. This necessary de-idealization of the father was preceded by another, rather hidden process, namely the de-personification of the psychic representation of this external ideal object. Freud called this psychic representation (actually an amalgam of self and object, invested with homoerotic libido) the ego ideal. As a result of the de-personification of this ego ideal, the values transmitted by the parental generation are preserved in idealized form, independent of the persons who may once have embodied them albeit imperfectly. The capacity for identifying with human imperfection while nonetheless striving for perfection by attempting to implement these values is felt as a tension between the ego and the ego ideal. And this tension can stimulate a creative potential, motivating many of our actions.

Freud did not distinguish clearly between the ego ideal and the superego. Sometimes he used both terms synonymously; sometimes he referred to aspects of one or the other. Most authors after Freud do distinguish, although often based on different reasoning (see. e.g., Chasseguet-Smirgelm, 1981, Chapter 7). But we can say that under *the umbrella structure of the superego* two parts may be distinguished by their function. If we understand the *ego ideal*, the residue of our narcissistic idealization, to be the bearer of our values, and the *conscience*, which arose out of the renunciation of the Oedipus complex, to represent what is forbidden, the *ego ideal* exerts a primarily *orienting function*, while the *conscience* exerts a *limiting function*. In other words, the *ego ideal* contains the commandments (*Gebote*) and the *conscience* the prohibitions (*Verbote*). Within the superego both the ego ideal and the conscience are engaged in a mutually reinforcing interaction by which compromises are continually worked out, and against which the ego is judged (often negatively). This in the end is how personality is shaped.

This theoretical parsing of the difference between the orienting function of the ego ideal and the limiting function of the conscience helps us to reflect on the foundations of the professional ethos of psychoanalysts and psychoanalytical associations. What is the professional ego ideal of psychoanalysts? What values do psychoanalysts uphold in their work? And what is the basis for the *guidelines* contained in the IPA's statement of mission? The answer is simple: the analyst bases his/her work on psychoanalytic theory, a theory that is constantly refined by the analyst's practice. This theory is contained in the psychoanalytic literature, at the time in the works of Sigmund Freud and his followers. And these works were publicly burned in Berlin on May 10, 1933. Banned were the works of Bernfeld, Böhm, Bonaparte, Brunswick, Deutsch, Anna Freud, Sigmund Freud, Ferenczi, Fromm, Groddeck, Klein, Pfister, Reik, and Zulliger, to name the most well-known authors. Freud's works were tossed into the flames with the words, "Against soul-shredding overemphasis on sexual instincts; for the nobility of the human soul." As Freud commented, "What progress we are making. In the Middle Ages they would have burned me. Now they are content with burning my books." (Freud in Jones 1957, Vol. III, p. 182)

This "progress" meant that as of May 1933 the psychoanalytic literature as a whole was on the Nazi Index; it disappeared from libraries and could be neither purchased nor owned. To the extent that the professional ideal of psychoanalysts, their orientation, is anchored in the works of psychoanalysis, it is clear that the immolation of the psychoanalytic literature meant the destruction of the psychoanalytic ego ideal. Let us be clear, however: I am not idealizing these works. Rather, what is at issue is the necessary orienting function that binds all psychoanalysts to their literature, and that is what the Nazis destroyed in May 1933. And while it is true that analysts still found ways to read what they needed, they did so clandestinely and at their own risk. And most crucially, any open discussion of psychoanalysis disappeared.

The next blow was directed at basic psychoanalytic terminology and concepts. To cite just two instances of many: people were no longer permitted to reference "psychoanalysis," only "mental healing" (*Seelenheilkunde*); and the Oedipus complex, the cornerstone of Freud's understanding of neurosis, was simply obliterated with no attempt made at replacement. It is not hard to imagine the collapse of the analyst's identity and professional competency associated with this destruction of language.

And furthermore, the Jews were subjected to contempt, persecution, and mass annihilation. Yet psychoanalysis is and remains the creation of Sigmund Freud, who was Jewish, and most of the best psychoanalysts and representatives of the psychoanalytic associations were Jewish as well. And these Jews were vilified by the Nazis, debased, and some of them were murdered. Thus psychoanalysts couldn't even reach back (*regress* in the sense of *reculer pour mieux sauter*) from adhering to psychoanalysis as a discipline (a de-personified ego-ideal) to the affectionate bond with their analytic father Freud (at the time most analysts had met him in person). They started to dissociate themselves from Freud and fell prey to the claim or belief that they could remain loyal to Freud's work even as they renounced its creator. For example, Felix Böhm and Carl Müller-Braunschweig tried to explain to the Sturmabteilung (SA), the paramilitary wing of the Nazi party, that although the psychoanalytic method had been developed by the Jew Freud, in Germany it was applied in "Aryanized" form, and they emphasized that in England only one single Jew was a member of the British Psychoanalytic Society (Brecht et al. 1985). However, with this dreadful

427

haggling for the continuation of their work permit, Böhm and Müller-Braunschweig betrayed not only Freud, their teacher and friend, but also their best colleagues, including Karl Abraham, with whom they had been in analysis. But even most importantly, they renounced the humanitarian character and ethos of psychoanalysis itself.

After the end of the war Freud had sporadically been accused of not having protested clearly enough against the attacks on psychoanalysis by the National Socialists. According to his accusers, he had tolerated too many of the harmful compromises sanctioned by the Berliners in order to salvage psychoanalysis in Germany (Lohmann & Rosenkotter, 1983, p. 1112). But the Mitscherlichs' interpretation allows us to better understand this German self-exoneration, which attempted to transform the betrayed father figure into the guilty party:

The foundering paternal authority ends by becoming the culprit after all. Now it is he who is the object of projections: all the crimes committed were committed for him and in his name. Once more the question of one's attitude to the father, to authority figures in general, has been sidestepped. What happens is that now feelings are mobilized by disappointment in the "leader" and in the evanescence of his omnipotence. (Mitscherlich & Mitscherlich, 1975, p. 49)

Furthermore, in his account, Böhm wrote that as early as 1933 Freud had become convinced that even Aryanization of the GPS board would not keep the Nazis from banning psychoanalysis. In 1937, on the occasion of a three-hour lament that Böhm delivered in Vienna on the precarious situation of analysts in Germany, according to Ernest Jones, Freud interrupted him testily: "'Quite enough! The Jews have suffered for their convictions for centuries. Now the time has come for our Christian colleagues to suffer in their turn for theirs. I attach no importance to my name being mentioned in Germany so long as my work is presented correctly there.' So saying he left the room." (Jones, 1957, p. 187)

Freud made clear that the issue was conviction, in this instance regarding the analytic ego ideal. He wanted his colleagues in Berlin to stand up for psychoanalysis. Freud was not concerned with his name or personal vanity or narcissistic injuries; what mattered to him was his work. And Freud also made clear that he was prepared to go along with events in Berlin only as long as psychoanalysis was presented *correctly*, as long as psychoanalysis was practiced in accordance with *his work*. Freud undoubtedly overestimated the maturity of his Berlin colleagues in expecting that they, too, were capable of holding on to a de-personified analytical ideal (that is, independent of Sigmund Freud), a professional ideal in the sense of a guiding principle, as it was presented and grounded in the psychoanalytic literature.

The analytic ego ideal, the professional ethos of the psychoanalyst, was severely damaged by the burning of the psychoanalytic literature in May 1933, by the Nazification of psychoanalytic terminology, and by the contempt for and persecution of everything Jewish. Any reference or regression to the father figure Freud was impossible because he was a Jew, and any possibility of group cohesion that might have saved the fledgling traditions of the psychoanalytic society was lost with the emigration of Jewish analysts. This raises the question of how German psychoanalysts dealt with this attack on their collective professional ego ideal.

The first recourse of Jewish psychoanalysts was emigration. But emigration should be understood as more than flight and the rescue of one's own life. It is also protestation. This is clear from the example of the non-Jewish analyst Bernhard Kamm. In 1935 the GPS recommended that its remaining Jewish members resign; Kamm's response was to renounce his membership in the society and emigrate to the United States. His reasoning is exemplary: where patients' paranoid fears of persecution and betrayal are exceeded by the real paranoia generated by the political system, the intellectual space needed for the analysis of unconscious fantasies is no longer available. Under these political conditions Kamm felt unable to function as a psychoanalyst in Germany, and so he left the country.

Edith Jacobson and John F. Rittmeister found other ways: they put their lives on the line in the political underground movements fighting the enemies of psychoanalysis. Both spent time in prison. And while Jacobson eventually fled to the United States in 1938, Rittmeister was executed in Germany in 1943. Both of them defended the intellectual freedom that is the minimum precondition for psychoanalytic work; by so doing they held on to the foundations of their professional ethos, their analytic ideal. Of course, their involvement in the German resistance movement was not aimed solely at preserving psychoanalysis; their goal was to fight the terror unleashed by the fascists. But because their resistance was also resistance to the destruction of psychoanalysis in Germany, the accusation by the GPS that Jacobson had done the association and the status of psychoanalysis great harm is nothing short of a betrayal.

Neither Müller-Braunschweig nor Böhm drew any such conclusions. Instead, they responded by adapting themselves and the GPS to the new rulers, modifying the intellectual traditions of psychoanalysis along the lines of National Socialist concepts of therapy. They supposedly did this with the good intention of allowing psychoanalysis to continue in Germany. Thus, in 1933 Müller-Braunschweig wrote an essay titled "Psychoanalysis and World View," in which he stated that, "Psychoanalysis attempts to transform incapable weaklings into competent human beings...those who are uninterested in life as a whole into servants of the whole. In so doing it provides an outstanding work of education and renders valuable service to the recently published [guide]lines for a heroic conception of life that is constructive and based in reality." (C. Müller-Braunschweig, 1933 [1983], p. 1139)

Müller-Braunschweig, who wanted to "make psychoanalysis palatable to the new rulers," later came to regret these statements. In any event, his hopes soon proved naïve, because in 1938 the Nazis revoked his right to teach anyway. He reacted, "with depression that fluctuated in intensity, and relented only with the end of the war seven years later" (ibid., p. 1143). Müller-Braunschweig was strongly criticized for these statements. However, in another section of the same essay, he shows how oppressive these compromises must have been for him when he rejected the Nazi's accusation of the deranged and merely materialistic nature of psychoanalysis by reference to "the ideal claims and evaluations of the superego," noting that "the ego and the super ego are constantly subjected to corruptions, seductions, and falsifications by the id, which cause the ego to make bad compromises, and what seems to sail under the flag of the ideal turns out to be much less than ideal." (ibid., p. 1183)

It seems that Müller-Braunschweig understood that considerably less ideal values had taken the place of the analytic ideal. Thorough psycho-analytic thinking had been compromised (or at least severely distorted) by the Nazi ideology: Hitler's *Mein Kampf* became the "scientific foun-dation" at the Göring Institute. Böhm's assessment that homosexuality should be seen as a symptom of inferior genetics and treated like any other crime (Brecht et al. 1985, pp. 155-157) shows just how far Böhm had distanced himself from the psychoanalytic ethos.

Let us consider at this point that a professional association is to some extent the physical representation of an idea put into social practice; its existence is justified solely by how it performs this task. If a professional association stops representing this idea it forfeits its reason for being. Furthermore, the quality of a professional association is dependent on the professional ethos of its members, their collective orientation toward scientific values, and on their expertise. Of course these values will develop over time and be subjected to vigorous dispute. However, disputes over theoretical differences are not the same as capitulation to an ideology. If we examine what happened within the GPS during the Nazi era, we must conclude that even if individual psychoanalysts at the Berlin institute made efforts, at least privately, to remain true to Freud and his theory, psychoanalysis as an institution in Germany was guilty of "self-alignment" (*Selbstgleichschaltung*). By capitulating to the goals of the National Socialists, it had lost what was essential to its theory long before the official dissolution of the GPS on November 19, 1938. At the 34th congress of the IPA in 1985, Klaus von Dohnanyi described the process accurately in his opening remarks, "In danger of losing the whole, they sacrificed piece by piece. Each step rational but simultane-ously leading in the wrong direction. Here a compromise with individuals, there one of substance, always done in the presumed inter-est of preserving the whole—which in the end had ceased to exist." (v. Dohnanyi, 1986, pp. 861-862)

There were three possible responses to the loss of a common, publicly acknowledged psychoanalytic frame of reference: emigration, resistance, and adaptation. Müller-Braunschweig and Böhm (as representatives of the GPS) chose the latter. By doing so they agreed to the abolition of their analytic ideal and to the take-over by the Nazis. This is the vantage point from which the three questions posed at the outset may be answered. Now devoid of their psychoanalytic frame of reference, the German analysts were incapable of interpreting correctly the implications of the political situation in 1933 in terms of Freud's understanding of mass psychology; nor were they in a position to resist the corruptive effects of fascist ideology. Finally, we may wonder what happened to the personal integrity of the German psychoanalysts at the Göring Institute.

In psychoanalytic terms, integrity may be defined as the maximum congruence of the ego with the superego (its conscience and ego ideal). As previously discussed, the ego ideal provides the goals toward which persons orient themselves, the conscience provides the limits to be observed. Naturally, a change in the ego ideal affects the functioning of the superego. For example, if the ego ideal personified by the Führer Adolf Hitler views the mass murder of the Jews as a positive value, as a service to humanity, the conscience (Thou shalt not kill!) will be stymied; hence the whole superego will function in a compromised, perverted way in the perpetrators, or at the very least neutralized (oblivious) in the Nazi followers. Whereas the conscience had previously banned murder absolutely and still banned the murder of Aryans, the murder of Jews became a commandment of the ego ideal. In this situation, if the ego enacts, knows about or witnesses the murder of Jews it is not in conflict with its conscience but congruent with the ego ideal, thus altogether with the superego; in other words, as horrible as it sounds, the murderer retains his integrity in his own mind. This explains the extraordinary lack of insight exhibited in court by Nazi war criminals, their profession of innocence, and the lack of any sense of guilt. Bela Grunberger provided a striking example: "As Eichmann listened to the enumeration of the horrific crimes of which he was accused, he never batted an eyelash.... But when the presiding judge ordered him to stand as the sentence was read, he apologized repeatedly, stuttering, his face red with shame." The mere thought of having transgressed court formalities troubled him more than the murders of which he stood accused.

Back to psychoanalysis at the end of the war. Those analysts who remained in Germany in 1938 and had aligned themselves with Nazi ideology, had continued working with the Nazi-approved psychothera-peutic groups at the Göring Institute more or less free of conflict and anxiety. Thus, they claimed, they had held a place for psychoanalysis, if only as Working Group A. After the defeat of Nazism, this latter claim enabled them to resume their psychoanalytic careers. One way or the other, the analysts were able to convince themselves that at no time had they lost personal integrity. Different attitudes toward psychoanalysis manifested at the end of the war, evidenced by the approaches taken by the two groups, the GPS and the new GPA. As early as 1927, Harald Schultz-Hencke began publicizing his neo-analysis in the GPS, a theory and clinical practice that differed from Freudian psychoanalysis in many respects, and he tried to convince the IPA to approve his neo-analysis at the new Berlin Psychoanalytic Institute (BPI). Thus Schultz-Hencke remained true to this ideal after the war; the fact that he collaborated with National Socialism, however, was swept under the rug. Böhm, who by the end had gone quite far in collaborating with the Nazis and, as he stated for the record in 1945, had always felt disadvantaged by the preponderance of Jews in the old BPI, proposed the idea of an "amalga-mated" training based on a variety of therapeutic approaches, basically "something of everything for everyone."

Burnt by his experiences at the Göring Institute, Müller-Braunschweig found this "something of everything" approach highly suspect. Conse-quently, he fought for a "purified" concept of psychoanalytic training in Berlin; now at last, an unadulterated psychoanalysis should once again be possible. His championing of an unambiguously Freudian psychoanalysis after the war may be seen as his attempt to distinguish clearly between analysis and ideology. At the same time, this return to Freud, this public profession of loyalty to him and his teachings, may also have been borne by his wish for reparation. Viewed in this light, we may assume that he experienced a sense of the loss of personal and professional integrity, which may have motivated him to now stand up for Freudian psychoanal-ysis as the basis of the new GPA.

Thus psychoanalysis as developed by Freud and his followers was reestablished after the war as a valid frame of reference in all therapeutic and institutional matters; it rehabilitated the analytic ego ideal of the

German analysts, supervised by the watchful eye of the IPA Of course, psychoanalysis has continued to develop since the early 1950s. Training analyses have become considerably longer, memberships have increased considerably, and the psychoanalytic literature has grown immeasurably. However, the three pillars of psychoanalysis—training analysis, theoretical seminars (including clinical and technical seminars based on Freud's teachings), and supervision—have remained basically the same since Max Eitigon, Müller-Braunschweig, and later Sándor Radó set them forth as systematic guidelines for the training of psychoanalysts at the BPI in 1923. From the perspective employed here, these three pillars allow for an organic development of the *analytic ego ideal*: this occurs first by way of a personification in the individual training analyst; second by a de-personification of this new ideal toward a focus on the analytic stance and function; third, through theoretical studies based on the psychoanalytic literature of Freud and his followers; fourth, by means of the encounter with school- and personality-specific variants of the analytic stance under a variety of supervisors; and fifth, as a result of work and discussion in local, national, and international associations, which represent the public face of this analytic ideal.

Psychoanalytic training has been criticized by both insiders and outsiders, and there is indeed much to criticize. In its practical implementation it can never be ideal, but it is what it is, namely, constitutive of the analytic ego ideal. And, as the history of German psychoanalysis under National Socialism demonstrates, the importance of that ego ideal should not be underestimated for maintaining the professional integrity of analysts and their resistance to ideological influences.

Postscript: In 1985 Germany hosted for the first time since the war the congress of the IPA in Hamburg, on "Identification and its Vicissitudes"; Berlin played host in 2007, on the topic of "Remembering, Repeating and Working Through." And after long and thorough deliberations the IPA accepted the GPS as a member of its organization in 2009.

References

Brecht, K. et al. (1985): "Hier geht das Leben auf eine sehr merkwürdige Weise weiter..." Zur Geschichte der Psychoanalyse in Deutschland. Katalog und Materialsammlung zur Ausstellung. Hamburg: Kellner.

Chasseguet-Smirgel, J. (1981): Das Ichideal. Psychoanalytischer Essay über die "Krankheit der Idealität". Frankfurt: Suhrkamp.

Dohnanyi, K. v. (1986): Eröffnungsrede zum 34. Kongress der Internationalen Psychoanalytischen Vereinigung am 28. Juli 1985. Psyche, 40, 860-863.

Freud, S. (1921): Group Psychology and The Analysis of the Ego. SE 18.

Grunberger, B. (1988). Narziss und Anubis. Die Psychoanalyse jenseits der Triebtheorie. Bd. 1, München, Wien: Verlag Internationale Psychoanalyse.

Jones, E. (1957): The Life and Work of Sigmund Freud. Vol. 3, The last phase. New York: Basic Books, Inc.

Lohmann, H.-M. & Rosenkötter, L. (1982): Psychoanalyse in Hitlerdeutschland. Wie war es wirklich? Psyche, 36, 961-988.

Lohmann, H.-M. & Rosenkötter, L. (1983): Psychoanalyse in Hitlerdeutschland. Wie war es wirklich? Ein Nachtrag. Psyche, 37, 1107-1115.

Mitscherlich, A. & Mitscherlich M. (1975). The Inability to Mourn. Principles of Collective Behavior. Translation by Beverley R. Placzek. New York: Grove Press.

Müller-Braunschweig, C. (1933). Psychoanalyse und Weltanschauung. Psyche, 1983, 37, 1136-1139.

Müller-Braunschweig, H. (1983). Fünfzig Jahre danach. Stellungnahme zu den in PSYCHE 11-1982 zitierten Äusserungen von Carl Müller-Braunschweig. Psyche, 37, 1140-1145.

CHAPTER 16

Images and Words—Fantasy and Reality[*]

Scene I. Some time ago, I saw an exhibition titled "The World as Myth." It contained drawings by Otto Dix and Max Beckmann depicting soldiers fallen in World War I. Looking at them, what struck me most was that each of these drawings was telling me more about the horror, pain, and despair—the war's human catastrophe—than any photograph from the battlefields I'd seen. These drawings depicted not just the wounded and dead, torn and sprawled within the rubble as they might be exposed to the photographer's lenses—shocking for sure, yet still dead bodies, merely the remaining outer shells from which the agony sustained in life had gone for good. No, the dead bodies drawn from these artists' creative imaginations displayed forever the acute horror these men were filled with at the end of their lives—the ineffaceable atrocities of war, any war, and what it does to the human heart and mind. The world as myth—the myth of war—myth or reality?

Scene II. The other day, my patient Andrea remembered, she had been sitting on a bench in the sun reading a book for school. A guy came along and offered her a free lunch in a nearby restaurant. He said the restaurant had just opened and this was being billed as a promotion day.

[*] A version of this paper was presented on September 4th 2014 at the FEPAL Meeting on *Fiction and Reality* in Buenos Aires.

437

Okay, she said and went with him. Andrea sat down at a window table. The chef came and invited her into the kitchen to let her choose from among different dishes. Andrea said the kitchen looked messy and smelled odd, but in order not to offend him she took a small piece of quiche and brought it back to her table. She didn't much like the quiche but indicated that it tasted fine. You don't have to pay, the guy reassured her. Andrea left. When she got home, she realized that her wallet was gone. She was sure that the guy who invited her had taken it from her purse when she was in the kitchen. While Andrea was talking, I noticed that I saw the scene she described before my inner eyes, and it was playing in a particular part of Zürich that I know. I saw the kind of guy who would do this and the kind of restaurant that would lure in the unsuspecting. But my patient had never been to Zürich, and I've never been to the place in the United States where she lived at the time this happened. So I had an image in mind very different from hers. Still, I think I got her right. The reality of her memory was not bound to the surface location; the reality was her experience of being lured in and robbed, and it found in me the image of a place that fit her story.

Scene III. Lukas the kid kicks a ball around the corner where no other kids hang out and he can be alone with thoughts of his own. His mother, leaning forward over the balcony, may just fly out to spy on him while he's having his private dreams. His father goes to work every day. Take me with you—I could work in the factory! Lukas strolls through the park, a small patch of mossy lawn fenced in by a tight hedge. He's feeling weird lately, his bones aching, his stomach knotted, his skin itchy. Little Sue is playing in the sandbox. An old man is sitting on the only bench nearby, reading a newspaper. He must be Sue's grandfather, dispatched to keep an eye on the little girl. Lukas decides to sit down on the grass. He stretches his legs. His mother crouches on a branch of the chestnut tree, her eyes glued to him. A passing train howls. Three o'clock and nowhere to go. One day I will have my own family—I will do stuff with them on weekends and on other days as well. First, I'll travel around the world, go West, always West, by car, boat, and plane. Maybe I'll never return. — His father has rolled up his shirt sleeves; he's checking the speed of the wallpaper print machine: too fast and the paper would rip; too slow and the print would turn mushy. He is into Asian design lately. How did that come up..? A noise in the bushes, a rustle, some giggles, then three guys standing around Lukas, looking down on him. Hey, weirdo, one says, preying on little girls? They laugh. One kicks Lukas's leg. I'm just sitting here, Lukas says. Just sitting, hee, one of the guys apes him, slapping his hand over Lukas's head. Another punches his knee in Lukas's back. One spits on him... and then in a split second Lukas is up on his feet, striking one in the face with his fist, kicking another in the groin, and knocking the third off his feet. All scream and jumble together, swearing and thrashing about. Lukas is flailing his arms like clubs, hitting hard and fast, faster than ever, mowing down his attackers one after the other. So it goes! Ha! He did it! All right! There we go! He's exhausted. He's hurting. He doesn't care. His head upraised, Lukas leaves the park. It's five o'clock in the afternoon.

Reality and fantasy need images to be captured and words to be communicated. This seemingly mundane relationship reveals its mysterious underbelly once we consider the endless flexibility, variability, and contingency of the images and words employed and combined. Psychoanalysis is a talking cure. The patient tries to articulate what he wrestles with. As he's lying on the couch, not seeing his analyst, he may immerse himself into the images of a memory train, thereby drifting into a fantasy; and the analyst, as she is listening, will see within her mind emerging images that lead her into the area where her patient is moving. By the end of the hour, they have shared a scene, a story that may not have been there before but thenceforth is part of their known world/the world they know.

Much of what we create may be to some extent imagination (scene I), even if memory seems to prevail (scene II), and some of it may get funneled into fiction (scene III). Yet once enunciated—regardless of the degree to which fantasy prevails—it is part of reality, a tale to tell like any other. That's the mystery: how we create new realities, the precursors of which have been there all along.

* * *

439

In his paper on *The Unconscious* (1915a), Freud explains that unacceptable thoughts and fantasies are repressed by being broken off. One part, the image (thing-presentation), becomes unconscious, while the other, the word (word-presentation), remains conscious. What happens next is confusing. We talk but don't really know what we refer to, and we imagine things that only our unconscious sees, things that aren't out there—all of which is what transference is about. It's only when the words and images are correctly reconnected that the once-repressed content becomes conscious again.

However, in the meantime, changes occur. In the unconscious, the repressed images "branch out in every direction into the intricate network of our world of thought" (Freud 1900, p. 525). Fantasies are in the making. Everything is worked over by the same mechanisms that churn and knead the ingredients of the dream—namely, displacement, condensation, and symbolization (representability). In this process, the repressed image—basically a drive's representation (the idea that represents the drive's aims)—moves and changes:

> It proliferates in the dark, as it were, and takes on extreme forms of expression, which when they are translated and presented to the neurotic are not only bound to seem alien to him, but frighten him by giving him the picture of an extraordinary and dangerous strength of the drive. [Freud 1915b, p. 149]

The alien appearance of our inner world comes about because the unconscious images attach themselves to whatever suits our drives' aims and is readily available in their surroundings; these images clump together with other groups, split off from them, and then associate again with anything remotely fitting. *Proliferation is displacement at work.* Thus, always moving and changing, these unconscious things can form extraordinary pictures—frightening monsters, bizarre objects. It is in this process "at some point where this meshwork is particularly close that the dream-wish grows up, like a mushroom out of its mycelium" (Freud 1900, p. 525).

The meshwork gets particularly close when *condensation* takes place, when all is crammed into a single image, a dense combination of elemental things, overdetermined metaphors. So we can see that primary process leads unconscious material into *expansion via displacement* and *contraction via condensation*—forming a conception of an unconscious as if breathing, in and out, the pulse of a living psyche. And so our unconscious fantasies are continuously in flux—yet perhaps they change more in their momentary appearance than in their essence. But what is their essence?

Let me illustrate with an example. My supervisee's patient attended an art course in which the task was to produce a self-portrait. What he painted, as he described it, was a soft-boiled egg, split in half and placed next to a knife. This image spontaneously came to him, baffling but somehow right. It could have come to him as a slip betraying his unconscious, or not unlike the way that a pictogram may jump into the analyst's mind. I find this image interesting: at the time, the patient is working on aspects of a negative Oedipus; so I'm thinking, his female self, the soft-boiled egg, stands in contrast to his male self, the knife; and the knife has cut open the egg, indicating castration, while simultaneously the egg is open to being penetrated by the knife. More associations are possible, each one elaborating or building on aspects of his anxious and wishful fantasy. However, in its immediacy, his surprising self-portrait seems to be a direct derivative of an unconscious fantasy. I suggest that his picture captures an early oedipal fantasy of who he wanted to be and how he wished and feared castration as a precondition for his father's love.

Images like this one symbolize unconscious fantasies in condensation and displacement: they have been displaced—progressed, really—away from the crude presentation (in the latter example of the concrete sexual organs, which would have been frightening) and condensed to their symbolic equivalents (egg and knife—as such, less scary). Such images, which come with a bit of a surprise and a tinge of oddity, carry the essence of an unconscious fantasy in a dense, dynamic package that may stir a dream, be elaborated in a fantasy-building process (Scarfone 2016), or be further unfurled in a piece of fiction. The clinically known persistence with which our patients produce a multitude of *variations of one and the same specific fantasy*, over and over, proves that the essence, the core of the unconscious fantasy, is consistently there. And it is personal, not interpersonal. What may be co-created in the *après-coup* between analyst and patient are the momentary and situational variations, the way these then-*conscious fantasies* are dressed up—not their essence, their unconscious meaning.

When Kazuo Ishiguro, winner of the 2017 Nobel Prize in Literature, published *The Remains of the Day,* he worried that he was just repeating himself, that people comparing it with his previous novels would say: "Oh, it's the same book again." Instead, "critiques saw the book as an extreme departure" (Alter and Bilefsky 2017). Ishiguro's worry may have betrayed a deeper insight than his readers could have guessed. If the writer's capacity to invent stories has anything to do with how unconscious fantasies work on his mind, then the core of his creativity may well be circumscribed ("the same again"), while the output could still be endlessly variable. Perhaps the elements of our unconscious fantasies are comparable to the limited number of colored glass pieces in a kaleidoscope: they remain the same, but with each turn they change their momentary overall pattern, each time displaying images not seen before.

*   *   *

The main difficulty with psychoanalysis—our patients' fears of lying on the couch and eventually freely associating—is to attach words to the emerging images. What will come up? In the beginning, our patients think it will be long-forgotten memories: the scary, shameful stuff that has been repressed. But over time, they may find an unrecognizable world that they have unconsciously created and now will create once more, consciously and anew: their inner truths, composed of a million bits and pieces of experiences, memories, wishes, and fantasies, contained in images and finally pulled into consciousness by the chain of words that lead them in directions unintended, unforeseen, or even arbitrary—sometimes just a funny rhyme, some consonant companion, the unbidden twist of an interfering remark. All these ideas! We never quite know where they come from or where they will thrust us....But once spelled out, they are there and remain there and need to be looked at, considered, and worked through. How is this reality and how is it fantasy or fiction?

We are used to strictly differentiating reality from fantasy. Did this really happen, or did you make it up? Reality testing is a crucial accomplishment in a child's development and an important strength we hope our patients bring to the couch, at least to a certain degree. But then again—is this what psychoanalysis is about? Or is it the courage and pleasure to look inside and see what's there—to develop the capacity for creating fantasy and fiction? This is where anxiety begins to flood: for moments and hours, we live in realities that aren't, but will be once we've shared them with our analysts or put them down in writing. The words we speak cannot be taken back, and the images we create will not easily fade. Even if they evaporate over time, for some days, at least, these carriers of our unconscious will linger as strange hybrids that aren't completely made up (parts of them stem from our perceptions) and yet aren't real (they are just thoughts—mere ideas). Is this the place we live in? Have we just not noticed? The psychotic cannot know the difference; he floats in a sea of angst to get lost. And we, too, get a taste of his fear—confusion and disorientation—whenever we allow our unconscious to take the lead.

The work of both patient and analyst in the throes of an emerging inner reality is as much a creative process as is an author's laborious way of writing fiction: it requires allowing transferentially and countertransferentially stirred unconscious images to connect with words and to be woven into the fabric of an unfolding tale, which in itself is never about actual realities, but rather about their inner versions, composed from more than these ultimately unknowable and to some degree unimportant facts of life. A patient who can differentiate between reality and fiction when he lies down on the analytic couch will learn how to creatively merge facts and fantasies without being restrained by too much fear or confusion, and in the end, he will discover that he has done this all along—just without knowing or appreciating it.

References

Alter, A. & Bilefsky, D. (2017). Kazuo Ishiguro is awarded the Nobel Prize in Literature. *The New York Times,* October 5.

Freud, S. (1900). *The Interpretation of Dreams. S. E.,* 4/5.

Freud, S. (1915a). The unconscious. *S. E.,* 14.

Freud, S. (1915b). Repression. *S. E.,* 14.

Scarfone, D. (2016). Fantasme et processus de fantasmatisation. *Revue française de psychosomatique,* 50.

CHAPTER 17

Intimacy in Writing Fiction*

T he place of greatest intimacy lies in the heart of the human mind. It's a place hard to reach, yet great to linger in. I went there many times. Each time I felt anxious. There is nothing particular that I fear; there is just this urge to move away. When writing fiction, the immediacy of this discomfort tells me that I'm getting into this state where ideas take over, ideas that are beyond my control. It feels like going into a dark room, and I don't know what I'll be stepping on; once I'm in, it's like flying—partly being carried by some uncanny matter, partly pushing ahead by my own moves, my intrigue. Or it's like an intimate exchange with an independent unknown other: what will emerge from our communication? I suppose it's an encounter with my unconscious, telling me something as though in a dream. Only if I dare to totally be where the images place me, only if I can, as it were, fiction-alize myself, can I translate this intimate inner dialogue into a narrative—a process then requiring further work not unlike the dream's secondary revision. A day residue or derivative of my unconscious may present itself in an image or in *a single sentence*, which may become the outset of creative writing, and this image, this sentence contains, encap-sulates a story, a scene on the cusp of exploding into the open—if captured before repression would shroud it again.

---

* Paper presented in 2017 at the IPA Congress on *INTIMACY* in Buenos Aires.

One day I wrote:

See Barren Land

Without warning, he grabs her hand and flings her into the back seat of his car. His clothes are piled up next to her. On the front passenger seat sits his computer. The car smells of cold smoke. Where are we going? You'll see, he says, and starts the car. The street is bumpy. They dash over potholes. Lukas pushes the engine to speed, speeds faster and faster. Ella's heart is racing. She knows they won't come back. She's left her diary—no time to snatch it from her shelf. Where's mother? You'll see, he says. He barks like a dog. A chewing gum's paper sticks to the back of his seat. Monterey, it says. Monterey..? She must have fallen asleep, dreaming a dream in a dream. Lukas shakes her. He's opened her door. Out, he shouts. She staggers out. Someone is pounding against from inside the trunk. What's that, Ella asks. You'll see, her father says. He lights a cigarette, burns a wisp of his hair that's hanging over his furrowed brows. Fuck! The place is bleak, just barren land, dry earth and rubble all around. Her father opens the trunk. Marlene jumps out, furious! How dare you, she yells! Ha, Lukas sneers, I told you! You see? He shrugs, turns around, gets into the car, and drives off! Drives off? Oh God! He's dumped them, dumped them at this place where there's nothing, nobody, nowhere! Her mother is besides herself, totally loses it, goes mad. She kicks a rock—there!—howls in pain, and holding her foot she starts sobbing, sobbing. Ella doesn't know what to do. Her mother wails and whines. Ella goes over and puts her hand on Marlene's shoulder. Oh, go away, her mother screams, it's all your fault, yours! Shocked, Ella flinches back. A short distance away, she crouches down. Cold winds are ripping over the land, whipping the shrubs. Here they will have to live, huddled in a dirt hole, covered by the crown of a fallen tree. Once in a while, some aborigines will come by. First they curiously look at them from afar. Later they approach them, touch their skin, probe it, scratch it. Marlene and Ella. They are scared. Do you have food, any food? And water, any water? The two whisper, can only whisper, starved and dried up, seared by fate, frail as dead leaves. The aborigines laugh and leave. Later they come back with two leather bags, one filled with water, the other with grain. They place them in front of the two and watch them eat. Marlene and Ella—voraciously they shovel the grain into their mouths and swallow it barely chewed up. Later they sit around an open fire waiting. Waiting for what? You'll see! Her father is gone. His trace is lost. The fire dims and goes out.

The next day, I sat behind Yvonne. (Yvonne was one of the first analysands I worked with after having moved to the US.) She tells me a dream: *Her friend Mary was in a terrible situation, in a hotel; Yvonne wanted to rescue her but couldn't get out of there on her own; still* (she tells me) *she could think about things and get her own perspective.*

Yvonne seems anxious. She returns to something she'd spoken about the previous day: she had visited her brother, whose little daughter at some point was supposed to take a nap but didn't want to and stubbornly refused; finally he got so mad at her that he'd just pushed her into her room and banged the door shut. Yvonne was shocked. It felt abusive. It still feels disturbing. It's horrible, she says, and it doesn't help. He'll see! And the casual way he then talked about it, it's not good, he'll see! (As she says this, and only then, at one stroke I *See Barren Land* and understand that, in my writing the previous day, I had picked up on her phrase *he'll see*. *He'll see* now appears to be its nucleus, the intimate core of this scene.)

Yvonne gets back to her dream, saying: when Mary laughs—she has a beautiful voice.... But in my dream she was in a terrible situation, and I couldn't get her out of it....Still, I could think about it, get my own perspective!—I say: you could see the despair.—Yvonne says: what I wanted to tell you—the oldest pain: *I know how it is to have a parent die.* (She cries.) I was alone with my grief—it's a book of sadness—you notice you can't stop, you cry and cry, and the sadness doesn't go away. As a kid, I was just thrown a bone—my mom said: God will take care of you. But I needed a mom, not a god! Why was I so sad? It's sad to think that I could see this. What makes sadness bearable is people, people saying: I am here. I was alone and couldn't do it. It was the worst feeling. (She briefly pauses and then continues.) The biggest loss in my adult life was when our dog died. I tried to make it go away, but Pete (her husband) could bear it, and then I could bear it too. You can't do it alone, it takes two.—Yeah, I say.

(After a while Yvonne continues.) It never occurred to me why I couldn't look at children's books that had a parent dying, like the lullaby of the old gray goose that dies. Why did my mom choose this lullaby for me? Her grandmother killed herself, her mother couldn't prevent it, it really happened, and somehow it got passed down. The kids are left behind without help. (Then Yvonne tells me about a man who fosters terminally ill children who don't have parents.) He takes them in and talks with them. He's my hero! Children feel intense pain and feel alone. And he goes with them through that grief, over and over.

(After a while, she goes on.) My father didn't want to have children; he was envious of the attention we got from my mother when we were little. I may have registered that.... Having a child is this radical, total, violent change of yourself and of the couple. And the second child is a much more difficult choice. (Yvonne is the second child of her parents, and at the time, she was thinking of having a second child herself. She continues.) Yesterday I saw a video—somebody was killed, it was so sad. How fragile things are!

I stop here. In reality, neither of Yvonne's parents died. Still Yvonne knows about the oldest pain, *having a parent die*. Her father had immigrated to the US from South America at a young age; her mother's parents had come from a European country. When Yvonne was little, the family moved around a lot—each time ripping her out of her home and throwing her into an unknown, as-if-barren land. Like her father, Yvonne experienced uprooting, perhaps without warning, maybe even with violence. She told me that her father had violent outbursts, sending her mother into states of dissociation, perhaps into barren land. Who dies when grief can't be shared? When a father violently abuses his child, he dies in her mind, drowns in her unending sadness, no longer her father. And yet he continues to be there, and he does it again, and dies again and again and again. His being there is like driving off and being gone. And a mother dissociating into barren land, with all her emotions sealed within her secret absence—she, too, dies for her child, and dies and dies. Lonesomeness knows no solace. A child cannot mourn alone; with no parent, she dies, too, dies alone, dies with them. Who is dead? Who will feed her? Who will rescue them? Are there still aborigines around, the origins that must be resorted to so as to survive? And what if all that gets mixed up with the violence of making babies? Is there then only barren land to flee to in order not to be killed?

And here I am, putting things together, intimately. In the 1940s, both my parents, still young and each on their own, fled from East to West Germany, fled through war's rubble, this ruined and barren land, losing their homes and leaving everything behind. They had to start from scratch, had to move several times when I was little, moved to make a living before they could settle down for good. Both lived to an old age. To bury my father I traveled to Hellerau, the town founded by my grandfather, where my father was born and grew up and where I've only been a few times for short visits. And yet, to my surprise, I felt deeply at home there, where *he*—not I—once was at home. Was this feeling a reflection of my father's unconscious transmission to me?

Seventeen years ago, I moved from Zürich, where I trained as a psycho-analyst, to Boston. Now I, too, live and work in a place far from my origins. I uprooted myself; it was my choice to move to the US in order to marry the man I love. I consider my life in Boston rich, full, and happy. And yet, professionally, I sometimes feel as though in a barren land, a place where Freud has been marginalized and relegated to the dead, where his profound thinking about the human mind has been shunned or forgotten, and psychoanalysis often seems reduced to a simple formula of repeating traumatizing childhood relationships. I'm not stating objective facts; I'm talking about my experience, the way I see it—*so you'll see!* I'm exploring an intimate feeling I'm struggling with. I lost my home, I mourned it, and still sometimes I miss it. Was I huddling with Yvonne under the crown of a fallen tree? Is Freud furiously driving off, leaving us with an impoverished version of psychoanalysis in a barren land? Freud's fascination with Michel-angelo's *Moses* comes to mind: Moses was furious, yes, but he stayed and kept the tablets from falling and breaking.

I didn't want Yvonne to be affected by *my* occasional woes... Yet I empa-thized with her when she complained about the lack of rigor at the graduate school where she teaches German literature, when she bemoaned the reluctance of her colleagues to engage the students in thorough textual analysis and theoretical thinking. Still, as familiar as this felt to me, I wanted her to keep trying to move things in what seemed to her the right direction, not to give up even when adversity seemed overwhelming. Yvonne loved to read Freud before she came to me. That was part of why she chose me as her analyst. So we had a common ancestor from the beginning. How much did she see and know and absorb from her parents, her husband, her friends and colleagues, and what did she take from her analyst—via this enigmatic phenomenon Freud called *unconscious communication*? We'll always be the children of our parents, be under the influence of their long journeys through life. What is theirs, what is ours? What was hers, what was mine? We have to sort it out. We can't stay home forever, nor shall we end in barren land. Life is on the move.

In analysis as in fiction writing, we never quite know where we're going. But we proceed, sometimes scared, sometimes delighted. *See Barren Land*—is it Yvonne's story, is it mine? Was it a co-creation in the analytic field, a reverie, a countertransference fantasy? Did it warn me of a potential collusion with Yvonne's unconscious dread of loss and destruction? I chose *See Barren Land* because—as it turned out—it so explicitly relates to my patient's statement *he'll see,* as well as to the terror she'd felt in many respects. Still, the terrible situation represented in *her dream* and the images and scenes in her mind during our sessions were of course different from the one I created. Our stories varied but may have converged and enhanced each other in some essential ways. Also, as much as it disturbed and pained Yvonne, her repeated claim of *he'll see!* showed her capacity for containment: she could hold the urge to interfere so that the other could learn to see for himself. *He'll see!* showed her capacity for representation: the distance necessary to *think about it and get her own perspective.* She could feel and bear the sadness, and she could know about it on her own. Analysis made it possible for her to now live within and beyond her inner world.

It's not so rare that patients in analysis begin to write poetry or stories. In contrast to the common fear that psychoanalysis kills a writer's creativity, it actually frees and enables the mind to dive deeper into the unconscious processes of creativity. I feel that writing fiction enriches my imagination, enhances the flexibility of my thinking about as-yet-unspoken possibilities, and increases my capacity for containment. Did writing this specific piece, *See Barren Land,* help me in my work with Yvonne? It's possible yet I'm not sure, or not sure to what extent. I felt immersed and connected in my sessions with Yvonne, so I may not have needed to write *See Barren Land* in order to understand and be with her in her process of working through. But *See Barren Land* seems to illustrate the inscape of her deep-seated pain. Once I had seen the link, I made use of it in one intervention about her dream: I said, *you could see the despair.*

The place of greatest intimacy lies in the heart of the human mind. That's why psychoanalysis is the royal road to intimacy. As Bollas (2012) has shown, talking to the analyst allows the patient to enter into an inner dialogue with herself, a dialogue that was disrupted long ago; via her analyst, the analysand learns to listen and to speak to herself, an inner conscious-unconscious conversation that is always fictitious. It's never about reality; it's always about fantasy, the stories that have been created to absorb and contain the crude facts of life.

In reading our psychoanalytic candidates' case reports over these past years, rarely have I been able to find the notion *unconscious* or *fantasy*, let alone *unconscious fantasy*. In supervision, a candidate may tell me about his patient's communications, and he may get caught up in what seems to be the patient's reality. As his supervisor, I try to expand his openness to the patient's implied stories, told in derivative, displaced, and transferential ways. To hear these hushed songs from afar sometimes requires the analyst to engage his creative mind, his imagination; this may lead to discomfort and an anxious move away, an urge to resort to what appears to be fact or reality. However, step by step, the candidate may begin to see—*he'll see*—what his patient tries to tell him. Some, though, may never get there.

But there is also a danger for the skilled senior analyst. She's heard it so often in so many ways that she may resort to the general template, to knowing what an unconscious fantasy most likely is about before having heard and seen its specific individual narrative. I mean: the senior analyst may get a little tired, tired of overcoming the subtle discomfort when engaging with her own and her patient's unconscious, tired of this wonderful but scary intimacy, tired of the work that needs to be done. A difficult analytic session leaves me as exhausted as writing a piece of fiction—but it's a good exhaustion.

When I trained in the 1980s in Switzerland, psychoanalysts were expected to read fiction. Reading fiction engages our imagination; it touches, stirs and works on our unconscious. In similar ways, writing fiction engages fantasy, part of which is always unconscious. Writing fiction strives to reveal, unfold, and free the core of sentences or images that come to the writer's mind, unbidden, arbitrarily, and on their own. If it's a sentence, it needs to be unfolded in an image, a scene. If it's an image, it needs to be elaborated in words. That's precisely how Freud described the process of making the unconscious conscious. If the writer is a psychoanalyst, she may catch such sentences from her patient's communications. When my patient said: *he'll see*—what did she want me to see? I didn't ask this question, but it played me.

Writing fiction is the elaboration of this intimate encounter between what is known and what is implied or hidden, between what is conscious and what is still unconscious. The anxiety that we have to tolerate in order to get to this place of utmost intimacy within ourselves and with our patients will never lessen. But if we aren't deterred by discomfort we may enhance our psychoanalytic work—or our fiction writing. *You'll see!*

Reference

Bollas, C. (2012). The psychoanalytic passage. *Bulletin of the European Psychoanalytic Federation*, 66:75-85.

CHAPTER 18

On Aging and Dying

S ome years ago, a colleague told me of her grandmother, who at age 105 was physically weak but mentally still as strong and clear as ever. She was well taken care of by her family and enjoyed daily encounters with an extended crowd of relatives. Still, one day she said she'd lived long enough and wanted to die. She was not in pain or distress; she just felt it was time to go. She reduced and then stopped eating and drinking, slept for most hours of the day, and two weeks later she quietly passed away.

Death did not seem to have frightened her. No longer was she driven to survive. How can we understand her final moves? I think she was no longer concerned with self-preservation (nor did she worry about the preservation of her family, since everybody was doing fine). After disinvesting or deactivating the solid mental structures of her preservative screens,[1] she didn't feel much hunger or thirst; her bodily functions slowed down without making her feel anxious. Maybe she died in the manner Freud once suggested: "It might be assumed that the death drive operated silently within the organism towards its dissolution" (1930, p. 119). In her last days she slept a lot. Sleep tries death, as the saying goes, and so it makes sense to suggest that the sleep screen is the last preservative screen we encounter before we enter the realm of death. She slept quietly.

---

[1] See *Surviving in Absence* in this volume.

Freud portrayed the work of the death drives as "unobtrusive" (1920, p. 63); they are, he suggested, "by their nature mute" (1923, p. 46) and "desire to be at peace" (ibid., p. 59). In this case, the fulfillment of her *wish to die* may have felt like a blessing, and for my colleague's grandmother, it may have crowned a life of self-determination. After having preserved her life over more than a hundred years, she granted herself the wish to die.

Maybe this example shows us that *the fear of death* does not arise from the death screen; rather, it is a necessary warning signal coming from the preservative structures, which sound an alarm when their survival needs are not met, when their strivings remain unsatisfied, and a life that wants to be continued is endangered. It is only when these preservative structures are decathected that we want to and are driven to die.

But before we get there—if life takes the average course—we age. Aging means approaching death. It challenges us with the loss of our previously available strength, mobility, balance, and mastery. Now we hurt, fall, err, and forget. Our capability to digest—in the broadest sense of its meaning—declines, and we have to reduce or renounce what we used to enjoy. We feel disheartened, insecure, self-conscious, and behind. All these occurrences tell us that our self-preservation is imperiled, and naturally, we increasingly turn toward issues of health and safety. Sit down with a group of older people, and you can be sure that sooner or later the conversation will turn toward and often lingers on questions about health and food, both central self-preservative issues. Reports of doctors' appointments, illnesses, and medical devices take center stage; our mere physical well-being becomes our preoccupation.

"If we now apply ourselves to considering mental life from a *biological* point of view, a 'drive' appears to us as a notion on the frontier between the mental and the somatic, as the psychical representative of the stimuli originating from within the organism and reaching the mind, as a measure of the demand made upon the mind for work in consequence of its connection with the body" (Freud 1915, p. 121f, italics in original).

The aging body increases its demands for self-preservation. Dental surgeries, eye surgeries, hearing aids, canes, walkers…all are designed to cope with physical impairments, yet they pose psychological challenges: they stir our self-preservative drives with worries. And as we're becoming more insecure in our physical (and mental) capacities, we may get more cranky and tend to react aggressively—a response to feeling endangered and attacked: we intensify our self-preservation; we fight for our survival.

At the same time, we have to struggle with challenges to our sexual drives. The decline of our physical attraction and sexual potency is an unavoidable narcissistic offense. All these wrinkles, the hair loss, the weight gain, the age spots, the swollen feet....Beauty isn't a natural given any longer; it needs to be worked on, thought about, and is only tediously achieved. Further, a discrepancy between our sexual desire and our physical readiness occurs, which unconsciously may resonate with the oedipal phase, when our erotic desires and fantasies were premature, hampered by our physiological unfitness, our bodily immaturity. Now, at the stage of sexual "post-maturity," we may not give up our sexual life, but we are confronted with its limits, which evidence a loss. And looking around, we may feel bypassed and marginalized. Others have already taken over.

This brief outline is meant to highlight the changing demands of our bodies on our minds; it concerns the psychoanalytic theory of drives—namely, the preservative and sexual drives. And since the drives make themselves known to us through ideas that come to our minds, we learn about our physical state through our thoughts, feelings, fantasies, and dreams. To realize (without denying) our increased preservative needs and our decreased capacity to fulfill our sexual desires gives us pause; it requires choices. We can give in to our worries about our physical ailments and give up our desires for the pleasures of Eros, or we can contain, limit, steer, sublimate, and control these tendencies and balance our interests. The task is to take good care of one's self without making self-preservation the sole or even major concern, e.g., by withdrawing to the super-safe, familiar place of home, or by insisting on rigid diets and schedules. The task is also to stay libidinally invested in our partners and friends, in the arts, politics, and new developments, which will inspire us and give us pleasure, simultaneously making us more interesting (attractive) to others. The sublimation of both drives is a lifelong process—a challenge as well as a liberating capacity of the mind. Aging is destiny, but then again it isn't *just* destiny—we can choose or at least contribute to *how* we age.

If we feel we have no choices and are scared or depressed about aging, we may need analytic work. The challenges to our psychic structures provoked by the threats of aging can lead to regressions or even mental breakdowns. Vulnerabilities that were earlier compensated for, or conflicts repressed or managed well enough through our younger years, may be activated and compound a mind in crisis. Psychoanalysis of older patients is a relatively new sector of treatment that invites opportunities for research, not only in the area of sexuality, but in particular with regard to the self- and object-preservative drives: how are they structured, how have the needs of self- and object-preservation been represented; what are the weaknesses, the secret addictions, neglects, and functional disorganizations? Psychoanalysis with older patients can be beneficial in reaffirming or even building structures that allow for more control of our changing bodily demands.

One fact of life, the arrival of grandchildren, often mitigates the challenges outlined above. It invites aging persons to invest their increased lethic energies in the care of little ones while helping their grown children with the tasks of child-rearing. Thus the lethic preoccupation with self-preservation, which narrows one's world, can be moderated by object-preservation, a broadened engagement that benefits the next generations. The lethic urge to take care can be divided between self- and object-preservation. The rewards will be bountiful.

One of the most painful human experiences is the death of one's own child—the child we're committed to protecting and preserving throughout life. This urge never vanishes from a parent's mind. It remains a lifelong aim of our object-preservative strivings. Thus it is very interesting that Freud, who never fully engaged with his own concept of the self-preservative drive, began his famous seventh chapter of *The Interpretation of Dreams* (1900) not with a dream about unconscious sexual desire or conflict, but with a father's reaction to the death of his child:

A father had been watching beside his child's sick-bed for days and nights on end. After the child had died, he went into the next room to lie down, but left the door open so that he could see from his bedroom into the room in which his child's body was laid out, with tall candles standing round it. An old man had been engaged to keep watch over it, and sat beside the body murmuring prayers. After a few hours' sleep, the father had a dream that *his child was standing beside his bed, caught him by the arm and whispered to him reproachfully: "Father, don't you see I'm burning?"* He woke up, noticed a bright glare of light from the next room, hurried into it and found that the old watchman had dropped off to sleep and that the wrappings and one of the arms of his beloved child's dead body had been burned by a lighted candle that had fallen on them.

The explanation of this moving dream is simple enough....The glare of light shone through the open door into the sleeping man's eyes and led him to the conclusion which he would have arrived at if he had been awake, namely that a candle had fallen over and set something alight in the neighbourhood of the body. [p. 509]

Freud adds to this explanation that some of what the child said in the dream may relate to actual events: "For instance, *"I'm burning"* may have been spoken during the fever of the child's last illness, and *"Father, don't you see?"* may have been derived from some other highly emotional situation of which we are in ignorance" (p. 510). I would add that the child's complaint *"Father, don't you see?"* may also speak of the father's guilt feelings, a self-reproach with regard to his object-preservation, his wish to *have seen in time* that his child needed care—the desperate (even though perhaps totally unrealistic) thought that he could have saved his child. The thought "If only I had or hadn't done x, y, or z" tells us that we are driven to preserve our objects—first and most of all, our loved ones. Survivor guilt even demands that we preserve our objects rather than ourselves.

But why didn't the father, on seeing the light, wake up and rush to the child's bedside right away, instead of first dreaming this dream? Freud's answer: the dream fulfilled the father's wish to see his child alive. Thus the driving wish of this dream was object-preservative: it pictured the child's survival. Freud doesn't specify the particulars of this dream's drive-wish, and having only a narrow notion of a sexual drive and a *self-*preservative one at this point, he probably would have thought of the dream's wish as a libidinal one. However, if we accept the concept of a preservative drive, it will be hard to dispute that this dream, which opens the chapter that introduces the first published presentation of Freud's theory of the mind (the psychical apparatus), exemplifies the fulfillment of an object-preservative wish.

References

Freud, S. (1900). The Interpretation of Dreams. *S. E.*, 5.

Freud, S. (1915). Instincts and their vicissitudes. *S. E.*, 14.

Freud, S. (1920). Beyond the pleasure principle. *S. E.*, 18.

Freud, S. (1923). The ego and the id. *S. E.*, 19.

Freud, S. (1930). Civilization and its discontents. *S. E.*, 22.

www.ingramcontent.com/pod-product-compliance
Lightning Source LLC
Chambersburg PA
CBHW060304030426
42336CB00011B/928